EXPLORING *the* BIBLE

EXPLORING *the* BIBLE:
A Guide to the Old and New Testaments

Three Books in One

R. LAIRD HARRIS, SAMUEL J. SCHULTZ, GARY V. SMITH,
AND WALTER M. DUNNETT

CROSSWAY BOOKS

A PUBLISHING MINISTRY OF
GOOD NEWS PUBLISHERS
WHEATON, ILLINOIS

Exploring the Bible: A Guide to the Old and New Testaments

Copyright © 2001, 2002 by Evangelical Training Association

Three-in-one edition first published 2007.

Published by Crossway Books
    a publishing ministry of Good News Publishers
    1300 Crescent Street
    Wheaton, Illinois 60187

Cover design: Jon McGrath

Cover illustration: Jessie McGrath

First printing 2007

Printed in the United States of America

Unless noted otherwise, Scripture quotations are taken from the Holy Bible, *King James Version*.

Scripture references marked NIV are from *The Holy Bible: New International Version*.® Copyright © 1973, 1978, 1984 by International Bible Society. Used by permission of Zondervan Publishing House. All rights reserved.

The "NIV" and "New International Version" trademarks are registered in the United States Patent and Trademark Office by International Bible Society. Use of either trademark requires the permission of International Bible Society.

Scripture quotations marked NASB are from *The New American Standard Bible*® Copyright © The Lockman Foundation 1960, 1962, 1963, 1968, 1971, 1972, 1973, 1975, 1977, 1995. Used by permission.

Scripture references marked ASV are from the *American Standard Version* of the Bible.

ISBN 13: 978-1-58134-864-4
ISBN 10: 1-58134-864-9

Library of Congress Cataloging-in-Publication Data
Exploring the Bible: a guide to the Old and New Testaments / R. Laird Harris . . . [et al.].
    p. cm.
    ISBN 13: 978-1-58134-864-4 (tpb)
    1. Bible—Criticism, interpretation, etc. I. Harris, R. Laird (Robert Laird), 1911– . II. Title.
BS511.3.E97   2007
220.6'1—dc22   2006028388

LB		17	16	15	14	13	12	11	10	09	08	07
15	14	13	12	11	10	9	8	7	6	5	4	3	2	1

CONTENTS

PART TWO: JOB—MALACHI

BOOK ONE:

EXPLORING THE BASICS OF THE BIBLE

R. LAIRD HARRIS

Chapter One

REVELATION AND INSPIRATION

THE BOOK OF GENESIS records how God created mankind in His own image and likeness. One of God's purposes was that Adam should have contact and communion with Him. It is clear from the account that God did care for Adam, talk with him, and give him commands. For the most high God to speak with people in this way was a wonderful revelation of God's word, His being, and His will.

After the sin of Adam and Eve, God could indeed have cast them off. They had deliberately disobeyed; the threat had been death. But God in boundless mercy interposed a divinely intended plan of salvation. So God sought out Adam in the garden and charged him with his sin. This was God's first revelation to fallen man.

SPECIAL AND GENERAL REVELATION

God spoke further with Adam, Eve, the serpent, Cain, Noah, and many others. This direct communication from God is usually called special revelation.

Much can be learned about God from the universe He has made. Such an enormous creation signifies an almighty God. The marvelous intricacy of the world argues for the infinite wisdom of God. Our consciences testify to us of a holy and benevolent God. These evidences of God in His creation are usually called general revelation.

This general revelation has often been denied. People say that what seems to be intricacy in nature is due to chance, and the "moral law within," called conscience, has been ascribed to society, early training, self-deception, etc. But Paul in Romans 1:19-23 clearly affirms that God can be seen in nature, and he clearly refers to conscience in Romans 2:15. Actually, it is an impressive phenomenon that the great majority of people have always believed in some kind of deity. Furthermore, although conscience can be denied, every known human culture has some moral rules. It would seem that natural revelation is well established. That it does not lead people to worship the true God is attributed by Paul to human wickedness (Rom. 1:18).

INSPIRATION

When God spoke to people in the early times, it was an oral special revelation. As far as we know, there was no writing until some time after the Flood. Some method of recording numbers of objects may have been used, but it seems that writing as we know it began in Mesopotamia and Egypt a little before 3000 B.C. God's oral revelation, however, was just as special and true and inspired as His later written words. When God spoke to Cain, it was not the voice of conscience within; Cain answered in anger. It was an objective speaking from God.

No one knows the names of many of the people to whom God spoke in the early days. Although the Old Testament records that Enoch "walked with God," the word here probably refers to habitual living rather than mere walking together. But in any case, it indicates a harmony and a fellowship including discourse. This fits with the New Testament reference to Enoch as a prophet (Jude 14). Noah received extensive revelations from God—even as to the dimensions of the ark, the animals to be assembled, etc. Without these specific revelations Noah would have perished too. He did not get the instructions for the ark from his heightened spiritual imagination.

A further lesson from Noah's life is that he ministered the word of God to his generation. The record in Genesis implies and 2 Peter states that Noah warned his generation of the coming judgment. This is the function of a prophet—having received the word of God, to speak it to the people.

While the Bible contains no information on God's revelation during the long years from Noah to Abraham, it says much after that. God spoke to Abraham many times. He gave him specific commands and promises that were fulfilled in ways Abraham could not have guessed. Abraham moved in society as a prince (Gen. 23:5) and as a worshiper of the true God (Gen. 14:22). By life and word he ministered to his generation, and through the record Moses wrote, he ministers also to us.

Moses was the first writing prophet. God spoke to Moses face to face (Num. 12:8). In addition, God ordered Moses to write His commands (Exod. 24:4-8). Most of the Pentateuch after Moses' call in Exodus 2 is governed by such expressions as "the LORD said to Moses." At the end of Deuteronomy, it says that Moses wrote down this law of the

Lord and instructed the people to obey its commands and to read it publicly at the Feast of Tabernacles every seven years (Deut. 31:9-13).

More will be said about the prophets and their work in chapter 4. For now, we shall study some of the consequences of this view of the Old Testament prophets as organs of revelation, God's spokesmen to the people (Exod. 7:1-2). Remember that a prophet in Israel was not just a highly spiritual man. A prophet was a man called of God to receive revelation from Him (Num. 12:2-8). The prophet's word was so much God's word that it was as if the prophet had eaten a scroll from heaven and had given it out orally to the people (Ezek. 2:7—3:3). The word spoken was God's word.

The same must be said of the words the prophets wrote. Not all prophetic messages were written down. Uriah prophesied in the name of the Lord as Jeremiah had done, but he was killed by King Jehoiakim, and his words were not written (Jer. 26:20-21). But when the Lord spoke through the prophets in ancient Israel, their words were truly God's word, whether they were merely spoken or also written down. Joshua wrote his record in the Book of the Law of God (Josh. 24:26). Much, if not most, of the Old Testament was spoken first and written afterward.

Some make a distinction between the prophetic speech and the prophetic writing, saying that only the writing was inspired, but the Old Testament makes no such distinction.

These examples illustrate what is meant by the term "inspiration of the Scriptures." A good definition is "that work of the Holy Spirit in chosen individuals by which the person is moved to speak or write in his own idiom the very words of God without error in fact, doctrine, or judgment." Chapters 2 and 3 will give further biblical evidence for this concept.

VERBAL INSPIRATION

This view of inspiration holds that the words themselves are truly God's words, inspired by the Holy Spirit. It is sometimes caricatured as a "dictation theory." But most conservatives today do not believe that God simply dictated His Word to scribes working like a modern secretary or a robot. God used the prophets and controlled them, but He did not violate their styles or personalities. The nearest thing to a theory of dictation is the teaching of the Roman Catholic Council of Trent in 1545, which said in Latin that the Scriptures were "*Spiritu Sancto dictante.*" But the Latin *dictante* does not mean "dictate" in the modern sense. It simply means "spoken" or "said."

INFALLIBLE AND INERRANT

Historically, the Bible has been called inspired, meaning that it is God's Word and fully true. Traditionally, it was also called infallible. That is to say, it is incapable of mistake. In more recent times conservative believers have considered belief in the Bible as "the only infallible rule of faith and life." They clearly meant to affirm that the Bible is infallible and that it is a rule of faith and conduct. But with the rise of liberalism, this vow was often reinterpreted to mean that the Bible was only infallible in matters of faith and morals. Thus the word *infallible* was watered down to allow errors of science and history, and this view is widely held among liberals today. To protect against this lower view of the Scriptures, conservative believers have found it necessary to use the additional adjective *inerrant*, which is to say that the Bible is without error.

To say the Bible is infallible ought to be enough. But in the current situation, we find it necessary to say also that the Bible is inerrant, if we mean that it is really true in all it says. The Bible is verbally inspired, it is infallible, and it is inerrant in the manuscripts as they were originally written. The statement of faith of the Evangelical Theological Society expresses it briefly but well: "The Bible alone, and the Bible in its entirety, is the Word of God written and is therefore inerrant in the autographs [original documents]."

Many think that this view of the Scriptures is too narrow. They say that in this twenty-first century, people cannot believe this. They say that the facts are against it, that the Bible's science is outmoded: We can no longer believe in a flat earth with heaven upstairs. They say that belief in a literal creation of a literal Adam or in the story of Jonah and other such tales must be denied. Indeed, they say, the Scriptures contradict themselves. They claim that there is a human element in Scripture that inerrancy does not allow for, and, therefore, by insisting on inerrancy, we will not reach modern people.

Some brief answers to these criticisms will be suggested here and will be developed in chapter 8. It may first be said that we should be slow to depart from an ancient doctrine—grounded as it has been on the teaching of Christ and His apostles—just to reach hypothetical "modern people." The prophets of old were commanded to preach the Word of God whether people would listen or not (see Isa. 6:9-10; Jer. 20:9; Ezek. 2:5-7).

Secondly, it is highly doubtful that the Bible pictures a flat earth with heaven upstairs. The claim is that it does if you "take it literally." But actually no one, not even the staunchest conservative, takes the Bible literally. The Bible is full of metaphors, parables, and poetry, which are to be interpreted as in any other piece of literature. How could anyone take "literally" such common expressions as "tickled to death," "a heart of gold," "ages since I saw you," etc. The objection depends on a crassly literal interpretation of various poetic passages and then says the Bible violates common knowledge. So would most poetry describing the moon, the trees, the mountains, and anything wonderful or beautiful.

Many forget that the standard astronomy of the New Testament world taught that the world is round. Eratosthenes had measured its circumference quite accurately in 250 B.C. It is curious that recent theologians who object to the idea that heaven is "up" speak of the "breaking in" of the kingdom of God. It is as strange to picture heaven this way, as outside a box, as it is to picture it as "up." But, as C. S. Lewis in his book *Miracles*[1] beautifully shows, all language about things that are not perceived by the senses must be metaphorical language. No other way can be found to describe the unseen.

So the Bible language does not mean to imply that the spiritual heaven is just upstairs (although Hebrew, like English, uses the same word for the heaven of stars and clouds and space where birds fly, which indeed is "up"). Similarly, "the ends of the earth" does not imply a falling-off place. The Hebrew word for "earth" is very often used for "land." The "ends of the earth" usually mean only distant places and the "four corners of the earth" refer only to wide areas in all directions (cf. Ezek. 7:2).

Thirdly, if people cannot believe in a literal creation, they must be able satisfactorily to ascribe to chance the marvelously intricate pattern of life, or, for that matter, the unique creature of intelligence, purpose, and moral consciousness that is known as man.

Finally, to object to the inerrancy of Scripture because of alleged contradictions neglects the years of study on these matters since the days of Justin who was martyred for the faith in A.D. 148 and who had written, "I am entirely convinced that no Scripture contradicts another" (*Dialogue with Trypho*, ch. 65).

It is obvious that the Bible contains some seeming difficulties and things that are hard to understand. Surely this is to be expected in a document from ancient times and from another culture. If culture shock is expected when traveling to foreign countries, how much more should surprising things be found in the Bible. But so many such difficulties have been solved by new discoveries about ancient practices and languages that an informed believer can attribute the few remaining problems to people's ignorance of the details of ancient life and history. Factual problems continue to be answered to the satisfaction of a host of scholars today.

Conservative believers do not accept the idea that Scripture contains real contradictions. Like the early Church Fathers, they believe that such alleged contradictions are due to lack of knowledge or to minor errors of copying.

BIBLE INTERPRETATION (HERMENEUTICS)

The Protestant Reformation was a great "back-to-the-Bible" movement. The emphasis was on giving the Bible to the laity. Wycliffe had stood for the principle previously, but Luther, Tyndale, and others carried on the work of translating the Bible into the languages of the people. The corollary was that the Bible is a plain book that the common people can read and understand.

Certainly the history of succeeding years has supported this view. This does not mean, however, that everyone can fully understand every passage. Rather, any reader can learn of God and His way of salvation and can by faith accept it. But the judgments of God are unsearchable and "his ways past finding out" (Rom. 11:33). Even references to historical incidents and ancient daily practices are difficult for anyone who does not have the ancient and Eastern background information.

So the interpretation of the Bible in detail requires studying of ancient languages, culture, history, etc. But a new approach to hermeneutics says that the Bible is not relevant to us today. Advocates of this position say that ancient Jews lived too differently from us. They were not interested in exact figures, chronological relationships, or historical accuracy. Critics say the Bible was not wrong by its standards, but errs by modern scientific standards.

Several things should be mentioned in reply. First, the ancients were not so careless as some think. The pyramids, built five hundred years before Abraham, are oriented to the North Star to within five degrees! Hezekiah's engineers in about 732 B.C. dug a winding tunnel through eighteen hundred feet of rock in Jerusalem. They started from both ends and met in the middle, being only a foot or two off in their alignment.

Secondly, no one is always exact. Every carpenter knows that a 2"x4" stud used in house construction is only approximately 1½"x3½". Being approximate is not being wrong. Historical errors have been alleged in the Bible, but many times later archeological discoveries have shown that the Bible was right after all.

The argument has been overworked that says the Bible is not relevant for today because it is the product of the ancient world. Millions of people who have found comfort, meaning, and salvation through the Scriptures testify otherwise. And, although ancient culture differs much from the modern, the differences do not overshadow the similarities. People lived, loved, ate, were ill, fought, thought, sinned, and died as they do today. It is not true that the ancient mind was too different from modern man's. E. D. Hirsch calls this the fallacy of the inscrutable past.[2] He remarks that there is less difference between modern people and the ancients than there is between various modern people. The Bible is understandable, and it is relevant.

Others today who call themselves evangelical nonetheless hold that there are errors in the Bible. They claim, however, that these errors are only negligible and do not affect the spiritual message. They say that a strict inerrancy does not allow for the human element in the Bible.

But this view is based on a misconception. The historical concept of verbal inspiration and inerrancy assumes the view that God by His Spirit works powerfully on people, although His work is behind the scenes. The process of inspiration is not all of God and none of man—this would be dictation. Neither was it all of man and none of God—this would be humanism. Nor was it 50 percent of God and 50 percent of man—then errors of major magnitude would be inescapable.

But the real picture is that God used men in their total activity, and yet He worked upon them powerfully, being 100 percent in control. Hence, verbal inspiration is possible only because the Spirit of God is perfectly able to work like that. The result was that the Bible's authors wrote as no ordinary people wrote, but "as they were moved by the Holy Spirit" (2 Pet. 1:21). Like most spiritual truth, this view involves mystery. But it is a wonderful mystery, and it has given us an inerrant Bible.

THE IMPORTANCE OF THE INSPIRED SCRIPTURES

The view of verbal inspiration or inerrancy has been held by the leaders of the church since early days.[3] A view so widespread would surely be basic. One of the main emphases of the Reformation was *sola scriptura*: "The Bible alone." This emphasis was vital to that great spiritual renewal.

Due to liberal influences, the doctrine of inerrancy was largely lost in Germany in the nineteenth century and in many areas of America in the early twentieth century. A revival of full trust and belief in the Bible accompanied a real resurgence of evangelical strength and outreach in the later twentieth century. It is not difficult to see the connection.

Without a real and true word from heaven, people are lost in a sea of human opinion and moral weakness. The Ten Commandments have been taken out of public schools. Their authority has been denied in many of our older church bodies. The result is disastrous. But the warning was given long ago by the beloved disciple. "For I testify unto every man that heareth the words of the prophecy of this book, If any man shall add unto these things, God shall add unto him the plagues that are written in this book: And if any man shall take away from the words of the book of this prophecy, God shall take away his part out of the book of life, and out of the holy city, and from the things which are written in this book" (Rev. 22:18-19).

The Scriptures are God's Word to us. We should personally read them, study them, meditate upon them, and, most of all, practice them. And then we should join with others of like precious faith to see that the Scriptures are honored and taught to the ends of the earth.

VOCABULARY ENRICHMENT

General revelation, special revelation, infallible, inerrant, hermeneutics

DISCUSSION QUESTIONS

1. What does Romans 1:18-32 teach regarding whether people can actually find the true God by natural revelation?
2. If all men have consciences and so have a moral standard, why do they not live good and perfect lives?
3. What does Exodus 7:1 teach regarding a prophet being a spokesman for God?
4. Did the prophets of Baal, who were supported by Jezebel, really speak for their god, or did they just say what was popular (1 Kings 22:6)?
5. Compare Job 26:7 and 9:6. How can you explain the seeming contradiction here?

Chapter Two

WHY CHRISTIANS BELIEVE THE BIBLE: OLD TESTAMENT

THE QUESTION "Why do Christians believe the Bible?" can be answered in many ways. Some answers are more important than others. One group of answers is based largely on reasoning. Another set is based on faith. Both are basic and will be considered one by one. This chapter will present the answers related to the Old Testament. The next chapter will develop the reasons believers can have faith in the New Testament.

CHRIST BELIEVED IT

The easiest and clearest answer as to why Christians believe the Old Testament is that Christ believed it. We trust His teaching. The Lord Jesus Christ is our final authority in all matters. By miracles, wonders, and signs, He fully proved Himself to have come from God. He proved Himself to be the Son of God with power by the resurrection from the dead. Paul summarizes it in Romans 1:4: "And declared to be the Son of God with power, according to the spirit of holiness, by the resurrection from the dead." To doubt Christ's teachings is to doubt all that is precious and basic in the Christian faith. Jesus believed the Old Testament and taught its truth. That alone should be enough.

It is clear that Christ did believe and teach that the Old Testament is God's Word. Many specific verses give His teaching plainly, and many other passages in the Gospels indicate His general attitude toward the Old Testament.

Of primary importance is Christ's teaching to the two disciples on the road to Emmaus after His resurrection. Read Luke 24:13-31. In this account it is clear that the disciples had not fully accepted the testimony of the women that Christ had risen. As He talked to the two disciples, He called them "fools, and slow of heart to believe all that the prophets have spoken" (v. 25). Then He went through the Old Testament, showing how it foretold these things. The Greek says, "He, beginning, expounded to them from Moses and from all the prophets in all the Scriptures the things concerning Himself" (v. 27). Notice how Christ reasoned out of a book known both as "the Scriptures" and as "Moses and all the prophets." The latter designation is a regular name for the Old Testament in the Dead Sea Scrolls and in the New Testament. It or "the law and the prophets" is used, with slight variations, several times in the New Testament. Jesus was declaring that they should have believed that book.

The same teaching is given forcefully in Luke 16:29-31. In this record of the rich man and Lazarus, great emphasis is placed upon belief in God's Word. The rich man was condemned to eternal torment from which there was no escape or relief. Lazarus, "the beggar," was in the place of eternal blessedness. The rich man pleaded with Abraham to send Lazarus from the dead to warn his five living brothers. Christ quotes Abraham's reply with obvious approval: "They have Moses and the prophets"—the Old Testament. The tormented man still begged for a special miraculous witness. Abraham replied, "If they hear not Moses and the prophets, neither will they be persuaded, though one rose from the dead" (v. 31).

Notice the force and application of this statement. The witness of the Old Testament is more valuable than a resurrection testimony would be. The Jewish leaders had made the Word of God of no effect through their tradition. Notice also how this truth is borne out in subsequent events. The Jews were not convinced by the resurrection of Lazarus of Bethany or even by the resurrection of Christ Himself. The testimony of the law and the prophets is final, just as Jesus has said.

Other passages bear the same witness. In John 10:33-39, Jesus quotes from Psalm 82:6 calling it their "law" and argues that since "the scripture cannot be broken," His own claims were justified. We are not now considering Christ's clear claim to deity. We are emphasizing the fact that He grounded His claims upon Scripture—the unbreakable Scripture. He had argued from the word *gods*. That one word was so certain that He could make it the solid basis of His claim.

"For had ye believed Moses, ye would have believed me: for he wrote of me. But if ye believe not his writings, how shall ye believe my words?" (John 5:46-47). Here Christ spoke of Moses as the author of the first five books of the Old Testament—the Pentateuch—and declares that we should believe these writings. Indeed Jesus ties up in the closest way belief in Moses' writings with belief in His own words. To doubt the Old Testament is to doubt Jesus. If we believe Jesus, we shall believe the Old Testament. These passages teach the importance of believing the Old Testament and the danger of denying it.

Further proof is recorded in Matthew 5:17-19 and Luke 16:16-17. Read these passages, which make it clear that Christ was referring to the Old Testament, "the law and the prophets." This title was used clearly enough to include just our thirty-nine Old Testament books. This book, "the law," is said to be letter perfect. The most stupendous claim is made for it: "It is easier for heaven and earth to disappear than for the least stroke of a pen to drop out of the Law" (Luke 16:17 NIV). Matthew is even more explicit: It is perfect "to the smallest letter . . . the least stroke of a pen." The *King James Version* says "the jot and tittle," which has become an English idiom. It is interesting to compare these passages with what Jesus said about His own words: "Heaven and earth shall pass away, but my words shall not pass away" (Matt. 24:35; Luke 21:33). Notice in passing that Jesus was not speaking of the preservation of His words, many of which have, of course, perished. He was speaking of their eternal truth and power—*the Word*.

Some people object to this appeal to Matthew 5:17, saying that Jesus proceeds to contradict the Scripture in the following verses. Here it is enough to say that Christ was not contradicting the Old Testament, but He was denying the traditional or scribal interpretations of it. For instance, in verse 43, "Ye have heard that it *hath been said* [not "it is written"], Thou shalt love thy neighbor, and hate thine enemy." Only the first part of this quotation (Lev. 19:18) is from the Old Testament. The last part is not. Jesus contradicted the last part—the Pharisaic addition. In similar verses, it can be shown that Jesus did not contradict the Old Testament itself. He exposed the scribal additions, mistranslations, and twistings. He honored the Old Testament itself as the sure Word of God.

Jesus' attitude toward the Old Testament is also shown in many general references. He quoted from it to banish Satan (Matt. 4:4, 7, 10). He began His ministry in Capernaum by reading Isaiah in the synagogue (Luke 4:16-19). To the assembled congregation He declared, "This day is this scripture fulfilled in your ears" (Luke 4:21). He told the Sadducees that they erred, "not knowing the scriptures" (Matt. 22:29). He appealed to the Scriptures to justify His own actions on the Sabbath (Matt. 12:5), His cleansing of the temple (Matt. 21:13), and His acceptance of the people's praise at His triumphal entry (Matt. 21:16). He declared that He must suffer in accordance with prophetic Scripture (Luke 18:31-34).

He affirmed that Judas's action was foretold (Mark 14:21; John 13:18; 15:25). Jesus even refrained from calling on the angels for help that "the scriptures be fulfilled" (Matt. 26:54). His whole attitude was one of submission to the Scriptures. It is summed up in the remarkable verse: "But the scriptures must be fulfilled" (Mark 14:49). If Jesus thus accepted the Scripture, who are we to question or to deny it? Christians should believe and obey the Word of God.

Much more could be said. Jesus accepted the Old Testament's *acts* as well as its *teachings*, its *history* as well as its *doctrines*. He believed it all. He referred to Jonah and the huge fish (Matt. 12:40 NIV), the creation of Adam and Eve by God (Mark 10:6), Noah's ark (Matt. 24:38), and Lot's wife (Luke 17:32). In all the Gospels and in many passages, Jesus is presented consistently as fully believing the Old Testament. Today even most unbelieving scholars admit that Jesus did believe in the Old Testament. These unbelievers simply do not believe Jesus. But for the Christian, Christ's word is enough.

THE APOSTLES BELIEVED IT

Further confirmation can be found in the attitude of the apostles who had learned from Christ. An outstanding example is in Paul's second letter to Timothy. This was Paul's last letter, and it is filled with serious admonitions. Paul wanted to leave Timothy with a solemn charge: "Preach the word" (2 Tim. 4:2). To emphasize this command, he reminds Timothy that "All scripture is given by inspiration of God, and is profitable for doctrine, for reproof, for correction, for instruction in righteousness" (2 Tim. 3:16).

Some have questioned the meaning of this verse, but there is no need to do so. The word *inspiration* does not mean "breathed in," but literally "God-breathed"—that is, spoken by God. There is no doubt as to what Scriptures are meant. Some would translate it, "Every Scripture inspired of God is also profitable" (RSV), as if only some Scriptures are in view. But the Scriptures referred to are made perfectly clear by verse 15. They were the Old Testament Scriptures that Timothy had learned at his Jewish mother's knee.

Peter's final epistle is equally explicit. He foresaw his coming death (2 Pet. 1:14) and was anxious to leave a worthy legacy. To keep his friends established in the faith, he recommends the prophetic Scriptures, which "came not in old time by the will of man: but holy men of God spake as they were moved by the Holy Ghost" (2 Pet. 1:21).

The other apostles quoted the Old Testament just as Jesus did.

Whereas Jesus said that David wrote Psalm 110 by the Holy Spirit (Mark 12:36), Peter declared that David was a prophet and thus predicted Christ in Psalm 16 (Acts 2:30-31). Paul quoted Isaiah 6 and said that the Holy Spirit spoke this through Isaiah (Acts 28:25). Hebrews says the same thing: "God . . . spake . . . by the prophets" (Heb. 1:1).

The proof is complete and satisfying. Christ and the apostles whom He had taught accepted the Old Testament as the true and trustworthy Word of God.

Notice that Bible scholars do not here merely prove the Bible from the Bible. This is not circular reasoning. They first accept the New Testament as the solid historical account of Christ's life and teachings. The New Testament is plainly such an account. Then they investigate the teachings of Christ, examining how Christ proved Himself to be the truth and the source of eternal life. But not only this, Jesus taught that the thirty-nine Old Testament books, known as "the law and the prophets," were the revealed Word of God, true and without error even in detail.

This doctrine that Jesus Himself taught is usually called verbal inspiration. And on His authority we accept it. In former days Christians meant the same thing when they referred to Scripture as infallible or spoke of the plenary ("full" or "complete") inspiration of Scripture. This view of the Bible has been held by believing Christians of all ages. It is based upon the best of reasons, the witness of Christ Himself.

FACTS CONFIRM IT

There are many other factors that confirm the divine origin of the Old Testament. Any serious Bible student should be alert to and be able to evaluate these confirmations.

The Demonstration of Miracles

The miracles done by God's prophets as recorded in the Scriptures indicate that these men spoke from God.

The Confirmation of Prophecy

The Word of God contains hundreds of prophecies. Many of these have already been fulfilled—such as the dispersion of the Jews and the world-wide preaching of the Gospel. Others, such as Christ's second coming, are to be fulfilled at some future time.

This argument from prophecy will be pursued further in chapter 8. But at present note that the prophecies are evidences of the supernatural character of the Bible. They were intended to prove that God had spoken. That a prophecy had come to pass was one of the tests of a prophet of God as found in Deuteronomy 18:20-22. Micaiah prophesied in advance Ahab's death at Ramoth-Gilead and staked his claim to revelation in its fulfillment (1 Kings 22:28). Long-range prophecies, such as the prediction in Isaiah 44:26-28 that Cyrus would rebuild the temple at Jerusalem, are examples. And the predictions are often startlingly definite. Other books not dependent on the Bible do not give such prophecies. The Koran or sacred books of the East or the Christian Science book, *Science and Health, with Key to the Scriptures*, or the books of Greek philosophy—none of these attempt what the Bible does in hundreds of places scattered through all its major divisions. Skeptical minds seek explanations for this phenomenon. No satisfactory answer can be given apart from belief that Bible prophecy is a message from God, giving not merely impressions and feelings but definite information and revelations from above.

The Reality of Spiritual Truth

The Bible deals with heavenly and spiritual realities such as conversion, victory in Christ, the efficacy of prayer, and Christian fellowship. These and a great host of other divine realities bear testimony that the Bible is God's Word.

The Testimony of History

Another argument is that for centuries many people have been consistent in telling of the one true God, even in times when all other cultures of antiquity were sunk in polytheism and degradation. If we can judge by its fruit, the Bible is indeed from God.

FAITH AFFIRMS IT

At the beginning of this chapter, it was stated that some people believe the Bible because reason explains it. This is, in itself, not sufficient. The fact is that the best reasons will not convince an unbeliever. God-given faith is the convincing proof that the Bible is the very Word of God.

This does not mean that the above arguments or reasons are poor or inadequate. It simply means that the unsaved are blind to the Gospel. "Spiritual things . . . are spiritually discerned" (1 Cor. 2:13-14). Color-blind people cannot experience the difference between green and red. Blind individuals cannot see the sunlight.

Only as the Spirit of God operates on unregenerate hearts will unbelievers be able to fully believe the Bible. The unsaved may believe the

Bible to be reliable history or sound advice. They may be impressed by its moral worth. But only the secret operation of the Holy Spirit can enable them to see the Bible for what it is—a revelation of God.

This truth is usually called the inner testimony of the Holy Spirit. We should be careful, however, that we understand this doctrine. Christians do not hear a voice saying, "This little black book is inspired." The Spirit does not give a witness or a light or revelation beyond the Bible. Rather He bears witness by and with the Word in our hearts. As Abraham Kuyper puts it, the Spirit witnesses to the "centrum," the basic facts of our salvation. The Bible gives us the way of salvation. The Spirit gives us eyes to see and accept and appreciate this salvation.

The Holy Spirit begets genuine heart faith through the preaching and teaching of the Gospel. People hear the facts of the gospel story—Jesus' life, death, and resurrection. They are convicted of sin by the Spirit and persuaded that Christ is the only Savior. "He that believeth on the Son of God hath the witness in himself. . . . And this is the record, that God hath given to us eternal life, and this life is in his Son. He that hath the Son hath life; and he that hath not the Son of God hath not life" (1 John 5:10-12). They have been converted and enabled to trust in Christ and to believe His teaching. These teachings include the fact that the Bible is the very Word of God. Such "believers" are children of God—Christians.

Christians "grow in grace" as they read and study the Bible. More and more they see the proofs of its divinity. They accept by *faith* and by *reason* the truth of its teachings about God, man, sin, and the Savior. The infallible proofs have been used by the Spirit to bring sinners to Christ and to open their eyes to accept "all that the prophets have spoken."

"These things have I written unto you that believe on the name of the Son of God; that ye may know that ye have eternal life, and that ye may believe on the name of the Son of God" (1 John 5:13).

VOCABULARY ENRICHMENT

Plenary inspiration, verbal inspiration.

DISCUSSION QUESTIONS

1. Using a concordance, locate all the New Testament occurrences of the term "Moses and the prophets" or the "law and the prophets."
2. What proof is there that Jesus taught the same thing about the Old Testament after His resurrection as before?
3. Memorize two or three texts showing Jesus' belief in the Scriptures.

4. What are your personal reasons for believing the Old Testament to be God's Word?
5. What did Jesus mean by His statement in Matthew 5:17?
6. Arrange a panel discussion, creating a probable situation in which a skeptic challenges a Christian with the question, "Why believe the Bible?"

Chapter Three

WHY CHRISTIANS BELIEVE THE BIBLE: NEW TESTAMENT

CHRISTIANS WHO BELIEVE THE Old Testament usually have no difficulty believing the New Testament. This is natural. The New Testament gives the gospel story of Christ and the detailed history of the founding and spreading of the early church. Since the New Testament was written in more recent times than the Old Testament, there is abundant testimony by those who were contemporary with the authors or their immediate followers.

Anyone whose eyes have been opened by the Spirit to Old Testament truths will readily embrace the New. It is important, nevertheless, to be explicit about our beliefs in these matters and to study the evidences for the truth of the New Testament. Furthermore, a knowledge of the New Testament and its origin will add to the understanding of the origin of the Old.

In the case of the Old Testament, it is possible to quote Christ to the effect that the whole book is perfect and complete. This cannot be done with the New Testament, for it was written in its entirety after Christ ascended to heaven. We must therefore establish the principles that bear upon our belief in the New Testament from what Christ said beforehand and from what apostles have recorded of His teachings.

THE APOSTLES TESTIFY

The claims of the apostles in these matters are very explicit. Some skeptical people have assumed that the apostles had no idea that their writings would be received, collected together, and treasured as the Word of God. In the minds of such skeptics, Paul wrote letters much as we write letters today, and it was only in later times that they were venerated and then collected. This view denies any special gifts of the Spirit to the apostles. It denies that these writings were inspired by God. Such skepticism opposes the frequent claims of the apostles that they were intentionally writing to be believed and obeyed. Finally, it contradicts the plain facts of history that these books were received and treasured, not hundreds of years later, but as far back as present-day evidence goes— back to the days of the apostles themselves.

It is necessary to look closely at the claims of the apostles. These claims were made most prominently in connection with problems that arose when disobedient churches rebelled against their teachers. It is well known that this happened, especially in Corinth. What claims does Paul make for his authority, especially to the Corinthians?

Paul

Briefly, but emphatically, Paul claims to speak and to write the Word of God. First Corinthians was written to a divided, sinful, and rebellious church. Some of its members claimed spiritual gifts but did not demonstrate a spiritual attitude. In chapters 12 to 14, Paul gave them directions for the use of spiritual gifts. He closed with the rather sharp reminder: "What? came the word of God out from you? or came it unto you only? If any man think himself to be a prophet, or spiritual, let him acknowledge that the things that I write unto you are the commandments of the Lord" (1 Cor. 14:36-37). Paul here clearly claims God-given authority for his writings.

In 1 Thessalonians 2:13, the first epistle he ever wrote, Paul speaks similarly. He commends the Thessalonian Christians for faithfulness and declares that they had received his instruction as the Word of God, which it truly was, not the word of men. Shortly thereafter he wrote 2 Thessalonians because they misunderstood the Second Coming. In this epistle he speaks strongly: "And if any man obey not our word by this epistle, note that man, and have no company with him, that he may be ashamed" (2 Thess. 3:14). Paul gave his churches the Word of God and expected them to believe it and to obey it as such. First Corinthians 2 is an equally forceful section. In defense of his ministry, Paul declared that he spoke "in demonstration of the Spirit" (v. 4), speaking "the wisdom of God" (v. 7), as revealed to him "by his Spirit" (v. 10). He knew the things of God so revealed (v. 12), and he spoke them not in man's words, but in words "which the Holy Ghost teacheth" him (v. 13).

It is possible to miss this point because Paul uses the plural "we" in part of this section. This pronoun could refer to Paul and the other apostles, as in 1 Corinthians 4:9. More likely it is an editorial "we" that Paul uses to speak modestly of himself. And in 2 Corinthians 10:8 he claims the same authority for "us" that he claims for himself personally ("my use of authority") in 2 Corinthians 13:10 (NASB).

Peter

Peter also believed that he wrote under the inspiration of God. In 2 Peter, his final letter, he emphasized the reliability of the Old Testament Scriptures. He also claimed that the gift of inspiration for the apostles was equal to that of the authors of the Old Testament: "Be mindful of the words which were spoken before by the holy prophets, and of the commandment of us the apostles of the Lord and Saviour" (2 Pet. 3:2). See also 2 Peter 1:16. These claims affirm that the Scriptures are to be received and believed.

Peter Approves Paul

Even more direct is Peter's reference to Paul: "Paul also wrote you with the wisdom that God gave him. He writes the same way in all his letters, speaking of them in these matters. . . . His letters contain some things that are hard to understand, which ignorant and unstable people distort, as they do the other Scriptures, to their own destruction" (2 Pet. 3:15-16 NIV). Here Peter asserts that Paul wrote Scriptures that, like the Old Testament, may be twisted, but only to the readers' peril. He specifically mentions certain "epistles" of Paul.

This passage in which Peter refers to the writings of Paul is remarkable as possibly the first instance of applying the term "Scripture" to other New Testament writings. Another place where this seems to have been done is 1 Timothy 5:18: "For the scripture saith, Thou shalt not muzzle the ox that treadeth out the corn. And, The labourer is worthy of his reward." This quotation consists of two statements. The first part is taken from Deuteronomy 25:4. The second quotation is identical (in the Greek) with Luke 10:7. It seems most natural to believe that Paul here quotes from the Old Testament and also from the third Gospel, calling both "Scripture."

A third passage of this nature is Jude 17-18. Here Jude recalls to mind "the words which were spoken before of the apostles of our Lord Jesus Christ." He quotes almost verbatim from 2 Peter 3:3. This quotation supports the apostolic authorship and early date of 2 Peter and shows the high regard for the apostolic company in those early days.

John

The concluding witness is the apostle John. In writing his gospel account, John clearly identifies himself as the beloved disciple who leaned on Jesus' breast at the Last Supper. He affirms that his writing and testimony are both true (John 21:20-24).

In the first epistle also, John presents a detailed claim that he was an eyewitness and that he was writing a message heard from God (1 John 1:1-5). He warns that false prophets are abroad and urges Christians to use discernment (4:1). Without hesitation he writes, "We are of God: he that knoweth God heareth us; he that is not of God heareth not us" (1 John 4:6). Meyer's commentary on this passage declares that it teaches that John and the other apostles spoke from God.

TESTIMONY OF REVELATION

Probably the most emphatic claims for New Testament Scripture are made by John in the book of Revelation. Many Christians apply these verses to the whole Bible, but their primary reference is to the book of Revelation. The principles, however, may be applied to the whole volume. The book, called "The Revelation of Jesus Christ Through John," has a salutation (1:4-5) like the writings of Paul. The book assures blessing for all who read, hear, and obey it (1:3). It pronounces a frightful curse on anyone who dares to "add unto" or "take away from the words of the book of this prophecy" (22:18-19). The reason is given by the revealing angel: "These sayings are faithful and true: and the Lord God of the holy prophets sent his angel to show unto his servants the things which must shortly be done. . . . blessed is he that keepeth the sayings of the prophecy of this book" (22:6-7). Later (v. 10) the Lord commands John to leave the sayings of the prophecy of this book unsealed. Note the contrast between this statement and Daniel 12:9 where the vision was to be "closed up and sealed till the time of the end." Revelation is actually put into the same class as the Old Testament. This was the apostolic position, and it must be our attitude toward the New Testament as a whole.

THE APOSTOLIC OFFICE

Why could the apostles speak thus of their own work? The answer is to be found in Christ's personal appointment of the Twelve and the fact that He personally promised their endowment with the Holy Spirit for their special work as teachers of the Word of God.

Consider the majesty of the office of apostle. Christ Himself selected the Twelve after His night of intercession (Luke 6:12-13). He later promised that they would "sit upon twelve thrones, judging the twelve tribes of Israel" (Matt. 19:28). Their names are inscribed on the twelve foundation stones of the New Jerusalem (Rev. 21:14). The church is "built upon the foundation of the apostles and prophets, Jesus Christ Himself being the chief corner stone" (Eph. 2:20). The apostles are first in the church (1 Cor. 12:28). The apostles, along with the Old Testament prophets, were ordained to this special privilege. The apostles were witnesses of Christ's resurrection (Acts 1:22). Christ promised that His Spirit would reveal to them God's Word.

In John's record of the Last Supper and subsequent events, many precious promises are given (John 13 to 17). In some cases, the apostles are distinguished from later Christians. In John 17:20, Jesus prayed, "Neither pray I for these alone, but for them also which shall believe on me through their word." John 14:26 and 16:13 are equally vivid. In John 14:26, the Holy Ghost was promised to the apostles. Though He comes to all Christians, this verse specifically promises that He would come to the apostles so that they might remember the words Jesus had spoken to them.

It is quite possible that the apostles had taken some notes of Jesus' messages. A system of shorthand was in use even in those days, and some of the apostles may have used it. Whether this was the case or not, the Holy Spirit was specifically promised to give them a remembrance of the gospel story. He was to guide them into all truth (John 16:13). Some Christians have uncritically held that this is a promise to the church at large. But the context clearly limits the promise of the Spirit's inspiring and revealing work to the apostles. He was promised to show "you things to come." This is not the Spirit's general illumination to all believers, but a specific promise to the Twelve.

What abundant proof of the New Testament's authenticity. Never cease to marvel at the way in which it was written. God who had spoken by the prophets sent His Son for our salvation. After Christ's ascension, the New Testament church was miraculously established at Pentecost. Its founders and leaders were chosen by Christ Himself. They were the apostles—with special gifts of inspiration and special apostolic signs to accompany their office. They claimed to speak and to write the Word of God the same as did the prophets of old. They called each other's writing "Scripture." They insisted that these writings should be read and obeyed. They spoke in Christ's name. They taught with His authority.

All branches of the church have historically held that the words of the apostles and of their assistants (such as Mark and Luke) are to be received as the very Word of God spoken. We are therefore fully justified in declaring that the New Testament, just like the Old Testament, was written by holy men of God moved by the Holy Spirit.

THE EARLY CHURCH FATHERS TESTIFY

The high regard for the apostles was shared by the early Church Fathers, who wrote immediately after the apostolic times.

Clement, Bishop of Rome

Clement, a bishop of the church in Rome, wrote a letter to the Corinthian Christians in A.D. 95. In it he referred to the "illustrious apostles," Peter and Paul. He said that the apostles preached the Gospel of Christ and were confirmed in the Word with full assurance of the Holy Spirit. He argued that they had perfect foreknowledge of church affairs. Finally, he said, "the blessed Apostle Paul" wrote to the Corinthians "under the inspiration of the Spirit" about the party strife that they showed toward the apostles (i.e., Peter and Paul) and "a man whom they have approved" (i.e., Apollos). Clearly, Clement revered the apostles and believed their writings.

Ignatius of Antioch

Ignatius lived in Clement's time. He was a bishop in the church at Antioch and was martyred either in A.D. 107 or 117. On his way to Rome for execution he wrote seven short epistles to different churches and individuals. Several times he contrasted himself with the apostles and lauded the apostles highly. For instance, in his letter to the Ephesians, he referred to "Paul the holy, the martyred, the deservedly most happy," who had written them an epistle. To the Romans he wrote, "I do not as Peter and Paul issue commandments unto you. They were apostles; I am but a condemned man."

Polycarp

Polycarp was also a famous martyr who gave his life for Christ at an advanced age. He died in about A.D. 155, having been a Christian (he said) for eighty-six years. In his youth he had known the apostle John. Ignatius wrote one of his letters to Polycarp. Polycarp's letter to the Philippians, written about A.D. 118, quoted from about half of the books of the New Testament. He referred to the apostles as parallel to the Old Testament prophets. He declared that he could not "come up to the wisdom of the blessed and glorified Paul," who had written them a letter. He referred to the martyrdom of Ignatius but reserved the classification of apostle for Paul and men like him.

Other Church Fathers

Other authors, such as Papias, Irenaeus, and Tertullian, provide more specific references to such things, so that we have much testimony from the next generation of men.

Chronology of Some Church Fathers and Writings

A.D.

95	Clement of Rome
117	Ignatius
118	Polycarp's Letter
130	Epistle of Barnabas
145	Papias
145	Justin Martyr, Barnabas, Hermas,
160	Epistles of Hermas
160	*Didache* (di-da-kay) or Teaching of the Twelve Apostles
170	Irenaeus, Muratorian Fragment
200	Tertullian, Clement of Alexandria

VOCABULARY ENRICHMENT

Apostle, Clement, early Church Fathers, Ignatius, Polycarp, Revelation.

DISCUSSION QUESTIONS

1. Compare the list of apostles in Matthew 10:2-4; Luke 6:14-16; and Acts 1:13, 26.
2. In 1 Corinthians 2:13 and 1 Thessalonians 2:13, how does Paul claim that his writings are true? What did he say regarding the inspiration of his public verbal teaching?
3. In what two passages do New Testament books call other New Testament books Scripture?
4. How did Paul fit the test that an apostle must be a witness of the resurrection of Jesus (1 Cor. 15:8-9)?
5. Can anyone properly be called an apostle today? What reasons can you give in support of your answer (Acts 1:22)?
6. What curses are given in Revelation for those who alter Scripture? What is promised for those who read it and keep it?
7. What reasons are there for personally accepting the New Testament as equally inspired as the Old Testament?
8. Examine the chronology chart above.

Chapter Four

WHO WROTE THE OLD TESTAMENT?

GOD COULD HAVE COMMUNICATED His will and His work to us in dozens of ways. He chose the writing of the Bible to reveal His wisdom and truth. Before Moses' day, God evidently spoke directly to Adam, Cain, Enoch, Noah, Abraham, and others. These men communicated God's Word to others by word of mouth. Apparently it was not written down. Indeed, there were ages during which writing had not yet been invented. Eventually, however, God commissioned certain men to write down the message He had given to them.

A study of inspiration shows that God wrote the sacred volume by His Spirit. The Bible is also a divine library with many human authors. It is our purpose to study these human authors, but we must always remember that the Bible is a single volume, one book, written by one Author, the Holy Spirit. This book has one great theme, redemption, and one great historical thread, God's saving dealings with fallen mankind.

MOSES

The first author of the Scripture was Moses, with whom God spoke "mouth to mouth, even apparently, and not in dark speeches" (Num. 12:8). Moses wrote the first five books called the Pentateuch or Law of Moses. The Jewish name is Torah (Law). He also wrote Psalm 90.

Never depreciate or minimize the work of the Holy Spirit when speaking of Moses' genius, for the Lord gave him his genius and his training. When God has a work to be done, He chooses the right man to do it. Moses was that man. Moses stood at the threshold of a new day. God had previously dealt with individuals and families. Now, in accordance with His promise to Abraham, He would weld Israel into a nation. Through God's providence, Moses, a slave by birth, "was learned in all the wisdom of the Egyptians" (Acts 7:22). He had learned of Israel's

God at his mother's knee, for she cared for her own son as Pharaoh's daughter's hired nurse.

At Pharaoh's court Moses studied reading, writing, and Egyptian culture. He learned the Egyptian and Akkadian (Babylonian) languages, in addition to his native Hebrew. He probably studied the Babylonian classics, civil administration, and military science. All this training and inborn ability was used in later years when God made him the leader of the nation, the judge of Israel, the captain of the army, the architect of the tabernacle, the people's poet, and the divine prophet and lawgiver. What a chosen vessel was Moses! What a man of God!

Moses was probably born about 1520 B.C., during one of the greatest periods of Egypt's history. His writings are known and loved around the world. He stands at the head of a long line of Old Testament prophets who revealed God's will to Israel for more than 1,000 years.

THE PROPHETIC LINE

God provided tests by which prophets were to be judged (Deut. 13 and 18). False prophets were those who disagreed with the true revelation already given and whose predictions did not come true. Exodus 4:1-5 shows that miracles also were given as a certification of the prophet's word. By these standards, Israel knew who God's true prophets were and which prophets were false. All the true prophets typified the great Prophet to come, Jesus Christ.

We do not know the names of all the prophets, but we do know many of them. Samuel wrote at least one book about the kingdom when Saul was anointed king (1 Sam. 10:25). He wrote a history of David's reign (1 Chron. 29:29) and delivered many prophecies. David, sweet singer and great king, was also a prophet (Acts 2:30). He wrote about half of the book of Psalms. From David to Malachi there were dozens of prophets. In this group were Elijah and Elisha, about 850 B.C.; Isaiah, Hosea, Joel, about 725 B.C.; Jeremiah, Nahum, Habakkuk, and Zephaniah about 600 B.C.; Ezekiel, Daniel, and others of captivity and post-captivity days to about 400 B.C.

There was also a succession of lesser-known prophets who recorded the history of the same period. These prophets are mentioned in a chain of references in Chronicles. For David's era, 1 Chronicles 29:29 mentions Samuel, Nathan, and Gad. For Solomon, 2 Chronicles 9:29 names Ahijah and Iddo. In 2 Chronicles 12:15, Shemaiah is also listed for the history of Rehoboam. Others were Jehu, the son of Hanani, who wrote of Jehoshaphat (2 Chron. 20:34), and Isaiah, who wrote of

Uzziah and Hezekiah (2 Chron. 26:22 and 32:32). Many other prophets are mentioned.

Most Old Testament books were written by prophets whose names we know. The others are included in the "more sure word of prophecy" (2 Pet. 1:19) and the books of the "prophets which are read every sabbath" (Acts 13:27). An examination of the Old Testament will reveal much detail about their writing.

Between the Pentateuch and David's time, Israel's history is given in Joshua, Judges, Ruth, and possibly Job. It is not specifically known who wrote Joshua, but Joshua himself probably wrote it or at least part of it. He was filled with the Spirit (Deut. 34:9), the people feared him as they had Moses (Josh. 4:14), and he wrote the words of the covenant in the Book of the Law of God (Josh. 24:26). He used the prophets' formula: "Thus saith the Lord" (Josh. 24:2). One apocryphal book, written in the time between the Testaments, calls Joshua the "successor of Moses in prophecies" (Ecclesiasticus 46:1).

Judges and Ruth present the period from Joshua to Samson. Judges portrays the sinfulness of those days (Judg. 17–21). Ruth is a beautiful picture of the godly who maintained the faith through dark days. Ruth was the great-grandmother of David. Judges–Ruth were united in one book in the old Hebrew enumeration and were probably written at the close of this period.

Job presents special considerations. Conservative scholars believe that this book is quite old, possibly written before Moses. It is argued that Job does not mention tabernacle worship. Instead, Job sacrificed at his sons' houses, much as Abraham offered private sacrifices. Other scholars have placed Job quite late. Their arguments are based on its style and its theology. These are the same arguments often given for the lateness of other books that the Bible specifically calls early. We cannot accept the arguments for its extreme lateness.

David, about 1000 B.C., is the chief author of the Psalms. Heman, Asaph, and other authors are referred to as prophets of God (1 Chron. 25:5; 2 Chron. 29:30). Eighteen psalms have no titles, but the Greek Septuagint translation assigns some to Haggai, Zechariah, and others.

Solomon wrote Ecclesiastes, the Song of Songs (Song of Solomon), and most of the Proverbs. It is now possible to place Solomon's reign at about 960-920 B.C. Archeological discoveries have shown Solomon's reign to be the time of Israel's greatest material success. Under his leadership, the worship of God at the new temple was established and furthered. He was a suitable author for the books that the Jews call Wisdom

Literature. The burden of Proverbs is that "the fear of the LORD is the beginning of wisdom" (Prov. 9:10). It is not merely a book of worldly-wise sayings. It contrasts good and evil and shows the necessity of trust in the Lord (Prov. 22:19). In Proverbs, the "wise" man is the godly man, and the "fool" is the sinner. The final chapters, called "prophecy" by men unknown to us (Prov. 30:1; 31:1), may have been added later.

Ecclesiastes, a book of philosophy, raises the question, "What is the chief end of man?" Various unsatisfactory answers are given and examined. The final answer of the "Preacher, the son of David, king in Jerusalem" is "Fear God, and keep his commandments" (Eccles. 12:13).

Solomon's Song of Songs is a poem of true love, typifying God's love for His people. Its conclusion may well be translated, "love is strong as death; jealousy is cruel as the grave. . . . Many waters cannot quench love" (Song of Sol. 8:6-7).

Solomon's writings, composed in his early years, were included in the Scriptures said to be given by God through "his prophets" (Rom. 1:2). Proverbs is quoted in the Dead Sea Scrolls of the second century B.C. with the phrase reserved for Scripture: "It is written."

Three great cycles of prophetic activity complete the Old Testament. In the 700s, God raised up great prophets to warn and comfort Israel during the Assyrian menace. These included Isaiah, the "evangelical prophet," and several of the Minor Prophets. Joel, Amos, and Jonah may have been the earliest of these. Isaiah, Hosea, and Micah soon followed. Obadiah is not dated but may be placed in this period because of its traditional position between Amos and Jonah. Of these, Hosea and Amos prophesied to the Northern Kingdom, which was carried off after several invasions to Assyria in 721 B.C.

During the century beginning about 625 B.C., Jeremiah ministered to the dying kingdom of Judah. This period also witnessed three Minor Prophets—Nahum, Habakkuk, and Zephaniah—all of whom predicted the downfall of Nineveh, the Assyrian capital. It fell in about 612 B.C. Shortly thereafter Nebuchadnezzar brought Babylon to the peak of its power. In expanding his conquests to the west, he broke the power of Egypt and finally demolished Judah in a series of attacks in 604, 597, and 586 B.C. The pitifully small group of captives taken to Babylon marked the end of real Jewish independence until A.D. 1948.

During the exile, Ezekiel and Daniel prophesied to the remnant in Babylon. These men did much to keep alive the true faith in those dark days. Their prophecies predicting the Messiah as Israel's hope brought into focus the great Messianic revelations of David, Isaiah, Micah, and others.

After the exile, the Jews returned to Palestine in three stages. In 538 B.C., Cyrus let the Jews return under Zerubbabel. At this time Haggai and Zechariah prophesied to the people in Jerusalem and encouraged them to build the second temple in 516 B.C. About this same time, Esther was written in Mesopotamia to show God's providential care over the captives who had remained behind, as well as to emphasize the dangers the Jews were exposed to while living under the pagan kings of Persia. Haman's massacre probably made many more Jews ready for the later stages of the return.

These later returns took place in 456 and 444 B.C. Ezra and then Nehemiah returned to rebuild the city and the wall. The first chapters of Ezra tell about the earlier return of Zerubbabel in 538 B.C. The rest of Ezra and all of Nehemiah trace the history to about 400 B.C. Malachi, last of the Minor Prophets, completed the Old Testament in about 400 B.C., after which the voice of prophecy was stilled. According to Jewish tradition and history, there was no prophet until John the Baptist announced the coming of a new age.

Thus the Old Testament was written from 1400 B.C. to 400 B.C. by more than twenty known authors and some unknown writers. The English Old Testament is conveniently divided into five groups of books. This division is a modification of the Latin Bible from the Greek Septuagint.

> 5 — The Law
> 12 — History
> 5 — Poetry
> 5 — Major Prophets
> <u>12</u> — Minor Prophets
> 39

Dates of Old Testament Books

B.C.

1400	Genesis, Exodus, Leviticus, Numbers, Deuteronomy
1400	Job (?)
1350	Joshua
1050	Judges-Ruth
1000	Psalms (the majority)
1000-575	1, 2 Samuel; 1, 2 Kings
950	Proverbs, Ecclesiastes, Song of Solomon
750-700	Isaiah, Hosea, Joel (?), Amos, Obadiah (?), Jonah, Micah
625-575	Jeremiah, Nahum, Habakkuk, Zephaniah
600-539	Ezekiel, Daniel
539-515	Haggai, Zechariah
475	Esther
456-400	1, 2 Chronicles, Ezra, Nehemiah, Malachi

The Hebrew Old Testament is now arranged in three divisions—the Law, Prophets, and Writings. There are five books of the Law, four books of earlier Prophets, four books of later Prophets (the twelve Minor Prophets count as one book), and eleven books of Writings. The total of twenty-four books includes, in various combinations, all of our thirty-nine books and no others.

Our present threefold division is perhaps due to liturgical usage and can be traced back to about A.D. 200. Before that a threefold division was used (along with the twofold "law and prophets"), but the books in each division were different. Two of the smaller books had been combined with others. Josephus (see below) put five books in the Law, thirteen in the Prophets, and four in a third division.

The Dead Sea Scrolls refer to the whole volume as "the work of Moses and the Prophets." Jesus referred to this book after His resurrection when He challenged His apostles to believe "all that the prophets have spoken" (Luke 24:25).

THE APOCRYPHA

Seven other complete books and a few additions are included in Roman Catholic Bibles. These additions are called the Apocrypha. A study of their origin will show why Protestants do not include them.

The Names of the Apocryphal Books

The Apocryphal books were evidently written during the period between the Old and New Testaments. Only one is dated. Two books, Judith and Tobit, tell of the Assyrian and Babylonian invasions. Two more, 1 and 2 Maccabees, record the Jewish War of Independence at about 165 B.C. Two more are books of wisdom—Ecclesiasticus and Wisdom of Solomon. One is an addendum to Jeremiah. There are also short additions to Esther and Daniel.

Several other books written during this period are not accepted by either Romanists or Protestants. These give the history and thought of the intertestamental period. They are such books as Enoch, Jubilees, and Testament of the Twelve Patriarchs. Fragments of these have been found among the Dead Sea Scrolls. These books were not received or quoted as Scripture. They are of some value but have never been in the canon.

Josephus, the Jewish Historian

How can we be sure these books should not be included in the Old Testament canon? It is certain they were not in the Scripture recognized and used by Christ and the apostles. The Jewish historian Josephus, who wrote in about A.D. 90, lived during the fall of Jerusalem in A.D. 70. His autobiography tells how the Emperor Titus gave him the sacred scrolls from the temple at Jerusalem when it was pillaged. He was qualified to know the canon of Jesus' day. In a significant writing, he says:

We have not an innumerable multitude of books among us disagreeing and contradicting one another, but only twenty-two books which contain the records of all the past times, which are justly believed to be divine. And of them, five belong to Moses, which contain his laws, and the traditions of the origin of mankind till his death. This interval of time was little short of three thousand years. But as to the time from the death of Moses till the reign of Artaxerxes, king of Persia, who reigned after Xerxes, the prophets, who were after Moses, wrote down what was done in their times in thirteen books. The remaining four books contain hymns to God and precepts for the conduct of human life. It is true our history hath been written since Artaxerxes very particularly, but hath not been esteemed of a like authority with the former by our forefathers, because there hath not been an exact succession of prophets since that time, and how firmly we have given credit to these books of our nation, is evident by what we do; for during so many ages as have already passed, no one hath been so bold as either to add anything to them, to take anything from them, or to make any change in them; but it has become natural to all Jews, immediately and from their very birth, to esteem these books to contain divine doctrines, and to persist in them, and, if occasion be, willingly to die for them.

This quotation teaches several things. First, the Jews believed in verbal inspiration. Second, they received the canonical books because these were written by prophets. Third, it was known that the Apocryphal books and others were not written by prophets. Fourth, the canon included all of our thirty-nine books and no others. Fifth, but very important, Josephus gives the first and only listing until about A.D. 170 of the Old Testament books. They were listed in three divisions, which are not the same as the three divisions common among the later Jews and found in modern Hebrew Bibles. Josephus placed the Pentateuch first, then all the books of Prophecy and History, then four books of Poetry and instruction (probably Psalms, Proverbs, Song of Songs, and Ecclesiastes). Sixth, he gave great prominence to prophetic authorship.

The New Testament quotes from almost all thirty-nine canonical books but not once from the Apocrypha. Jesus referred to the Old Testament once as "the law of Moses," "the prophets," and "the psalms"

(Luke 24:44). The New Testament often cites the Old Testament in two divisions—the Law and the Prophets or Moses and all the Prophets (Matt. 5:17; Luke 16:29; 24:27). It never cites the Apocrypha.

Dead Sea Scrolls

The Dead Sea Scrolls supply further confirmation. They indicate that the Scriptures are the word of Moses and the prophets. They quote many Old Testament books as Scripture but none of the Apocrypha.

Septuagint

The situation is a closed case except for one problem. Present-day copies of the Septuagint contain the Apocrypha. Since the New Testament frequently quotes from the Septuagint Old Testament, many scholars argue that the New Testament sanctions the Apocrypha. It is important, however, to know that our Septuagint copies come from a late time—about A.D. 325. There is no evidence that the early Septuagint contained the Apocrypha. Indeed there is evidence against it.

Early Church Fathers

Most of the early Church Fathers who touch on this subject excluded the Apocrypha. Melito, a bishop of Sardis in A.D. 170, listed the Old Testament books paralleling our listing, and he excluded the Apocrypha. The learned Origen of Egypt in A.D. 250 also excluded the Apocrypha. Jerome, who translated the Apocryphal books into Latin, explicitly said they were non-canonical. Only two ancient councils, and those not widely authoritative, approved the Apocrypha. A later one was the Roman Catholic Council of Trent in A.D. 1545, when the Romanists, in opposition to the Protestants, insisted that the Apocrypha was inspired. There is hardly a shakier point in Roman Catholic theology.

We believe that the thirty-nine canonical books of the Old Testament are the inspired Word of God. The Apocryphal books are not. The thirty-nine were approved by Jesus and the apostles. The others were not. Most of these thirty-nine were clearly written by prophets. If Samuel and Kings are the work of the succession of prophets mentioned in Chronicles (1 Chron. 29:29; 2 Chron. 9:29; 12:15; 20:34; 26:22; 32:32), and if Solomon received visions as a prophet from God, then at least thirty of the Old Testament books were written by prophets. The other nine may have been written by prophets. They are included with the thirty as the work of prophets by the New Testament, the Dead Sea Scroll authors, and Josephus. The Apocrypha and other books have no such claim to be a revelation from God. We may read the Apocrypha for information and insights into the history and culture of the intertestamental period and what life was like at the time of Christ, but we reserve our faith and confidence for the books approved by Christ. "They have Moses and the prophets; let them hear them" (Luke 16:29).

VOCABULARY ENRICHMENT

Apocrypha, Pentateuch, Septuagint, Torah

DISCUSSION QUESTIONS

1. Memorize the names of the Old Testament books. Check your spelling and pronunciation of these names.
2. Could a prophet also be a king (Acts 2:30)? A priest (Ezek. 1:3)?
3. What prophet was predicted as yet to come when the Old Testament closed (Mal. 4:5; Matt. 17:12-13; Luke 1:17)?
4. Compare our popular division of the Old Testament into five parts with the Hebrew three-part division.
5. Try to obtain a copy of the works of Josephus and read what he says about the Old Testament books in *Against Apion*, book 1, chapter 8.
6. How do the Hebrew Scriptures of twenty-two books include all thirty-nine books of our Old Testament canon?
7. What is meant by apocryphal books?
8. Why are apocryphal books not included in the canonical list?
9. Study the chart "Dates of Old Testament Books" in this chapter. Arrange the books in their correct time periods under the following headings: Beginnings to Wilderness Wanderings, In the Promised Land, In Exile, The Exiles Return.

Chapter Five

WHO WROTE THE NEW TESTAMENT?

PETER REFERS TO THE whole Bible when he admonishes us to "be mindful of the words which were spoken before by the holy prophets, and of the commandment of us the apostles of the Lord and Saviour" (2 Pet. 3:2).

Any study of the writing of the New Testament must emphasize the importance of the apostolic office. It should consider the details of the various books, their dates, and their authorship. Also such study would be incomplete without a brief review of the Christian literature written immediately after the days of the apostles. These writings provide external evidence of the various books' authorship and their acceptance and recognition as parts of the Bible.

THE CHURCH FATHERS

The previous chapters have already discussed some of the early Church Fathers, or "Apostolic Fathers," as they are often called. These include Clement of Rome, Ignatius of Antioch, and Polycarp. These men were discussed in relationship to New Testament authority. They are also important in establishing New Testament authorship. We shall see below how their writings support the genuineness of Paul's writings and the writings of other apostles in the New Testament.

Papias

An important link is Papias, who lived about A.D. 140. He tells how he had diligently searched out the traditions of the apostles from those who had personally heard them. In this context he mentioned seven of the twelve apostles. It is known that he wrote a five-volume book on the Gospels. This book has, however, been lost, but some quotations from it tell how the Gospels were written. These excerpts are preserved in Eusebius's *Church History*, written about A.D. 300.

Justin

Slightly later than Papias is Justin, about A.D. 145. Before being martyred for his faith, he wrote several books, seven of which are left. His witness to the Gospels is examined later in this chapter.

General Writings of the Fathers

Several other writings of about this time are known, but their authorship is uncertain. These include *The Epistle of Barnabas*, *Teaching of the Twelve Apostles* (called *Didache*), and the allegory called *The Shepherd of Hermas*. Numerous other early books have been lost. The so-called *Gospel of Truth*, written about A.D. 140 and long lost, has recently been rediscovered. It is not itself valuable, but is a good witness to the early use of many of our New Testament books.

The above list covers the literature to about A.D. 145—fifty years after the last apostle's death. The writing that has been preserved is interesting and valuable. It breathes the air of real Christian devotion.

After A.D. 170, the literature that remains is much more extensive. A work by Irenaeus in A.D. 170 covers more than 250 large pages of English text. His writing is especially important because he was a pupil of Polycarp and therefore linked closely with the apostle John.

This same period provides an invaluable catalog of New Testament books called the Muratorian Fragment, part of which has been destroyed.

Dating about A.D. 200 are extensive writings by Tertullian, who lived in North Africa across from Spain. Clement of Alexandria, Egypt, also wrote at this time (see chart on p. 29).

These early witnesses tell much about the formation of the New Testament. But it is the student's task to combine the ancient, external, Christian witness with the internal witness that the New Testament bears to its own authorship and formation. Therefore, we turn to the New Testament writings themselves and combine with their internal evidence the testimony of the Fathers introduced above.

PAUL'S WRITINGS

The writings of Paul are of primary importance because many of his epistles tell us when they were written. Thirteen epistles, from Romans to Philemon, begin with statements that include Paul's name. Today even critical students admit that most of these letters were written by Paul. There is no objective evidence against the Pauline authorship of any of them.

In Galatians Paul tells something about his life. He saw Peter in

Jerusalem three years after his conversion (Gal. 1:18). Over fourteen years later, he went to Jerusalem again with Barnabas and Titus (Gal. 2:1).

The information and other data in Corinthians and in Acts indicate that Paul was converted in the early thirties and was with Peter in Jerusalem in about A.D. 37 or 38. Paul's witness to the events of Christ's life, therefore, goes right back to the earliest apostolic community in Jerusalem. This is extremely important since it validates Paul's detailed witness to Jesus' resurrection (1 Cor. 15:1-20). Reading the record makes it possible for the reader, as it were, to stand by the empty tomb in Jerusalem within about five years of Christ's resurrection.

Acts teaches the facts of Paul's three missionary journeys and his imprisonment in Palestine for two years and then in Rome for two years. Various hints make it clear that he wrote no epistles on the first journey in southern Asia Minor. During his second journey, which took him through Greece, he stayed at Corinth almost two years and wrote two epistles, 1 and 2 Thessalonians. These should be studied in the light of Acts 18. They are brief epistles dispatched after Paul had received good news of the infant church at Thessalonica. They stress salvation through the divine Christ (1 Thess. 1:9-10) and clearly demonstrate the authority of the apostle (1 Thess. 2:13; 2 Thess. 3:14-17).

Next Paul wrote the so-called major epistles. Galatians was probably written at the start of his third journey. During this time, he stayed at Ephesus about three years and wrote three epistles—Romans, 1 and 2 Corinthians (read Acts 19). Romans and Galatians should be studied together because of similarity in structure, subject matter, and phraseology.

At the end of the third missionary journey, Paul was taken prisoner in Jerusalem. An interesting phenomenon occurs in the book of Acts. In some passages, such as Acts 16:10, the author says "we" went on certain journeys. In others (Acts 20:13-14), the "we" refers to one group of the missionary party traveling on while Paul went a different way by himself. The logical conclusion is that Acts was written by someone who usually traveled with Paul. These "we" sections show that the author went with Paul on his last trip to Jerusalem. This man was undoubtedly free in Palestine for two years while Paul was in jail. Later he accompanied Paul on the shipwreck journey to Rome (Acts 27:2) and was free in Rome for two years while Paul was in bonds there. The Muratorian Fragment, Irenaeus, and other early witnesses name this helper as Luke.

While Paul was in bonds at Rome, he wrote the four important Prison

Epistles—Ephesians, Philippians, Colossians, and Philemon. Colossians and Ephesians have much in common and should be studied together.

Philippians 1:12-25 indicates that Paul was expecting trial and release. This evidently happened, for as he traveled, he left his coat and books at Troas (2 Tim. 4:13). During this time, he wrote the Pastoral Epistles—Titus and 1 and 2 Timothy. First Timothy and Titus are quite similar and help to explain each other. Each gives details about the organization of churches and the qualifications of church officers.

Table of Paul's Writings

Journeys	Writings
First Missionary Journey (in Asia Minor only)	No epistles
Second Missionary Journey (through Asia Minor and Greece; two years at Corinth)	1 Thessalonians 2 Thessalonians
Third Missionary Journey (same territory as second; three years at Ephesus)	Romans 1 Corinthians 2 Corinthians Galatians (or earlier)
Imprisonment in Palestine for two years	No epistles Luke's Gospel (see p. 47)
First Imprisonment in Rome for two years	Prison Epistles Ephesians Philippians Colossians Philemon Acts (see p. 47)
Period of Liberty Travel to Troas and Spain (?)	1 Timothy Titus Hebrews (?)
Second Imprisonment in Rome and martyrdom	2 Timothy

Second Timothy was Paul's last epistle. He was arrested again and doubtless executed (2 Tim. 4:7-8). Clement of Rome in A.D. 95 said that Paul preached in the "extreme limit of the West," fulfilling his desire to visit Spain (Rom. 15:24) after his first Roman imprisonment.

The Pauline Epistles are all used by writers before A.D. 120—thirty years after the death of the last apostle. Some of them were referred to by name.

For instance, Clement, writing in A.D. 95 to the Corinthians, refers expressly to Paul's having written to them. Ignatius in A.D. 117, writing to the Ephesians, refers either to Paul's epistles to them or to his epistles in general. Polycarp, writing to the Philippians in about A.D. 118, refers to Paul's epistle to them and quotes from six of Paul's other epistles.

LUKE'S GOSPEL

Luke was intimately associated with Paul. Acts 1:1 explains that Acts was the author's second writing to Theophilus. Obviously, from Luke 1:1-3, we see that the Gospel of Luke was Luke's first one. The New Testament does not specifically state that Luke was the author of Luke's Gospel or the Acts of the Apostles, but it is clear from the "we" sections that some companion of Paul wrote them. Also the history of the book of Acts has been supported even in small detail by the research of William Ramsey[1] and others. The name and title of Gallio (Acts 18:12), the titles of Sergius Paulus (Acts 13:7) and other officials, and also other historical details are so precise that the most natural conclusion is that it was written by a man contemporary with the events. Luke's Gospel, of course, preceded Acts (Acts 1:1).

Luke's Gospel and Acts were used by both Ignatius and Polycarp. Justin Martyr quoted from the three Synoptic Gospels and probably from John, calling them together "The Memoirs of the Apostles." He gives an interesting description of a Sunday service in which "the Memoirs of the Apostles or the Writings of the Prophets" were read, followed by a sermon. He spoke of the Gospels as the "memoirs which I say were drawn up by His apostles and those who followed them." In this quotation, he shows that Luke and Mark were not directly written by apostles, although elsewhere he calls these books the work of apostles.

In A.D. 170 the Muratorian Fragment and Irenaeus explain that Luke wrote the Gospel, but wrote in some sort of association with Paul. Tertullian, about A.D. 200, ascribed it to Luke, writing under Paul's supervision. He intimates that it can be called Pauline. Origination by the apostle seems to fit all the facts. In 1 Timothy 5:18, Paul quotes briefly from Deuteronomy and from Luke 10:7 in connection with salaries for ministers. In 1 Corinthians 9:7-18, he had argued that same subject quoting extensively from the Old Testament, but not from Luke. The "Table of Paul's Writings" clearly demonstrates that between the writing of 1 Corinthians and 1 Timothy, Paul was imprisoned in Palestine, while Luke was free. These reasons and other evidence lead to the belief that Luke gathered his material and wrote the third Gospel at that time. The book of Acts would have been written shortly afterward, probably during Paul's Roman imprisonment. Both books could have been written by Luke as Paul's understudy.

THE HEBREW EPISTLE

Was the Epistle to the Hebrews written by Paul? If so, when and how? Devout scholars do not agree on the answers to these questions. Some believe that it was written somewhat like Luke and Acts—by one of Paul's helpers under his supervision.

The Epistle to the Hebrews was known and used as early as Clement of Rome in A.D. 95. It was first accepted widely, then questioned in the West, and finally accepted by the entire church. There is little question about its canonicity. The main problem has been its obscure authorship. Wherever its Pauline authorship has been believed, the Epistle has been accepted without question. In Egypt the tradition of Pauline authorship dates back to Clement of Alexandria (A.D. 200), and before him to Pantaenus. Like Polycarp, Pantaenus lived to a great age and connected the Alexandrian church with the early days.

All the facts seem to harmonize when the Epistle is considered Pauline, but indicate that it probably was written down or even translated by Luke or Barnabas or someone similar. It is fairly well established that Paul used stenographers, as Romans 16:22 shows. Origen (d. A.D. 250) has often been quoted as saying, "Who wrote the epistle, in truth, only God knows."[2] But in the context, Origen is talking about the penman and argues that Paul is behind the epistle. In his work *De Principiis*, Origen refers to Hebrews over half a dozen times as by Paul,[3] and in his book *Ad Africanus* he claims specifically that Paul can be proved to be the author.[4] The Chester Beatty Papyrus of the Pauline Epistles comes from about A.D. 200, and it includes Hebrews, placing it between Romans and Corinthians. In any event, Hebrews was probably written during Paul's later life.

MATTHEW'S GOSPEL

The Gospel of Matthew is the one to which we have earliest outside reference. It is used by Clement, Ignatius, Polycarp, and others. Barnabas quoted it with the phrase "it is written." It was never questioned in antiquity. Papias suggests that Matthew wrote in Aramaic, and the Gospel was translated later. If this is true, the Aramaic original has perished. Matthew himself may have published the book in Aramaic and Greek. This was frequently done because both languages were used in Palestine.

This much is obvious: Matthew's Gospel was written with special attention to the Jews who formed the bulk of the earliest Christian church.

MARK'S GOSPEL

Mark wrote the second Gospel, according to Papias, as Peter's helper or interpreter (i.e., translator) in Rome. Justin Martyr used Mark. Irenaeus and Clement of Alexandria agreed as to Mark's authorship. Opinions differ as to whether Mark wrote while Peter was alive. Papias and Clement both believed that Mark wrote under Peter's direction. This is the simplest view, since Justin includes Mark among "The Memoirs of the Apostles." The usage of Mark by the earliest Fathers is difficult to trace because about fifteen-sixteenths of Mark is also found in Matthew or Luke. Many quotations from Mark are identical with Matthew or Luke. Papias's witness, however, is positive and early. Clearly Mark was written for the Gentiles, probably the Romans to whom Peter ministered.

JOHN'S WRITINGS

The writings of John cover most of the rest of the New Testament. John, the beloved disciple, moved to Ephesus and lived to a great age. Polycarp knew him there. Patmos, the island of John's exile, was near Ephesus. Irenaeus, Polycarp's student, tells us that John lived until the days of Trajan (A.D. 98–117). Christians have always held dear the writings of John because they speak with such tender and intimate knowledge of Christ. They claim to be written by John "the beloved."

Their similar style strengthens the claim of each individual book. Both Clement of Rome and Ignatius refer to John's Gospel. Polycarp used 1 John. Papias probably knew John's Gospel, 1 John, and Revelation. Justin testified concerning John's Gospel and Revelation. The incomplete Muratorian Fragment cites by name John's Gospel, Revelation, and two epistles, probably 2 and 3 John. It also quotes 1 John 1:1. The testimony is quite sufficient.

An additional witness is now available. A small scrap of papyrus was discovered in Egypt in 1917 and published in 1931. Handwriting experts date this Rylands Papyrus at about A.D. 125, only thirty years or so after the death of John. This papyrus contains parts of five verses of John 18. Justin or Polycarp could even have seen it in their day.

In 1957 a more extensive papyrus of the Gospel of John was published. This Papyrus Bodmer II is dated about A.D. 200 and covers most of John's Gospel. It was a book, not a scroll, and only a few pages are missing. It is the earliest known extensive portion of the New Testament.

Later another similar papyrus was published, Bodmer XIV-XV, containing nearly all the Gospel of Luke and two-thirds of John bound together. It is possibly a little earlier than Papyrus Bodmer II. These were also books and are a precious early witness to the use and to the text of these Gospels.

PETER, JAMES, AND JUDE

The smaller epistles of Peter, James, and Jude have only limited witness in antiquity, but that witness is positive. Clement alludes to James, Polycarp to 1 and 2 Peter, Papias to 1 Peter. The Muratorian Fragment mentions Jude. Tertullian assures us that Jude was written by an apostle. Second Peter has strong internal testimony. It states that it is the second epistle by Peter, an apostle who witnessed Christ's transfiguration (1:1, 18; 3:1-2). It is of equally great interest that Jude (vv. 17-18) quotes from Peter's epistle and calls it the work of an apostle (2 Pet. 3:3). Another Papyrus Bodmer (VII-IX), dated before A.D. 300, is now available containing 1 and 2 Peter and Jude.

The identity of James and Jude, who were brothers (Jude 1), has been the subject of much discussion. There apparently were brothers James and Jude among the Twelve (Luke 6:16) and also brothers James and Jude who were half-brothers of the Lord (Matt. 13:55). Some scholars suggest that these half-brothers were really cousins of Christ and were identical with the James and Jude in the company of the Twelve. The evidence is perhaps indecisive, and it is not known which of the pairs, if there were two, wrote the epistles.

The dates these smaller epistles were written are not known. These and all other New Testament books were written by the apostles and their helpers "under the inspiration of the Spirit" as Clement of Rome says of Paul's letter to the Corinthians. Christian workers, leaders, and teachers should learn more about the time, authorship, and the circumstances related to all these epistles. Much can be learned by diligent study of the books themselves. The early authors confirm an intelligent faith in these books as the true, apostolic, and inspired Word of God.

No other books have been so widely considered, and we have no positive testimony that any other books were written by apostles. The early Fathers agree that some false writings were undoubtedly circulated (2 Thess. 2:2; 3:17). But these were promptly exposed, and only a few people were deceived. Though Christ never gave a list of New Testament books, He did appoint twelve apostles, then Paul, to be the foundation of the church. These men, divinely appointed and divinely endowed with the Spirit, wrote the New Testament of our Lord and Savior Jesus Christ. The Bible-believing Christian rejoices in this written Word of God.

VOCABULARY ENRICHMENT

Muratorian Fragment, *Didache* (pronounced di-da-kay).

DISCUSSION QUESTIONS

1. Make a table of the New Testament authors and their books.
2. By reviewing this chapter, verify the statement that "thirty years after the death of John only the single chapters of Jude and 2 John and 3 John are not attested in the works of the Fathers."
3. Who was Ignatius, and what of his writings do we have?
4. Who was the first Church Father whose writings remain?
5. Using 2 Peter 3:15-16 and Jude 17-18, explain the regard the apostles had for each other's words.
6. What proof is there that the apostles regarded their own works as inspired?
7. Trace the missionary journeys of Paul on a Bible map and list the order in which his epistles were written.
8. Why do we receive only twenty-seven books as the New Testament canon?

Chapter Six

PRESERVATION OF
THE BIBLE:
NEW TESTAMENT

MOST CHRISTIANS HAVE NOT thought seriously about how the New Testament writings were preserved. They can easily secure copies of the Bible and suppose that access to the Bible has always been available. Like all other blessings, however, this one should not be taken for granted. Men and women have died that the Bible might be preserved, translated, and published. Even in our day, in certain countries of the world, the Scriptures are scarce.

The history of the preservation of the New Testament can be divided into two periods—before the invention of the printing press and after. During the 1400s, three historical events were of inestimable benefit to the modern world. Columbus in 1492 discovered the New World, and America would become the world's cradle of liberty. Johann Gutenberg invented the printing press in 1456. And in 1493 Martin Luther, the founder of the Protestant Reformation, was born. These events have profoundly influenced the scope and effect of Christianity in modern times.

PRINTING THE BIBLE

The first book to come from Gutenberg's press was the Latin Bible. Copies of that first edition are preserved to this day. Soon afterward the Greek New Testament and the Hebrew Old Testament were both printed. Preserving the Scriptures after that became a relatively simple matter, for the Bible was produced by the thousands. After Tyndale translated the Bible into English, it was printed in Holland and smuggled into England. For a while the English bishops tried to burn all the copies, but they were unsuccessful. In a few years Tyndale's Bible and its successors were easily obtained all over England.

After the printing press was invented, it became relatively easy to

The opening verses of Genesis from the Gutenberg Bible, first published in 1456. Gutenberg's invention of movable type paved the way for distribution of the Bible in English seventy years later, with the publication of Tyndale's first edition of the New Testament in 1526.

Tyndale's translation of the opening words in Genesis, shown from a first edition of Tyndale's Pentateuch published in 1530.

reproduce the Bible without mistakes. Previously, a person copied many pages by hand and was apt to make a few mistakes. If he discarded that work and started all over again, he probably would avoid those mistakes, but make others. Today in printing a book, it is a simple matter to correct any mistakes and leave the rest untouched. By careful proofreading, the Bible can be produced without any mistakes. In preparing plates for the printing of Bibles, the copy is proofread many, many times. Proofreaders may work in pairs, one reading from a correct copy and the other watching the proof sheets, or proofreaders may read through the copy while listening to an audio version of the Bible. In less expensive Bibles, there may be misprints because they are not so carefully checked. Most ordinary books are not so carefully proofread, and they are likely to have at least a few typographical errors.

Sometimes it was not a question of a mistake in copying, but rather of the style to be used. During the century after the 1611 *King James Version* was translated, a printer had to be a grammarian to know what spellings to change in successive reprints of the original *King James Version*.

For this reason, an old copy of the English Bible is different from recent editions. The differences are not mistakes or misprints. They reflect the practical adjustment of a changing language.

The KJV translation we use today is not an exact copy of that printed in 1611. Here is a reproduction of the original KJV with modern type but using the original spelling. An examination shows many strange forms and spellings that were modified throughout the first hundred years after it was published. For instance, "son" was spelled "sonne," "year" was "yeere," "he" was "hee," and music was "musick." The present-day Authorized Version contains all the changes made to approximately 1750.

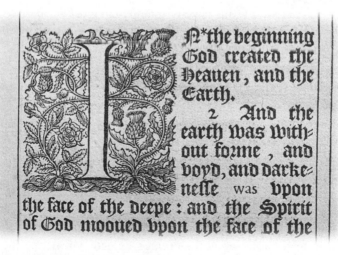

The King James Version translation of the opening verses of Genesis, from a first edition of the King James Bible published in 1611.

EARLY COPIES

To comprehend how the New Testament was preserved, the student needs to understand the history of the ancient Roman Empire. In apostolic days the Roman Empire included the entire Mediterranean area—Spain, France, Italy, Greece, Turkey, Syria, Palestine, Egypt, and North Africa around Algiers. The empire also extended into Britain and parts of Germany. Latin was the government language, but most people used Greek.

Christianity was especially strong in Egypt, Palestine, Asia Minor, Rome, and North Africa. But Christianity was a forbidden religion, and at least ten different bitter persecutions broke out against its followers. Again and again Christian books were burned. Many Christians died rather than deliver their sacred books to the flames.

Finally Emperor Constantine the Great was converted in A.D. 313, after which he gave the famous Edict of Milan allowing freedom of religion. In succeeding decades, the Roman Empire weakened under attack from the barbarian Goths in Europe and from other peoples coming through Europe from Asia. In A.D. 410 Rome fell. Those were the days of Jerome, who made his Latin translation of the Bible called the Vulgate. Augustine was another leader whose name is still well known. Shortly after Rome fell, the empire was divided, with Constantinople as capital of the Eastern division and Rome as capital of the Western. The Eastern empire used Greek during the whole Middle Ages while the West used Latin.

The scholar who wants a New Testament as close as possible to that written by the apostles will treasure the Greek copies more than the Latin. Some early Greek copies date from before Jerome.

By God's providence, the student of the New Testament is favored in having many ancient copies. The original copies, called "autographs," were probably written on papyrus or leather scrolls. By A.D. 125, however, it was customary to use the form of the book called a codex, instead of a scroll. In this form it was easier to combine many writings into one volume. These books were copied and recopied in Greek. Before long, perhaps by A.D. 200, the church in Antioch and the area of Mesopotamia to the east wanted the Word in Syriac, its predominant language. Syriac is quite similar to Hebrew. By this time the church in North Africa wanted the Gospel in Latin; so an Old Latin translation was made. Later this translation was superseded by Jerome's Vulgate. Until A.D. 400, however, Greek continued to be the main biblical language.

Early copies of the New Testament were written in small letters.

Medieval Greek manuscripts were also written this way. These copies are called "cursives." In the 300s it became the practice to make especially fine copies of the Bible on parchment, printed carefully in capital letters. These manuscripts are called "uncials," meaning capitals.

Several of these great uncial manuscripts have been preserved till today. For generations they were housed in the libraries of ancient monasteries, and only a few out of hundreds have withstood the ravages of time and waves of persecution. The latter was probably their worst enemy. When the Muslims invaded Egypt in the seventh century, they burned the great Alexandrian Library of 100,000 volumes, including the treasures of antiquity. About the same time, they burned the great Eusebian Library in Caesarea of Palestine with its treasures of early Christian antiquity. But in God's providence, many copies escaped the flames. It is said that there are about 3,000 copies of the Greek New Testament or parts of it. Of these, a dozen or more are over 1,500 years old.

THE OLD MANUSCRIPTS

What are our oldest manuscripts? What are they like? In the last two centuries, several important early manuscripts have been discovered. These manuscripts provide added information about the early text of the Bible.

The Alexandrian Text

In 1859 Constantine Tischendorf discovered a priceless manuscript among old works in the monastery of St. Catherine on the slopes of Mt. Sinai. This manuscript is called Codex Aleph, or Codex Sinaiticus, dating from the 300s of our era. Codex means book, not scroll, and aleph is the first letter of the Hebrew alphabet.

In 1868 the Vatican Library published another old manuscript from the 300s called Codex B (sometimes called Vaticanus because it was found in the Vatican Library). These two manuscripts, Codex Aleph and Codex B, contain very similar wording, and it seems clear that they were copied from the same or similar master copies. They belong to the same family of manuscripts that has been called the Neutral Text, now better called the Alexandrian Text.

The Koine

Most copies made during the Middle Ages form another family of manuscripts differing in details of wording. It is called the Koine, meaning "common." It is also referred to as the *Textus Receptus*. This family was used by the King James translators. The Alexandrian Text was used by the Revised Version and Revised Standard Version committees. It is easy to compare these two families of manuscripts by comparing the King James Version and the Revised Versions of the New Testament. Most of the recent New Testament translations follow in general the Alexandrian Text, but the evidence for each questioned reading is usually considered afresh.

Other Manuscripts

In recent times even earlier copies have been found among piles of papyri unearthed in Egypt. The Chester Beatty Papyri cover much of the New Testament and come from the 200s.

The Rylands Papyrus, from about A.D. 125, is a valuable, though very small witness to the New Testament text. It is almost identical to the Alexandrian Text.

The Bodmer Papyri of John, also mentioned in chapter 5 in another connection, confirm the Alexandrian Text of that book. Most of the newer translations use these recently found manuscript readings.

TEXTUAL CRITICISM

The study of ancient manuscripts is called textual criticism, or lower criticism to distinguish it from destructive higher criticism. Textual criticism is an ancient, valuable study. It has been practiced by Christian scholars at least since Origen, of A.D. 250, but it must be done by those thoroughly trained in language. New Testament textual criticism has been put on a firmer basis since the work of Tischendorf, Westcott, Hort, and others.

Textual criticism can aid Christians in two ways. First, it can help to recover in most passages the very words written by the apostles. The copies presently available were made several generations after the originals were written. By comparing the testimony of the early families of manuscripts, the scholar can usually decide what words were originally written. Second, in some passages it is difficult to decide upon the original text. Did it say "Simon" or "Peter," "Jesus" or "Jesus Christ"? It may not be easy to decide, but when complete families of manuscripts agree, whichever wording is used, no great difference is involved.

It is usually held, on adequate evidence, that the Alexandrian family is closest to the original, though it must always be checked against other witnesses. And the Koine family, which most think to be more defective in detail, is still practically as good as our best. The differences only concern occasional details. The major differences between those modern translations done by believing scholars who made an earnest effort to translate accurately are not differences of the text families, but differences of interpretation and of wording. The remark of Westcott and Hort in 1881 is often quoted and is worth remembering:

> *If comparative trivialities . . . are set aside, the words in our opinion still subject to doubt can hardly amount to more than a thousandth part of the whole New Testament.*

More recent discoveries have confirmed and strengthened the conclusion of Westcott and Hort.

Our New Testament has been preserved by monk and scholar, by martyr and missionary, through laborious handwriting and by careful printing. In critical texts and numerous translations, the words of God by the apostles have been faithfully preserved and industriously spread over all the world. Christians may read and study their Bibles with confidence, knowing that this is the very Word of God.

"Heaven and earth shall pass away, but my words shall not pass away" (Matt. 24:35).

VOCABULARY ENRICHMENT

Autographs, cursives, text, textual criticism, uncials, Koine, *Textus Receptus*.

DISCUSSION QUESTIONS

1. How close is the date of the earliest New Testament manuscript segment to the life of its author, John?
2. What three great copies of the New Testament made before A.D. 400 are preserved in large portions?
3. Compare the resurrection narrative (John 20) in the King James and Revised versions.
4. What basis do we have for confidence in even our poorest New Testament text?

Chapter Seven

PRESERVATION OF THE BIBLE: OLD TESTAMENT

THE OLD TESTAMENT COMES from a much earlier age than the New. Malachi, the last Old Testament book, was probably written about 400 B.C. Until recently, not much information has been available for the textual study of the Old Testament. However, the discovery of the Dead Sea Scrolls in 1947 provided a wealth of new textual material.

ANCIENT PRESERVATION

Moses and the other prophets wrote the Old Testament over a period of approximately 1,000 years—1400 B.C. to 400 B.C. During that time the sacred copies of the Scriptures were partly controlled by the temple priests, partly under the supervision of the king, and partly cared for by prophets to whom God gave His Holy Spirit for the revelation of His will. Prophecy was sometimes scarce in Israel, as in the days of Eli: "And the word of the LORD was precious in those days; there was no open vision" (1 Sam. 3:1). The nations often sank into idolatry, as in the days of Ahab. In all those periods, God raised up faithful prophets who were inspired by the Holy Spirit. These prophets loved and treasured the Word of God and gave it out courageously.

There is a lack of evidence about those times in Palestine from sources outside the Bible. However, the Bible contains internal evidence about its own composition and preservation. Secular literature, both writings and books, were doubtless composed during those days but have been lost. Multitudes of stories, histories, and poems are preserved on the imperishable clay tablets of Mesopotamia. In Egypt the writings were on papyrus, which, though fragile, has survived in that very dry climate. Traders from Palestine bought the Egyptian papyrus in exchange for cedar wood and olive oil. Papyrus was convenient for their use, but almost all these papyrus manuscripts perished in the rainy seasons of the hills of Palestine. Only in the hot, dry Dead Sea area have the ancient papyrus and leather scrolls been preserved. Thus the secular literature of Palestine was lost, and the biblical scrolls were worn out.

As the old scrolls were worn out or destroyed, they had to be recopied. What happened to these copies of the Bible after the last prophets finished their work in about 400 B.C.? Beginning at this end of history, we will work back to that ancient time 2,400 years ago.

An authentic Hebrew scroll opened to the beginning verses of Genesis

THE MIDDLE AGES

During the Middle Ages, the Hebrew Old Testament was preserved by the Jews. During that time, the lamp of learning in Europe burned very low. The Latin church used Jerome's Vulgate translation since none of its scholars seemed to know Hebrew. The Greek Orthodox Church in the Eastern Mediterranean area used the Greek Septuagint, and none of its theologians seemed to have paid any attention to the original Hebrew. And the Jews, despite cruel persecutions, spread everywhere and treasured their Scriptures and ancient customs and traditions.

Jewish tradition teaches that medieval rabbis copied the Scriptures with great care. They even counted the verses in a book and marked the middle verse. The result was a remarkably faithful transmission of the text.

Furthermore, when the Hebrew Bible is compared with the Latin translation made by Jerome in about A.D. 400 (the Vulgate), it is evident that Jerome worked with a Hebrew text much like the one in use today. Indeed, some translations were made into Greek in about A.D. 200 by various Jewish scholars. (These should not be confused with the Septuagint, which was made earlier.) These reveal that the Hebrew Bible of that day was close to present-day Hebrew. These "minor Greek translations" have not been preserved in their entirety, but even so, they help trace the history of the Hebrew text.

From before A.D. 200, however, there were no Hebrew copies until recently, and no important earlier translations were made until the Septuagint of 200 B.C. There was a Syriac, a Samaritan, and an Aramaic Targum, but their dates were uncertain, and they were relatively unimportant. There was, therefore, imperfect evidence for the careful preservation of the Hebrew text, at least before the year A.D. 200.

DEAD SEA SCROLLS

In 1947 an Arab shepherd threw a stone into a cave near the Dead Sea and heard the tinkle of breaking pottery. All the world now knows the story of the Bedouin who took seven manuscripts out of that cave, leaving hundreds of fragments. Since then other caves have yielded additional Old Testament manuscripts and related Jewish material. Thousands of fragments are still being patiently pieced together and studied. The Dead Sea Scrolls, buried long ago by the scribes of the sectarian community of Qumran, open up new and valuable evidence on the preservation of the Hebrew text in antiquity.

Nonbiblical Scrolls

The treasure includes two kinds of writings, the first of which are the nonbiblical scrolls. These writings show that the sect at Qumran regarded the books of the Old Testament as the product of God by His Spirit through the prophets. Repeatedly they refer to "the Law of Moses and the Prophets" or "what God spoke through Moses and all the Prophets." Their attitude toward the Old Testament and their terminology are similar to that of Christ and His apostles.

Biblical Scrolls

The second type of Dead Sea material is the biblical scrolls. These ancient copies of manuscripts have been compared directly with our Hebrew Bible. They demonstrate how accurately the ancient scribes did their work.

All the Old Testament books except one have been found in the caves. The book of Esther has not yet been identified. Some books, such as Psalms, Deuteronomy, and Isaiah, are represented in many copies. Others, such as Chronicles, are present only in fragments. The greatest scroll is Isaiah, preserved completely and in good condition. Apparently it can be dated at about 125 B.C. Some fragments are older. Portions of Job, Jeremiah, Samuel, and Psalms can be dated to 200 B.C. or earlier. One portion of Psalms is unofficially dated at about 300 B.C. A copy of Ecclesiastes dating from 150 B.C. is of special interest because some extreme critics have insisted that Ecclesiastes was written at a much later date. Copies of Daniel dating from the second century B.C. are significant because they are so close to the crucial date of 165 B.C. when critics claim the book was written.

Summary

The Dead Sea Scrolls are remarkably like our Hebrew Bible. They prove that those who copied the Hebrew Bible through all the years back to the second century before Christ did an extremely careful job. It is established that our Hebrew Bible in nearly its present form was used by the Jews 200 years before Christ, since some of the Dead Sea Scrolls are older than the Isaiah scroll. With confidence, it may be asserted that there is no known event in Israel's history that made any change in the Jews' habits of copying between Ezra's day and 200 B.C. Therefore, we conclude that the Old Testament is, in essentials and in detail, like the Scripture that Ezra caused to be read to the Jews in Jerusalem after his return from Babylonian captivity.

Such proof is enough for all ordinary purposes. However, today's scholars can trace the history of our Old Testament to an even earlier date. The Greek Septuagint, translated about 200 B.C., has been preserved in numerous copies made by Christian scribes, and an English translation has been made. Thus a student who does not know Greek and Hebrew can now compare the Septuagint with the King James Version. This is a great help, but it does raise some questions. The New Testament sometimes quotes from the Septuagint where the latter disagrees with the Hebrew. Is the Septuagint sometimes better than the Hebrew? Was this translation into the Greek done carefully?

Today there is positive evidence to answer these questions. Some Dead Sea manuscripts date from around 200 B.C. They are so much like the Septuagint that they represent the type of text used by the Septuagint translators. Where the Septuagint differs from our Hebrew, it is probably because there were already two or more different Hebrew texts running side by side as early as 200 B.C. The new evidence has solved several of the problems in New Testament quotations. It has shown that in these cases the Septuagint and the New Testament were undoubtedly right. It is remarkable that in all the centuries since then, these two types of texts have been preserved—one in Hebrew and the other in the Septuagint.

Of what value is a knowledge of the different "families" of Old Testament text? First, by careful comparison, the original reading can usually be determined. Second, the care with which the copiers handled all the texts in antiquity can be seen. Third, by comparing the two types as a whole, one can establish conclusively that neither text is far from the great early copies from which both families originated.

TEXTUAL COMPARISON

Two additional arguments reinforce the belief that the Old Testament has been copied with great accuracy from the earliest days. First, the passages of Scripture that quote each other agree quite closely. Second, the names appearing in both the Old Testament and in ancient inscriptions are in closest agreement. A few samples must suffice.

Agreement of Parallel Passages

There are more parallel passages in the Old Testament than most Bible readers realize. Psalm 18 is the same as 2 Samuel 22; Psalm 14 equals Psalm 53; Psalm 108 is made up of parts of Psalm 57 and Psalm 60. Isaiah 36–39 is the same as 2 Kings 18:13–20:19. Large parts of 2 Samuel and Kings are quoted in Chronicles.

Agreement of Names

Names provide an interesting "spot check." The Bible contains many complex names such as Shishak, Chedorlaomer, Azariah, Tiglath-Pileser, and Jehoiakim. Robert Dick Wilson stated that out of 184 letters of forty names preserved in our Hebrew copies, scarcely any are incorrectly preserved. Clay tablets found since Wilson's day have added other examples.

ANCESTRY OF THE ENGLISH BIBLE

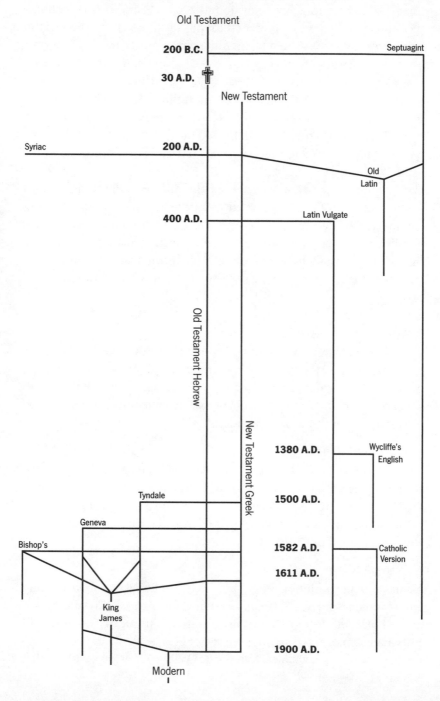

A striking example is Jeremiah 39:3. For centuries the men mentioned here were unknown. Recently the names of Nebuchadnezzar's officers have been found and can be checked with this verse. The names were confused with titles and were misread, but every letter was preserved accurately. It should read "Nergal-sharezer of Samgar,[1] Nebo-sar-sechim the Rab-Saris, Nergal-sharezer the Rab Mag." Such accuracy in copying proves that the Old Testament text has been transmitted with marvelous fidelity. To all intents and purposes, the Bible student can affirm that the writings of the prophets have been preserved without any error that would affect the message of the Word of God. The text is reliable, and it may be used with the same confidence that was shown by Christ and the apostles.

VOCABULARY ENRICHMENT

Dead Sea Scrolls, external evidence, internal evidence, parallel passages, textual comparison, transmission, Vulgate.

DISCUSSION QUESTIONS

1. How do we know that our Old Testament has been copied without any significant changes since A.D. 400? A.D. 200?
2. What is the Septuagint, and when was it made?
3. What two kinds of manuscripts were found in the caves around Qumran?
4. How many Old Testament books are represented among the Dead Sea Scrolls?
5. What are the approximate dates of some of the Old Testament scrolls and fragments?
6. How do the Dead Sea Scrolls show that the Old Testament was carefully copied in the centuries before Christ?
7. Compare the Septuagint text to today's Hebrew Old Testament.
8. What does textual criticism demonstrate about the Old Testament?
9. Read carefully 2 Samuel 22 and Psalm 18, noting the minor differences. Explain how slight alterations of the Hebrew text have caused this variation.
10. Prepare a display of pictures, written articles, and books that would show how the Old Testament was transmitted and preserved. Up-to-date encyclopedias, both secular and religious, contain explanatory articles and photographs of recent archeological finds. Make this display available to the entire Sunday school and church.

Chapter Eight

BIBLE PROBLEMS

THE BIBLE IS THE most *important* book ever written. It is much larger than the average reader realizes. In ordinary-size type, without extensive notes, it covers about 1,300 pages. It is not surprising that skeptics and unbelievers find some problems in such a volume.

The Bible is a *strange* book—different from all other books. It deals with spiritual things that cannot be understood "naturally." Spiritual things are "spiritually discerned" (1 Cor. 2:14-16). Unfriendly critics, therefore, discover problems even where no real problems exist. Nicodemus exclaimed to Christ, "How can these things be?" (John 3:9). People unwilling to accept the Bible's spiritual message cannot understand it.

The Bible is an *ancient* book. It was written in Hebrew, Aramaic, and Greek by prophets, kings, tax gatherers, and scholars. Its historic setting changed from the Bronze Age to the Iron Age to Roman times. Its events occurred in Canaan, Egypt, Greece, and Asia Minor. No wonder it has puzzled some readers.

These supposed difficulties are the result of ignorance of Bible lands, customs, and languages. Most problems fade away under deep, earnest, and prayerful Bible study. The sincere Christian student should exercise faith and spiritual discernment.

The Bible contains remarkably few difficulties in comparison to its size and unusual background. The wonderful harmony of the book is a well-established fact. It was written over a period of sixteen centuries by approximately thirty-five authors. It tells one story and presents one consistent message. Its very harmony has been cited as one proof that it is inspired.

Some major classes of problems, however, have been raised. Several of these are related to miracles, prophecies, and the alleged contradictions of the Scriptures. In examining these, the student will discover the answers to other related problems and questions.

MIRACLES

Many miracles are recorded in the Bible. Some affected large areas and many people—like the crossing of the Red Sea (Exod. 14). Some were smaller, less conspicuous—such as Elisha making an iron axe head float (2 Kings 6:1-7). Some were healings—Jesus healing the blind man (John 9). Others were in the realm of nature—Jesus feeding five thousand with a few loaves and fishes (Mark 6:34-44).

How important are these miracles? What do they teach? Can twenty-first-century Christians believe them? How? Why? In order to answer these questions, we must know what biblical miracles are.

All biblical miracles had one thing in common: They were related to the natural world. Iron floated, water turned into blood, leprosy was healed, deafness was cured, lame men walked, storms were stopped.

Biblical miracles were also unusual events, contrary to ordinary experience. They were unbelievable and impossible for mere man to accomplish. People do not walk on water. Iron does not float. Fire does not come down from heaven and lick up a sacrifice—water, stones, and all. Miracles resulted from direct intrusion by supernatural powers. A miracle is a remarkable event in the natural world, totally beyond man's ability to produce.

Today it is popular to deny the possibility of miracles. David Hume argued that it would take infinite evidence to prove that miracles exist. Scientists insist that fixed laws govern the universe, and no exceptions are possible. They maintain that ancient, unenlightened, gullible people believed that God ran the universe directly and could easily change anything He wanted to. Some scientists say, "We know that God—if there be a God—operates through regular natural laws that admit to no exception."

The Bible clearly shows, however, that early peoples were not gullible. True, they did not have scientific data, but they knew that people could not walk on water (Matt. 14:25; Mark 6:49; John 6:19). When they saw Christ so doing, they were terrified and thought He was a ghost. When Paul healed the lame man (Acts 14), the people were convinced that the gods had appeared in the likeness of men. They knew that mere human power could not do this. The blind man whom Jesus healed said, "Since the world began was it not heard that any man opened the eyes of one that was born blind" (John 9:32). He knew that Jesus had done something that was impossible for mere man to do.

The science of that day was elementary, but the people believed in the regularity of nature and in the law of cause and effect. They believed the miracles not because they were gullible, but because the sensory evidence was inescapable. They believed that the God of miracles had entered this sinful world in His own revealing power.

Some critics have gone to great lengths to discredit the miracles. They suggest that Jesus healed by psychology, that the disciples did not see Him on the water but on the reeds near the shore. The feeding of the five thousand is explained away by assuming that the people had brought their lunches, and the lad's unselfish example had shamed them into sharing with each other. Such unscientific, foolish theories found in many modernistic books do not deal with the plain evidence in the case.

The crowning miracle of all, Christ's resurrection, is totally unexplainable by natural means (Matt. 28; Mark 16; Luke 24; John 20). The strongest argument for His bodily resurrection is the transformation Christ wrought in the disciples. Those who had forsaken and fled (Mark 14:50) became bold witnesses, ready to die for their faith.

Those who explain away the miracles, including Christ's resurrection, have nothing left but empty religion without power, joy, or salvation—a vain philosophy without God's blessed revelation. Theirs is the darkness of midnight without the light of life. True Christians have no problem with miracles. Miracles are at the heart of the Christian's faith. Their reality as recorded in God's Word is a final, exclusive proof of the validity of Christian hope and confidence.

Paul had the answer for all skepticism. When he appeared before Festus and Agrippa, the governor refused to believe Paul's doctrine. He declared that Paul was mad (Acts 26:24). Paul's answer to Agrippa was a sober argument: "Why should it be thought a thing incredible with you, that God should raise the dead?" (Acts 26:8). Anyone who believes God has no difficulty accepting miracles. The consistent, sensible, merciful miracles of the New Testament are proof that the merciful God has spoken indeed. Miracles are an essential witness to, and proof of, our faith.

PROPHECIES

The argument from prophecy is equally striking. Bible prophecy includes definite, positive, often long-range predictions that no observer could expect, no matter how wise. Of course, shrewd observers can predict certain things. The weatherman attempts a limited forecast. Political "pollsters" attempt to predict election results weeks in advance. But true predictive prophecy is supernatural.

Old Testament Fulfillment

Bible prophecies were not double-tongued predictions like those of the Greek oracles. A Greek oracle predicted that if a certain king would fight, he would destroy a great empire. He did so. The empire he destroyed was his own. In contradistinction, Hebrew prophets foretold the future with definiteness, often predicting the dates and the names of the participants. The prophets spoke because God gave them supernatural insight and detailed information about future things. This is one of the vital proofs of the entire Bible's authenticity. Every evangelical Christian believes this truth.

How do skeptics treat these prophecies? Very cleverly. When a chapter in Isaiah predicts Cyrus's reign, they say, "That chapter was written after Cyrus came to the throne." If the books of Kings predict Josiah by name, they erroneously teach that "Josiah's name was slipped into the verse by a later copyist after Josiah arose." If Daniel predicts the days of Antiochus Epiphanes, that is held to be positive proof that Daniel was written after 165 B.C. The liberal scholars' attitude toward predictive prophecy is the reason they insist that the Old Testament was written at a later date and by authors other than the books allege.

What is the answer to such objectionable criticism? First, the bias against supernaturalism must be pointed out. Next, it can be shown that both internal and external evidence favor the earlier dating. Among the Dead Sea Scrolls are copies of Daniel made in about 110 B.C. that prove that Daniel could not have been written by a false Daniel in a hoax at about 165 B.C. It could hardly have been copied and recopied widely and its false origin kept hidden and its canonical authority recognized all in the space of fifty-five years. The Dead Sea material strongly supports the earlier date for Daniel, and that makes Daniel predictive prophecy.

Second, many Bible prophecies refer to the first coming of Christ or to events during this age that happen long after any possible date for the prophetic utterance. Many instances could be cited. The prophecy of the virgin birth of Christ is a case in point (Isa. 7:14). Critics say that the word *virgin* means "young woman" and referred to Isaiah's son soon to be born or to an expected child of Ahaz. In the context this child, Immanuel, is also called "Wonderful," and is promised to be of David's line (Isa. 9:6-7). Isaiah already had a son, Shearjashub, so the passage could not refer to him. Nor could it apply to Ahaz's son, Hezekiah, who by this time was over nine years old. Hezekiah was twenty-five when he succeeded Ahaz, and Ahaz had reigned for sixteen years. As further proof, the word *virgin*, used six other times in the Old Testament, is never applied to a married woman. At least three times it clearly means a virgin. Further, the Septuagint translation uses a word specifically meaning "virgin." Long before Christ's birth, the Jews accepted this clear prophecy of the Virgin Birth. Only critical bias prevents the acceptance of this great prediction.

Consider Daniel's prophecy of the seventy weeks (Dan. 9:24ff.). It plainly says that from the time of the commandment being given to build Jerusalem to the coming of Messiah the Prince shall be seven weeks and sixty-two weeks, and after the sixty-second week the Messiah shall be cut off, and the city shall be destroyed. Critical scholars have unsuccessfully attempted a different translation of this passage and have dissolved its meaning by claiming that the time periods are only symbolic.

Two explanations should be noted. First, the word *week* refers to a unit of seven years as observed by the Jews. The Hebrews counted time in sevens and fifties—weeks and jubilees. Debts were to be forgiven after seven years, and everyone was to go back to his family holdings in the fiftieth Year of Jubilee. The practice was as old as the Levitical legislation. The intertestamental *Book of Jubilees* dates events in Genesis by their jubilee, week, year, month, and day. Obviously, "week" means a seven-year period. Seven and sixty-two weeks are therefore sixty-nine weeks of years, or 483 years. An additional week mentioned in verse 27 accounts for the total of seventy.

Second, there were various commandments to restore and rebuild Jerusalem. The first one was by Cyrus about 539 B.C. This was later revoked, and only the temple was built. The next such decrees were in the time of Ezra and Nehemiah, between 456 B.C. and 444 B.C. Ezra 9:9 implies that Ezra's decree included building Jerusalem. So Ezra rebuilt the city, and his friend Nehemiah finished the wall. Some therefore count from Nehemiah's date, using years slightly shorter than usual (because Revelation 11:2 compared with 12:6 refers to years 360 days long). It seems more natural to use normal years such as the Jews regularly used and count from Ezra's date. Thus 456 B.C. minus 483 years equals A.D. 26. (There is no 0 year, so the result is not A.D. 27.) This is exactly when Christ was announced by John the Baptist as the Messiah of Israel. Shortly afterward this Messiah was cut off. Forty years later the city was destroyed in a bitter siege by the Romans. On any theory of the dating of Daniel, the prophecy, strictly interpreted, refers to events long after Daniel. The argument from prophecy thus is strong here.

Opinions may differ as to the fulfillment of the seventieth week. Premillennialists (of whom the writer is one) believe that it remains to be fulfilled in accordance with the indications given by Christ in Matthew 24:15ff.

New Testament Fulfillment

Many New Testament predictions are being fulfilled today. Jesus made a bold prediction when He told a few fishermen, "the gospel must first be published among all nations" (Mark 13:10). Yet from its small beginning, the Christian church has grown to cover all the major areas in the world. Jesus also predicted, "This generation [NIV footnote—nation] will certainly not pass away until all these things have happened" (Matt. 24:34). The Jews have persisted even when they were dispersed, persecuted, outlawed, and massacred. Their present return to Palestine is a further vital fulfillment of ancient prophecies (Zech. 12:1ff.).

These predictions are neither a problem nor an embarrassment to personal Christian faith. The abundance of fulfilled prophecies is a supernatural proof that God has spoken.

ALLEGED CONTRADICTIONS

Liberals charge that there are a number of contradictions in the Bible. These are not as serious as the critics affirm. It is impossible in this study to answer all of them. John Haley surveyed the literature of modern criticism and reviewed all the difficulties that they mentioned. His carefully prepared answers have been accepted because of their faithfulness to the facts. They are worthy of consideration. Additional suggestions have been made by other evangelical scholars.

One such alleged contradiction is Judas's suicide. Matthew 27:5 reports, "He . . . went and hanged himself." Acts 1:18 says, "And falling headlong, he burst asunder in the midst." The original word translated "hanged" in Matthew does not necessarily refer to hanging, but to suicide in general or to strangling. It is used in 2 Samuel 17:23 to translate the Hebrew *hanaq*, a root used only in Nahum 2:12 and Job 7:15 to mean not specifically "hang" but any kind of strangulation. Death by hanging was not common in Old Testament times. Of course, if Judas's body was undiscovered, it would bloat and burst. The alleged contradiction may be due to over-precise translation.

Mark 14:30 and 72 record Peter's threefold denial before the cock crowed twice. The other Gospels refer only to the cock crowing. Some of the oldest manuscripts of Mark do not include the word *twice*, thus agreeing with Matthew and Luke. In 2 Chronicles 36:9, Jehoiachin was eight years old when carried captive, but 2 Kings 24:8 says he was eighteen. Some Hebrew texts and the Greek Septuagint translation say eighteen years old in both places. This was clearly the original reading in both books. Textual criticism solves this problem.

Another example is that of the blind man healed as Jesus was leaving Jericho (Mark 10:46-52). Parallel accounts seem to disagree. Matthew 20:30 reads, "And, behold, two blind men sitting by the way side." Luke 18:35 mentions "a certain blind man" healed as Jesus came near Jericho, meaning that he was healed in the vicinity of Jericho. At that time there were two Jerichos—the old city and the one housing Herod's winter palace. The company of disciples could be leaving the one city and in the vicinity of the other. These accounts are not contradictory; one simply tells more than the others.

Many other supposed contradictions are not contradictory narratives, but rather are supplementary accounts. The inscription over the cross is of this nature, with slight variations in the four Gospels. The inscription was in Greek, Latin, and Hebrew. Other trilingual inscriptions from those days were not identical in all languages. The variation indicates that one Gospel gave part of the title; others gave additional parts.

Most alleged contradictions are not serious. A good reference Bible often suggests answers. The problems usually lie in our limited knowledge or misinterpretation of the situation.

Skeptical minds overemphasize the problems in the Bible. In spite of their assaults, the Bible stands, and multitudes of ordinary Christians and faithful scholars find in it the light of life and the truth of God. We should remember Peter's confession of faith: "Lord, to whom shall we go? thou hast the words of eternal life" (John 6:68). Many people turn back because of the difficult sayings of Christ, but "we believe and are sure that thou art that Christ, the Son of the living God" (John 6:69).

THE BIBLE AND SCIENCE

The idea is abroad that modern scientific advances make it impossible to believe the Bible. This is not true for the Bible believer who really studies the Word. The Bible is inspired and is true not only in spiritual matters, but also when it touches science and history. It is not a textbook on science. It seldom bears on physics, chemistry, mathematics, or electricity. The major conflict between the Bible and science is in the first chapters of Genesis, usually relating to evolution. This controversy revolves mainly around three subjects: the great antiquity of the earth, the fixity of species, and the origin of man.

The Antiquity of the Earth

Geology claims that the earth is four or five billion years old. How does this fit the Bible? Only the briefest answer is possible. Some Bible scholars have suggested that the six creative days are really long periods of time and not literal twenty-four-hour days. The first three "days" occurred before the sun was set to mark time.

Those holding this view also suggest that these days need not be of equal extent. The first may have been extremely long. The creation of plant life, the final phases of formation of the sun and moon, and the beginning of animal life could have occurred fairly close together, followed by a long period of growth and further creation.

On the other hand, other Bible scholars holding to the literal six twenty-four-hour days of creation argue that God could have created the world with the appearance of age. It must be clear that the Bible is true regarding the antiquity of the earth.

The Fixity of Species

In this problem much depends on the meaning of the word *species*. There is no all-embracing definition. In biology species are identified as *plants or animals having similar characteristics*. As thus defined, species are not fixed. For instance, cabbage, cauliflower, and brussels sprouts look very different, and yet they interbreed freely. If we define species, however, as *organisms that interbreed with each other but not with other species*, then the species is fixed, with only rare examples of crossing over the species boundary.

The Age of Man

There has been no established figure on how long human beings have been on the earth. Older theories of evolution had held that primitive humans appeared during the Glacial Period, the so-called Pleistocene, some 500,000 years ago. They were followed by Neanderthal man about 60,000 years ago and by Cro-Magnon man only 25,000 years ago. These theories have changed through recent discoveries. Carmel man was discovered with some modern characteristics, though he was dated to about 125,000 years ago by glacial correlations. That dating has more recently been changed to 35,000 by the carbon-14 method, which itself still has considerable uncertainty. The Swanscombe man and Kanjera man were discovered with many modern characteristics, though they were dated to 300,000 years ago. The date, based also on glacial phenomena, is quite questionable. Scientists now agree that the Neanderthals were not so primitive as formerly believed. The whole subject of dating by science is undependable and is constantly being restudied.

New discoveries in these fields are coming rapidly with the finds of Louis Leakey in Olduvai Gorge, Africa, and his son, Richard Leakey, farther north, Donald Johanson, and others. Although the cited ages of these creatures is excessive (two or three million years old), the earliest specimens claimed by Richard Leakey have an upright stature, human-like tooth structure, and tool-making ability. The evidence here may be for variation within the human race, but not evolution.

The Bible itself, while being definite about the facts of creation, gives no specific dates for creation. Most Bible scholars, however, believe in a young creation, perhaps only ten to fifteen thousand years old.

Growing experience with Scripture and a sincere faith in its divine origin will lead the student to a deep confidence that, when all the facts are known, *true* science will be in harmony with a sober, careful, strict interpretation of the Bible.

VOCABULARY ENRICHMENT

Alleged contradictions, critical bias, evolutionary theory, miracle, science.

DISCUSSION QUESTIONS

1. Identify the eight nonhealing miracles in the Gospels.
2. How can the devil and his minions perform miracles (cf. Exod. 7.22, Rev. 13:14)?
3. Read Peter's sermon in Acts 2 and Paul's sermon in Acts 13 and list the prophecies that are fulfilled in Christ.
4. In the light of modern science, give reasons why Christians can continue to believe the Bible.
5. State some contradictions not covered in this chapter that you may have discovered. How can these problems be answered?

Chapter Nine

HIGHER CRITICISM AND THE BIBLE

ALL BIBLE STUDENTS SHOULD learn something about the attacks that have been leveled against the Bible. By so doing, they will be prepared to try the spirits and be able to resist being led away by those who are unstable and distort the Scripture to their own destruction (2 Pet. 3:16). Similarly, a medical student studies diseases in order to learn how to keep people healthy.

There have always been people who disbelieve the Bible. In our day there is a particular type of unbelief expressed in *higher criticism*. We need not study all the details of this viewpoint, but it is wise to know that such criticism does exist.

DEFINITION

Higher criticism includes the study of the date and authorship of Bible books. Many higher critics hold that some or all of the books of the Bible were not written by the men that the books claim as authors, that the books were not written when they claim to be written, and that they were often not unified books but composed of several documents pieced together.

Today some orthodox scholars use the term higher criticism in a somewhat different sense. They admit there is a place for the right kind of higher criticism, something altogether different from the vicious, unbelieving higher criticism of the liberals. Orthodox higher critics study the authorship and background of Bible books. They use the techniques of higher criticism, but they do it reverently. The orthodox type of higher criticism is merely another name for what has been called "Bible introduction."

The phrase "higher criticism" usually refers to the unbelieving type outlined above. It has been and is destructive of faith and is fatal to Christian endeavor. If the Bible is a mass of falsehood (as the liberal critics teach), why read it at home or preach it abroad? Why teach our children to keep the Ten Commandments if the commandments themselves bear false witness to Moses' experience with God on Sinai?

In order to understand this erroneous theory, it is necessary to review certain historical backgrounds. In 1753 a French physician, Jean Astruc, noticed that the name for the deity in the book of Genesis is sometimes "God" (Hebrew, *Elohim*) and sometimes "Jehovah" or *YHWH* (LORD in the *King James Version*). Astruc suggested that the variation was the result of Moses' having used two different sources when he composed Genesis, one called an "E source" and the other a "J source." Astruc did not deny that Moses was the author, but he concluded that these two sources woven together make up our book of Genesis.

OLD TESTAMENT CRITICISM

Later writers in the rationalistic era of French and German thought extended Astruc's theory and said that the Pentateuch was actually the work of someone much later than Moses. "E" was said to be the early document and "J" the later.

In 1853 Hupfeld of Germany turned things around. He declared that the "E" document was itself made up of two parts, one of which was very late. Later German critics, especially Wellhausen (1878), went further and claimed that they could find four documents in the Pentateuch. Their names and dates are:

J   document, 850 B.C. (now placed a bit earlier—named from the use of "Jehovah" for Lord)
E   document, 750 B.C. (named from the use of "Elohim" for God)
D   document, 625 B.C. (largely made up of Deuteronomy)
P   document, 450 B.C. (having a major priestly emphasis)

Wellhausen held that none of the Pentateuch was written by Moses and presumed that the whole record of the priestly or sacrificial system had been compiled by men living 1,000 years after Moses.

Mosaic Authorship of the Pentateuch

Higher criticism does not stop with denying the Mosaic authorship. It denies also the truth and value of the Pentateuch. It declares that there never was any wilderness tabernacle. It holds that those stories were made up by postexilic priests.

Some of the early critics even declared that Moses did not know

how to write—if there was a Moses. They called the histories of the patriarchs "a mass of later legend." The exodus from Egypt was often doubted
completely (Exod. 12ff.). The Sinai legislation was called spurious
(Exod. 20ff.). The miracles of the ten plagues (Exod. 7:9ff.), crossing
the Red Sea (Exod. 14:21ff.), giving of manna (Exod. 16:14ff.), and
others were all explained away. More serious yet was the higher critics'
denial that God had revealed Himself to early people as the true, holy,
and only God. Higher critics insisted that the patriarchs in Abraham's day
were crude *animists* (worshipers of stones and trees); by Moses' day
they were *polytheists* (worshipers of many gods); David was a *henotheist*
(believing that every nation had its own particular God); *monotheism*
(belief in one God) was the discovery of the eighth-century prophets.
This diabolical reconstruction of Israel's early religion and history was
the "fully assured result" of German rationalistic criticism at the beginning of the twentieth century. To deny this view was to be labeled as
backward and ignorant of the facts. Thank God, many thousands of
Bible-believing Christians never surrendered to the subtle attacks of the
liberal higher critics.

David, Isaiah, and Daniel

Higher criticism went far beyond the Pentateuch. It was inevitable that
the entire Word of God should be discounted. If David was not a
monotheist, he could not have written the psalms, for they speak of
one holy, living, and true God. For these and other reasons, the critics set
the writing of most of the Old Testament books at a later date. Isaiah
was supposed to have been written by one, two, three, or more men.
They say that Isaiah did not predict the coming of Cyrus 175 years in
advance. It was the writing of Deutero-Isaiah, or a second Isaiah, who
lived during Cyrus's time. They also claim that Daniel did not predict
the succession of the great empires of Babylon, Medo-Persia, and Greece
down to Antiochus Epiphanes in 165 B.C. The book was presumed written at a later time when Antiochus Epiphanes was fighting the
Maccabees, and it was actually ancient history instead of the prophecy
it pretended to be. Thus the higher critics did not limit their destruction to the structural details of the text. They struck at the very basic
truth and value of almost every Old Testament book.

Christ's Approval of the Old Testament

Higher criticism affects our view of both the Old Testament and the New.
It is quite clear, as studied in chapter 2, that Christ and the apostles
fully believed the Old Testament. Jesus taught that "it is easier for heaven

and earth to pass, than one tittle of the law to fail" (Luke 16:17). He declared that the Old Testament was more convincing than if one should rise from the dead (Luke 16:29-31). He believed the historical reality of Adam and Eve, Jonah and the huge fish, the manna from heaven, and all the other Old Testament events. Christ was not a higher critic. Modern criticism, therefore, pictures Christ as a person of His time, subject to the simple, noncritical, erroneous teaching of His day. Liberal critics teach that He gradually became aware of His Messiahship, was mistaken about His second coming, and died not as the divine substitute (1 Pet. 2:24-25) but as a human martyr. Higher criticism strips the Old Testament of its value and robs the New Testament of its Lord.

And, sad to say, this view has become widespread and deeply entrenched. It is the very basis of what is often called modernism. In the early days of the twentieth century, promising young theologians went to Europe to take advanced training and often came back infected with the modernistic teachings of the German learning. Most of the older, larger theological schools accepted this liberalism as the basis of their theological teaching, and their graduates for years preached these ideas. Most local Christian workers and leaders can hardly realize the extent of this influence. It has been resisted by the Bible institutes and Bible colleges and by a goodly number of orthodox, evangelical colleges and seminaries, especially those seminaries founded after 1920. But it has affected a large percentage of the Protestant preachers of our generation. The effects of higher criticism should be thoroughly understood by every Christian worker and Sunday school teacher.

THE OLD CRITICISM

The hallmarks of the older liberal higher criticism are references to the J, E, D, P documents, the denial of the unity of Isaiah, the holding of a late date (after the exile) for most of the psalms, the Maccabean date of Daniel (165 B.C.), the idea of the evolution of Israel's religion (rather than its revelation), the discovery of monotheism by eighth-century-B.C. prophets, and many similar denials. By logic and in point of fact, a person who believes part of higher criticism believes other parts too. One who believes in "two or three Isaiahs" will hardly believe that Daniel was written in 550 B.C. One who believes that Moses did not write anything will also refuse to believe that David did write the psalms attributed to him. Higher criticism is a system, and at every basic point it is opposed to orthodox Christianity.

Fortunately, higher criticism itself is under attack today. In the providence of God there have been remarkable archeological discoveries since about 1920. These have convinced scholars, even many of the unorthodox, that the histories of Genesis are true, that Moses may well have been monotheistic, that many psalms were written as early as David. According to a very prominent scholar, W. F. Albright, the old Wellhausen theory has suffered a "total breakdown." The old positions are being greatly modified. The new archeological discoveries actually support the old orthodox position. However, not many are suddenly returning to orthodoxy. Instead, they are propounding new types of critical views that have not been accepted by all scholars. These are just as wrong as the earlier views.

THE NEW CRITICISM

The newer criticism is not as unified as critical views were earlier in the twentieth century, and it cannot be followed out in detail. There is an oral tradition theory that holds that nothing was written down until exilic times, and that all of Israel's traditions were passed on orally. A more usual view holds substantially to the documentary theory of the J, E, D, and P sources but tries to trace the oral traditions behind such sources. Other views subdivide the sources into J1, J2, P^A, P^B, etc. A common view now holds that the documents J, E, and P can be traced only through Genesis, Exodus, Leviticus, and Numbers (the so-called Tetrateuch) and that the "Deuteronomist" author, editor, or school wrote Deuteronomy, Joshua, Judges, Samuel, and Kings at a time near the exile. Of course the work of the Deuteronomist is not a unit. He used older material, and much has been inserted into his work, according to these scholars, in the later days.

The arguments for these views are quite subjective, which is why they can be so diverse. They begin with the old arguments used by Wellhausen about parallel passages, contradictory statements, and characteristic wordings and concepts and proceed to divide the text as these hints impress them. It is interesting that the extent of the P document in Genesis, for instance, as given by Driver almost a century ago agrees rather closely with the view held today by Martin Noth[1]. The main difference is that Noth finds no P document in Genesis 14 and 24. Genesis 14 was called quite late, even Maccabean (i.e., about 165 B.C.) by early critics.

Today archeological study has shown that it fits the times of the patriarchs and no later. That the belief in the J, E, D, and P documents is still held so persistently and with little change is surprising, since no archeological discovery has given evidence of such documents. On the contrary, many finds have supported the historicity of these biblical texts in major and in minor matters. For further study of the complicated details of these critical analyses, see the works of Archer, Allis, Unger, and Young listed in the Resources for Enrichment section at the end of this text.

VOCABULARY ENRICHMENT

Animist, evangelical, henotheist, higher criticism, liberalism, monotheist, orthodox, polytheist.

DISCUSSION QUESTIONS

1. Mention several interrelated ideas of higher criticism in connection with Old Testament books.
2. Give several reasons why higher criticism is harmful to the Christian faith.
3. Explain what higher criticism believes in regard to predictive prophecy and the reality of miracles.
4. What modern factor is helping to disprove the old higher criticism?

Chapter Ten

ARCHEOLOGY AND THE OLD TESTAMENT

VOLUMES HAVE BEEN WRITTEN on the relationship of archeology to the Old Testament. In this chapter, it is impossible to do more than define archeology, show the limits of its study, and demonstrate how it bears on the Old Testament.

DEFINITION

Archeology is "the study of ancient things." For all practical purposes, it is limited to that study of ancient history that is illuminated by the digging up of buried cities, tombs, and other relics. Biblical archeology is mainly concerned with the archeology of Palestine, Egypt, and Mesopotamia.

Archeologists proceed by carefully digging up ancient remains, photographing, recording everything exactly as found, and interpreting the results. They also translate and study the documents produced.

HISTORY

In the Middle Ages, the paintings and writings in Egyptian temples were thought to be magical. In about 1700 archeologists discovered the Rosetta Stone, written in three languages, including Greek. This gave scholars the key to the Egyptian language.

In the 1800s, the Behistun inscription of Darius the Great was deciphered. This inscription was also in three languages and gave the key to the Assyrian-Babylonian language. Scholars now call this the Akkadian language, after the city of Akkad mentioned in Genesis 10:10. The Akkadian language was written by using a wedge-shaped stick to make various combinations of marks on soft clay tablets usually about the size and shape of a bar of soap. These tablets were then sun-dried and are often beautifully preserved. This writing is called cuneiform (wedge-shaped).

In Palestine and Egypt most of the writing was done on papyrus, a paperlike material made from the papyrus plant. Papyrus rots quickly in the damp rainy season of the Palestinian winter, so only a little writing has been preserved in Palestine. An exception is the recent discovery of many leather scrolls and fragments in the caves of the hot, dry Dead Sea district. These scrolls date from about 200 B.C. to A.D. 50. Aside from these, Palestinian writing is restricted to a few inscriptions, seals, and writings on pottery.

Early archeologists were unskilled and unscientific in their approach. They dug through the ancient ruins in accidental fashion, hoping to find written material, well-preserved statues, or other treasure. They finally discovered that the ancient cities of Palestine and Mesopotamia were built in layers, one on top of another. The earliest cities were abandoned in time of war, famine, or pestilence. The mud-brick houses and walls tumbled down. Later new groups of settlers moved in, leveled out the old ruins, and built a new level right on top. As many as twenty-three layers or cities have been found on a single location. Later archeologists uncovered the strata in excavation sites one by one. Thus they could get the relationships of one group of inhabitants to another.

The study of archeology grew slowly until World War I. About that time, archeologists realized that the layers of each period were marked by characteristic types of pottery. A careful examination and study of the types of objects, especially pottery, made it possible to compare the layers of one city with the layers of cities uncovered in other locations. Further comparison with occasional inscriptions allowed these layers to be dated, often very accurately. It is therefore said that archeology became a science in about 1920. Archeological works older than that may have contained valuable facts, but they had to be restudied by the more accurate procedures and methods of later archeology.

The advances of archeology in the past half-century have been tremendous. A hundred years ago, little was known about the history of Egypt, Mesopotamia, or Palestine before 800 B.C. Now there are brilliant illuminations back to 3000 B.C. and earlier. Scientists know the names of the ancient kings of Babylon, Assyria, and Egypt. These kings are also mentioned in the Bible, and the names and even the pictures of some of them have been discovered. Ancient battles, laws, languages, and cultures have come to life under patient investigation.

What bearing has this had upon the Bible itself? Naturally, a great deal. Recent discoveries have confirmed and illuminated the Bible and in many cases have effectively answered Bible critics.

CONFIRMATION

Many parts of the Old Testament cannot yet be confirmed. No archeologists can prove that "The Lord is my shepherd, I shall not want." Archeology is concerned with Bible history. It can confirm facts in the historical and prophetical books, but it cannot bring spiritual discernment.

Archeological discoveries have confirmed Shishak's war against Rehoboam (1 Kings 14:25-26), the kingship of Omri and the power of Ahab (1 Kings 16:22), the rebellion of Mesha of Moab (2 Kings 3:5), the fall of Samaria (2 Kings 18:10), the digging of Hezekiah's tunnel (2 Kings 20:20), the invasion of Pharaoh-Nechoh (2 Kings 23:29), the fall of Jerusalem and the deportation of Jehoiachin (2 Kings 24:10-15).

It is most striking when some detail long forgotten by everyone, except the Bible authors, is confirmed. Such proven conclusions argue that the books of the Bible were written by eyewitnesses or by other men who knew the facts intimately and who lived in the age concerned. Two examples are sufficient for illustration.

Baruch's Seal

Baruch, Jeremiah's scribe, was doubtless a minor personage. No one but a contemporary would know about him. He is not mentioned outside of the book of Jeremiah where his name occurs twenty-three times in chapters 32, 36, 43, and 45. But in Jerusalem a seal was discovered with the inscription: "Belonging to Baruch, son of Neriah, the Scribe." In the same cache, a seal was found with the inscription "Belonging to Jerahmeel, son of the King" (cf. Jer. 36:26, 32). The most natural conclusion is that the book of Jeremiah was written by a contemporary.

The Ironsmiths

A different type of illustration is found in 1 Samuel 13:19-21 where the Philistines did not allow the Israelites to have smiths, lest the Israelites make themselves swords. This passage had long been difficult to translate. It seemed odd that there were no Hebrew "smiths," since metalworking had existed for centuries all over the Near East. Later information proves that these verses reflect accurately the situation in Israel just at that time. The Philistines introduced the Iron Age into Palestine and at first maintained a strict monopoly on iron-working. There were no ironsmiths in Israel, for the Philistines kept iron-working a military secret.

The phrase "They had a file for the mattocks" is now illustrated by the discovery of a weight inscribed with a form of the word translated "mattock." Evidently this word does not mean "mattock," but refers to the price charged for sharpening agricultural tools. The knowledge of such a detail is clear proof that the author of 1 Samuel was in full possession of his facts. Later copyists who did not know the complete picture misinterpreted the verse. We now see what the original author meant. Thus we can translate the Hebrew word correctly.

ILLUMINATION

Other examples can be given of the use of archeology in illustrating and illuminating the Old Testament. These confirm the Bible and show the background against which it should be fitted. Illumination is important, however, in its own right, because the Bible cannot be fully appreciated until it is understood. Adequate knowledge will save the student from many serious errors of interpretation. Here again only a few scattered illustrations can be given.

The Horites

A group of people called Horites or Horims are mentioned in Genesis, Numbers, and Deuteronomy and were apparently connected with Edom. The Horites seem to have been related to the Jebusite dwellers in Jerusalem. The word *hor* in Hebrew means "hole." For this reason, one of the standard older lexicons (a book containing an alphabetical arrangement of the words in a language, with the definition of each), such as the one by Brown, Driver, and Briggs, stated that the name Horite "probably equals cave-dweller." This statement implies that there was a race of cavemen in Palestine in the patriarchal days. Now archeology has recovered these Horites, and they were not cave-dwellers. They were as advanced as anyone else of antiquity, and it is now known that Abraham had a thousand years of high culture behind him. The Horites are now called Hurrians. Excavation of the Mesopotamian town of Nuzi (1929) revealed legal and family customs. The Hurrian language is now taught in some universities.

Solomon

Solomon is fabled for his wisdom. However, ancient history is so silent about him that some scholars wondered if his wealth and wisdom were not exaggerated by the biblical records. However, several discoveries have greatly illustrated and confirmed the biblical picture, even though archeology has not discovered any tablets or inscriptions of Solomon. First, the town of Megiddo was excavated (1925–39). The buildings showed

Solomon's ability and interest in architecture. They verified his practice of establishing various chariot cities for defense (1 Kings 10:26). It is interesting to note that a six-pointed star is scratched on one of the slightly later buildings at Megiddo. This is the shield of David—which appears today on the flag of Israel. Later excavations in Hazor of Galilee (1955-59) show a similar prosperity in the Solomonic layer. The gateway at Hazor is said to be almost identical to the Solomonic gateway at Megiddo.

The researches south of the Dead Sea by Nelson Glueck are a further proof of Solomon's era. Glueck found several copper mines with crude smelting furnaces in the valley south of the Dead Sea. Pottery showed that the mines had been worked in the time of Solomon. Copper was evidently taken to Ezion-Geber (modern Eilat) on the eastern arm of the Red Sea. Glueck excavated a remarkable city in 1938, evidently planned and built as a unit and used for refining and casting copper and as a center of trade. The Bible says that Solomon's ships left Ezion-Geber for distant ports, bringing home rich cargoes (1 Kings 9:26–28). Archeology confirms the truth of the Bible. Solomon's ships exported copper and brought him rich revenue. He was a copper magnate of antiquity.

ANSWERING CRITICISM

The higher criticism carried on by liberal scholars has always been infused with skepticism. Though essentially an investigation of the Bible books' authorship and dates, it has had sad results for Christian teaching.

Higher criticism arose in a time of great ignorance of the Bible backgrounds. It assumed and taught that Palestine and Mesopotamia were as backward as Greece in 1500 B.C. It taught that Moses did not know how to write. The stories of the patriarchs were said to be the unbelievable and legendary folklore of the Hebrews of 900–700 B.C. They were *explanation stories,* like the Native American stories about how the bear lost its tail. Liberal critics said that the Genesis stories did nothing more than attempt to tell how family life began, why women hated snakes, and such.

Such error was difficult to answer in the days when the early history of the Near East was virtually unknown. Today such skepticism is foolish. It has been proven that in the days of Moses an educated man could write three or four languages. The patriarchs moved in a world of great powers and advanced cultures.

Of special importance are the advances that archeology has made in patriarchal backgrounds and in the Hebrew language. In 1929 the ancient town of Nuzi in Northern Mesopotamia was discovered. It yielded a wealth of tablets, generally dating back to about 1500 B.C. These illustrated the daily life and legal customs of the Hurrians and of the north Fertile Crescent. Outstanding archeologists—E. A. Speiser, W. F. Albright, and others—have shown how these customs support and explain even in detail many of the peculiar family customs of the patriarchs.

For example, Nuzi wedding contracts specify that if a wife is barren, she shall give a slave girl to her husband to provide an heir. Such a child shall have the right of a firstborn. But if the legal wife later bears a son, the earlier heir shall give way to him. These and many other customs exactly fit the patriarchal families. They do not fit the Israelite practices of 900-700 B.C. Some scholars have therefore become convinced of the historicity of the Genesis narrative.

It is most encouraging to see many of the citadels of liberalism so effectively overturned. Today even this newer liberalism is on the defensive. However, not all archeologists believe in verbal inspiration. Many things about the Old Testament cannot be proven by archeology. The Christian takes them on faith, trusting in the approval given them by Jesus Christ. At the same time, archeological discoveries have not required orthodox scholars to make any important revision in their viewpoint regarding the Bible's authenticity. It is reasonable to assume that further archeological study will give additional, welcome light and confirmation.

VOCABULARY ENRICHMENT

Archeology, cuneiform, Fertile Crescent, lexicon, tablets, illumination.

DISCUSSION QUESTIONS

1. Give a brief history of archeology.
2. Give two examples of how archeology confirms the Bible.
3. Which came first, higher criticism or scientific archeology? What can be learned from this sequence?
4. Give an example of the way archeology has confounded higher criticism.
5. Use your concordance to list the references to the Horites.
6. Describe the archeological discoveries related to Solomon.
7. Examine at least one orthodox book on archeology.

Chapter Eleven

HELPS FOR
BIBLE STUDY

THE BEST HELP FOR Bible study is the Bible itself. There is no substitute for a thorough knowledge of God's Word. Bible students should possess the best reference works and should give much thought to the edition of the Bible they are going to use.

The purpose and progress in Bible knowledge will influence greatly the decision as to what edition of the Bible to secure. Some people prefer a small Bible for ease in carrying. Others want a large-type Bible for ease in reading, especially in public reading. You should get a Bible that will last a reasonable length of time. When you become familiar with a Bible and have study notes in its margin, it is not easy to change.

You may want to get a Bible with thumb-notch indexes for the different books. Some like this feature; others do not. Anything that helps you to use your Bible conveniently and quickly is worth getting.

You probably will want a Bible with a concordance in the back if it does not make the Bible too bulky. A concordance lists and locates the words used in the Bible. An exhaustive concordance does this for every word in the Bible. An abridged concordance lists only the important words. It is the abridged concordance that is usually found in the back of many Bibles, and this tool is useful for quickly locating many verses.

REFERENCE BIBLES

Reference editions of the Bible are available from several publishers. Their notes or comments really constitute a brief commentary on the Bible. Such works are useful to the earnest, serious student. It is necessary, however, to distinguish carefully between what the Bible says and what the commentary notes say about the Bible. It is well to compare several commentaries or reference Bibles so as to understand various views. The *Scofield Reference* edition of the *King James Version* has been used by millions since its publication in 1908. It is now available in other versions.

The *Thompson Chain Reference Bible* has much material in the form of a concordance and Bible dictionary. It does not have the paragraph headings in the text but has them plainly marked in a wide margin. The wide margin itself is helpful for student notes. This edition also is available in several versions.

The Zondervan Publishing Company has also published a *New International Version Study Bible* with concordance and extensive explanatory notes, tables, and cross-references. The *Life Application Bible*, published by Tyndale House, is also a very helpful resource. Other good reference Bibles are also available.

TRANSLATIONS

Most important translations have been done by believing men. A few translations have been made by liberal scholars. Sometimes when translation is easy and the meaning is clear, this may make little difference. In other cases, when the meaning of the words is not so clear or where doctrinal matters are of importance, the liberals may allow their background to influence their translation. This is especially true in translations of the Old Testament prophecies of Christ.

King James or Authorized Version

This translation has been used for many years. Its translators were gifted scholars. They took time to do good quality work and were extremely conscientious and faithful. Its language may be slightly outmoded, and there are some modern discoveries that can be used to improve the translation here and there. But for general accuracy and time-honored beauty, it is still a favorite.

The *New King James Version* is a revision of the 1611 translation that uses more modern English forms and takes advantage of recently discovered manuscripts.

English Revised and American Standard Version

The *English Revised Version* of 1885 and *American Standard Version* of 1901 are also quite accurate. New Testament translators used more recently discovered Greek manuscripts and textual study in an attempt to improve upon earlier translations. These revised versions may seem somewhat stilted because the translators frequently used the Hebrew and Greek word order rather than the English. The result is that they do not have the excellent English of the *King James Version*. If the revisers had really brought the language up-to-date, the revision would be more acceptable for modern study. But their improvements are not of sufficient strength to overbalance their deficiencies.

Revised Standard Version

The *Revised Standard Version* reflects modern scholarship and presents some improvements. This was an ambitious work done over a long period. Unfortunately, many of the translators represented the modern critical position and did not believe all the truth of the Bible they were translating. Unless students can refer to the Hebrew and Greek, they do not know whether any particular verse is an accurate translation or not. Many times where the Hebrew is difficult, the translators decided that the text had become corrupt. In such cases they often changed the Hebrew text without manuscript evidence and then translated the supposed reading. Most of these places are marked in the footnotes as a "correction" (Cn.). The *New English Bible* did the same thing, marking such conjectures as the "probable reading."

The RSV translators seldom utilized any newly discovered text of the Old Testament. Whenever they have done so, they seem to have worked by conjecture or by unscientific use of the Septuagint or other old versions.

In recent years an updated version of the RSV, titled the *New Revised Standard Version Bible*, has appeared. The text has been carefully recast in fresh vocabulary and construction and reflects changes in the English language that have occurred since the original translation was published.

Even more recently a group of conservative evangelical scholars undertook a complete revision of the *Revised Standard Version*, seeking to correct the problems mentioned above. The Bible they have produced, titled the *English Standard Version*, is an essentially literal translation. It embraces the ideal of word-for-word exactness while at the same time taking into account the differences between modern English and the original languages. Translators sought the English words that most closely captured the meaning of the original. The result is a Bible that is both accurate and readable.

The *New English Bible* is the British counterpart of the *Revised Standard Version* in England, but the former is even more extreme. Again, the NEB is less reliable in the Old Testament. Actually the editors do not strictly translate. In many cases, they change the text in order to solve a difficulty. For instance, the psalm titles are omitted, and numerous passages in Job are dislocated. The *New English Bible* is beautifully written, modern in expression, and easy to read; however, its readings must be constantly checked for accuracy of translation and fidelity of text.

Other Translations

Several other translations are now available. They are of three kinds: liberal, conservative paraphrases, and conservative with strict principles of translation.

Of the first kind is the Roman Catholic *Jerusalem Bible*, which is liberal in its translation and extremely liberal in its extensive footnotes. The Roman Catholic *New American Bible* is much better in these regards. The *Good News Bible* is quite modern in expression and not fully conservative. For instance, it replaces references to the blood of Christ with references to His death. This alteration misses the Old Testament sacrificial connections.

A modern conservative paraphrase, *The Living Bible*, is very readable. However, it sometimes imparts a meaning to a verse that is not there. It should be compared with other versions for careful study. The *Amplified Bible* is somewhat different in that it offers several variant readings for particular words. It is interesting for private study, but difficult for general church use.

In the last category, several newer versions should be mentioned: the *New American Standard Bible*, the *New International Version*, and the *New Living Translation*. The *New American Standard Bible* is a careful, thorough revision of the *American Standard Version* done by competent evangelical scholars. Some think that this Bible is not done in the smoothest modern English. But it is accurate and faithful both to the text and to the spirit of the original. The *New International Version* was prepared by a large group of competent scholars. It is also true to the text, but gives a sentence-equivalence treatment rather than a word-for-word translation. The result is a smooth, highly readable translation suitable for study, reading, memorization, and public reading. It appears to be the most widely accepted version today. The *New Living Translation* is a thought-for-thought translation that can be readily understood by the average person. This translation adopts the vocabulary and language structures used by people today.

YOUR LIBRARY

Serious Christian workers need a library—at least a small library—and they should use it. Good leaders teach out of a fullness of material.

Effective teachers do not face their classes just a jump ahead of them in the manual.

Christian workers should have some books of a sound, popular nature on all the main divisions of Bible study. They need Bible dictionaries for technical helps, commentaries for explanation of hard passages, church histories for the study of the spread of the Gospel, books on Bible introduction for information on authorship and background, theology books for doctrinal study, and practical books for guidance in teaching, missions, and devotional life. The many evangelical publishers of our day should be patronized by Christians and their worthwhile books widely read.

A word of caution is in order. The study of liberal books may have a place for the well-grounded Christian. Their challenging statements may cause believers to rethink the basis of their faith and be ready to give an answer. New Christians or beginning students, however, cannot afford to give large place to these writers. Strychnine in small quantities is a stimulant. In larger amounts, it is deadly.

Commentaries

There is no one best commentary. For one purpose one commentary may excel; for another purpose, another. But the Bible student who has not had technical training will probably want one or two general purpose commentaries. For many years Matthew Henry; Jamieson, Fausset, and Brown; and Adam Clarke have been the favorites. These are valuable devotional commentaries and are still well accepted. The *New Bible Commentary: Revised* and the *Wycliffe Bible Commentary* are helpful. For more extensive study, the Tyndale Commentary series is good. For technical matters, the *New International Commentary* volumes can be consulted or *The Expositor's Bible Commentary*. Much newer information bearing on the Bible has been discovered in recent times, and these newer commentaries are worth consulting. Publication information about the above commentaries may be found in the Resources for Enrichment section at the end of this text.

Concordances

For those who need more help than the abridged concordance in the back of their Bible can provide, complete standard concordances are available. Two of these, Young's and Strong's, have about equal merit. In *Strong's Exhaustive Concordance*, every word is followed by a number. This number appears in the back of the book as a key to the original Hebrew or Greek word, transliterated in English letters.

Strong's Concordance

2051. זְדָן **V⁰dân,** *ved-awn';* perh. for 5730; *Vedan* (or Aden), a place in Arabia:—Dan also.

2052. וָהֵב **Vâhêb,** *vaw-habe';* of uncert. der.; *Vaheb,* a place in Moab:—what he did.

2053. וָו **vâv,** *vaw;* prob. a *hook* (the name of the sixth Heb. letter):—hook.

2054. וָזָר **vâzâr,** *vaw-zawr';* presumed to be from an unused root mean. to *bear guilt:* *crime:*— × strange.

2055. וַיְזָתָא **Vay⁰zâthâ',** *vah-yez-aw'-thaw;* of for. or.; *Vajezatha,* a son of Haman:—Vajezatha.

2056. וָלָד **vâlâd,** *vaw-lawd';* for 3206; a *boy:*—child

2057. וַנְיָה **Vanyâh,** *van-yaw';* perh. for 6043; *Vanjah,* an Isr.:—Vaniah.

2058 וָפְסִי **Vophçîy,** *vof-see';* prob. from 3254; *additional; Vophsi,* an Isr.:—Vophsi.

2059. וַשְׁנִי **Vashnîy,** *vash-nee';* prob. from 3461: *weak; Vashni,* an Isr.:—Vashni.

2060. וַשְׁתִּי **Vashtîy,** *vash-tee';* of Pers. or.; *Vashti,* the queen of Xerxes:—Vashti.

child▲   See also CHILDBEARING; CHILDHOOD; CHILDLESS; CHILDREN; CHILD'S.
Ge 11:30 Sarai was barren; she had no *c'*.   2056
16:11 her, Behold, thou art with *c'*,   2030
17:10 Every man *c'* among you shall   *
12 every man *c'* in your generations,*
14 the uncircumcised man *c'* whose*
19:36 both the daughters of Lot with *c'* 2030
21: 8 the *c'* grew, and was weaned: 3206
14 and the *c'*, and sent her away: "
15 cast the *c'* under one of the shrubs."
16 Let me not see the death of the *c'*. "
37:30 The *c'* is not; and I, whither shall "
38:24 she is with *c'* by whoredom.   2030
25 am I with *c'*: and she said,   "
42:22 Do not sin against the *c'*;   3206
44:20 and a *c'* of his old age, a little one; "
Ex 2: 2 saw him that he was a goodly *c'*,
3 and put the *c'* therein; and she   3206
6 had opened it, she saw the *c'*:   "
7 women, that she may nurse the *c'* "
9 Take this *c'* away, and nurse it   "
9 the woman took the *c'*, and nursed "
10 And the *c'* grew, and she brought "
21:22 hurt a woman with *c'*, so that her 2030
22:22 afflict any widow, or fatherless *c'*.

In *Young's Analytical Concordance to the Bible*, the Hebrew or Greek word is printed with the English word. A section at the back tells what English words are used to translate each original word. For instance, you can look up the word *paidia*, "child," and find that it is translated twenty-five times "child," four times "damsel," twelve times "little child," and ten times "young child." These English words give a complete picture of the Greek word. This is no substitute for actually reading the Greek or Hebrew, but this tool is a great help. A Hebrew dictionary that can be used by nontechnical students is the *Theological Wordbook of the Old Testament*. Since its entries are keyed to Strong's *Concordance*, it can be used in a limited way by those with little or no Hebrew.

Bible Dictionary

Do you want to know how a word is used or what it means? What is a pomegranate, a farthing, a cherub? How old is Jerusalem? Where is Ai? A Bible dictionary or encyclopedia gives the answers to questions such as these.

In this field the *International Standard Bible Encyclopedia* has been the standard for many years among orthodox scholars. A similar work is Merrill Tenney's five-volume *The Zondervan Pictorial Encyclopedia of the Bible*. Less exhaustive but very suitable is the one-volume *The Zondervan Pictorial Bible Dictionary* by the same editor. J. D. Douglas's *New Bible Dictionary* also is valuable, as is the *Wycliffe Bible Encyclopedia*. Charles Pfeiffer has a general reference dictionary on archeology, *The Biblical World*. See the Resources for Enrichment section for further information about these resources.

Bible Introduction

Who wrote Judges? When did Paul visit Rome? When was the Old Testament canon closed? Which Gospel was written first? Bible dictionaries and encyclopedias give partial answers. Books on Bible introduction have more complete, satisfactory answers to these questions.

Some books deal with specialized or limited subjects. Some are technical, but Christian students should not be afraid of a little study. In this field as in some others, however, it is wise to avoid books tainted with liberalism, since they do not usually present all the evidence. This leaves students with a half truth that is dangerous, especially if they are not able to study further. In the New Testament field, the *Introduction to the New Testament* by Thiessen is a standard. The Old Testament field is more technical. Unger's *Introductory Guide to the Old Testament* may be valuable. The writer's own book, *Inspiration and Canonicity of the Bible*, and *Survey of Old Testament Introduction* by Gleason L. Archer, Jr., deal with some of these subjects in a more popular way. O. T. Allis's *The Five Books of Moses* is standard for discussion of the Pentateuch.

Theology Books

Benjamin B. Warfield, great theologian of the past generation, said, "The best theological professor is a Christian mother." Every Christian mother should work faithfully at her teacher's task. At an early age the author was taught a complete system of theology by his mother. She made him memorize the Westminster Shorter Catechism. Actually such creeds as the Westminster Confession of Faith and Catechisms, the Heidelberg Catechism, and the Lutheran Augsburg Confession are theology textbooks in a small yet vital compass.

A readable work on theology is by Dr. J. Oliver Buswell, Jr., *A Systematic Theology of the Christian Religion*. An excellent short study on theology is *In Understanding Be Men* by T. C. Hammond of England. It has a scriptural, popular approach. Widely used and good are *Basic Christianity* by John R. W. Stott and *Mere Christianity* by C. S. Lewis. An older book by A. A. Hodge, *Outlines of Theology*, also deserves careful study. There are many other well-written, conservative texts in theology; so students need not feel limited in their study.

Miscellaneous Reading and Study

Have you read any church history? It is fascinating. Try F. F. Bruce's *The Spreading Flame*. This is the first in a series of popular books on the history of the church. Earle E. Cairns's *Christianity Through the*

Centuries covers the whole field in one volume. How many biographies have you read? The stories of D. L. Moody, Charles Hadden Spurgeon, Morrison of China, Judson of Burma, William Carey of India, Hudson Taylor of China, George Mueller of England, and many others are fascinating reading. Many books are available on modern experiences, such as Corrie Ten Boom's *The Hiding Place*, or on modern problems, such as Francis Schaeffer's *Escape from Reason*. And then there are the widely known books of C. S. Lewis on many subjects. Fill your life with such literature.

VOCABULARY ENRICHMENT

Bible introduction, commentary, concordance, reference Bible.

DISCUSSION QUESTIONS

1. Compare the translation of Hebrews 1 in the *King James Version,* the *New International Version*, the *American Standard Version,* and the *Revised Standard Version.*
2. Do the same for Psalm 45.
3. Evaluate the merits and weaknesses of the *King James Version,* the *New International Version*, the *American Standard Version,* and the *Revised Standard Version.* Explain your position.
4. Trace in Young's or Strong's concordance the uses of the Hebrew word *tsur,* "rock." (There are seventy-six usages, with the Hebrew translated by nine English words or phrases.) In how many of these is God called a rock?
5. Use a Bible dictionary or encyclopedia to look up the dates of the reign of Sargon, king of Assyria, and tell something about him.
6. Try to find five of the books mentioned in this chapter. Do you have any of these in your own library? If not, your pastor may let you check his library. What about your church or Sunday school library?

Chapter Twelve

BIBLE STUDY METHODS

"HOW CAN I IMPROVE my knowledge of the Bible?" "How can I really study and understand God's Word?" These companion questions are frequently asked by serious-minded Christians. They deserve careful thought because the contents of the Bible are so varied, and the backgrounds are so different. The study of God's Word has occupied many people of great ability through the centuries. How can you unlock its treasures?

Two things must be considered—how to appreciate and understand the Bible better and how to get more of the Bible's blessing for daily living. The first concerns Bible study; the other is related to devotional life. Unfortunately, it is possible to have one without the other. The well-taught, well-balanced Christian understands the Word of God and takes it to heart.

DEVOTIONAL READING

Nothing can substitute for daily reading of the Bible. It should be devotional reading—prayerful, thoughtful reading with a prepared heart. All kinds of devotional helps are available today. And certainly everyone agrees that the Holy Spirit is the great Teacher.

For devotions, do not read too much at a time. It is better to cover half a chapter, underlining the striking verses and jotting down the lessons learned, than to read hurriedly through three chapters without taking any of it to heart. Though it takes time and discipline, it is a good practice to memorize verses and chapters. These should be reviewed frequently and shared with others.

Some portions are well adapted to devotional reading. Others, like the genealogies and laws of cleanliness, do not adapt to devotional reading, even though they are true and important.

New Christians will find it helpful to begin devotional reading by using the Psalms or the four Gospels, especially John. The Acts and the shorter Epistles are helpful. But wherever people begin, they should keep their hearts open for God's blessing.

A word of caution may be said on devotional helps. Numerous devotional books and quarterlies have been written by liberal authors. Some have the idea that quietness, emotionalism, and stained-glass windows are the essence of devotion. If so, Paul had a meager devotional life. A pamphlet that quotes a verse of Scripture out of context and tells a story about a little boy who gave his allowance to his brother and closes with a prayer, "O Lord, help us to help one another," is no help to devotion.

Does your devotional guide exalt the Lord Jesus Christ as the supernatural, miracle-working, sin-bearing, resurrected Savior? Does it encourage you to seek positive answers to prevailing prayer? Does it offer the meat of the Word adequately interpreted? If not, scrutinize it again. Choose from the many sound books, such as *Daily Light, My Utmost for His Highest,* and *Streams in the Desert.* Biblically sound radio and TV devotional programs also are helpful.

BIBLE STUDY

Christian workers need more than devotional reading of the Bible. Teachers and leaders especially need to know the facts, doctrines, and backgrounds of the Bible. Without thorough Bible knowledge, they will not be able to answer the questions of others or to bring out the rich truths of the Word.

How shall we study the Bible and master it? Any answer implies a willingness to study. Mathematics, French, and chemistry are not learned without application. This is equally true of the Bible.

Bible study involves the use of books written by Bible scholars. Why? The early Christians did not debate extensively the meanings of the Epistles. They knew the language and the backgrounds of the writings. Today most Christian workers do not know either Greek or Hebrew. Nor do they have a broad, general knowledge of ancient times. So they must depend on those who do know this information. It is, therefore, important to use such studies intelligently. In a fundamental seminary or Bible college, the Bible is studied from a variety of angles. Most teachers, workers, or officers of the local church have not had such formal training, but they can study the Bible diligently and consistently.

Dr. Wilbur M. Smith, in his useful book *Profitable Bible Study*, advocates several methods of approach—a book at a time (often too much for a beginner), studying by chapters, by paragraphs, by verses, and by words. He suggests the study of Bible biographies and prayers and reminds us that all the material should be related to Christ and His work for us. He quotes Miss Grace Saxe's ten questions to ask of each chapter:

What is the leading subject?

What is the leading lesson?

What is the best verse?

Who is the principal person?

What does it teach of Christ?

Does it show an example to follow?

Is there any error to avoid?

Is there a duty to perform?

Does it give a promise to claim?

Is there a prayer to echo?

Dr. Smith quotes Dr. Howard A. Kelly, famous Christian surgeon of Baltimore, who said that "the greatest secret of Bible study is simply to do it!"

What appears to a beginner as a great knowledge of the Bible is thus often only the natural result of a persevering use of the simplest of all methods—namely, reading the book day by day until it becomes extremely familiar in all its parts.

Bible Book Study

Study of the books or portions is called exegesis or interpretation. Several steps lead to success in this type of study. First, the book should be read many times. Then an outline should be made to analyze the book. The general contents should be placed in plain view, showing the relationship of each part to every other. It will be of help to ask these questions.

Does the book have a main theme?

How is the theme developed?

If the book is historical, what is the historian's viewpoint?

What does the author emphasize?

In some books, such as the Psalms, the themes are not easily unified. Such a book should be studied by individual units.

LITERARY DIVISION

You may want to study a verse at a time or to treasure certain verses apart from context. Louis M. Sweet's *The Study of the English Bible* is a healthy protest against this piecemeal approach. Sweet's book follows the method of Dr. W. W. White, that of observing the literary units of paragraphs and larger wholes. Many Bibles have the paragraphs or literary units marked. The natural division should be carefully kept in mind in study.

BIBLE INTRODUCTION

It is important to know the background of each book and the reason for its writing. A good book on Bible introduction will provide this information. For instance, in the study of Colossians, you will discover that this book is one of four Prison Epistles written by Paul from Rome. This fact explains the agreement between Ephesians and Colossians—a similarity so striking that the one helps to explain the other. Both were written against a background of the growing heresy of Gnosticism. Therefore, Paul emphasized the uniqueness of Christ. This background information enriches your interpretation. An extensive study of history and archeology will also help in attaining the goal of increased Bible knowledge.

Doctrinal Study

This study, known as systematic theology, can be as exhaustive as your time and ability will allow. Doctrinal study strengthens interpretation, and correct interpretation is necessary for doctrinal study.

A study of "Christ" in Hebrews 1 shows the error of the claim of some liberal theologians that Colossians 1:15 teaches that Christ is firstborn among equals. Rather it reveals Him as the unique Son of God who existed before any of the things that He Himself created. Comparison of Scripture with Scripture is proper and profitable because the Holy Spirit is the Author of it all. He directs and guides as you trace each doctrine through the entire book.

Careful study of "Christ in the Prison Epistles" will uncover truths usually missed in general book study. Doctrinal study has a stabilizing influence and helps produce virile Christians.

It may be difficult to remember all the texts bearing on "the nature of sin," but a brief doctrinal statement from a catechism or a book on systematic theology will summarize the Bible's teaching on this subject. This is useful in Christian life as well as in Christian study.

Historical Study

Another fruitful method of study is by historical periods. This is important in the Old Testament where the books are not arranged chronologically. Companion books should be studied together. The following grouping will help.

OLD TESTAMENT

The Pentateuch (Genesis-Deuteronomy) is a unit and concerns the early times.

The psalms of David go with the books of Samuel.

Proverbs, Ecclesiastes, and the Song of Solomon fit in with the early chapters of 1 Kings.

Isaiah should be read with the first six Minor Prophets—Hosea, Joel, Amos, Obadiah, Jonah, and Micah.

Jeremiah, Ezekiel, Daniel, and the three Minor Prophets Nahum, Habakkuk, and Zephaniah are approximately of the same time period.

Ezra, Nehemiah, and the last three Minor Prophets are of the post-exilic times.

Passages in 2 Samuel should be read and compared with 1 Chronicles to see if they are parallel or supplementary passages.

Likewise, 2 Chronicles should be compared with 1 Kings and 2 Kings.

NEW TESTAMENT

In the New Testament the time span is shorter, but the historical background is equally important. An interesting way to study Acts would be to stop at each place where Paul wrote an epistle. Before continuing, read the corresponding epistle. This method interweaves the book of Acts and the Pauline Epistles, enriching the interpretation.

Word Study

The aim of all exegesis is simply to find out what the Bible says. When we read magazines or newspapers, we do not have to engage in exegesis because we are thoroughly familiar with the language. Occasionally we meet a strange word, and then we consult a dictionary. In reading more difficult material, we use exegesis more.

The Bible was written in Greek, Hebrew, and Aramaic. These are strange languages to us, and the customs of antiquity are unfamiliar or perhaps unknown. The biblical material concerns deep and wonderful divine truths. Therefore, we must probe deeply into the meaning of the Bible's text. Word study is often helpful in this process. This investigation of a word's usage and derivation involves the use of dictionaries and other reference books.

For instance, Jesus said, "I am the bread of life" (John 6:35). What did He mean? Is Jesus bread? How do "bread" and "life" fit together? Here is deeper truth to be gained by study. For such word study, look up all Jesus' references to bread, especially to His being bread. He evidently was not talking about physical life or physical bread. Notice that Christ also claims to give the "light of life" (John 8:12) and the "living water" (John 7:38). Study the other metaphors using the expression, "I am"—"I am the door" (John 10:9); "I am the way, the truth, and the life" (John 14:6). Word study will bring out the deeper truths.

Some words are strange to us. A much debated word is *baptize*. Word study will not provide an absolutely final answer. If it did, all discussion would cease. But you should look up all the uses of this word. Whatever your view, you should investigate the biblical data. Take Young's or Strong's concordance, find how many ways the Greek word *baptizo* is translated. Check all these references. Your investigation of the evidence will enable you to make sure your view is based on facts. Word study is a valuable tool in exegesis.

Combinations of Bible Study Methods

All methods of Bible study are interrelated. You do not learn all the doctrines before you begin exegesis. Nor do you study a whole book and its component paragraphs before you investigate its background. The fact is, all methods should be used at all times. No one should use book study or the verse-by-verse method of interpretation without using the others. Conscientious students who use supplementary materials will improve their personal lives and ministry. A major purpose of this course has been to give guidance and suggestions in this further Bible study. Full-orbed Bible study is a blessing.

"Blessed is he that readeth, and they that hear the words of this prophecy, and keep those things which are written therein; for the time is at hand" (Rev. 1:3).

VOCABULARY ENRICHMENT

Catechism, chronology, doctrinal study, exegesis, Gnosticism, historical study, interpretation, systematic theology, textual study, word study.

DISCUSSION QUESTIONS

1. Give two reasons why New Testament exegesis is more of a problem today than it was for the early Christian church.

2. Why should Christians study the Bible both devotionally and technically?
3. What information would a close study of an epistle such as 2 Timothy reveal about what time in Paul's life and under what circumstances it was written?
4. Using the Westminster Shorter Catechism, Heidelberg Catechism, or any other catechism, look up the doctrine of the person of Christ.
5. Describe the Bible study methods you have used.

NOTES

1 REVELATION AND INSPIRATION

1. C. S. Lewis, *Miracles* (New York: Macmillan, 1947), p. 74.
2. E. D. Hirsch, *The Aims of Interpretation* (Chicago: University of Chicago, 1976), p. 41.
3. Norman L. Geisler, ed., *Inerrancy* (Grand Rapids: Zondervan Publishing, 1980), chapters 12, 13.

5 WHO WROTE THE NEW TESTAMENT?

1. Cited and defended by Donald Guthrie, *New Testament Introduction*, Vol. 3 (Downers Grove, Ill.: InterVarsity Press, 1965), pp. 321-22.
2. Quoted by Eusebius in his *Ecclesiastical History*, vi, 25.
3. Alexander Roberts and James Donaldson, eds., *Early Church Fathers, The Ante-Nicene Fathers*, Vol. 4 (Hendrickson, MA: 1994), pp. 310, 333, 361ff.
4. Ibid., p. 388.

7 PRESERVATION OF THE BIBLE: OLD TESTAMENT

1. See the article "Nergal-sharezer" by E. M. Yamauchi in *Wycliffe Bible Encyclopedia*, ed. Charles F. Pfeiffer, H. F. Vos, and J. Rea (Chicago: Moody Press, 1975).

9 HIGHER CRITICISM AND THE BIBLE

1. Martin Noth, *A History of Pentateuchal Traditions*, tr. B. W. Anderson (Chico, CA: Scholars Press, 1981), pp. 17-18.

RESOURCES FOR ENRICHMENT

Albright, William F. "Recent Discoveries in Bible Lands." Supplement of *Young's Analytical Concordance to the Bible*. Rev. ed. Grand Rapids: Wm. B. Eerdmans Publishing, 1955.

Allis, Oswald T. *The Five Books of Moses*. Grand Rapids: Baker Book House, 1977.

_____. *The Unity of Isaiah*. Grand Rapids: Baker Book House, n.d.

Archer, Gleason L., Jr. *A Survey of Old Testament Introduction*. Rev. ed. Chicago: Moody Press, 1973.

_____. *Encyclopedia of Bible Difficulties*. Grand Rapids: Zondervan Publishing, 1982.

Bruce, F. F. *The New Testament Documents: Are They Reliable?* 5th rev. ed. Grand Rapids: Wm. B. Eerdmans Publishing, 1960.

_____. *The Spreading Flame*. Grand Rapids: Wm. B. Eerdmans Publishing, 1980.

_____. *New International Commentary on the New Testament*. Grand Rapids: Wm. B. Eerdmans Publishing, 1994.

Buswell, J. Oliver, Jr. *A Systematic Theology of the Christian Religion*. Grand Rapids: Zondervan Publishing, 1962.

Cairns, Earle E. *Christianity Through the Centuries*. Grand Rapids: Zondervan Publishing, 1967.

Carson, D. A., and Woodbridge, John D., eds. *Scripture and Truth*. Grand Rapids: Zondervan Publishing, 1983.

Douglas, J. D., ed. *The New Bible Dictionary*. Grand Rapids: Wm. B. Eerdmans Publishing, 1962.

Finegan, Jack. *Light from the Ancient Past: The Archaeological Background of Judaism and Christianity*. 2nd ed. 2 vols. Princeton, N.J.: Princeton University Press, 1970.

Gaebelein, F. *The Expositor's Bible Commentary*. Grand Rapids: Zondervan Publishing, 1979.

Geisler, Norman L., ed. *Inerrancy*. Grand Rapids: Zondervan Publishing, 1980.

Geisler, Norman, L., and Nix, William E. *From God to Us: How We Got Our Bible*. Chicago: Moody Press, 1974.

Gish, Duane T. *Evolution: The Challenge of the Fossil Record*. El Cajon, Calif.: Creation-Life Publishers, 1985.

Greenlee, J. H. "Text and Manuscripts of the New Testament." *The Zondervan Pictorial Encyclopedia of the Bible*. 5 vols. Ed. Merrill C. Tenney. Grand Rapids: Zondervan Publishing, 1975.

Guthrie, Donald. "Canon of the New Testament." In vol. 1 of *The Zondervan Pictorial Encyclopedia of the Bible*. 5 vols. Ed. Merrill C. Tenney. Grand Rapids: Zondervan Publishing, 1975.

_____. *New Testament Introduction*. 3 vols. Chicago: InterVarsity Press, 1965.

Guthrie, Donald, and Motyer, J. A., eds. *The New Bible Commentary: Revised*. Grand Rapids: Wm. B. Eerdmans Publishing, 1970.

Haley, J. W. *An Examination of the Alleged Discrepancies of the Bible*. Nashville: B. C. Goodpasture, 1958.

Hammond, T. C. *In Understanding Be Men*. London: InterVarsity Press, 1936.

Harris, R. Laird. "Canon of the Old Testament." In vol. 1 of *The Zondervan Pictorial Encyclopedia of the Bible*. 5 vols. Ed. Merrill C. Tenney. Grand Rapids: Zondervan Publishing, 1975.

_____. *Inspiration and Canonicity of the Bible*. Rev. ed. Grand Rapids: Zondervan Publishing, 1969.

_____, ed. *Theological Wordbook of the Old Testament*. Chicago: Moody Press, 1980.

Harrison, R. K. "Dead Sea Scrolls." In vol. 2 of *The Zondervan Pictorial Encyclopedia of the Bible*. 5 vols. Ed. Merrill C. Tenney. Grand Rapids: Zondervan Publishing, 1975.

_____, ed. *New International Commentary on the Old Testament*. Grand Rapids: Wm. B. Eerdmans Publishing.

Helm, Paul. *The Divine Revelation*. Chicago: Good News Publishers, 1982.

Jensen, Irving L. *Enjoy Your Bible*. Chicago: Moody Press, 1969.

Lewis, C. S. *Mere Christianity*. New York: Macmillan Co., 1960.

_____. *Miracles, A Preliminary Study*. New York: Macmillan Co., 1947.

Orr, James, ed. *The International Standard Bible Encyclopedia*. Chicago: Howard Severance Co., 1930.

Parker, Gary. *Creation, the Facts of Life.* El Cajon, Calif.: Creation-Life Publishers, 1980.

Perry, Lloyd M., and Culver, Robert D. *How to Get More from Your Bible.* Grand Rapids: Baker Book House, 1979.

Pfeiffer, Charles F. *Dead Sea Scrolls and the Bible.* Grand Rapids: Baker Book House, 1969.

_____, ed. *The Biblical World, a Dictionary of Biblical Archaeology.* Grand Rapids: Baker Book House, 1966.

Pfeiffer, Charles F., and Harrison, E. F., eds. *The Wycliffe Bible Commentary.* Chicago: Moody Press, 1962.

Pfeiffer, Charles F., and Vos, H. F., eds. *Wycliffe Bible Encyclopedia.* 2 vols. Chicago: Moody Press, 1975.

Pun, Pattle P. T. *Evolution: Nature and Scripture in Conflict?* Grand Rapids: Zondervan Publishing, 1982.

Schaeffer, Francis A. *Escape from Reason.* Downers Grove, Ill.: InterVarsity Press, 1979.

Scroggie, W. Graham. *A Guide to the Gospels.* Old Tappan, N.J.: Fleming H. Revell, 1975.

Sproul, R. C. "The Case for Inerrancy." *God's Inerrant Word.* Ed. J. W. Mungor. Minneapolis: Bethany Fellowship, 1974.

Stott, John R. W. *Basic Christianity.* Grand Rapids: Wm. B. Eerdmans Publishing, 1957.

Tasker, R. V. G., ed. *Tyndale New Testament Commentary.* Grand Rapids: Wm. B. Eerdmans Publishing, 1979.

Ten Boom, Corrie. *The Hiding Place.* Minneapolis: Billy Graham Assn., 1971.

Tenney, Merrill C. *New Testament Survey.* Rev. ed. Grand Rapids: Wm. B. Eerdmans Publishing, 1961.

_____, ed. *The Zondervan Pictorial Bible Dictionary.* Grand Rapids: Zondervan Publishing, 1967.

Thiessen, Henry C. *Introduction to the New Testament.* Grand Rapids: Wm. B. Eerdmans Publishing, 1971.

Thompson, J. A. *The Bible and Archeology.* Rev. ed. Grand Rapids: Wm. B. Eerdmans Publishing, 1981.

Unger, Merrill F. *Archeology and the Old Testament.* Grand Rapids: Zondervan Publishing, 1954.

_____. *Introductory Guide to the Old Testament*. Grand Rapids: Zondervan Publishing, 1951.

Vos, Howard. *Effective Bible Study*. Grand Rapids: Zondervan Publishing, 1956.

Wald, Oletta. *The Joy of Discovery in Bible Study*. Minneapolis: Augsburg Publishing House, 1975.

Warfield, B. B. *The Inspiration and Authority of the Bible*. Nutley, N.J.: Presbyterian and Reformed Publishing, 1948.

Wenham, J. W., "Christ's View of Scripture," and Blum, E. P., "The Apostles' View of Scripture." *Inerrancy*. Ed. Norman L. Geisler. Grand Rapids: Zondervan Publishing, 1980.

Wiseman, D. J., ed. *Tyndale Old Testament Commentaries*. Chicago: InterVarsity Press.

Young, Edward J. *An Introduction to the Old Testament*. Grand Rapids: Wm. B. Eerdmans Publishing, 1958.

CONTENTS

PART TWO: JOB—MALACHI

INTRODUCTION

STUDY OF THE OLD TESTAMENT offers a fascinating experience for all who desire to understand more clearly the workings of God. Well-known Bible stories take on a new dimension when seen in the perspective of a sweeping panoramic overview. *Exploring the Old Testament* and its companion text, *Exploring the New Testament*, provide this overview of the entire Bible. A capable teacher of others must first develop spiritual depth and biblical knowledge. These books will assist in attaining both of these goals.

Here in easy-to-read form is a survey of the interesting and challenging Bible books of history, law, poetry, and prophecy. To avoid duplication of historical background information, the study is arranged in sequence according to the date the Bible book was written or when the prophet ministered, not in the order they appear in most Bibles.

Also, to avoid specific differences in interpretation, the book simply presents what the Bible says rather than the various ways individuals and groups have interpreted some passages. For those who feel specific interpretations are necessary as well, we suggest that you consult additional sources. The bibliography found at the end of the text should provide you with more in-depth resources for gathering this information.

Each chapter is followed by suggested questions and exploration activities. Questions are content centered and can profitably be used for reviewing historical fact and development. The project and discussion portion will direct you to deeper study of the Word, helping you rethink and crystallize its major truths and apply them to your daily life.

Dr. Smith was Professor of Old Testament at Bethel Theological Seminary in St. Paul, Minnesota, for fifteen years and currently is Professor of Old Testament at Midwestern Baptist Theological Seminary in Kansas City, Missouri. He has helped with several Bible translations and is the author of books and articles.

Dr. Schultz is a recognized Bible scholar who communicates the Old Testament message with a refreshing contemporary approach. He retains scholarship within the framework of a challengingly spiritual approach. His comprehensive work on the Old Testament, *The Old Testament Speaks,* is an excellent source of more detailed consideration of this same portion of the Word.

No text, however, can ever substitute for a study of the Bible itself. Nor can the most capable of teachers apply the message of the Book to human hearts. The one who would benefit most from this study must first read the portion of the Word of God under consideration. Read it as many times as possible. Read it in various good translations. Read it; then read it again.

Since "the New is in the Old concealed, and the Old is in the New revealed," a study of the Old Testament is an imperative foundation for clarity of both Old and New Testament Bible teaching. It will enrich a believer's knowledge and life and make for better teaching to the glory of God.

PART ONE:

GENESIS—ESTHER

Chapter One

BEGINNINGS

THE BIBLE IS THE world's bestseller. The message of God is considered so vital to man that translators and Bible agencies have produced parts of the Scriptures in 2,237 languages, according to the fourteenth edition of *Ethnologue: Languages of the World*. At least 95 percent of the world's population has portions of the Scriptures in a language available to them.

WHY STUDY THE OLD TESTAMENT?

The Old Testament has had the widest acclaim of all writings in the fields of literature, history, and religion. Jews, Muslims, and Christians find their beginnings in the Old Testament. It continues to attract and challenge the keenest scholars and meet the needs of even the humblest of every generation.

In contemporary Christianity, the Old Testament is more neglected than the New. Because of the prominence of law in the Old Testament, and of the Gospel in the New, readers do not always clearly understand that God's grace operated throughout the history of His dealings with people. Those who portray the God of the Old Testament as a God of wrath and judgment, and think of God in the New Testament as a God of love, should not ignore the fact that Moses (Deut. 4–6), Jeremiah (9:23, 24), and others represented Him as the God of love and justice. The apostle Paul, who was thoroughly versed in the Old Testament, called God the "Father of mercies" (2 Cor. 1:3).

The Old Testament provides the historical background by which we are able to understand the New. This is apparent in the fact that the New Testament contains over 600 references or allusions to the Old. Jesus and the apostles constantly appealed to it in their teaching. Paul used the Old Testament with great effectiveness as he went from synagogue to synagogue to convince the Jews that Jesus was the Christ (cf. Acts 17:3, 11-13; 18:5, and others). Neither human nature nor God has changed since Old Testament times. Our study of man's relationship with God guides us today and leads us to the proper response of faith and obedience.

THE HISTORY OF OLD TESTAMENT TIMES

The history of the Old Testament is found primarily in the first seventeen books (Genesis–Esther) of our English Bible. After a brief account of the developments from Adam to Terah, biblical history is basically concerned with God's chosen nation beginning with Abraham (ca. 2000 B.C.), and continuing until the time of the rebuilding of the walls of Jerusalem under Nehemiah (ca. 450 B.C.). The poetic and prophetic books reflect various periods of history and allow insight into prevailing political, religious, and cultural situations.

As we may learn from the Old Testament itself, the historical books are more than the national records of the Jewish nation and tell us more than its history. Both Jews and Christians hold that the Old Testament discloses God's revelation of Himself to man. Jesus gave it His stamp of approval as Holy Writ and taught that it had predicted His coming (Luke 24:44 and others). Paul called Old Testament Scripture "the oracles of God" (Rom. 3:2).

While it is sacred history, the Old Testament gives an account of natural events, guided by and interwoven with the supernatural activity of God. In times of both blessing and adversity in Israel, God was accomplishing His purposes in national and international developments. Consequently, the Old Testament can be interpreted properly only when both the natural and the supernatural are recognized in its pages.

Old Testament history may be divided into the following periods:

The era of beginnings	Genesis 1–11
Patriarchal times	Genesis 12–50
Israel becomes a nation	Exodus—Deuteronomy
Conquest and occupation	Joshua, Judges, Ruth
The united kingdom	1 Samuel; 2 Samuel; 1 Chronicles; 2 Chronicles 1–9; 1 Kings 1–11
The divided kingdom	1 Kings 12–2 Kings 25; 2 Chronicles 10–36
The postexilic era	Ezra, Esther, Nehemiah

Era of Beginnings

Scripture Survey: Genesis 1–11
Extent of Time: From the Beginning to About 2000 B.C.

Genesis 1–11 is introductory to the whole Bible. In spite of its brevity, this section covers a longer span of time than the rest of the Old Testament—that is, from Abraham to Malachi. Throughout the Scriptures are numerous references that amplify and expound the meaning of this brief section. These chapters are essential to a proper understanding of the whole written revelation.

This introduction is vital to the rest of Genesis and to the other four books of the Pentateuch. Beginning with Genesis 12, God's promise of redemption is focused on Abraham and his family. Exodus through Deuteronomy describes an established nation under Moses' leadership, growing out of the descendants of the patriarchs. Moses, who was intimately associated with the events and laws recorded in these four books, is recognized throughout the Bible as the author of the five books called the Pentateuch. Both written and oral sources available to Moses may have provided him with the basic material for Israel's history as recorded in Genesis. Consequently, the book of Genesis is properly regarded as Moses' introduction to the rest of the Pentateuch (cf. Gen. 17:12; John 7:23).

The period of beginnings may be outlined as follows:

The account of creation	Genesis	1:1–2:25
The universe and its contents		1:1–2:4a
Man in his first dwelling place		2:4b-25
The Fall and its consequences		3:1–6:10
Man's disobedience and expulsion		3:1-24
Cain and Abel		4:1-24
The generation of Adam		4:25–6:10
The Flood: God's Judgment on man		6:11–8:19
Preparation for the Flood		6:11-22
The Deluge		7:1–8:19
Man's new beginning		8:20–11:32
The covenant with Noah		8:20–9:19
Noah and his sons		9:20–10:32
The Tower of Babel		11:1-9
Shem and his descendants		11:10-32

The Creation Account

Scripture Survey: Genesis 1–2

Simple but profound is this account of the origin of the universe, and in particular of God's creative activity as manifested on the earth. The record assumes the existence of God who created the universe including the earth and all life upon it. The account clearly states that God created all things. God is the subject of the verb here as well as in most places where this verb appears. Whenever an object is used with this verb, no preexisting material is indicated. Although *bara* normally refers to creation *ex nihilo* (out of nothing), it sometimes expresses God's creative power in history (Exod. 34:10; Num. 16:30; Jer. 31:22; Isa. 45:7, 8; 48:7).

A DIVINE PLAN IN CREATION

Order and purpose are expressly stated. Genesis 1:2b could be interpreted to refer to a divine restoration of a chaotic condition. In this view, the opening verse (1:1) presents an original creation that was subsequently reduced to chaos (1:2a) through judgment and destruction. Usually Isaiah 45:18 is quoted in favor of this view, interpreting the Hebrew word *bohu* to mean "void." Further support is adduced by equating the "prince of Tyre" in Ezekiel 28 with Satan himself and applying Jeremiah 4:23-26 to a pre-Adamic condition. According to this view, verses 1 and 2 represent the summary of all that the Scriptures reveal of God's original creation, and the following verses are an account of the process of restoration. This is known as the Gap-Restoration view.

On the other hand, it is reasonable to interpret this account of creation as giving an orderly series of divine acts in which verse 2 is simply one logical step in the process of creation. Taking this view of the passage, we may see an orderly preparation being made for proper conditions to maintain life on earth, as follows:

1. Heaven and earth were created to provide the basis for an orderly state.
2. Atmospheric conditions were regulated.
3. Dry land was established above the receding water level to make vegetation possible.
4. Lights or luminaries, which very likely were included in creation (1:1), were made available to regulate time and the cycles of rotation and revolution of the earth and moon.
5. Animal life appeared on the earth.
6. Human beings representing the epitome of God's creative acts were placed on the earth as responsible individuals.

On the whole, modern geology presents the same order as given in the Scriptures.

The amount of time required for this process is not indicated in the account, beyond the statements that the whole period of creation is summarized by or in some sense related to six days. The length of each day is not stated, and consequently many varied interpretations have been offered. In the first eleven chapters, not to mention the rest of the Bible, the word *day* may refer to a long period of time (2:4) or to a twenty-four-hour period (8:12). Those holding to the twenty-four-hour-day interpretation often accept the Gap-Restoration theory of 1:2b.

GOD AS CREATOR AND SUSTAINER

Throughout the first unit of this account of creation the name of "God" (Elohim) is used, whereas beginning at chapter 2:4b the composite name "Lord God" (or "Jehovah God" in the ASV) occurs. The former word portrays God in His relationship to the universe and all contained therein as the great Creator (cf. Col. 1:16; Heb. 1:2). The latter term speaks of God in His relationship to mankind as the One who lovingly cares and provides for them. While human beings appear only toward the end of the account in Genesis 1, it is immediately clear that they are the center of interest beginning with chapter 2:4b.

MAN'S RELATIONSHIP TO CREATION

The biblical view of man is that of a highly intelligent and responsible being. Clearly distinct from and superior to animals when God created him, Adam was given the privilege of naming the animals, ruling over them, and tilling the Garden of Eden. He was capable of fellowship with God. The distinction between man and animals is further apparent in the fact that man found no companionship until God created Eve to be his mate (i.e., "a helpmeet for him," 2:20). God's loving care for human beings may be clearly seen in the provision of the Garden of Eden for their enjoyment and occupation.

The Fall and Its Consequences
Scripture Survey: Genesis 3:1–6:10

The fall of the human race into sin is the most significant event in their personal history prior to the coming of Christ to provide redemption for them. We are dependent upon God's revelation concerning human origins and the Fall, since the Fall took place before any written records. Various Scriptures assert that the history of the Fall and its consequences is literal, especially 1 Timothy 2:13, 14.

ADAM AND EVE'S DISOBEDIENCE AND EXPULSION

The crucial issue in Adam and Eve's relationship with God was their disobedience. They yielded to the tempter and were disobedient because of doubt and defiance. It is clear from passages such as John 8:44, Romans 16:20, 2 Corinthians 11:3, Revelation 12:9 and 20:2

that the serpent stood for more than the physical presence of the reptile. Judgment was solemnly pronounced on all parties—the serpent and Satan, Eve and Adam.

However, mercy preceded judgment—a principle seen frequently in Scripture—in the Messianic promise that the seed of the woman would be victorious over the seed of the serpent (3:15). Messianic promises were later amplified in Genesis 12:1-3; Numbers 24:17, 19; 1 Chronicles 17:11-14; Isaiah 7:14; 9:6, 7, and others. The promise of a Savior was given to them in the Garden of Eden, before they were expelled and subjected to the effects of the curse. God's gracious provision of skins as a covering is a hint of the shedding of blood as the means of redemption.

MAN'S HOPE OF REDEMPTION

The hope of redemption from the punishment meted out to Adam and Eve is expressed by Eve when Cain is born (4:1). After they were disappointed in Cain and over the death of Abel, Adam and Eve renewed their expectation upon the birth of Seth (4:25). Later generations cherished the hope of obtaining relief from the curse, as in the case of Lamech, who prophesied at the birth of Noah (5:28-30). And from generation to generation, the promise of redemption through the seed of the woman was passed along.

THE FIRST MURDER

Cain became the first murderer. His willful defiance was evident when he brought a sacrifice that did not please God. It seems reasonable to infer from subsequent developments that God had made known what kind of sacrifice was required and that Cain acted contrary to those instructions. When Abel's sacrifice was accepted by the Lord, Cain was provoked to murder his brother.

THE UNGODLY LINE OF CAIN

The civilization of Cain and his descendants is summarized in a genealogy that may cover an extended period of time (Gen. 4:17-24). We read that Cain built a city. Its inhabitants were largely dedicated to raising flocks and herds. In the course of time arts developed, and musical instruments were invented. The science of metallurgy came with the extensive use of bronze and iron. It seems, then, that the people began to have a false sense of security. Lamech, the first polygamist, displayed an attitude of scoffing and boasting, priding himself that he could destroy life with his superior weapons. Any recognition of or reference to God is conspicuously absent from the record of Cain's descendants.

THE GODLY LINE OF SETH

After the murder of Abel and with the birth of Seth (4:25ff.), Adam and Eve's hope was renewed. In the days of Enos men began to turn to God. Generations and centuries later another godly man appeared in the person of Enoch. His life of fellowship with God did not end with death but with his translation. And when Noah was born, as noted above, his father Lamech expressed again the hope that mankind would be relieved of the curse under which it had suffered since Adam and Eve were expelled from Eden.

The Flood: God's Judgment
Scripture Survey: Genesis 6:11–8:19

In the days of Noah, godlessness reached a new intensity that brought about judgment from God. People increasingly used God's good gifts for their own pleasure and ignored the Giver. Corruption and violence increased so that all their doings were full of evil. God is said to have regretted creating men and women and planned to destroy the race from off the earth (6:17). Again mercy preceded judgment in that people were warned of impending destruction over a period of 120 years. While the race as a whole continued to corrupt the earth and increase in its lust for power, God assured Noah that He would establish His covenant with him and his descendants (6:12, 18).

God commanded Noah to build an ark that would provide safety for them during the coming flood. This ark, which was 450–600 feet long, 75–100 feet wide, and 45–60 feet deep (depending on the exact length of the cubit), provided enough room for two of each of the unclean species and for seven of each of the clean. For just over one year life was preserved in the ark according to God's provision and instruction.

The Deluge was the most universal and severe judgment upon the human race in Old Testament times. Its purpose was to destroy sinful humanity and at the same time renew the human race through a godly remnant. Only Noah and his family escaped death. Subsequent references to this divine judgment point to it as a warning for the rest of mankind (cf. Luke 17:27; Heb. 11:7; 1 Pet. 3:20; 2 Pet. 2:5; 3:3-7). Through the Flood God's purpose was accomplished and His covenant established, this time with Noah and his family.

New Beginnings for the Human Race
Scripture Survey: Genesis 8:20–11:32

People found a new opportunity in a renovated world. Noah's first act after leaving the ark was to worship God with an animal sacrifice.

GOD'S COVENANT WITH NOAH

The rainbow was a sign of the covenant between God and man, assuring him that the human race would never again be destroyed by a flood. Noah and his sons, after receiving the basis for a new hope, were commissioned to repopulate and possess the earth. God now provided for their sustenance, giving them animals, properly slaughtered, and plants for food. All people, however, would be held strictly accountable to God for shedding human blood.

Canaan, a son of Ham, was cursed because of Ham's disrespectful treatment of Noah. Many centuries later the Canaanites were divinely judged when the Israelites, under Joshua, were commanded to destroy them.

THE TOWER OF BABEL

While it was a racial and linguistic unit, the human race remained for an indefinite period in one area (11:1-9). Defying God's command to spread abroad over the earth and proud of their own achievements, they undertook to build the Tower of Babel on the Plain of Shinar. But God intervened and put an end to their endeavor by confusing their language. Consequently, the race was scattered according to God's original intention.

THE DISPERSION OF NOAH'S SONS

The geographic and ethnic distribution of the human race is described in chapter 10. Japheth and his sons moved westward toward Spain via the Caspian and Black Seas (10:2-5). The sons of Ham migrated southwestward to Africa (10:6-14), while the Semites (10:21-31) occupied the area north of the Persian Gulf.

THE MESSIANIC LINE OF SHEM

The record of the developments during the age of beginnings is finally narrowed down to the Semites (11:1-32). By means of a genealogical listing of ten generations, the record focuses attention upon Terah, who migrated from Ur to Haran. A climax is reached upon the introduction of Abram, whose name is later changed to Abraham (17:5). He became the father and founder of a chosen nation, Israel. Within that nation were the hopes of universal blessing and for the fulfillment of the messianic promises (Gen. 22:15-18; cf. Matt. 1:1, 2). The rest of the Old Testament is principally the history and literature of God's chosen people, Israel.

DISCUSSION QUESTIONS

1. Why is the study of the Old Testament basic to understanding the New Testament?
2. What was the crucial issue in Adam and Eve's relationship with God?
3. How was God's mercy manifested in the account of the Fall?
4. What were the moral causes of the Flood?
5. What was the sign and significance of the covenant with Noah?
6. What motivated the people to build the Tower of Babel?
7. Trace the steps of disobedience in the story of the Fall of the human race. Compare and contrast this with human behavior today.
8. Write a paragraph to explain the emphasis the New Testament puts upon the following events:

    Creation (John 1:1, 2; Acts 14:15; Heb. 1:10; 11:3; Rev. 4:11; 10:6)

    People created in the image of God (1 Cor. 11:7; Col. 3:10; James 3:9)

    The Flood (Matt. 24:37-39; Luke 17:26, 27; 1 Pet. 3:20)
9. Compare and contrast the line of Seth with the line of Cain. Relate this to the spiritual man and the natural man.
10. Trace the evidence of God's interest in men and women in Genesis 1–11. Give at least five evidences of His interest in mankind today.

Chapter Two

THE PATRIARCHS

DURING THE EARLY PART of the second millennium B.C., the patriarchs lived in the midst of Near Eastern cultures. Abraham emigrated from the Tigris-Euphrates Valley to Palestine, and Jacob and his sons settled in Egypt at the close of the patriarchal era. The area between the Nile and the Tigris-Euphrates is known as the Fertile Crescent.

At that time the great pyramids had already been constructed in Egypt. In Mesopotamia various codes of law regulating commerce and social relationships had already been written. Merchants traveling with camel and donkey caravans frequently passed through Palestine to carry on trade between the two great cultural centers of the ancient world.

The patriarchal period is covered in Genesis 12–50. It may be outlined as follows:

Abraham	Genesis 12:1–25.18
Isaac and Jacob	25:19–36:43
Joseph	37:1–50:26

ABRAHAM

Abraham is one of the greatest and best-known characters in history. In both Judaism and Islam Abraham is a patriarch. In Christianity he is remembered as a man of great faith and as the father of the faithful. The chapters dealing with Abraham will be outlined in this way:

Abraham established in Canaan	Genesis 12–14
His moves from Haran to Shechem, Bethel, and the South Country	12:1-9
Sojourn in Egypt	12:10-20
Separation of Abraham and Lot	13:1-13
The land promised	13:14-18
Lot rescued	14:1-16
Abraham blessed by Melchizedek	14:17-24
Abraham awaits the promised son	15–24

BACKGROUND AND TIME

Abraham was born into an idolatrous family and environment (Josh. 24:2, 3). His father may have participated in the worship of the moon at Ur and later at Haran. In response to God's call, Abraham left Haran and traveled into Palestine, about 400 miles away.

Abraham's moves may be traced in the Genesis narrative. Most of the places he visited can be identified today. Shechem, some thirty miles north of Jerusalem, was his first stopping place. Later he lived at nearby Bethel. Near Hebron tourists can still see the oaks of Mamre where Abraham built an altar and had fellowship with God. Other cities where he lived were Gerar in the Philistine country and Beersheba to the south. A trip to Egypt is also noted in the Scriptures.

Most of these chapters deal with the twenty-five years of Abraham's life prior to the birth of Isaac (12–20). Chapters 21–25 give us relatively little detail from the seventy-five remaining years of his life.

TEMPORAL PROSPERITY

Genesis tells of the great wealth of Abraham. The statement in 12:5, "all their substance that they had gathered, and the souls that they had gotten in Haran," merely suggests the extent of his riches. But the fact that he could muster a force of 318 trained servants to deliver Lot indicates that he had vast resources (14:14). The ten-camel caravan used by Abraham's servant on his trip to Mesopotamia points to extensive wealth, since one camel represented a larger investment than the average person could afford (24:10). Servants were added to Abraham's household by purchase, gift, and birth (16:1; 17:23, 27; 20:14). Local chieftains recognized Abraham as a prince, and they made alliances and concluded treaties with him (14:13; 21:32; 23:6).

CUSTOMS AND CULTURE

Abraham was a man of his times. His decision to sojourn in Egypt when pressured by famine may indicate a lack of faith, and his behavior before pharaoh definitely represents a period of spiritual declension. As Sarah's husband, he might have been killed. But as her brother, he expected to be honored. Decency and strict truthfulness were both bypassed, and Abraham was later ushered out of Egypt in disgrace (12:11-20).

Laws prevalent in the Mesopotamian culture from which Abraham came also explain why he considered making his eldest servant Eliezer his heir (15:1-3). Nuzu laws provided that if a man and his wife were childless, they could adopt a servant as a son with full legal rights and the assurance of receiving the inheritance in return for constant care and proper burial at death. As Abraham weighed this possibility, God renewed His promise (15:4, 5).

At Sarah's suggestion, Abraham accepted the idea of having a son by Hagar, Sarah's handmaid. This, too, was in agreement with the custom of the age. A childless couple could also adopt the son of a handmaid as a legal heir. After ten years in Canaan, without any prospect of the promised son, Abraham and Sarah may have expected that this method would bring about the fulfillment of God's promise. Thirteen years later, when Abraham was ninety-nine, God rejected these plans and this time assured him that Sarah would bear him the promised son. At this time the covenant was renewed, and circumcision was instituted as its visible sign (17:1-27; cf. 12:1-3; 13:14-18; 15:18-21; Col. 2:11).

There was another spiritual lapse in Abraham's life, when he lied about his wife to Abimelech at Gerar (20:1-18). However, God intervened on Abraham's behalf so that he was enabled to pray for the king and his household.

From the expulsion of Hagar (21:9-21) and Abraham's concern for her welfare, it appears that he had contemporary laws in mind. It was illegal to sell a handmaid into slavery after she had given birth to a child for her master. While the case is not strictly parallel, Abraham expelled Hagar only after he had God's assurance that this was His will. Even then he made provision for her and her son when they departed.

Again when Sarah died, Abraham is seen as a man of his times. When he bargained with the Hittites for a burial place (23:1-20), he wanted to purchase only the cave of Machpelah. However, Ephron insisted on selling the field with the cave. In this way Abraham also became subject to taxation under Hittite law. Had he acquired only the cave, he might have been free from that liability.

A Man of Faith

Through faith in God's promises, Abraham rose above the religious level of his times. From the beginning he responded with obedience. Wherever Abraham sojourned in Canaan, he erected an altar and gave public testimony of the fact that he worshiped "the God of heaven and earth" (24:3) in the midst of a pagan environment (cf. 12:7, 8ff.).

Consider the sixfold promise God made to Abraham:

1. "I will make of thee a great nation."
2. "I will bless thee."
3. "I will make thy name great."
4. "Thou shalt be a blessing."
5. "I will bless them that bless thee and curse him that curseth thee."
6. "In thee shall all the families of the earth be blessed."

This multiple promise has had far-reaching implications in history down to the present time—more extensive than Abraham could comprehend during his lifetime. It is true that Abraham was richly blessed while he lived, and before his death he could understand that many nations could yet be born through Ishmael, Isaac, and his other sons. Today, by way of contrast, the name of Abraham is held in great honor among Jews, Muslims, and Christians. The promise that Abraham would be a blessing to all the families of the earth unfolds in Christ. Matthew begins his gospel with the assertion that Jesus—the Savior of the world—is the "son of Abraham" (1:1; cf. Gal. 3:6-9).

The Abrahamic Covenant

As we study the life of Abraham in subsequent chapters, it is apparent that Abraham's grasp of the promises was progressively enlarged. In times of crisis Abraham gained fuller understanding of them. He showed great generosity when he offered Lot the choice of the land (Gen. 13). While Lot's decision was based on the prospects of immediate material gain in a godless environment, Abraham received confirmation from God that the land was to be his and for his posterity.

When Abraham rescued Lot, he refused to accept a reward from the king of Sodom and was concerned about the legal arrangements for the future. But God revealed to Abraham more about the time to come. He promised that his descendants would be as numerous as the stars of heaven, but that they would dwell in Egypt for 400 years. We read that Abraham believed God, and that it was accounted to him for righteousness (cf. Rom. 4:3, 22).

God's covenant with Abraham was enlarged and confirmed when Abraham was ninety-nine years old. The terms of the covenant were distinctly given (17:1-27). While the birth of the promised son was still a year away, circumcision was given as the distinctive sign of the covenant for Abraham and his descendants (cf. Rom. 4:9-12).

A FRIEND OF GOD

It may be seen from Genesis 18 and 19 that there was friendship between Abraham and God (cf. Isa. 41:8; James 2:22, 23). When God shared with Abraham the secret of His plans concerning Sodom and Gomorrah, Abraham was moved to prayer. He rested his case with the rhetorical question, "Shall not the God of all the earth do right?" God showed that His justice was tempered by mercy when He assured Abraham that the cities would be saved if ten righteous people were found in them. Only because there were not that many the cities were destroyed, though Lot and his family were rescued.

MORE TESTINGS AND TRIALS

Abraham faced the greatest test of his faith after Isaac's birth. God asked him to sacrifice his only son on Mount Moriah. Abraham obeyed, exhibiting faith that God was able to raise someone from the dead (cf. Heb. 11:19). He was obliged to give an answer to the most disturbing question ever posed by a son when Isaac asked about the sacrifice. By faith Abraham reached beyond the visible evidence to give a prophetic reply, assuring Isaac that God Himself would provide the sacrifice (22:1-19; cf. 1 Cor. 5:7; Heb. 9:26; Rev. 13:8). First God provided a ram, and centuries later, His own beloved Son.

ABRAHAM'S SEED

Isaac was Abraham's son to whom God's promises would be repeated. The story of the way Abraham provided a bride for Isaac (Gen. 24) is fascinating and exciting. The account contains numerous lessons in the way God guided Abraham's servant through prayer. Finally he was able to take Rebekah back to the land of patriarchal promise to be Isaac's wife.

The Scriptures tell us little about him. His life was uneventful in comparison to that of his father and his sons. He lived most of his life in southern Canaan in the vicinity of Gerar, Rehoboth, and Beersheba. Isaac was a necessary link in the process of fulfilling God's promises to Abraham. From the record (27:27-33) we recognize him as a man of faith who invoked future blessings upon his sons (cf. Heb. 11:20).

Abraham had other sons. The best known of these were Ishmael, the father of the Arabs, and Midian, the father of the Midianites. To each of these other sons Abraham gave gifts as they went out from Canaan, leaving the territory to Isaac, the heir of all of Abraham's possessions.[1]

TWIN BROTHERS

A study of the lives of Isaac's two sons, Esau and Jacob, is both intriguing and disappointing. Jacob took advantage of Esau in buying the birthright—the right of the firstborn to preeminence in the tribe—and connived with his mother Rebekah to deceive Isaac and steal the blessing. On the other hand, Esau lacked faith in God, a true sense of values, and appreciation for his birthright (25:29-34). Later he disregarded the ideals of his parents and married a Hittite woman (26:34). The author of Hebrews calls him "profane" or "irreligious." The history of Esau's descendants, the Edomites, deserves separate study.

Jacob's Adventures

Although Jacob left Canaan with his father's blessing, he passed through many hard experiences before he became a man of faith. He was afraid that Esau would seek revenge. His parents, hoping to keep him from marrying a Hittite woman, sent him to Mesopotamia. On the way, while he slept at Bethel, Jacob had a dream and responded to God with a tentative commitment. Jacob prospered greatly while he worked for Laban, acquiring not only a large family, but great wealth in flocks.

Back to Canaan

Conscious now of God's direction, Jacob made plans to return to Canaan. A strained relationship had developed between Jacob and Laban, and Jacob took the opportunity to depart while Laban was on a sheep-shearing mission. Laban pursued him quickly, but since Jacob had a three-day advantage, he reached the hill country of Gilead before Laban overtook him.

Laban claimed that his household gods had been taken. The teraphim, which Rachel hid beneath her skirts, undoubtedly had more than mere religious significance for Laban. According to Nuzu law, a son-in-law who possessed the household gods might claim the family inheritance in court. Though Laban could not find the idol, he nullified any advantage that might accrue to Jacob by means of a covenant between Jacob and himself, barring Jacob from the land.

At the Jabbok River Jacob learned that Esau was coming against him with 400 men. In order to appease Esau, he sent his possessions and family, with gifts for his brother, ahead of him. Through the night he wrestled with an assailant whom he sensed to be God Himself. In that encounter his name was changed from "Jacob" to "Israel," meaning "he who strives with God." The blessing implied in the new name expressed a new relationship. Hereafter Jacob would not be the deceiver; instead, he would have victory with God.

After being reconciled with his brother, Jacob moved southward to Shechem. There Levi and Simeon aroused the enmity of the community through scandal and treachery (34:1-31). As Jacob separated to move to Bethel, where he had previously made a commitment to God, he removed the remaining idolatry from his household. At Bethel he built an altar, and in response God renewed His covenant, assuring him that a company of nations and kings should emanate from Israel (35:9-15).

Eventually Jacob settled in Hebron, the home of his father Isaac. While they were on the way, Rachel died and was buried in the vicinity of Bethlehem. Later when Isaac died, Esau came from Seir where he had settled, to accompany his brother Jacob at the burial of their father.

THE LIFE OF JOSEPH

Joseph, Rachel's older son, was Jacob's pride and joy. Jacob made him a full-length tunic which, according to the Septuagint and the Targum Jonathan, was "a coat of many colors." It seems that such a coat was the distinctive mark of a tribal chief. Joseph's older brothers already hated him because he reported their evil conduct to Jacob. Now they hated him all the more. And when Joseph's dreams indicated that he would be exalted over them, they sold him to Ishmaelite and Midianite traders who were passing by their camp at Dothan. When Joseph was taken into Egypt, his brothers never expected to see him again. They led Jacob to believe that Joseph had been torn to pieces by wild animals.

Joseph, the favorite son	Genesis 37	
Hated by his brothers		37:1-24
Sold to Egypt		37:25-36
Judah and Tamar[2]	38	
Joseph—a slave and a ruler	39–41	
Joseph demoted to prison		39:1-20
Interpreting dreams		39:21–41:36
Ruler next to pharaoh		41:37-57
Joseph and his brothers	42–45	
First trip—Simeon kept as hostage		42:1-38
Second trip includes Benjamin—		
Joseph identifies himself		43:1–45:28
Joseph's family established in Egypt	46–50	
Goshen allotted to the Israelites		46:1–47:28
The patriarchal blessings		47:29–49:27
Jacob's burial in Canaan		49:28–50:14
Joseph's hope for Israel		50:15-26

A SLAVE IN EGYPT

Whether in adversity and suffering or success, over the years that Joseph spent in Egypt, he continually honored God. Because he did not want to sin against God nor against his master, he would not yield to the temptation put before him by Potiphar's wife (39:9). When he was asked to interpret dreams, Joseph gave God the credit for the ability to do so (40:8). He also acknowledged God before pharaoh, boldly asserting that, through pharaoh's dream, God was revealing that a specific number of years of plenty and famine were to follow (41:14-36). In naming his son Manasseh (which means "forgetting," 41:51), he testified that God had helped him to forget his sorrow. When he revealed his identity to his brothers, he acknowledged that God had brought him to Egypt. After Jacob's death Joseph reassured them that God had ordered the events of history for the good of all and that they should not fear him as though he were in God's place (50:15-21).

SAVIOR OF HIS FAMILY

Joseph's recognition of God and his trust in Him through many difficulties was rewarded by his promotion. In Potiphar's house he was so trustworthy that he was made the overseer. Later, though imprisoned on false charges, he soon became the warden and was able to use his position to help his fellow prisoners. A butler, who for two years had forgotten Joseph's help, suddenly remembered and arranged to have Joseph brought before pharaoh to interpret his dreams. This was an opportune moment—pharaoh needed the help of a man of wisdom such as Joseph. Now as chief administrator for pharaoh, Joseph guided Egypt through the crucial years of plenty and famine and incidentally saved his own family from starvation. His position of power enabled him to allot the broad pasturelands of Goshen to the Israelites when they migrated to Egypt. There they were able to tend their flocks and those of pharaoh as well.

Jacob's words of blessing provide a fitting conclusion to the patriarchal age. We may regard his deathbed pronouncements as his last will and testament. Though he was in Egypt, his oral blessing would be legal and binding. And in keeping with God's promises, Jacob's blessing was also prophetic.

Before Joseph died in Egypt, he voiced his confidence in the covenant that God had made with Abraham, Isaac, and Jacob. The promises had been faithfully conveyed to each generation, and Joseph believed that God would fulfill them in bringing the Israelites back to the land that had been promised to them (cf. Gen. 15:1-21; 50:24-26).

DISCUSSION QUESTIONS

1. Who were the patriarchs?
2. Outline the main events of Abraham's life.
3. Why were the altars Abraham built to worship God significant?
4. Why is Abraham called a man of faith?
5. What was the sign and significance of God's covenant with Abraham?
6. How did Abraham's servant discern God's guidance in choosing Isaac's bride?

7. Describe the circumstances leading to Joseph's release from prison.
8. In what ways did Joseph indicate forgiveness toward his brothers when they came to Egypt?
9. Trace the patriarchal promise in Genesis 12–50. What is its significance today?
10. On a map locate the cities associated with the patriarchs. Which of these have prophetic significance today?
11. Note the origin of the following peoples in Genesis: Moabites, Ammonites, Midianites, Arabs, and Edomites. Which of these are in world news today?
12. Compare and contrast the characters of Jacob and Esau. What particular personality traits make them typical of mankind?
13. What do the following New Testament references reveal about these Genesis characters:

> Abraham (Rom. 4:1-22; Gal. 3:16, 17; 4:22-31; Heb. 11:17, 18)
> Isaac (Luke 13:28; Rom. 9:7, 10; Gal. 4:28; Heb. 11:9, 18; James 2:21)
> Esau (Rom. 9:13; Heb. 12:16, 17)
> Jacob (Matt. 1:2; 8:11; Luke 13:28; John 4:12; Rom. 9:13; Heb. 11:9, 20, 21)
> Joseph (Acts 7:11-14; Heb. 11:21, 22; Rev. 7:8)

14. What laws and customs seemed to influence the behavior of the patriarchs? To what extent should culture govern Christian ethics? Suggest at least two cultural factors that involve the question of Christian standards. Discuss the practical biblical solution to these.

Chapter Three

GOD'S
HOLY NATION

SACRED HISTORY TAKES ON new dimensions with the book of Exodus. Centuries had passed in silence since the death of Joseph. Meanwhile the patriarchal descendants had become exceedingly numerous. A pharaoh came into power who viewed this growing population with disfavor, enslaving and oppressing them. Under the leadership of Moses, the Israelites were delivered from slavery, transformed into an independent nation, and prepared for the conquest and occupation of Canaan.

The spiritual significance of this deliverance can hardly be overemphasized. The rest of the Pentateuch, approximately one-sixth of the entire Old Testament, is devoted to this development.

Let us look at the scope of movement and time involved as we preview these four books in the following outline:

Israel's enslavement, 400 years	Exodus 1, 2
Egypt to Sinai, less than 1 year	Exodus 3–18
Encampment at Sinai, ca. 1 year	Exodus 19–Numbers 10
Wilderness wanderings, ca. 38 years	Numbers 10–21
Encampment before Canaan, ca. 1 year	Numbers 22–Deuteronomy 34

Egypt was one of the most advanced centers of civilization during the period when Israel emerged as a nation. The New Kingdom began in the sixteenth century B.C. with the expulsion of the Hyksos people who had occupied Egypt for nearly two centuries. From about 1550–1100 B.C. Egypt maintained a well-established empire. One of its greatest military leaders was Thutmose III (ca. 1500–1450) who repeatedly marched his armies through Palestine or sailed the Mediterranean to extend Egyptian control to the Euphrates River. He is often compared to Alexander the Great or Napoleon.

FROM SLAVERY TO NATIONHOOD

In a relatively short period under the leadership of Moses, the Israelites were delivered from oppression to become an independent nation consciously aware of its covenant relationship with God. The biblical account may be divided as follows:

Israel freed from slavery	Exodus	1:1–13:19
Conditions in Egypt		1:1-22
Moses—birth, education, and call		2:1–4:31
The contest with pharaoh		5:1–11:10
The Passover		12:1–13:19
From Egypt to Mount Sinai		13:20–19:2
Divine deliverance		13:20–15:21
En route to the Sinaitic encampment		15:22–19:2

OPPRESSION OF THE ISRAELITES

When the clan of Jacob migrated to Egypt, they were favored by the Egyptian rulers, who were indebted to Joseph for guiding them successfully through an extensive famine. Settled in the rich fertile grazing area of the land of Goshen in the Nile Delta, the Israelites prospered and increased greatly during a period of several centuries. With the rise of the eighteenth dynasty at the beginning of the New Kingdom, new policies were introduced, designed to alleviate the pharaoh's fear of a rebellion by the Israelites. Subjected to hard labor assignments in building the cities of Pithom and Rameses (Exod. 1:11), the Israelites multiplied so prolifically that the fears of the Egyptian rulers increased. Not only was the oppression intensified, but an edict was also issued to drown at birth all the male children born to the Israelites (Exod. 1:15-22). Decades later when Moses challenged the power of pharaoh, the Egyptians even withheld the straw (Exod. 5:5-19) that was helpful to the Israelites in producing bricks.

LEADERSHIP PREPARED

Dark were the days of Israel's history when Moses was born. Moses, however, was adopted by pharaoh's daughter, exposed to educational opportunities in the foremost center of civilization, and trained in the wisdom of the Egyptians (Acts 7:22).

The second phase of Moses' training was provided in the desert of Midian where he spent the next forty years. His attempt to help his people ended in failure. In Midian he married Zipporah, the daughter of Reuel, a priest of Midian, who was also known as Jethro. While shepherding flocks in the area surrounding the Gulf of Aqaba, Moses acquired a thorough knowledge of this territory even though he was not aware that he would some day lead the nation of Israel through this desert.

Consider the call of Moses (Exod. 3:1–4:17) in the light of his background and knowledge of the royal court in Egypt and the apparently hopeless condition of the Israelites. Moses knew that the pharaoh of Egypt was not disposed to take orders from anyone. Note the problems Moses realistically reflected and the answers God gave as paraphrased below:

Moses: "Who am I to face mighty pharaoh?"

God: "I will be with thee."

Moses: "By whose authority shall I go to face my own people?"

God: "I AM—the God of Abraham, Isaac, and Jacob—sends you."

Moses: "The Israelites will not believe me."

God: "Use the rod in your hand to perform miracles before them."

Moses: "I am not an orator."

God: "I will send Aaron to speak for you."

With this assurance Moses returned to Egypt to do God's bidding.

THE CONTEST

In a series of ten plagues Moses challenged the might of the pharaoh of Egypt who persistently refused to release Israel. The purpose of the plagues (Exod. 9:16) was to demonstrate God's mighty power to the Israelites as well as to the Egyptians. Pharaoh had the opportunity of complying with God's will, but in the course of this experience, he hardened his heart.[1] His basic attitude never changed. Although the plagues came through natural phenomena, the supernatural power of God was apparent in intensification, in discrimination, and in time control. These plagues may have been directed against the various gods of the Egyptians.

THE PASSOVER

The Passover and death of the firstborn brought this contest to an eventful climax. Every home in the land was affected. The Egyptian homes were made conscious of the judgment of the God of Israel in the death of the oldest son in each family. The Israelites in every home by contrast were made conscious of God's redeeming power as they put blood on the doorposts, ate the lamb, and then in haste made their journey out of Egypt (cf. Matt. 26:26-28; 1 Cor. 5:7; Heb. 9:14, 15).

THE MIRACLE OF DELIVERANCE

The shortest route from Egypt to Canaan was a well-traveled road along the Mediterranean coast. But Moses, divinely instructed, led this multitude of liberated slaves through the Red Sea to the Sinai Peninsula. The miracle of deliverance was followed by numerous divine interventions and provisions for Israel's safety and sustenance. God's pillar of cloud by day and of fire by night not only served to protect in time of danger, but also to provide guidance en route (cf. 1 Cor. 10:1).

LAWS FOR A HOLY NATION

Israel's religion was a revealed religion. It was not adopted from surrounding nations but stood in sharp contrast to the religious standards and practices of the heathen nations of that period.

The biblical content of God's revelation to Israel at Mount Sinai may be outlined as follows:

God's covenant with Israel	Exodus	19:3–24:8
Preparation for meeting God		19:3-25
The Decalogue		20:1-17
Ordinances for Israel		20:18–23:33
Ratification of the covenant		24:1-8
The place of worship		24:9–40:38
Preparation for construction		24:10–31:18
Idolatry and judgment		32:1–34:35
Building of the tabernacle		35:1–40:38
Instructions for holy living	Leviticus	1:1–27:34
The offerings		1:1–7:38
The priesthood		8:1–10:20
Laws of purification		11:1–15:33
The Day of Atonement		16:1-34
Heathen customs forbidden		17:1–18:30
Laws of holiness		19:1–22:33
Feasts and seasons		23:1–25:55
Conditions for God's blessings		26:1–27:34

THE MOSAIC COVENANT

Redemption from Egypt obligated Israel to be God's holy nation. God, who had made a covenant with Abraham and his descendants, had delivered the Israelites and entered into a covenant with them as a nation (Exod. 19:3–24:8). The key to a right relationship with God was obedience. Their observance of the laws would result in their being a holy people and distinguish them from the heathen nations about them.

Most important for the Israelites were the Ten Commandments commonly known as the Decalogue (Exod. 20:1-17). These are usually classified as moral laws and are repeated in the New Testament, with the exception of the Sabbath observance. The distinctive feature of the Decalogue sets forth monotheism (worship of one true God), not even allowing the Israelites images. This set Israel apart in sharp contrast to the pagan practices of surrounding nations.

Expansion of these moral laws and additional regulations were designed to guide the Israelites in their conduct (Exod. 21–24; Lev. 11–26). Simple obedience to these moral, civil, and ceremonial laws would mark them as God's holy people. Many of the practices forbidden to Israel were common in Egypt and Canaan. Marriage of brother and sister, practiced in Egypt, was forbidden to the Israelites. Regulations regarding motherhood and childbirth not only reminded the Israelites that man is a sinful creature, but these laws stood in sharp contrast to sex perversion, prostitution, and child sacrifice associated with the religious rites and ceremonies of the Canaanites. In Egypt the slaughter of animals was associated with idolatry. Some of the restriction in food and slaughter of animals can be better understood in the light of prevailing practices known to the Israelites. It was fitting that the Israelites, having vivid memories of slavery, should be instructed to leave gleanings for the poor at harvest time, provide for the helpless, honor the aged, and constantly render righteous judgment in all their relationships. Many of these civil and ceremonial laws were temporary in nature and were abrogated in the course of time as conditions changed.

THE TABERNACLE

In contrast to many temples in Egypt, Israel was to have one sanctuary. Construction of the tabernacle was under the supervision of two foremen, Bezalel and Aholiab, who were filled with the "Spirit of God" and "ability and intelligence to supervise" (Exod. 31, 35, 36). Laymen who were motivated to help assisted with building, and freewill offerings were accepted from the people to supply the materials.

The tabernacle itself was forty-five feet long and fifteen feet wide, divided into two parts. The entrance from the east opened into the holy place thirty feet in length. Beyond it was the Holy of Holies. Surrounding the tabernacle was a court having a perimeter of 450 feet and a thirty-foot entrance from the east. The eastern half of this enclosure was the worshiper's square where stood the altar of sacrifice or brazen altar where the Israelites made their sacrifices. Between this altar and the tabernacle was the bronze laver where the priests washed their feet in preparation for officiating at the altar of sacrifice in the tabernacle.

Three pieces of furniture were in the holy place. On the right was the table of shewbread for the priests, on the left was the golden candlestick, and before the veil separating the holy place from the Holy of Holies was the altar of incense.

The ark of the covenant was the most sacred object in Israel. This and this alone was placed in the Holy of Holies. On the lid of the ark facing each other were two cherubim of gold with their wings overshadowing the place between them known as the mercy seat. This mercy seat represented the presence of God, and unlike the heathen, the Israelites had no material object to represent their God. The *Shekinah* (Hebrew–"to dwell") glory of Jehovah God dwelled with Israel in the tabernacle. Here the high priest sprinkled blood once a year on the Day of Atonement in behalf of the nation. Subsequently, stored in the ark were the Decalogue (Exod. 25:21; 31:18; Deut. 10:3-5), a pot of manna (Exod. 16:34), and Aaron's rod that blossomed (Num. 17:10). Before Israel entered Canaan, the Book of the Law was placed next to the ark (Deut. 31:26).

THE PRIESTHOOD

In patriarchal times the head of the family officiated in making a sacrifice. Since the seed of Abraham had become a large nation, it was necessary to have priests officiate for orderly ministration and effective worship. Aaron, the brother of Moses, was appointed as the high priest, assisted by his sons, two of whom were smitten in judgment for bringing unholy fire into the tabernacle (Num. 3:2-4; Lev. 10:1, 2). By virtue of having escaped death in Egypt, the firstborn of every family belonged to God. Chosen as substitutes for the oldest son in each family, the Levites assisted the priests in their ministration (Num. 3:5-14; 8:17). In this way the entire nation was represented in the priestly ministry.

The priests represented the people before God, officiated in the prescribed offerings (Exod. 28; Lev. 16), taught the Law to the laity, and were responsible for ministering at the tabernacle. The sanctity of the priests as described in Leviticus 21:1–22:10 reflects a contrast with heathen practice.[2]

THE OFFERINGS

The practice of offering sacrifices characterized God-fearing people from the time of man's expulsion from the Garden of Eden. Whether or not the various kinds of offerings were clearly distinguished and known to the Israelites when they left Egypt may be debatable. As a free nation and God's covenant people, they were given specific instructions regarding their sacrifices (Lev. 1–7).

Four kinds of offerings involved the shedding of blood:

Burnt offering—The distinctive feature was that the entire sacrifice was consumed, signifying complete consecration (cf. Heb. 10:1-3, 10, 11).

Peace offering—This was a voluntary offering in which part of the sacrificial animal was eaten by the priest and the offerer, signifying fellowship between God and man (cf. Eph. 2:13, 14).

Sin offering—This sacrifice was required for sins of ignorance committed inadvertently (cf. John 1:29; 6:51).

Trespass offering—Infringement on the rights of others necessitated this offering and restitution where possible (cf. Col. 2:13).

The grain offering did not involve the shedding of blood but consisted of the products of the soil representing the fruits of man's labor (Lev. 2:1-16; 6:14-23; cf. Mark 8:15; 1 Cor. 5:8; Gal. 5:9). Apparently the grain was never brought as an offering by itself but was brought in addition to other offerings. When expiation for sin had been made through the shedding of blood, then the offering of gifts was acceptable to God.

FEASTS AND SEASONS

Through appointed feasts and seasons, the Israelites were constantly reminded that they were God's holy people. To observe these holy periods was part of their covenant commitment. Briefly note the times designated for their observance:

> *Sabbath*—Weekly, by rest and cessation from work, they were reminded of God's creative work and their deliverance from Egyptian bondage. Note that this was included in the Decalogue (Deut. 5:12-15; cf. Mark 2:27, 28).
>
> *New Moon and Feast of Trumpets*—Trumpet blasts proclaimed the beginning of each month. The first day of the seventh month was designated as the Feast of Trumpets, ushering in the climax of religious observances (Num. 29:1-6; cf. Col. 2:16).
>
> *Sabbatical Year*—Upon entrance into Canaan, the Israelites were to leave the fields unseeded and the vineyards unpruned every seven years. The cancellation of debts and the freeing of slaves every seventh year reminded the Israelites of their deliverance from Egypt (Exod. 21:2-6; Deut. 15:12-18; cf. Heb. 4:1-11).

Year of Jubilee—After seven observances of the Sabbatical Year came the Year of Jubilee. This marked the year of liberty in which family inheritance was restored to those who had the misfortune of losing it, Hebrew slaves were freed, and the land was left uncultivated (Lev. 25:8-55; cf. Acts 4:36, 37; 11:29; 1 Cor. 7:23).

Passover and Feast of Unleavened Bread—First observed in Egypt, it annually reminded each family of their deliverance from Egypt. The Passover was the principal event, followed by a week when only unleavened bread was eaten. The Passover was observed on the fourteenth day of Nisan, the seventh month of their civil year, but the first month of their religious year (Exod. 34:17, 18; Deut. 16:1-7; cf. Matt. 26:26-29; Luke 22:7-13; 1 Cor. 5:68).

Feast of Weeks—Observed fifty days after the Passover. Offerings on this day consisted of grain or flour, acknowledging that the family's daily bread was provided by God (Lev. 23:15-20; cf. Acts 1:5; 2:1).

Feast of Tabernacles—The final festival of the religious year held at the end of the harvest season. By living in booths during this week, they were to remind themselves of their wilderness sojourn. Every seven years at this time the Law was read publicly (Deut. 31:9-13; cf. John 7:2).

Day of Atonement—The most solemn observance during the entire year! (Lev. 16:1-34; 23:26-32; Num. 29:7-11; cf. Heb. 7:27).

The instructions given to the Israelites at Mount Sinai made it possible for them to adopt a pattern of living that would distinguish them from the heathen environment in Egypt as well as in Canaan. The Law, the tabernacle, the priesthood, the offerings, and the feasts and seasons were provisions and means for them to live in conformity to God's plan for His covenant people. Obedience and faith were essential in maintaining this covenant relationship.

DISCUSSION QUESTIONS

1. Give the major movements of Exodus through Deuteronomy as outlined in the text.
2. Why did pharaoh intensify the oppression of Israel?
3. What training did Moses receive in the desert that helped prepare him for future leadership?
4. What problems did Moses present to God as objections to His call?
5. What answers did God give to assure Moses?

6. What was the purpose of the plagues?
7. What plague climaxed the contest between pharaoh and God?
8. What was the condition of Israel's covenant relationship with God (cf. Exod. 19:1-5)?
9. How did Israel differ from the Egyptians in their worship of God?
10. Trace the supernatural events throughout Exodus that made the Israelites aware of God's interest and care. What part does the supernatural play in God's manifestation of His concern for His people today?
11. With a concordance trace the use of the word *Passover* throughout the Scriptures. Why is this event given such prominence? In what way is the Lord's Supper a comparable Christian activity?
12. Make a simple diagram of the tabernacle and its court, showing the furniture in each part. Indicate possible symbolic teaching found in the tabernacle and its furnishings (Exod. 25–28; 35–40).
13. Show how the feasts, offerings, and priesthood aided the Israelites in serving God. How did these point to the redemptive work of Christ?
14. Show how the plagues were related to the gods of Egypt.

Chapter Four

LOOKING FORWARD TO CANAAN

ISRAEL'S ENCAMPMENT IN THE environs of Mount Sinai lasted for nearly one year. While they were there, additional instructions were given to the new nation. These are recorded in the first part of the book of Numbers. After an eleven-day march to Kadesh, spies were sent into Canaan, precipitating a crisis and the divine verdict that prolonged the wanderings. Thirty-eight years later the Israelites proceeded to the Plains of Moab where Moses gave his farewell speeches as found in the book of Deuteronomy.

ORGANIZATION OF ISRAEL

Detailed instructions regarding organization for their encampment and journey are summarized in Numbers. These chapters are not necessarily in chronological order. They may be outlined as follows:

Numbering Israel	Numbers 1:1–4:49
Military census	1:1-54
Camp assignments	2:1-34
Levites and their duties	3:1–4:49
Camp regulations	5:1–6:21
Restrictions of evil practices	5:1-31
Nazirite vows	6:1-21
Religious life of Israel	6:22–9:14
Tabernacle worship instituted	6:22–8:26
The second Passover	9:1-14
Provisions for guidance	9:15–10:10
Divine manifestations	9:15-23
Human responsibility	10:1-10

Israel was numbered before leaving Mount Sinai. Very likely this census also represented a tabulation of the count taken when they left Egypt a year earlier (Exod. 30:11ff., 38:26). Excluding women, children, and the Levites, the count was about 600,000. Almost forty years later, after the rebellious generation had perished in the wilderness, their manpower was approximately the same (Num. 26).

MARCHING ORDER

Law and order were essential for God's people. The Levites were substituted for the firstborn of each family and assigned to care for the tabernacle. In the camp of Israel the tabernacle was in the center with the Levites surrounding the tabernacle and three tribes in each direction beyond the Levites. When they traveled, six tribes preceded the Levites who carried the tabernacle, and six tribes followed.

TABERNACLE DEDICATED

Impressive in the memory of the Israelites must have been the events during the first month of the second year after they left Egypt. The tabernacle with all its furnishings had been completed and erected. With Moses officiating, the tabernacle was dedicated and became the center of Israel's religious life (Exod. 40:1-3; Num. 6:22–9:14). Offerings were presented, Aaron and the Levites were publicly presented and dedicated for their services, and the congregation was divinely blessed with these words:

> "The LORD bless thee and keep thee:
> The LORD make his face to shine upon thee, and be gracious unto thee:
> The LORD lift up his countenance upon thee, and give thee peace" (Num. 6:24-27).

The observance of the Passover marked their first anniversary of deliverance from Egypt. Special emphasis was given that everyone, even strangers, should participate.

ON TO CANAAN

On the twentieth day of the second month, the Israelites were alerted to break up camp in preparing for their journey to Canaan. Divine guidance was provided in the pillar of cloud by day and the pillar of fire by night. Observe carefully the importance of divine guidance, as well as the requirement for efficient organization and procedure. Proper coordination of the human and divine are exemplified in these instructions for Israel and deserve consideration and application for the mission of the church today.

WILDERNESS WANDERINGS

Israel's movement from Mount Sinai to the Plains of Moab is briefly summarized in Numbers 10:11–22:1. Comparatively little is known about the thirty-eight years they spent in wilderness wanderings, as may be observed in the outline below:

From Mount Sinai to Kadesh	Numbers	10:11–12:16
Order of procedure		10:11-35
Murmurings and judgments		11:1–12:16
The Kadesh crisis		13:1–14:45
The spies and their reports		13:1-33
Rebellion and judgment		14:1-45
The years of wandering		15:1–19:22
Laws—future and present		15:1-41
The great rebellion		16:1-50
Vindication of appointed leaders		17:1–19:22
From Kadesh to the Plains of Moab		20:1–22:1
Death of Miriam		20:1
Sins of Moses and Aaron		20:2-13
Edom refuses Israel passage		20:14-21
Death of Aaron		20:22-29
Israel avenges defeat by Canaanites		21:1-3
The brazen serpent		21:4-9
March around Moab		21:10-20
Defeat of Sihon and Og		21:21-35
Arrival on the Plains of Moab		22:1

En route to Kadesh the Israelites complained and rebelled. Seventy elders were appointed to share responsibility with Moses in controlling the people as they murmured about the manna. When an abundant supply of quail was divinely provided, the people were so intemperate and indulgent that many died in the resultant plague. Even Aaron and Miriam complained against Moses, whom God vindicated as leader.

THE KADESH CRISIS

Spies were sent into the land of Canaan as Israel moved north to encamp at Kadesh, approximately forty miles south and somewhat west of Beersheba. The twelve men unanimously reported both the excellency of the land and the potential strength and ferocity of the inhabitants. But as to the prospects for conquest, they disagreed. Ten declared that occupation was impossible and stirred up public sentiment for an immediate return to Egypt. Two—Joshua and Caleb—confidently asserted that with divine aid, conquest was possible. The people were swayed by the majority's report and became an insolent mob, threatening to stone Joshua and Caleb and even considering selecting a new leader to replace Moses.

Divine judgment followed. This generation that less than two years before had seen God's mighty acts in delivering them from the clutches of pharaoh should have had enough evidence to believe that God would aid them in the conquest of Canaan. When God contemplated annihilation, Moses intervened. Even though pardon was extended to the nation, the ten spies and all people aged twenty and older were consigned to death in the wilderness because of their lack of faith.

THE YEARS OF WANDERING

The great rebellion led by Korah, Dathan, and Abiram represents two mutinous groups, mutually strengthened through their cooperative effort (Num. 16:1-50).[1] Korah and his supporting Levites challenged the leadership of Aaron and his family, who were responsible for the priestly ministry in Israel. Dathan and Abiram aspired to replace Moses as political leader, since they were the descendants of Reuben, the oldest son of Jacob. Both Moses and Aaron were vindicated when the earth swallowed up Dathan and Abiram and their families and Korah.[2] Before this rebellion completely subsided, more than 14,000 people had perished in the camp of Israel. Aaron's place as priest was also confirmed by the miraculous sign of the budding rod.

EN ROUTE TO THE PLAINS OF MOAB

After marking time for approximately thirty-eight years in the area of Kadesh—a time during which many more murmurings and rebellions may have occurred than are recorded here—Israel was led by the way of the Gulf of Aqaba to the Plains of Moab. Among the numerous events along the way, it is significant to note that Moses in response to the complaints of the Israelites became irate and impatient. For his disobedience in smiting the rock instead of commanding it to bring forth water, Moses was denied the privilege of entering Canaan. The experience of the Israelites when punished by a scourge of serpents is also significant. Through simple obedience and faith, those who looked at the bronze serpent erected by Moses were saved. The Lord Jesus used this incident as a symbol of His death on the cross, applying the same principle—anyone who turned to Him would not perish but have eternal life (John 3:14-16).

By moving southward, the Israelites circumvented Edom and later Moab as they settled in the plains north of the Arnon River and east of the Dead Sea. Although forbidden to fight against Moab, the Israelites fought against Sihon, king of Heshbon, and Og, the king of Bashan, as they occupied this land north of Moab.

INSTRUCTIONS FOR ENTERING CANAAN

The experiences and instructions that came to Israel while encamped on the Plains of Moab conditioned God's holy nation for possessing the land of promise. A brief survey of these developments is provided in the following outline:

Preservation of God's chosen people	Numbers 22:2–25:18
Balak's design to curse Israel	22:2-40
Balaam's blessings	22:41–24:24
Seduction and judgment	24:25–25:18
Preparation for conquest	26:1–33:49
The new generation	26:1-65
Inheritance problems	27:1-11
A new leader	27:12-23
Sacrifices and vows	28:1–30:16
Vengeance on the Midianites	31:1-54
Transjordan apportioned	32:1-42
Review of Israel's journey	33:1-49
Anticipation of occupation	33:50–36:13
The land to be conquered	33:50–34:15
Leaders appointed for allotting the land	34:16-29
Levitical and refuge cities	35:1-34
Inheritance regulations	36:1-13

Balaam and Balak

King Balak of the Moabites was disturbed when the Israelites encamped to the north of him. He endeavored to persuade Balaam to come to his aid, hoping that this prophet would curse Israel. Enticed by the reward offered, Balaam went but was shockingly reminded by his donkey and the angel that he was limited in this mission to speak God's message only. Four times Balaam blessed Israel and subsequently was shamefully dismissed by Balak. However, through Balaam's advice (Num. 31:16), the Moabites seduced many Israelites into immorality and idolatry, which brought judgment upon God's people. Balaam was killed in a battle between the Israelites and Midianites. God, however, would not allow His people to be cursed.

DECISIONS AND INSTRUCTIONS

The territory east of Jordan appealed to the Reubenites and Gadites as excellent grazing land. In response Moses reluctantly granted permission to Reuben, Gad, and half of the tribe of Manasseh to settle east of the Jordan but exacted a promise from them to participate in the conquest of Canaan. Three cities of refuge were appointed in this territory.

Most significant among other instructions and plans outlined by Moses was the designation of Joshua as the new leader (Num. 27). He had already distinguished himself as a military leader when they repulsed the Amalekites (Exod. 17) and as a man of faith when he was sent in to spy out the land.

RETROSPECT AND PROSPECT

Moses' ministry was nearing completion. In the wake of new leadership and conquest and occupation of the Promised Land, Moses addressed the nation he had led out of Egypt in a number of public addresses. They may be considered under the following divisions:

History and its significance	Deuteronomy 1:1–4:43
Review of Israel's failures	1:1–3:29
Admonition to obedience	4:1-40
Transjordan cities and refuge	4:41-43
The Law and its significance	4:44–28:68
The covenant and the Decalogue	4:44–11:32
Laws for living in Canaan	12:1–26:19
Blessings and curses	27:1–28:68
Final preparation and farewell	29:1–34:12
Israel's choice of blessing or curse	29:1–30:20
Joshua commissioned	31:1-29
The song and blessing of Moses	31:30–33:29
The death of Moses	34:1-12

The messages Moses delivered to his people were vital and significant. No one knew the Israelites any better than Moses. No one else was in a better position to anticipate the future developments.

HISTORY

In his first address Moses reviewed Israel's history. He began with their encampment and departure in the Sinai Peninsula. He highlighted this review by reminding them that the generation that came out of Egypt murmured and rebelled repeatedly and in consequence was denied entrance into the land of promise. Clearly and distinctly he pointed out that the conditions for obtaining God's favor were obedience to the Law and a wholehearted devotion to God.

LAW

In his second address Moses vividly reminded them that they were God's covenant people. He repeated the Ten Commandments and pointed out that these were basic to a life acceptable to God. Genuine love for God would issue in a life of obedience, which would maintain them as God's holy people in the midst of pagan surroundings. Idolatry together with idolatrous people were to be removed. Moses also set forth rules and ordinances to guide them in their civil, social, and domestic responsibilities. The blessings and curses outlined by Moses were to be read publicly to the entire congregation after they entered Canaan.

FAREWELL

When Moses resigned, he entrusted Joshua with the leadership and the priests with his teaching ministry. He provided them with a copy of the Law. How complete this copy was is not indicated, but it was stored with the ark, making it available to be read publicly to the congregation every seven years according to provisions previously made. Moses once more recounted the birth and childhood of the nation that he had led from Egyptian slavery to the border of Canaan and uttered a blessing for each tribe. Before he died, Moses was instructed to ascend Mount Nebo from which he viewed the land the Israelites were about to enter.

DISCUSSION QUESTIONS

1. What was the population count of Israel before they left Mount Sinai?
2. How did the Israelites celebrate their first anniversary after the Exodus?
3. Where was the tabernacle located when Israel was encamped or en route?
4. What precipitated the crisis causing Israel to remain in the wilderness for an extended period?
5. How did Joshua and Caleb propose the conquest of Canaan?
6. Who were the leaders of two rebellions against Moses and Aaron?
7. How is the incident of the serpent used in the New Testament?
8. What nation refused to let Israel use their highway?
9. Who was Balak?
10. Why was Moses denied entrance into Canaan?

11. Trace the movement of Israel from Mount Sinai to the Plains of Moab via Kadesh-barnea. What spiritual lessons still applicable should have been learned as the result of these travels?

12. Study the means of guidance provided through the pillar of cloud and the trumpets in Numbers 10. What means does God use to guide His children today?

13. Point out how Deuteronomy 4–6 can be helpful to parents in rearing their children. Discuss practical ways to apply Deuteronomy 6:7 in family life.

14. Evaluate the character of Balaam as a prophet of God. Does God use similar individuals today?

Chapter Five

POSSESSING THE PROMISED LAND

FROM THEIR ENCAMPMENT NORTHEAST of the Dead Sea, the Israelites could view the land of Canaan across the River Jordan. Before Moses died, Joshua had been appointed to lead them in conquest and occupation.

CONDITIONS IN CANAAN

Politically the land was under the control of people who lived in city-states. A walled city situated on top of a mound could resist an invading force for almost an indefinite period as long as their water and food supply lasted. Consequently, for Israel conquest and occupation seemed a formidable and impossible assignment.

The Canaanites were polytheistic in their religion. El, the chief god, was called "father bull" and creator. His wife's name was Asherah. Foremost among their many offspring was Baal, meaning "lord" (1 Kings 18:19). He was the reigning king of the gods, who were believed to control heaven and earth and fertility.

The brutality and immorality in the stories of these gods were unsurpassed in our present knowledge of Near Eastern gods during that period. This lack of morality was reflected in the religious rites and ceremonies of the Canaanites. Archaeologists have pointed out that the evidence of Canaanite culture of Joshua's time indicates that the people practiced child sacrifice, religious prostitution, and snake worship in their religious rites and ceremonies.[1] The conditions, however, were known to Moses, and he warned the Israelites that if they did not destroy these wicked people, the Israelites would be ensnared in the sins of the Canaanites (Lev. 18:24-28; 20–23; Deut. 12:31; 20:17, 18).

This divine judgment coming upon the Canaanites through the Israelites was preceded by a long period of mercy. The patriarchs while living in Canaan had erected their altars in numerous places, exemplifying the worship of the true God of heaven and earth. When God promised Abraham the land of Canaan for his descendants (Gen. 15:16), the Bible states that the iniquity of the Amorites was not yet full and that the Israelites would dwell in Egypt for four centuries. After this long period, the Canaanites had become worse, so that the time for judgment was ripe as Israel entered to occupy the land.

THE CONQUEST UNDER JOSHUA

Joshua came to this responsible position of leadership with a background of experience and training under Moses' tutelage. At Rephidim (in the wilderness) Joshua led the Israelites in victory, repulsing the Amalekite attack (Exod. 17:8-16) as Moses continued in intercessory prayer for him. As a spy, he gained firsthand knowledge of Palestine and heroically, in face of opposition, asserted that by faith in God they would be able to conquer the land (Num. 13, 14). Thus he had witnessed God's power exercised in their behalf from Egypt to the borders of Canaan, even though an entire generation was denied the privilege of entrance because of unbelief.

ENTRANCE INTO CANAAN

The first four chapters narrate the events of Israel's movement into Palestine. These may be outlined as follows:

Joshua assumes leadership	Joshua	1
Two spies sent to Jericho		2
Passage through the Jordan		3
Memorials		4

Joshua was assured of success if he would be careful to heed the instructions given in the Book of the Law that had been given through Moses. Under God's command and with assurance of God's presence, he assumed this task of leading God's chosen nation. Two spies who were sent to Jericho learned from Rahab that the stories of God's mighty acts in behalf of Israel were circulating among the inhabitants of Canaan.

The miraculous passage through the Jordan should have made every Israelite of this new generation conscious of God's intervention for them. They erected two twelve-stone memorials—one in or near the Jordan and another at Gilgal—to remind coming generations of this great event.

THE MAJOR CAMPAIGNS

In six chapters the summary of Joshua's campaigns is given. Note the following developments:

Preparation for the campaigns	Joshua	5
Central campaign—Jericho and Ai		6
Southern campaign—Amorite League		9
Northern campaign—Canaanite League		11:1-15
Tabulation of the conquest		11:16–12:24

Four events made the whole nation of Israel conscious of the fact that they were in the land of promise:

1. They erected two memorials of stones to perpetuate the memory of divine deliverance.
2. They observed the Passover, reminding the new generation of their deliverance from Egypt.
3. They observed the rite of circumcision, making them conscious of the fact that they were God's covenant people.
4. Manna ceased, and their sustenance came from the land they had entered.

In addition, Joshua was personally reminded through a theophany (a physical manifestation of God) that he was but a servant and subject to the Commander of the army of the Lord (5:13-15).

The central campaign was directed against Jericho and Ai. The former was a sample victory, making all Israel aware of God's supernatural power released in their behalf. Peculiar to this victory was the fact that the Israelites were not allowed to retain any spoils of conquest. (Ai was conquered according to regular military strategy after Achan's sin had been removed.) After this victory the Israelites were allowed the livestock and other property.[2] Following the occupation of central Canaan, the Israelites assembled between Mount Ebal and Mount Gerizim for a convocation to hear the reading of the Law of Moses.

In the southern campaign the Amorite League was defeated. Through deception and insensitivity to divine guidance, the Israelites entered into a league with the Gibeonites. In consequence, the other cities of this league attacked Israel, but through the divine intervention of hailstones, in addition to a surprise counterattack and extension of daylight, the Israelites were able to rout the enemy in a smashing victory.[3] Although such city-states as Gezer and Jerusalem were not conquered, the whole area from Gibeon down to Kadesh-barnea came under the control of Joshua.

The northern campaign is briefly described. In a great battle near the waters of Merom, the Canaanites were defeated. The city of Hazor was utterly destroyed. Recent excavation under the Israeli expedition begun in 1955 indicates that this Canaanite city may have had a population of over 40,000 at this time.

In summary, thirty-one kings were defeated in the conquest of Canaan. Although the inhabitants of Canaan were not destroyed as extensively as Moses had instructed the Israelites, Joshua was able to allot the land.

DIVISION OF THE LAND

The remaining chapters of Joshua describe the allotment of the Promised Land and the farewell advice of Joshua as follows:

Plan for division	Joshua	13–14
Tribal allotment		15–19
Refuge and Levite cities		20–21
Farewell and death of Joshua		22–24

After tribal boundaries were established, six cities were designated as cities of refuge—three on each side of the Jordan River. Forty-eight cities were assigned to the Levites, who were scattered throughout the land in order to meet their responsibilities in religious service. Shiloh was designated as the religious center of Israel. Here the tabernacle was erected (Josh. 18:1). Before Joshua died, he assembled the Israelites at Shechem, reminding them that Abraham had been called from idolatry and admonishing them to fear the Lord.

LEADERSHIP OF JUDGES

The events in Joshua and Judges are closely related. The exact chronology of this era is very difficult to establish, but for approximately two or three centuries the destiny of Israel is surveyed under the leadership of judges who rose to deliver their people from the oppressing enemies.[4] Most of these leaders ruled locally, and, consequently, the years allotted to each may have been synchronous with the preceding or succeeding judge.

PREVAILING CONDITIONS

A general description of the times of the judges is given in the opening chapters of Judges as follows:

Unoccupied areas	Judges	1:1–2:5
Religious-political cycles		2:6–3:6

Throughout the land, Canaanites had retained strongholds during Israel's conquest and occupation. As a result, the Israelites encountered continual difficulties, even though at times the inhabitants of such city-states as Jerusalem, Megiddo, Taanach, and others were subjected to hard labor and taxes. In times of spasmodic leadership in Israel, these heathen peoples gained the upper hand.

Fourfold cycles occurred repeatedly in Israel. Association with the pagan population led the Israelites into apostasy and idolatry. Judgment followed in the form of oppression by invading nations. In the course of time, the Israelites repented, which resulted in divine deliverance. The religious-political cycles may also be characterized by the following words: sin, sorrow, supplication, and salvation.

OPPRESSING NATIONS AND DELIVERERS

The history of Israel during this period is recorded with special interest in the oppressing nations and the judges that were raised to free the people from the invaders. Below is a list as given in Judges:

Mesopotamia—Othniel	Judges	3:7-11
Moab—Ehud		3:12-30
Philistia—Shamgar		3:31
Canaan (Hazor)—Deborah and Barak		4:1–5:31
Midian—Gideon (Jerubbaal)		6:1–8:35
Abimelech, Tola, and Jair		9:1–10:5
Ammon—Jephthah		10:6–12:7
Ibzan, Elon, and Abdon		12:8-15
Philistia—Samson		13:1–16:31

Most of these individuals apparently performed great feats on behalf of the Israelites, even though some of them are only mentioned by name. The oppressing nations came from the neighboring territories, gradually invading various areas of tribal possessions, taking their crops, and occupying the land. Some of these nations would exact taxes that became a terrible burden to the Israelites.

The stories of a number of these judges deserve careful study. Five of them—Barak, Gideon, Jephthah, Samson, and Samuel—are listed among the heroes of faith in Hebrews chapter 11. Individual deeds and battles exhibiting supernatural strength restored to the Israelites the consciousness that God was intervening on behalf of His people. For some of the judges very little information is given concerning their activities.

CONFUSED CONDITIONS

The last five chapters of the book of Judges and the four chapters of the book of Ruth relate the blessings and adversities of various groups and families. These may be briefly outlined as follows:

Micah and his idolatry	Judges	17
Migration of the Danites		18
Crime and civil war		19–21
The story of Ruth	Ruth	1–4

Historical details in these chapters are lacking so that at best these events can be dated in the days "when the judges ruled" and when there was "no king in Israel" (Ruth 1:1; Judg. 21:25). Certainly the national developments are not given, and the statement "Every man did that which was right in his own eyes" (Judg. 21:25) characterized the plight of Israel during the times of the judges.

DISCUSSION QUESTIONS

1. What were the conditions for Joshua's success?
2. How were future generations to be reminded of Israel's crossing the Jordan?
3. What did Rahab know about Israel when she conversed with the spies?
4. How did Israel observe its entrance into Canaan?
5. Why were the Israelites forbidden to take any spoils after the fall of Jericho?
6. Where did Joshua assemble the people for the reading of the Law of Moses?
7. How did the Gibeonites deceive Joshua?
8. Where did the Levites live in Canaan?
9. What judges are listed in Hebrews 11?
10. What were the prevailing religious-political conditions during the time of the judges?
11. Trace the major events in the conquest of the land of Canaan. In each instance indicate the determining factor for victory or defeat. Which of these factors are significant in Christian experience? (Cf. Rom. 6–8; Eph. 1–6)
12. Locate on a map the five cities conquered in the southern campaign. To what degree did divine intervention utilize physical factors in giving success?
13. What characteristics and abilities seen in Joshua's leadership are essential to effective Christian leadership?
14. How does the story of Ruth illustrate the truth that God has never left Himself without witness? How does this account advance the messianic hope?

Chapter Six

TIME OF
TRANSITION

THE THREAT OF PHILISTINE supremacy hung over Israel. Settled in the maritime plain in the southwestern part of Palestine, the Philistines began to overrun the Israelites in the days of Samson. The Israelites lacked centralized national leadership, and they failed to repulse the invaders. Even though Samson was endowed with supernatural power, he failed to use this to the best advantage of Israel's national interest.

Philistine superiority over Israel is best explained by the fact that they held the secrets of smelting iron. Although the Hittites in Asia Minor had been iron founders before 1200 B.C., the Philistines were the first to use this process in Palestine. They guarded this monopoly carefully, and as a result had Israel at their mercy. "There was no smith found throughout all the land of Israel" (1 Sam. 13:19-22). Consequently, the Israelites were dependent upon the Philistines for the production of spears and swords as well as for the sharpening of their farm implements.

Politically, the Philistines occupied at least five cities in the maritime plain, which were independently ruled by a "lord." The names of these cities—Ashkelon, Ashdod, Ekron, Gaza, and Gath—appear in the biblical records.

The Scriptures reflect this struggle between the Philistines and the Israelites during several generations. Under the leadership of Eli, Samuel, and Saul, the tribes of Israel were united to some extent in their resistance against the Philistines. There were times when it seemed as though the Israelites were on the verge of being subjected to hopeless slavery. By about 1000 B.C. under David, the power of the Philistines was broken.

ELI AS PRIEST AND JUDGE

The events related in 1 Samuel 1–4 occurred during the days of Eli's leadership. They may be briefly outlined as follows:

Birth of Samuel	1 Samuel 1:1–2:11
Tabernacle service	2:12-26
Two warnings to Eli	2:27–3:21
Judgment on Eli	4:1-22

Shiloh, where the tabernacle was erected in the days of Joshua (Josh. 18:1), apparently continued to be Israel's religious center. Here Eli served as high priest and provided religious and civil leadership for the people. Although the narrative already is focused upon Samuel, the conditions existing during the days of Eli are vividly portrayed.

RELIGIOUS APOSTASY

The religion of Israel was at an all-time low when Eli was in charge. He failed to teach his sons to revere God as Moses had clearly instructed Israelite parents to do (Deut. 4–6). Eli's sons, Hophni and Phinehas, "knew not the Lord" (1 Sam. 2:12). Nevertheless, they were allowed to assume priestly responsibilities, taking advantage of the people as they came to sacrifice and worship. Not only did they rob God in demanding the priestly portion before sacrifice was made, but they conducted themselves in such a manner that the people abhorred bringing their sacrifices to Shiloh. They profaned the sanctuary with the baseness and debauchery common in Canaanite religion. Consequently, it is not surprising that Israel continued to degenerate into increasingly corrupt religious practices.

This religious atmosphere in Shiloh was the environment to which Samuel was exposed as a growing child. Transferred from the care of a God-fearing mother, Samuel was subjected to the evil, degrading influences of the sons of the high priest in the national religious center. It was to the benefit of Israel that Samuel reacted against this godless pressure and became conscious of God's call in the early years of his life.

IMPENDING JUDGMENT

Eli's laxity provoked God's judgment. Twice he was warned. An unnamed prophet clearly pointed out to him that he was honoring his sons more than he honored God (1 Sam. 2:30). His lack of parental discipline extended to his priestly office as the sons assumed responsibilities at the tabernacle. With the call of Samuel, a second message of warning was conveyed to Eli (1 Sam. 3).

The day of judgment affected the entire nation. In the course of a battle against the Philistines, the sons of Eli yielded to the pressure of the people to take the ark of the covenant out of the Holy of Holies in the tabernacle and bring it into the battlefield, hoping this would force God to give them victory.

The defeat of Israel was crushing. The ark was stolen, the sons of Eli were slain, and the report of these reverses for Israel shocked Eli so that he collapsed and died. In all likelihood Shiloh was destroyed. When the ark was returned, it was placed in a private home. No mention is made of Shiloh or the tabernacle. Shortly after this, priests officiated at Nob (1 Sam. 21:1).

So demoralizing was this defeat of Israel that when Eli's daughter-in-law gave birth to a son, she named him "Ichabod" because she sensed that God's blessing had been withdrawn from Israel.

SAMUEL AS PROPHET, PRIEST, AND JUDGE

Brief but significant are the chapters in 1 Samuel that project the religious and political changes that took place under the leadership of Samuel. Consider the following outline:

The ark restored to Israel	1 Samuel 5:1–7:2
Revival and victory	7:3-14
Summary of Samuel's ministry	7:15–8:3
Request for a king	8:4-22
Saul anointed	9:1–10:16
Public acclaim and victory	10:17–11:11
Saul's inauguration; Samuel's pledge	11:12–12:25

Samuel has a unique place in Israel's history. He was the last of the judges who exercised civil jurisdiction over Israel in that capacity. Although he was not of the lineage of Aaron, he officiated as the leading priest. He also gained renown as a prophet and established schools of the prophets who influenced the kings of Israel in succeeding generations.

EFFECTIVE LEADERSHIP

Samuel erected an altar in his home town of Ramah. Although the ark was returned, it was stored in the home of Abinadab until the time of David. Samuel established circuits throughout Israel in performing his priestly duties and effective teaching ministry. Places mentioned in the biblical account are Mizpah, Ramah, Gilgal, Bethlehem, Bethel, and Beersheba. In the course of time, prophetic bands gathered about Samuel, as all Israel from Dan to Beersheba became conscious of the fact that he was established as a prophet of the Lord.

The purging of Canaanite cultic worship from the ranks of Israel was also effected under the influence of Samuel. When Samuel gathered the Israelites for a convocation of prayer, fasting, and sacrifice at Mizpah, the Philistines attacked. In the midst of the battle, the Philistines were confused and fled as a result of a severe thunderstorm. Samuel acknowledged God's help and intervention by erecting a stone, which he named Ebenezer, meaning "Hitherto hath the Lord helped us" (1 Sam. 7:12). Not again did the Philistines attack the Israelites while Samuel was in charge of Israel.

REQUEST FOR A KING

Reluctantly Samuel listened and finally consented to Israel's demand for a king. Samuel eloquently implored his people "not to impose upon themselves a Canaanite institution alien to their own way of life." Sensitive to divine guidance, Samuel agreed and turned the affairs of state over to a new leader (1 Sam. 8:7-22).

SAUL ANOINTED AS ISRAEL'S FIRST KING

Saul was God's choice to be Israel's first king after the people clamored for a leader like the other nations had. Saul was privately anointed and publicly acclaimed in a convocation at Mizpah, as the people enthusiastically shouted, "Long live the king." The nature of kingship in Israel, however, was uniquely set forth in the statement that Saul was to be "captain of His [God's] inheritance" (1 Sam. 9:16; 10:1).

The deliverance of Jabesh-gilead from the Ammonite threat under the leadership of Saul projected the new king into the national limelight. In a public meeting at Gilgal after this victory, Samuel publicly endorsed Saul as king with the warning that prosperity was dependent upon the obedience of the king as well as his subjects to the Law of Moses. This message was confirmed by a sudden rain and thunder during the wheat harvest, about May 15 to June 15. This was considered a miracle, since normally Palestine has virtually no rain from April to October. Samuel, however, assured his people of his sincere interest in their future welfare in his public statement: "God forbid that I should sin against the LORD in ceasing to pray for you."

Saul's leadership of Israel is vividly and dramatically portrayed in the remaining chapters of 1 Samuel. For a survey account, we may divide this into three outline units as indicated in the following pages.

Saul fails to wait for Samuel	1 Samuel 13:1-15a
Philistines defeated at Michmash	13:15b-14:46

| Surrounding nations subdued | 14:47-52 |
| Disobedience in an Amalekite victory | 15:1-35 |

Saul led his nation in numerous military victories. On a hill three miles north of Jerusalem, he established Gibeah as a strong palace-fort that apparently served as his capital while he was king of Israel. Saul routed the Philistines at Michmash and defeated numerous other nations in addition to the Amalekites (1 Sam. 14:47, 48).

King Saul had numerous advantages in his favor as he assumed the kingship. He was successful as a military leader and gained the national acclaim of his people. He also had the spiritual support of the nationally known prophet, Samuel, who assured the king as well as the people of intercessory prayer. Success and public acclaim, however, did not obscure the personal weaknesses in Saul's character. These became evident in his impatience to wait for Samuel at Gilgal, where Saul assumed priestly duties, and his disobedience to God's command through the prophet to utterly destroy the Amalekites. Sternly Samuel rebuked him in the warning that "to obey is better than sacrifice." In failing to recognize his sacred trust, Saul was reminded that he had forfeited the kingdom.

DAVID'S RISE TO NATIONAL FAME

David's anointing by Samuel was unknown to Saul. In this experience the prophet Samuel learned the lesson that man is prone to look on the outward appearance, but the Lord appraises the heart. David in his youthful days had extensive preparation. During this time, he not only learned how to play instruments, but he also developed his strength and ingenuity in fighting off lions and bears. At the same time, he learned to place his trust in God for divine aid. On an errand of serving his older brothers who were in the army, David heard Goliath challenging the Israelites. David reasoned that God would help him kill the giant. By killing Goliath, David suddenly gained national recognition. While David had been brought before the king on previous occasions as a musician to calm Saul's troubled spirit, he now served the royal court on a permanent basis.

David's rise to national fame	1 Samuel 16–17
Saul seeks to ensnare David	18–19
Friendship of David and Jonathan	20
David's flight and its consequences	21–22
Saul's pursuit of David	23–26

Saul yielded to jealousy as David arose in national fame. When subtle schemes devised to ensnare David failed repeatedly, Saul began to persecute David. In the meantime, one of the noblest friendships in the Old Testament developed between Jonathan and David. Their relationship enabled David to be constantly aware of the king's malicious designs. Eventually David was forced to take refuge in the Judean desert. During the times that Saul pursued David and his men, David twice had the opportunity to take the king's life but always refrained, affirming that he would not touch the Lord's anointed.

The Philistine-Israelite conflict:

Philistines afford David refuge	1 Samuel 27:1–28:2
Saul seeks help in Endor	28:3-25
David recovers his possessions	29:1–30:31
Death of Saul	31:1-13

David's fear that Saul might overtake him unexpectedly caused David to seek refuge in the land of the Philistines. During the last year and a half of Saul's reign, David was granted permission by Achish to reside in the Philistine city of Ziklag. He was denied, however, the privilege of joining the Philistines in their warfare against Saul.

When the Philistines faced the Israelite armies encamped on Mount Gilboa, Saul had more to fear than this enemy whom he had previously defeated. Samuel, long ago ignored by Saul, was not available for interview. Saul was panic-stricken as he turned to God and received no answer by dream, by Urim, or by prophet. In desperation he turned to spiritualistic mediums that he himself had banned in the past.

As Samuel had predicted, Saul's life ended with dismal night as he renewed his encounter with the Philistines. The invaders won a decisive victory, gaining control of the fertile valley of Megiddo from the coast to the Jordan River and occupying numerous cities. The termination of the reign of Israel's first king was tragic. Although God-chosen and anointed by the praying prophet Samuel, Saul failed to realize that obedience was essential in the sacred and unique trust afforded him by God—to be "captain over his inheritance" (1 Sam. 10:1).

DISCUSSION QUESTIONS

1. How did the Philistines maintain temporal control over the Israelites?
2. How was Eli warned about his laxity in his home and his office?

3. Why was the ark not returned to Shiloh?
4. Why did Saul stop at the home of Samuel?
5. Why did the Israelites request a king?
6. What cities were included in Samuel's circuit as a judge and prophet?
7. What talent of David brought him before the king?
8. Who was David's closest friend in the royal family?
9. What was David's attitude toward Saul?
10. Where was Saul's life terminated?
11. What evident qualities in Samuel's life are necessary for effective Christian leadership?
12. On a map of Palestine list the leading cities mentioned in 1 Samuel. What earlier and later events added to their historical significance?
13. Trace the steps in Saul's downfall. Which of these inevitably lead to spiritual difficulties?
14. What qualities evidenced in David's life are always commendable? What experiences of his life prepared him for effective leadership?
15. Compare and contrast the qualities required for kingship in Israel with that in heathen nations.

Chapter Seven

THE REIGN OF DAVID

DAVID WAS THE OUTSTANDING king in the entire history of Israel in Old Testament times. His reign represents the epitome of Israel's national achievements and is so recognized throughout the holy Scriptures.

Politically and religiously, David distinguished himself as a great leader. He was successful in uniting the tribes of Israel into an effective union and extending its territory from the river of Egypt and the Gulf of Aqaba to the Phoenician coast and the land of Hamath. Through military success and friendly overtures, David gained for Israel international respect and recognition that remained unchallenged until the death of Solomon.

Religiously, David organized the priests and Levites for effective participation in the ritual and ceremonial activities of the entire nation. Even though he was denied the privilege of building the temple, David made elaborate preparation for its erection during the reign of Solomon.

Two books in the Old Testament report the account of David's reign. Second Samuel depicts the Davidic reign in great detail and provides an exclusive account of the sin, crime, and rebellion in the royal family. First Chronicles traces the genealogical background of the twelve tribes and focuses attention upon David as the first king of the ruling dynasty of Israel. Saul is hardly mentioned. Much attention is given to the political and religious organization of Israel and the extensive description of David's preparation for building the temple.

The outline of David's reign as given in this chapter represents a suggested chronological arrangement of the events as recorded in 2 Samuel and 1 Chronicles.

THE KING OF JUDAH

	2 Samuel	1 Chronicles
Genealogical background		1–9
David laments Saul's death	1	10
Disintegration of Saul's dynasty	2–4	

Israel was in serious trouble when they lost their king and three of his sons in Saul's last battle with the Philistines. Abner, who had served as captain of Saul's army, was able to restore enough order to have Ishbosheth (Eshbaal) anointed as king in Gilead east of the Jordan. Philistine interference or occupation may have delayed the accession of Saul's son for five years, since he ruled only two years during the seven and one-half years that David reigned at Hebron.

David was in Philistia when news reached him of Saul's death. After mourning the deaths of Saul and Jonathan, David returned to Hebron where he was anointed as king by the leaders of Judah. Although civil strife prevailed in Israel, with the tribe of Judah supporting David and the rest of the nation loyal to Ishbosheth, mediation was soon effected when all Israel realized that David held no animosity toward the family of Saul. In the course of these negotiations, both Abner and Ishbosheth were slain without the consent of David. After seven and one-half years David gained recognition of all the tribes of Israel without malice or vengeance.

JERUSALEM—THE NATIONAL CAPITAL

	2 Samuel	1 Chronicles
The conquest of Jerusalem	5:1-9	11:1-9
David's military strength	23:8-39	11:10–12:40
Recognition by Philistia and Phoenicia	5:10-25	14:1-17
Jerusalem—center of religion	6:1-23	13:1-14
		15:1–16:43
An eternal throne	7:1-29	17:1-27

David's kingship at Hebron may have been no serious concern of the Philistines, but when David won the acclaim and recognition of the entire nation of Israel, the Philistines were seriously alarmed. Twice David defeated them and may have found their opposition an aid to the unification of Israel.

Jerusalem had remained a Jebusite stronghold throughout the time that Israel had occupied Canaan. After David decided that this would be a strategic location for a national capital, Joab succeeded in expelling the Jebusites. As a reward he became commander of David's army. The particular site David occupied was known as Ophel and may have been higher at that time than the hill to the north where the temple was built under Solomon. This fortress was known as the "city of David" (1 Chron. 11:7) and was frequently referred to as Zion in subsequent Old Testament literature because it represented the seat of authority in Israel.

When David assumed national leadership, he organized the entire nation. The men who had been with him as a fugitive and at Hebron were now appointed as princes and leaders. He built a magnificent palace in Jerusalem, contracting with the Phoenicians for his material (2 Sam. 5:11, 12).

Jerusalem was also made the religious center of Israel. In time the ark was brought to Jerusalem and housed in a tent or tabernacle. Priests and Levites were assigned their respective duties, and worship was reestablished on a national scale.

David was vitally interested in building a temple. Although Nathan the prophet at first approved, he was subsequently divinely instructed that the building of the temple would be postponed until David's son was established on the throne. This was because David was essentially a man of war, and though he was a man after God's own heart, David's son Solomon would build the temple. The magnitude of the promise made to David, however, extends far beyond the scope and time of Solomon's kingdom. David was assured that his throne would be established forever. Sin and iniquity in David's posterity would be temporarily judged and punished, but God promised not to withdraw His mercy indefinitely.

No earthly kingdom or dynasty has ever had eternal duration. Neither did the earthly throne of David—without linking his lineage to Jesus, who is specifically identified in the New Testament as the Son of David. This assurance, given to David through the prophet Nathan, constitutes another link in the series of messianic promises given in Old Testament times. A fuller revelation of the Messiah and His eternal kingdom is given by the prophets in subsequent centuries.

PROSPERITY AND SUPREMACY

	2 Samuel	1 Chronicles
List of nations conquered	8:1-13	18:1-13
David shares responsibility and blessing	8:15–9:13	18:14-17
The famine	21:1-14	
Defeat of Ammonites, Syrians, and Philistines	10:1-18 21:15-22	19:1–20:8
Song of deliverance (Ps. 18)	22:1-51	

The expansion of Davidic rule from the tribal boundaries of Judah to a vast empire stretching from the River of Egypt and the Gulf of Aqaba to regions of the Euphrates receives scant attention in the biblical record. Historically, however, this is very significant since the Davidic and Solomonic kingdom of Israel was the leading nation in the Fertile Crescent at the beginning of the tenth century B.C.

The observations that the Philistines had the monopoly on iron in the days of Samuel (1 Sam. 13:19, 20), and that near the end of David's reign it was freely used in Israel (1 Chron. 22:3), suggest that a long chapter could have been written on the economic revolution in Israel. David's period as a fugitive and Philistine resident not only afforded him experience in military leadership, but also gave him firsthand acquaintance with the formula and methods used by the Philistines in the production of arms.

The Arabah Desert, which extended southward from the Dead Sea to the Gulf of Aqaba, was strategically important for Israel. The iron and copper deposits in this area were necessary to break the Philistine monopoly. In all likelihood this was the reason that David conquered and occupied Edom and established garrisons throughout the land to control these natural resources (2 Sam. 8:14).

In addition to defeating the Philistines and the Edomites, David subdued the Moabites and Amalekites, exacting silver and gold from them. David also defeated the Ammonites and Arameans, extending his power east and north to gain control of the trade routes that came through Damascus and other points. With the Phoenicians who carried on lucrative naval trade, David concluded a treaty.

The story of Mephibosheth given in the narratives of Israel's expansion illustrates David's magnanimous attitude toward his predecessor's descendants. David not only allotted Mephibosheth a pension from the royal treasury but also provided a home for him in Jerusalem.

Mephibosheth received special consideration during a famine that came as a judgment upon Israel for Saul's terrible crime of attempting to exterminate the Gibeonites, with whom Joshua had made a covenant (cf. Josh. 9:3ff.). Realizing that this sin required atonement (Num. 35:31ff.), David allowed the Gibeonites to execute seven of Saul's descendants. Mephibosheth, however, was spared. At this time David transferred the bones of Saul and Jonathan to the family sepulcher in Benjamin.

As king of Israel, David did not fail to acknowledge God as the One who granted Israel military victories and material prosperity. In a psalm of thanksgiving (2 Sam. 22; Ps. 18), David expressed his praise. This represents but a sample of many psalms that he composed on various occasions during his varied career as a shepherd boy, a servant in the royal court, a fugitive, and finally as the architect-king and builder of Israel's largest empire.

SIN IN THE ROYAL FAMILY

Character imperfections in the leaders of Israel are not minimized in the Bible. Indulging in sin, David could not escape the judgments of God. However, when he acknowledged his iniquity as a penitent sinner, he qualified as a man who pleased God (1 Sam. 13:14).

David's crime and repentance	2 Samuel 11:1–12:31
Amnon's crime and results	13:1-36
Absalom's defeat in rebellion	13.37–18:33
David recovers the throne	19:1–20:26

David practiced polygamy (2 Sam. 3:2-5; 11:27). In Davidic times a harem at the royal court was a status symbol and freely practiced by surrounding nations. Polygamy seems to have been tolerated in Old Testament times because of the hardness of Israel's heart, but was definitely forbidden in the fuller revelation of the New Testament. Kings were especially warned about the multiplicity of wives (Deut. 17:17). For David, the marriages to Michal the daughter of Saul and Maacah the daughter of Talmai, king of Geshur, had political implications. Like others, David had to suffer the consequences as the crimes of incest, murder, and rebellion unfolded in his family life.

From a human standpoint, David's sin of adultery with Bathsheba and the murder of Uriah constituted a perfect crime. (This account is exclusively recorded in 2 Samuel.) Not accountable to anyone in his kingdom, David very likely concealed these developments from everyone but temporarily failed to recognize that his thoughts and deeds were known to God. For a despot in a heathen nation, adultery and murder might have passed unchallenged, but not so in Israel where kingship was a sacred trust. When confronted with his sin by Nathan the prophet, David repented. David's spiritual crises found lofty expressions in Psalms 32 and 51. He was granted forgiveness, but grave, indeed, were the domestic consequences (2 Sam. 12:11). The grace of God is seen in the fact that God spared David from death by stoning, the scriptural punishment for adultery. It is further seen in that David's illegitimate child was overshadowed by Bathsheba's giving birth to Solomon, who later became king.

David's lack of discipline and self-restraint set a poor example for his sons, who became involved in immorality and murder. Amnon's immoral behavior with his half-sister resulted in his assassination by Absalom. Incurring David's disfavor, Absalom found refuge with Talmai, his grandfather in Geshur, for three years but then returned to Jerusalem through Joab's mediation. After spending about four years in Jerusalem in a public relations effort to win the hearts of the people, Absalom staged a rebellion against David. It appeared to have all the marks of success when David, taken by surprise, was forced to flee from Jerusalem.

David was a brilliant militarist. Given time to organize his forces, David routed the armies of his rebellious son. Absalom was killed. David, who mourned his son's death instead of celebrating the victory, was rebuked by Joab for neglecting the welfare of the Israelites who had given him loyal support. After another rebellion led by Sheba, a Benjaminite, was suppressed, David recovered his throne.

Through nearly a decade following David's crime, the solemn words spoken by Nathan the prophet were realistically fulfilled. God indeed had forgiven and pardoned David's sin, but David had to suffer the consequences that fermented in his own house.

RETROSPECT AND PROSPECT

	2 Samuel	1 Chronicles
Sin in numbering the people	24:1-25	21:1-27
Solomon charged to build the temple		21:28–22:19
Duties of Levites		23:1–26:28
Civil officers		26:29–27:34
Charge to officials and people		28:1–29:22
Last words of David	23:1-7	
Death of David		29:22-30

David made elaborate plans and detailed arrangements for building the temple. Although he had defeated surrounding nations in his expansion of the Israelite empire, David had made a treaty with the Phoenicians, who carried on extensive naval commerce throughout the Mediterranean world. He negotiated with them for the materials to build the temple. Local and foreign labor was organized for this purpose, and even the details for religious worship in the proposed structure were carefully outlined.

The military census of Israel and the punitive consequences for the king and his people were closely related to David's elaborate plans for building the temple. Even though the reason for divine punishment upon the king and his people is not clearly stated, it seems that David was motivated by pride and reliance on military strength for Israel's national achievements. Perhaps Israel was punished for the rebellions under Absalom and Sheba. Although Joab objected to taking the census, David overruled.

Punishment for this sin was announced by Gad the prophet. Given the choice of punishment, David resigned himself and his nation to God's mercy by choosing the pestilence. During these days of judgment, David and the elders offered intercessory prayer on the threshing floor of Ornan, the Jebusite, directly north of Jerusalem. Instructed by Gad, David purchased this site. As he offered a sacrifice there before God, he became conscious of a divine response as the pestilence ceased.

This site, Mount Moriah, was designated by David as the location for the altar of burnt offering and the temple. Very likely this was the spot where Abraham, approximately a millennium earlier, had been willing to offer his son Isaac. Although Mount Moriah was outside the city of Zion (Jerusalem) as originally occupied by David, it was included in the capital city under Solomon.

David reflected on the fact that he had been a man of war and bloodshed. The first seven and one-half years at Hebron had been a period of preparation and civil strife. During the next decade, Jerusalem was established as the national capital, and many surrounding nations were defeated in the expansion of the kingdom. David's sin and the subsequent rebellions may have disrupted the major part of the third decade of his reign. During the last decade, David focused his attention upon the preparation for building the temple that he was not permitted to erect.

David charged Solomon with the responsibility to obey the Law as it had been given to Moses and to acknowledge his accountability to God. In a public assembly, David charged the princes and priesthood to recognize Solomon as his successor.

The last words of David (2 Sam. 23:1-7) reveal the greatness of Israel's most honored hero. He speaks prophetically about the eternal endurance of his kingdom. God had spoken to him, affirming an everlasting covenant. This testimony by David would have made a fitting epitaph for his tomb.

DISCUSSION QUESTIONS

1. What part of David's reign is exclusively recorded in 2 Samuel?
2. Who were the army captains under Saul and David?
3. How did David show his kindness to the family of Saul?
4. Why was David denied the privilege of building the temple?
5. Name two prophets in the reign of David.

6. What economic resources did David secure from the Sinaitic area?
7. How did David's exile in Philistia prepare him for the future?
8. Why was Absalom ostracized from Jerusalem?
9. Who misguided Absalom in his strategy?
10. Whom did David designate as his successor?
11. Compare and contrast the content and approach to history found in the books of 2 Samuel and 1 Chronicles. What is the place of God in current historical events?
12. List the nations conquered by David and show on a map how his kingdom expanded. How does this compare with the borders of the land God gave as an inheritance to Israel (Gen. 15:18)? What spiritual application can be made from this study?
13. Trace the consequences of David's sin during his reign. What aspects of God's manner of judgment for sin have not altered since David's time? Give biblical verification for your answer.
14. Compare and contrast the characters of Saul and David. What characteristics in their lives exemplify characteristics of leaders you know personally?
15. What traits of David's kingship foreshadowed Israel's greater King, Christ?

Chapter Eight

THE SOLOMONIC KINGDOM

PEACE AND PROSPERITY—THESE two words describe the golden era of Solomon's reign over Israel. He reaped the benefits of his father's military efforts in uniting the nation, expanding the borders of Israel, and gaining international recognition.

Solomon's reign of forty years, as given in these two accounts, is difficult to outline in any chronological order. The building and dedication of the temple that occurred during the first decade receive the most consideration. The building of the palace was completed thirteen years later. Many activities that are barely mentioned have been illuminated in recent years through archaeological excavations. Lacking a chronological perspective, the biblical content is considered topically in this analysis of the accounts in 1 Kings and 2 Chronicles:

	1 Kings	2 Chronicles
Solomon emerges as sole ruler	1:1–2:46	
Prayer for wisdom at Gibeon	3:1-15	1:1-13
Wisdom in administration	3:16–4:34	
Trade and prosperity		1:14-17

SOLOMON ESTABLISHED AS KING

Solomon inherited the throne of his father David. Although Adonijah, another son of David, enlisted the support of Joab and Abiathar, the priest at Jerusalem, to have himself anointed as king, the appeal of the prophet Nathan and Solomon's mother Bathsheba to David resulted in his recognizing Solomon as king. The new king was anointed on the eastern slope of Mount Ophel by Zadok, the officiating priest at Gibeah. In a public acclaim, "Long live King Solomon," the people of Jerusalem expressed their support so effectively that the supporters of Adonijah dispersed.

In a subsequent convocation, Solomon was officially crowned and recognized by the nation (1 Chron. 28:1-5). With officials and statesmen representing the whole nation present, David delivered a charge to the people outlining their responsibilities to Solomon, the king of God's choice. Privately David reminded his son that he was responsible to obey the Law of Moses (1 Kings 2:1-12).

Numerous changes occurred as Solomon was established on the throne. Adonijah's request to marry Abishag, the Shunammite maiden, was interpreted by Solomon as treason, resulting in Adonijah's execution. The removal and banishment of Abiathar to Anathoth marked the fulfillment of the solemn words spoken to Eli (cf. 1 Sam. 2:27-36; 1 Kings 2:26, 27). Joab's treasonable conduct in supporting Adonijah and his crimes during David's reign brought about his execution.

As a young man possibly in his early twenties, Solomon sensed his need for wisdom as he assumed national leadership. Sacrificing at Gibeon where the tabernacle and the bronze altar were located, he received the divine assurance that his request for wisdom would be granted. Conditioned on his obedience, he was also assured of riches, honor, and long life.

Solomon's wisdom as king of Israel became a source of wonderment. His wise judgment in the case recorded in 1 Kings 3:16-28 very likely represents but a sample of many decisions that exhibited his wisdom before his people. His fame spread internationally through extensive trade (2 Chron. 1:14-17).

Solomon's kingdom may have been very simple at the beginning, but it became a vast organization in the course of controlling his vast empire. The king himself constituted the final court of appeals. Appointments of various officers are listed in 1 Kings 4:1-6 and represent an increase over those under David. For taxation purposes the nation was divided into twelve districts. In rotation each district supplied provisions for the central government during one month of each year from a store city or from warehouses where these supplies were collected during the rest of the year. One day's supply for the king and his court of army and building personnel consisted of over 300 bushels of flour, almost 700 bushels of meal, 10 fattened cattle, 20 pasture-fed cattle, 100 sheep, plus other animals and fowl (1 Kings 4:22, 23).

Solomon also added to his armed forces 1,400 chariots and 12,000 horsemen, which were stationed in Jerusalem and chariot cities throughout Israel. This increased the burden of taxation to include a regular supply of barley and hay. Through efficient organization and wise administration, Israel maintained a state of prosperity and progress.

THE BUILDING PROGRAM

The temple constructed by Solomon represented a high point in Israel's religious history. It marked the fulfillment of David's desire to establish a permanent place of worship. The significant events include:

	1 Kings	2 Chronicles
The temple in Jerusalem	5:1–7:51	2:1–5:1
Solomon's palace	7:1-8	
Dedication of the temple	8:1–9:9	5:2–8:16
Settlement with Hiram of Tyre	9:10-25	

Through treaty arrangements with Hiram, the wealthy and powerful ruler of Tyre and Sidon who had extensive commercial contacts throughout the Mediterranean world, vast resources were available to Solomon. Advanced in architecture and workmanship of costly building materials, the Phoenicians not only furnished building supplies but also thousands of architects, technicians, and foremen who supervised building the temple in Jerusalem. Solomon made payment in grain, oil, and wine.

The temple was erected on the top of Mount Moriah located directly north of Zion where David had built his palace. On this place, where Abraham had gone to sacrifice Isaac, Solomon's temple stood until it was destroyed in 586 B.C. by Nebuchadnezzar. It was rebuilt in 520–515 B.C. and demolished again in A.D. 70. Since the seventh century A.D. the Mohammedan mosque, the Dome of the Rock, has been located on this site, regarded as the most sacred spot in world history. Today this temple area very likely is larger than it was in Solomon's time, covering about thirty-five to forty acres.

The temple itself was twice as large as the Mosaic tabernacle in its basic floor area. As a permanent structure, it was much more elaborate and spacious, with appropriate additions and a much larger surrounding court. Although no archaeological remains are known to modern excavators, it is quite likely that the art and architecture were basically Phoenician. Descriptions indicate that the temple and its furnishings were very elaborate, with gold being used freely. The splendor and beauty of this temple apparently were never equaled in the history of Israel.[1]

DEDICATION OF THE TEMPLE

The dedication of the temple was the most significant event in the religious history of the nation since Israel left Mount Sinai. The chronological notation in 1 Kings 6:1 relating the deliverance of Israel from Egypt and the building of the temple is important. Whereas the pillar of cloud hovered over the tabernacle, the glory of God was manifested in the dedication of the temple, signifying God's blessing and benediction. The temple was dedicated as the Israelites gathered in Jerusalem to observe the Feast of Tabernacles, which also reminded them that they once were pilgrims in the wilderness. With Solomon as king, the kingdom of Israel was divinely confirmed as anticipated by Moses (Deut. 17:14-20).

Solomon was the key person in the dedication ceremonies. Under the covenant all Israelites were God's servants (Lev. 25:42, 55; Jer. 30:10, and other passages) and viewed as a kingdom of priests unto God (Exod. 19:6). Solomon, in his unique position as king of God's chosen people, took the position of a servant of God in representing his nation in the dedication ceremonies. This relationship with God was common to prophet, priest, layman, and king in true recognition of the dignity of man. In this capacity Solomon offered prayer, delivered the dedicatory address, and officiated at the offering of sacrifice.

Solomon also built an elaborate palace for himself that took thirteen years to complete. It contained government offices, living quarters for the daughter of pharaoh, and his own private residence. In addition, the maintenance of the powerful army and the administration of the kingdom required building numerous cities, such as Megiddo, throughout the land.

INTERNATIONAL RELATIONS

David had already taken control of Edom and the vast natural resources extending south to the Gulf of Aqaba. Recent archaeological findings[2] indicate that Ezion-geber was a large refining center of iron and copper in the days of Solomon. Aided by Phoenician engineers, the city became the "Pittsburgh of Palestine."

	1 Kings	2 Chronicles
Naval ventures at Ezion-geber	9:26-28	8:17, 18
The Queen of Sheba	10:1-13	9:1-12
Revenue and trade	10:14-29	9:13-31

Control of this metal industry placed the Israelites in an advantageous position in commerce and trade. Through the aid of the

Phoenicians, Solomon built ships that took iron and copper as far as southwest Arabia (modern Yemen) and the African coast of Ethiopia. From there they returned with gold, silver, ivory, and monkeys. Phoenician commerce provided favorable contacts with the Mediterranean world. As a result, Solomon accumulated extensive wealth.

The king acquired horses and chariots from the Hittites through the Arameans. Although David hamstrung or lamed all the horses he captured, with the exception of 100 (2 Sam. 8:4), it is obvious that Solomon accumulated a considerable force. These were helpful for controlling the commerce that crossed Israel's territory. Additional wealth accrued to Israel due to vast camel caravans promoting the spice trade between Southern Arabia, Syria, Phoenicia, and Egypt.

International respect and recognition increased Solomon's wealth by gifts from rulers far and near. People from afar came to hear the wisdom of this Hebrew king expressed in his proverbs, songs, and speeches. The visit of the Queen of Sheba may represent but a sample of the international acclaim. Her 1,200 mile trip by camel very likely was motivated by commercial interests. The wealth and wisdom of Solomon were never exceeded by any Israelite king.

APOSTASY AND DEATH

The final chapter of Solomon's reign as reported in 1 Kings 11 is tragic and disappointing. The simple facts are that the king who had reached the zenith of success and fame in wisdom, wealth, and international acclaim under divine blessing terminated his reign in failure. Like the Israelites in the wilderness after God's revelation to them at Mount Sinai, Solomon departed from wholehearted devotion to God. He broke the very first commandment by his inclusive policy of allowing idol worship at Jerusalem.

FOREIGN WIVES AND IDOLATRY

Solomon also conformed to contemporary culture by making alliances with foreign rulers and confirming this by marriage (1 Kings 11:1-8). By taking wives from Egypt, the Moabites, Ammonites, Edomites, Sidonians, and Hittites, Solomon permitted idolatry to prevail in the environs of the temple he had erected to God. The multiplicity of wives resulted in his ruination, as his heart was turned away from God (Deut. 17:17). Some of the gods for whom Solomon built high places were not removed until the times of Josiah, three and a half centuries later (2 Kings 23:13).

JUDGMENT AND ADVERSARIES

While Solomon was still living, the stage was set for the disruption of the kingdom. Because of disobedience, the kingdom was to be divided according to the words of the prophet Ahijah (1 Kings 11:9-43). For David's sake, the judgment was withheld until after the death of Solomon. Enemies and strong leaders such as Hadad the Edomite, Rezon of Damascus, and Jeroboam, to whom the prophet Ahijah gave ten pieces of his mantle to indicate that he would rule over ten tribes, began to threaten the rule of Solomon. Even though the kingdom was not divided until after his death, Solomon was subjected to the anguish of rebellion at home and secession in various parts of his empire as a result of his personal failure to obey and serve God faithfully.

DISCUSSION QUESTIONS

1. What was Solomon's greatest concern when he became king?
2. Who furnished architects, foremen, and building supplies for the temple?
3. Describe briefly the temple itself.
4. How did Solomon make payment for the building material?
5. Describe briefly the dedication of the temple.
6. How was God's presence apparent at the dedication?
7. Why did the Queen of Sheba come to see Solomon?
8. What physical factors aided Solomon in accumulating great wealth?
9. How did foreign wives influence Solomon?
10. Why did God withhold judgment upon Solomon during his life?
11. What characteristics and abilities made Solomon a great king and leader? What characteristics and weaknesses led to his decline? Which of these are applicable to Christian leadership today?
12. Compare and contrast the reign of Solomon with the reign of his father, David. What factors of parental influence can be observed in this study?
13. Trace the events leading to the division of the kingdom. What specific sin was at the root of the problems? Discuss the extent of its consequences.
14. What great principles of prayer worthy of emulation can be observed in Solomon's dedicatory prayer?
15. Compare the dedication of the temple with the dedication of the tabernacle. What aspects of these dedications could be applied in the dedication of a new church building?

Chapter Nine

THE NORTHERN KINGDOM

REBELLION AFTER THE death of Solomon resulted in the division of the Davidic empire. To the north ten tribes rebelled against the Davidic dynasty ruling in Jerusalem and established the Northern Kingdom under the leadership of Jeroboam. Beyond the Northern Kingdom to the northeast, the Syrians or Arameans declared their independence under the leadership of Rezon with Damascus as their capital. Rehoboam, the son of Solomon, retained only the tribes of Judah and Benjamin for his kingdom, continuing to use Jerusalem as his capital.

The biblical account of the Northern Kingdom is given in 1 Kings 12 to 2 Kings 17. Interwoven with it are the contemporary events in the Southern Kingdom. Although the name Israel was originally given to Jacob and subsequently used to designate his descendants, it was normally used during the divided kingdom era to refer to the Northern Kingdom. Another name for this kingdom was Ephraim (cf. Isa. 7; Hosea), which originally referred to Joseph's son and later to one of the tribes.

The Northern Kingdom lasted approximately two centuries (931–722 B.C.). Changes in ruling families or dynasties occurred quite frequently. For our study purposes the developments in the Northern Kingdom may be conveniently divided as given below. Of special interest also are the prophets who ministered during these centuries, confronting the kings and the people with God's message.

Dynasty of Jeroboam, 931-909 B.C.	1 Kings 12–15
Dynasty of Baasha, 909-885 B.C.	1 Kings 15–16
Dynasty of Omri, 885-841 B.C.	1 Kings 16–22; 2 Kings 1–9
Dynasty of Jehu, 841-752 B.C.	2 Kings 10–15
Last Kings of Israel, 752-722 B.C.	2 Kings 15–17

THE ROYAL FAMILY OF JEROBOAM

Jeroboam distinguished himself as an efficient administrator under Solomon, who placed him in charge of constructing the wall of Jerusalem, known as Millo. A prophet named Ahijah dramatically conveyed to Jeroboam the future developments by giving him ten pieces of his mantle, signifying that Jeroboam would rule over ten tribes (1 Kings 11). Arousing the suspicion of Solomon, Jeroboam temporarily took refuge in Egypt, but he returned to Shechem when the elders of Israel rebelled against Rehoboam. Here he was recognized as the first king of the Northern Kingdom, reigning for twenty-two years. Although civil warfare and bloodshed were averted at this time of secession, periodic wars between Jeroboam and Rehoboam erupted, which are merely noted in the biblical record (2 Chron. 12:15).

Religious Trends

In religious matters Jeroboam took the initiative in leading his people astray. Fearing that the people might be diverted in their political loyalty by going to Jerusalem to worship, Jeroboam instituted idolatry by erecting golden calves at Bethel and Dan. Ignoring Mosaic restrictions, he appointed priests and allowed the Israelites to offer sacrifices at high places throughout the land. Jeroboam even officiated at the altar and changed feast days (cf. 1 Kings 12:25-33).

Warned by Two Prophets

The experience of an unnamed prophet from Judah is dramatically portrayed in 1 Kings 13. Jeroboam is realistically confronted with a warning that tempered his aggressiveness in promoting idolatry. The sequel to the faithful ministry of this unnamed prophet deserves careful study. Perhaps the tomb of this prophet, who was killed by a lion and brought back to Bethel for burial, serves as a reminder to succeeding generations that obedience to God is essential even for a messenger of God.

Another prophet who warned Jeroboam was Ahijah. When Jeroboam's wife inquired of Ahijah regarding the prospect of the recovery of their son, Abijah, the king of Israel was not only informed that his son would die but that the dynasty of Jeroboam would be exterminated. This was divine judgment for failure to obey the commandments of God. When Jeroboam died, his son Nadab ruled only two years. Nadab was assassinated by Baasha.

THE DYNASTY OF BAASHA

Little is known about Baasha, of the tribe of Issachar, who became the next king of Israel. Apparently he made Tirzah the capital. When many of his people seemed to desert to Judah, Baasha began to fortify the city of Ramah where the two main roads from the north converge, leading to Jerusalem only five miles south. Fearing these developments, King Asa of Jerusalem bribed Benhadad of Damascus to attack Israel. When Benhadad took control of such cities as Kedesh, Hazor, Merom, and Zephath and acquired the rich fertile acreage west of Lake Galilee, the Syrians accrued the lucrative returns from the caravan trade to the Phoenician coast. As a result, Baasha abandoned his fortification of Ramah, averting war with Judah.

THE PROPHET JEHU

Jehu, the son of Hanani, was active in proclaiming God's message during the reign of Baasha. He reminded the king that he should serve God, who had entrusted him with the kingship, but unfortunately Baasha continued in the sinful idolatrous ways of Jeroboam.

ELAH THE KING

Elah, the son of Baasha, ruled less than two years. While drunk, Elah was assassinated by Zimri. The prophetic words of Jehu were fulfilled as Zimri exterminated the friends and relatives of this ruling family. Zimri, however, ruled only seven days.

THE ROYAL FAMILY OF OMRI

The most notorious dynasty in the Northern Kingdom was established by Omri. Best known in this family was his son Ahab, who was succeeded by his two sons, Ahaziah and Joram. During this period Israel not only regained much territory lost in Syria but also gained international renown.

OMRI THE KING

When Zimri slew Elah, the Israelite troops—encamped against Gibbethon—were under Omri's command. Omri marched his troops against Tirzah, and Zimri secluded himself in the palace while it was reduced to ashes. When Tibni, who apparently was a strong leader, died six years later, Omri was sole ruler of Israel.

Omri's twelve-year reign is summarized in eight verses in the Bible (1 Kings 16:21-28). His reign, however, was very significant. He built the city of Samaria on a site seven miles northwest of Shechem. Strategically located on the road leading to Phoenicia, Galilee, and Esdraelon, Samaria was secured as the impregnable capital of Israel for over a century and a half, until it was conquered by the Assyrians in 722 B.C.

Omri promoted an international policy that established Israel's prestige. Apparently he subjected the Moabites, exacting taxes from them. He made an alliance with Phoenicia, which was sealed by the marriage of his son Ahab to Jezebel, the daughter of Ethbaal, the king of the Sidonians. This relationship was commercially advantageous to Israel, but it resulted in a degrading religious fusion in the next generation. Very likely Omri regained the economic and territorial losses Baasha had suffered under Syrian aggression. So great and extensive was Omri's international fame that in subsequent times the Assyrian records referred to Israel as the land of Omri.

AHAB AND JEZEBEL

Ahab, the son of Omri, expanded the political and commercial interests of Israel during his twenty-two-year reign. Increasing trade with the Phoenicians represented a serious threat to the lucrative trading interests of Syria. A policy of friendship with Judah, sealed by the marriage of Ahab's daughter Athaliah to Jehoram, the son of Jehoshaphat, strengthened Israel against Syria. From Moab, Ahab exacted a heavy tribute of livestock. With wealth accruing to Israel through these economic policies, Ahab was able to build and fortify many cities, including Jericho, and to lavish wealth on himself by building an "ivory house" (1 Kings 22:39).

AHAB'S RELIGION

Baal worship was promoted under Ahab and Jezebel. To this god of Tyre the king of Israel built a temple in the city of Samaria. Ahab brought hundreds of prophets into Israel, and Baalism became the religion of his people. Consequently, Ahab gained the reputation of being the most sinful of all the kings who ruled Israel. Jezebel is portrayed as the degrading influence behind the throne.

ELIJAH THE PROPHET

Elijah stepped forth in this era of rank apostasy as a forthright spokesman for God. After a three-and-one-half-year drought, he dramatically challenged Baalism and supervised the execution of Jezebel's prophets on Mount Carmel. Fearing the queen, Elijah retreated to the Sinai Peninsula where he received a threefold commission—to anoint

Hazael as king of Syria, to anoint Jehu as king of Israel, and to call Elisha as his successor. On his return to Israel, Elijah called Elisha to be his associate in the prophetic ministry.

A final encounter between Elijah and Ahab took place in Naboth's vineyard (1 Kings 21:1-29). Ruthless Jezebel, who had no respect for Israelite law and gave no heed to Naboth's conscientious refusal to sell his inherited possession to the king, engineered the stoning of Naboth. As Ahab took possession of this vineyard, he was severely rebuked by Elijah. For this gross injustice in shedding innocent blood, the Omride dynasty was doomed. Ahab's repentance tempered this judgment only by postponement until after his death.

WARFARE WITH SYRIA

Toward the end of Ahab's reign there seemed to have been frequent warfare with Syria. When faced by a common enemy, however, Israel and Syria joined forces, as is indicated by the battle of Karkar. Shortly after this, Ahab persuaded Jehoshaphat, the king of Judah, to join him in a battle against Syria (1 Kings 22:1-40). After Ahab was warned by the prophet Micaiah that he would be killed in this battle, Ahab disguised himself so that the Syrians would not recognize him. However, a stray arrow pierced Ahab, wounding him fatally and fulfilling the words of Elijah (1 Kings 21:19).

AHAZIAH—KING OF ISRAEL

This son of Ahab ruled only one year. He failed to suppress the rebellion of Moab and unsuccessfully launched naval expeditions with Jehoshaphat at the Gulf of Aqaba. Elijah's last encounter with the Omride dynasty in the biblical account was the warning to Ahaziah that he would not recover (2 Kings 1).

JORAM—THE SON OF AHAB

The twelve-year reign of Joram terminated the Omride rule in Israel in 841 B.C. During these years intermittent warfare was carried on between Israel and Syria. Apparently Syria increased in military strength so that when Joram's reign ended, Syria emerged as the dominating kingdom in Palestine.

ELIJAH AND ELISHA

These two prophets had cooperated in establishing schools for prophets throughout Israel. Apparently Elijah's ascension occurred near the beginning of Joram's reign so that Elisha became the leading prophet in Israel.

Numerous events are recorded in which Elisha was closely associated with Joram in his military problems as he sought to regain control of Moab and fight against Syria.

Elisha's ministry was known not only throughout Israel but also in Syria as well as in Judah and Edom. Through the healing of Naaman and the peculiar encounter of the Syrian armies with this prophet, Elisha was recognized as the "man of God" even in the Syrian capital Damascus. Near the end of Joram's reign, Elisha made a visit to Damascus to inform Hazael that he would be the next king of Syria (2 Kings 8:7-15). While Joram was recovering at Jezreel from a wound he had received in battle, Elisha sent his servant to anoint Jehu king of Israel. Being commander of the Israelite army, Jehu proclaimed himself king and killed Joram, the king of Israel, as well as Ahaziah, the king of Judah.

THE DYNASTY OF JEHU

This ruling family occupied the throne of the Northern Kingdom for a longer period than any other dynasty—nearly a century (841-753 B.C.). During this time Israel rose from an extremely weakened position to a strong kingdom reaching its peak in international prestige and prosperity under Jeroboam II.

JEHU

A bloody revolution brought Jehu to the throne. Not only did Jehu dispose of the royal family, including Jezebel, but he also exterminated Baalism, making a clean sweep in religion and politics. By exterminating the Omride family, Jehu incurred the disfavor of Phoenicia and Judah. Seeking to avert Assyrian aggression, he sent tribute to Shalmaneser III but thereby faced the antagonism of Hazael, king of Syria, who enlarged his kingdom southward by claiming Gilead and Bashan at Israel's expense. Idolatry, however, still prevailed under Jehu.

JEHOAHAZ

When Jehu died in 814 B.C., Hazael took further advantage of Israel during the reign of Jehoahaz. So weak was Israel at this time that Hazael advanced his armies through Israel to capture Gath and threaten Jerusalem (2 Kings 12:17). Jehoahaz was so helpless that he was ineffective in resisting invasion by the Edomites, Ammonites, Philistines, and Tyrians. Although Jehoahaz temporarily turned to God for relief from this pressure, he did not depart from idolatry nor destroy the images of the gods in Samaria (2 Kings 13:1-9).

JEHOASH

During the reign of Jehoash (798-782 B.C.), Israel's successes revived. With the death of Hazael (ca. 800 B.C.), Syrian power declined. Israel built up a strong fighting force, placing Benhadad II of Syria on the defensive and reclaiming much territory. When Jehoash was challenged by Amaziah of Judah, the Israelite army invaded Judah, broke down part of the wall of Jerusalem, plundered the palace and temple, and even took hostages back to Samaria.

Elisha the prophet was still living when Jehoash began to reign. The silence of the Scriptures warrants the conclusion that neither Jehu nor Jehoahaz had much to do with Elisha, but Jehoash went down to see Elisha on his deathbed. In a dramatic incident the prophet assured victory over Syria to the king of Israel. Although Jehoash was disturbed over the loss of Elisha, he did not serve God nor turn from his idolatrous ways. His reign, however, marked the turning point in the blessings of Israel as Elisha had predicted.

KING JEROBOAM II

Jeroboam, the fourth ruler in Jehu's dynasty, was the outstanding king in the Northern Kingdom. He ruled forty-one years, including a twelve-year co-regency with his father (793-753 B.C.). The vast political and commercial expansion of Israel under his leadership is summarized in the prophecy given by Jonah (2 Kings 14:23-29). With Syria being threatened by Assyria, it was possible for Jeroboam to regain Israelite borders to the east and north. The wall of Samaria was widened and the city refortified. Peace and prosperity unequaled since the days of Solomon brought to Israel wealth and luxury reflected in the books of Amos and Hosea. With prosperity came the moral decline and religious indifference these two prophets boldly challenged.

When Jeroboam died in 753 B.C., he was succeeded by his son, Zechariah, whose reign lasted only six months. Zechariah was murdered by Shallum.

THE LAST KINGS—753–723 B.C.

These three decades mark the decline and fall of the Northern Kingdom as the Assyrians extended their control into the land of Palestine. From its highest peak of commercial and political prosperity, Israel fell in this short period to a state of Assyrian vassalage.

MENAHEM AND PEKAHIAH

Menahem ruled Israel for approximately ten years after Shallum's one-month rule ended in his assassination. Facing aggression by Tiglath-pileser III, or Pul, who ascended the Assyrian throne in 745 B.C., Menahem paid tribute in order to avoid invasion. Pekahiah, his son, maintained the same policy of subservience during his two-year rule.

PEKAH—739–731 B.C.

Pekah very likely led a movement of revolt against Assyria and was responsible for the assassination of Pekahiah. In Syria a new king, Rezin, provided aggressive leadership. Facing a common foe, these two kings formed an alliance to resist Assyria. Judah up to this time had provided aggressive leadership in resisting Assyria, but in 735 Ahaz was enthroned in Jerusalem by a pro-Assyrian party. Although the Syro-Israelite alliance tried to coerce Judah to support them by invading Judah (2 Kings 16:5-9; 2 Chron. 28:5-15; Isa. 7:1–8:8), the attempt ended in failure. In 732 B.C. Tiglath-pileser conquered Syria by occupying Damascus. Rezin was killed. In Samaria the Israelites killed Pekah and enthroned Hoshea as a vassal of the king of Assyria.

HOSHEA—THE LAST KING

When Shalmaneser V succeeded Tiglath-pileser III on the Assyrian throne in 727 B.C., Hoshea discontinued his tributary payments to Assyria, depending on Egypt for help. By 726 the Assyrian king besieged Samaria. After a three-year siege Hoshea was forced to surrender. This ended the Northern Kingdom.

Under the Assyrian policy of scattering conquered people, 28,000 Israelites were taken captive and dispersed into the regions of Persia. In return, colonists from Babylonia were settled in Samaria, and Israel was reduced to the status of an Assyrian province.

For over two centuries the Israelites had followed the pattern set by Jeroboam I who led his people into idolatry, breaking the first commandment in the Decalogue. Prophet after prophet warned the kings as well as the people of impending judgment. For their gross idolatry and their failure to heed the admonition to serve God, the Israelites were subjected to captivity (2 Kings 17:1-23).

DISCUSSION QUESTIONS

1. By what other names was the Northern Kingdom known?
2. How did Ahijah inform Jeroboam that he would be a king?
3. Why was the prophet from Judah killed on his return trip?
4. Why did Baasha abandon his fortification of Ramah?
5. What did Omri do to establish Israel as a strong nation?
6. How did Ahab promote the religion of Baal?
7. How did Elijah oppose Ahab?
8. Why was the Northern Kingdom so weak under Jehu?
9. Who predicted the expansion of Israel under Jeroboam II?
10. What finally caused the fall of the Northern Kingdom?
11. What leadership qualifications that Elijah and Elisha possessed led to spiritual interest on the part of the people?
12. Give evidences of the grace of God manifested toward the Northern Kingdom.
13. Trace the religious conditions throughout the period of the Northern Kingdom. Compare the conditions to those in the Southern Kingdom.
14. Show how God's power was manifested through the miracles performed by His prophets Elijah and Elisha during this period. What was the evident response to these miracles? To what degree are miracles necessary if people are to follow God?

Chapter Ten

THE KINGDOM OF JUDAH

Rehoboam—Jotham

ONLY TWO TRIBES REMAINED loyal to the Davidic dynasty ruling in Jerusalem after the death of Solomon. Whereas ruling families and capitals changed frequently in the Northern Kingdom, the descendants of David, with one exception, retained continuous royal leadership in the capital city established by David.

Judah, also known as the Southern Kingdom, continued its established rule for nearly three and a half centuries, beginning with Rehoboam, the son of Solomon (931-586 B.C.). A total of twenty kings ruled in Judah during this period. Twelve of these were contemporary with the rulers in the Northern Kingdom.

This long period of Judah's history can conveniently be considered by focusing attention upon four kings who exerted outstanding leadership. For each of these kings we suggest an approximate date that highlights this period chronologically:[1]

Jehoshaphat	850 B.C.
Uzziah	750 B.C.
Hezekiah	700 B.C.
Josiah	630 B.C.

The biblical account of the Southern Kingdom is given in the books of 1 and 2 Kings in its relationship to the developments in the Northern Kingdom. Supplementary information is provided in 2 Chronicles, which is primarily devoted to the history of the Davidic dynasty.

THE ERA OF JEHOSHAPHAT

An abrupt change took place in Jerusalem after Solomon died in 931 B.C. Rehoboam faced rebellion and a disruption of the great empire that he inherited. Numerous leaders—Jeroboam in the northern tribes, Rezon in Damascus, and Hadad in Edom—championed the cause of their own people and challenged the rule of the Solomonic successor.

CAUSE OF DISRUPTION

Two reasons are given in Scripture for the termination of the union of Israel that had been established by David. The northern tribes rebelled against the excessive taxation and the threat of heavier levies by Rehoboam. The biblical narrative also points explicitly to Solomon's apostasy and idolatry as a cause for divine judgment (1 Kings 11:9-13). For David's sake this division did not occur until after the death of Solomon (2 Sam. 7:12-16).

Rehoboam made plans to suppress the Israelite rebellion. When he called for troops, only the tribes of Judah and Benjamin responded to support him. A prophet Shemaiah advised Rehoboam not to fight against the seceding tribes. In the early years of his reign, Rehoboam was further humbled by an invasion by Shishak, the ruler of Egypt. Shemaiah assured the leaders of Judah that they would not be destroyed, even though the Egyptians raided Jerusalem and appropriated some of the temple treasures.

Although Rehoboam apparently began his reign with sincere religious devotion, he soon succumbed to prevailing idolatrous influences. His seventeen-year reign and the short three-year rule of his son Abijam were characterized by apostasy and idolatry, even though the service of God in the temple was maintained. The prophet Iddo may have warned these kings of their sinful ways.

ASA'S REFORMS

Asa's forty-one-year reign (910–869 B.C.) prepared the way for the religious revival that prevailed under Jehoshaphat. Asa began a program of reform, admonishing the people to keep the Mosaic Law. When attacked by the Ethiopians from the south, Asa repulsed them with divine aid. Admonished by the prophet Azariah, King Asa removed idols throughout the land, crushed and burned the image of Asherah—the Canaanite goddess of fertility—in the valley of Kidron, and removed Maacah as queen mother.

When the religious celebrations in Jerusalem attracted the people from the Northern Kingdom, Baasha began to fortify Ramah, five miles north of Jerusalem. Fearing this as a military threat, Asa sent a bribe to Benhadad, king of Syria. When Syria seized Israelite territory in the north, Baasha withdrew his forces from Ramah.

For this alliance with Syria, the king of Judah was severely rebuked by a prophet named Hanani. Asa should have trusted God instead of depending upon the help of a heathen king. Unfortunately Asa did not respond favorably to God's warning, for he imprisoned the prophet. Two years before his death, Asa was stricken by a fatal disease.

THE REIGN OF JEHOSHAPHAT

The twenty-five-year reign of Jehoshaphat (872–848 B.C.) was one of the most encouraging and helpful eras in the religious history of Judah. Since Jehoshaphat was thirty-five years old when he began to reign, he very likely had come under the influence of Judah's great religious leaders during the early years of his life. Under a well-organized program he sent princes, priests, and Levites throughout the land to teach the people the Law.

Internationally this was a period of peace. The Philistines and Arabs acknowledged the superiority of Judah by bringing presents and tribute to Jehoshaphat. This enabled the king of Judah to build fortresses and store cities throughout the land where he stationed military units. In addition, he had five army commanders in Jerusalem who were directly responsible to him.

When Jehoshaphat was threatened by a terrifying invasion of Moabites and Edomites from the southeast, he proclaimed a fast in all the cities of Judah. In the court of the temple the king himself led a prayer expressing his faith in God in the simple words "neither know we what to do; but our eyes are upon thee." Through Jahaziel, a Levite of the sons of Asaph, the assembly received the divine assurance that even without fighting they would see a great victory. When Judah marched toward the enemy, the invaders were thrown into confusion and massacred each other. After collecting spoils for three days, Jehoshaphat led his people triumphantly back to Jerusalem, and the fear of God fell on the nations round about.

ALLIANCE WITH THE OMRIDE DYNASTY

Friendly relations prevailed between Judah and Israel during the days of Jehoshaphat. For his alliance with the godless ruling family in the Northern Kingdom, Jehoshaphat was severely rebuked on numerous occasions. Very likely this affinity between these two royal families began early in Jehoshaphat's reign. He sealed the alliance with the marriage of his son Jehoram[2] to Athaliah, the daughter of Ahab and Jezebel. Even though this relationship with the Omride dynasty provided Judah with a friendly nation to the north as a protection from other nations, Jehoshaphat was rebuked by at least four prophets.

MICAIAH

Before Israel and Judah joined in the battle against Syria in which Ahab was killed, Jehoshaphat had an uneasy conscience when the 400 Israelite prophets predicted success in this venture. To pacify Jehoshaphat, the prophet Micaiah was called before the kings, solemnly warning that the king of Israel would be killed (1 Kings 22). Jehoshaphat narrowly escaped death.

JEHU THE PROPHET

When Jehoshaphat returned to Jerusalem from this battle, he was confronted by Jehu with the words: "Shouldest thou help the ungodly, and love them that hate the Lord?" (2 Chron. 19:2).

ELIEZER

After Ahab's death Jehoshaphat continued his affinity with Israel in an alliance with Ahaziah, the son of Ahab. Together these kings launched ships at Ezion-geber for commercial purposes. In accordance with the prediction of the prophet Eliezer, these ships were wrecked (2 Chron. 20:35-37).

ELISHA

When Joram, the son of Ahab who succeeded Ahaziah on the throne of Israel, attempted to suppress Moab, Jehoshaphat joined in this military venture. At one point the armies of Judah, Israel, and Edom were in a desperate condition for lack of water, and the prophet Elisha appeared before the three kings in charge. In the presence of this prophet, Jehoshaphat was once more made conscious of the fact that he was in an alliance with ungodly kings (2 Kings 3:1-27).

Within a decade the results of Jehoshaphat's policy of ungodly alliances unfolded in Judah. When Jehoshaphat died in 848 B.C., Jehoram as king not only executed six of his brothers but also espoused the sinful ways of Ahab and Jezebel. This change in religion may reasonably be attributed to Athaliah. According to 2 Chronicles 21:11-15, Elijah the prophet severely reproached Jehoram, who died in 841 B.C. of an incurable disease.

Ahaziah, the son of Jehoram, ruled for less than a year. Visiting his Uncle Joram, the son of Ahab, Ahaziah was killed by Jehu, who exterminated the Omride dynasty and began to reign in Samaria. In Jerusalem

Athaliah, the mother of Ahaziah, seized the Davidic throne and began a six-year reign of terror. To secure her position, she began the execution of the royal family. What Jezebel had done to the prophets in Israel, Athaliah did to the royal family to whom the Davidic promise had been made of an eternal throne (2 Sam. 7:12-16). Providentially, a son, Joash, was saved, and the Davidic dynasty was restored after the execution of Athaliah.

THE ERA OF UZZIAH (AZARIAH)

Joash was enthroned at the age of seven in 835 B.C. and reigned until 796 B.C. During the early decades of his reign, Joash was guided and influenced by Jehoiada, a priest who was responsible for his enthronement. The temple with its services had suffered under the three preceding rulers but was now restored. However, when Jehoiada died, apostasy swept the kingdom of Judah so extensively that when Zechariah, the son of Jehoiada, warned the people that they would not prosper if they continued to disobey the commandments of the Lord, he was stoned in the court of the temple.

Joash was threatened by Syrian aggression. When the Syrians conquered Gath, Joash stripped the temple of its dedicated treasures and sent them to Hazael to avoid invasion. Presumably, failure to pay tribute brought the Syrian armies to Jerusalem after the turn of the century. Judah's capital was invaded, and before the Syrians left with the spoils, they killed some of the princes and wounded Joash, who was subsequently slain by his palace servants. This judgment came upon the king who permitted apostasy to permeate Judah and even tolerated the shedding of innocent blood.

AMAZIAH

Amaziah, who is credited with a total of twenty-nine-years' rule (796-767 B.C.), actually ruled only a short period. Uzziah apparently was made co-regent with his father in 791.

The death of Hazael in Damascus at the turn of the century provided relief from Syrian aggression for the kingdom of Judah as well as for Israel. Amaziah developed his military strength sufficiently to recover control over Edom. Proud of his military victory, he challenged Jehoash of Israel to a battle. As a result Judah was invaded by the Israelites, who not only plundered Jerusalem but also broke down part of the wall and took royal hostages. King Amaziah was also captured and probably held captive in Israel until 782 when Jehoash died.[3]

The Reign of Uzziah or Azariah

When Amaziah broke the peace that had existed between Judah and Israel for almost 100 years, the national hopes of the Southern Kingdom sank to the lowest point since the division of Solomon's kingdom. Apparently Uzziah was made co-regent in 791 and guided the affairs of state during the remainder of Amaziah's reign, assuming full control in 767 when his father was assassinated.

Gradually but constructively Uzziah initiated policies that brought about the restoration of Judah. Very likely he rebuilt the walls of Jerusalem. Judah's vassalage to Israel must have terminated, at the latest, with Amaziah's death or perhaps with his release fifteen years earlier. Apparently a policy of friendliness and cooperation prevailed between Jeroboam II and Uzziah.

With a program of military preparedness and economic expansion, Uzziah brought the Philistines, the Edomites, and Ammonites under his control, extending Judah's borders to the Gulf of Aqaba. Throughout the kingdom, he provided wells needed for large herds in desert areas and erected towers for the protection of vinedressers as they expanded their production. Copper and iron mining industries, which had flourished under Solomon, were revived in the Sinai Peninsula. Judah's growth and influence during this period were second only to those experienced in Davidic and Solomonic times.

Uzziah's prosperity was directly related to his dependence upon God (2 Chron. 26:5, 7). Zechariah, a prophet otherwise unknown, effectively instructed the king, who until about 750 B.C. had a wholesome and humble attitude toward God. At the height of his success, however, Uzziah assumed that he could enter the temple and burn incense. With the support of eighty priests, the high priest Azariah confronted Uzziah with the fact that this was the prerogative of those consecrated for this purpose (cf. Exod. 30:7; Num. 18:1-7). In anger the king defied the priests. As a result of divine judgment, Uzziah became leprous. For the rest of his reign he was ostracized from the palace and denied ordinary social privileges. He could not even enter the temple. Jotham was made co-ruler in 750 B.C. and assumed the royal responsibilities for the remainder of his father's life.

With the death of Jeroboam in 753 B.C., the Southern Kingdom that had been so solidly built under Uzziah emerged as the strongest power in Canaan. Very likely Uzziah cherished hopes of restoring the whole Solomonic empire to Judah, but these were soon shattered by the rising power of Assyria. When Tiglath-pileser III of Assyria began in 745 B.C.

to move his armies westward, Azariah, the king of Judah, is mentioned as leading the opposition. In the meantime, Menahem paid tribute to the Assyrian king in behalf of Israel.

Jotham assumed sole control of Judah when Uzziah died in 740 B.C. This marked a crucial year in the history of Judah, with the passing of the king who had restored Judah from its vassalage to Israel and made the Southern Kingdom the most powerful nation in Palestine. The impending threat of Assyrian invasion clouded future national hopes. This was also the year in which Isaiah was called to be the prophet of God in Jerusalem. Jotham continued an anti-Assyrian policy as he assumed the leadership of Judah, but in 735 B.C. a pro-Assyrian party elevated Jotham's son Ahaz to the throne.

DISCUSSION QUESTIONS

1. How does the account in Kings differ from the account in Chronicles?
2. What were the causes of the disruption of the Solomonic kingdom when Rehoboam became king?
3. What did Asa do to promote a religious revival?
4. Why was Jehoshaphat concerned about joining Ahab in battle?
5. Whose influence did Athaliah reflect when she reigned in Judah?
6. How did the influence of Jehoiada affect the kingdom of Judah?
7. How did the aggressive policies of Hazael in Syria affect Judah?
8. How did Uzziah establish Judah economically?
9. Why was Uzziah smitten with leprosy?
10. What was Uzziah's policy toward Assyria?
11. Compare the religious influence of Jehoshaphat in Judah and in Israel. What dangers of association or friendship with the ungodly are seen in Jehoshaphat's experience?
12. How were the central movements in this study directly resultant from failure to keep the commands of God? What one commandment was consistently broken? Do world kings and leaders face similar situations today? What words of warning do they need from God's messengers?
13. Trace the evidences of the grace of God manifested toward the Southern Kingdom.
14. What was the extent of the influence the prophets exercised over the kings studied in this chapter? To what degree should the clergy influence politicians?
15. List the messianic line of kings in the Southern Kingdom.

Chapter Eleven

THE KINGDOM OF JUDAH

Ahaz—Zedekiah

HEZEKIAH AND JOSIAH ARE the best-known kings during the last century and a half (735–586 B.C.) of Judah's existence as a kingdom. Both kings were reformers who took the initiative in leading their people back to God and postponing the judgment announced by the prophets upon Jerusalem.

AHAZ—FATHER OF HEZEKIAH

The nations in Palestine were on the verge of being overrun by the Assyrian armies when Ahaz was enthroned (735 B.C.) in Jerusalem by a pro-Assyrian party in the kingdom of Judah. Simultaneously, Pekah in Israel and Rezin in Syria formed an anti-Assyrian alliance. To secure themselves against attack from the south, these two kings waged the Syro-Ephraimite war against Judah, taking thousands of Judeans captive. Warned by a prophet named Oded, the king of Israel released the prisoners of war.

ISAIAH'S WARNING

When Ahaz faced the threat of invasion, Isaiah was sent to meet him with the admonition to place his trust in God. Isaiah told Ahaz that the two kings from the north would be dethroned (Isa. 7–9). Ignoring and defying Isaiah, the king of Judah appealed to Tiglath-pileser, the king of Assyria, for aid. This brought immediate results. As a result of Assyrian aggression, the kingdom of Syria was terminated with the death of Rezin, and Israel was made tributary with Hoshea replacing Pekah in 732 B.C. Ahaz himself met the Assyrian king in Damascus, participating with him in pagan religious rites and pledging his loyalty.

AHAZ'S CONTINUED IDOLATRY AND EVENTUAL DEATH

Ahaz promoted the most obnoxious idolatrous practices. Taking the measurements of the altar in Damascus, Ahaz ordered Urijah the priest to duplicate this altar in the temple in Jerusalem. Ahaz took the lead in pagan worship, had his son walk through the fire according to heathen customs, and took treasures from the temple to meet the demands of the Assyrian king. Even though he guided his nation successfully through this period of international crises, he incurred God's wrath. In subsequent periods the Assyrian power extended into Judah like a razor in God's hand (Isa. 7:20) and like a river (Isa. 8:7), according to the prediction of Isaiah.

HEZEKIAH—A RIGHTEOUS KING

When Hezekiah began his reign in 716 B.C. in Jerusalem, the Northern Kingdom had already capitulated to the Assyrian advance with the fall of Samaria in 722. Throughout his twenty-nine-year reign, Hezekiah reversed the political and religious policies his wicked father had initiated.

With a keen realization that Israel's captivity was the consequence of a broken covenant and disobedience to God (2 Kings 18:9-12), Hezekiah placed his confidence in God as he began an effective reform. Levites were called in to repair and cleanse the temple for worship, idols were removed, vessels were sanctified, and sacrifices were initiated, accompanied by liturgical singing. In an attempt to heal the religious breach that had prevailed between the two kingdoms since Solomon's death, Hezekiah sent invitations to the people of the northern tribes to participate in the observance of the Passover in Jerusalem. At no time since the dedication of the temple had Jerusalem experienced such a joyful celebration. Even the bronze serpent erected by Moses (Num. 21:4–9), used by the people as an object of worship, was destroyed.

Politically, Hezekiah acknowledged the overlordship of Sargon II (721–705 B.C.), since Judah had already been committed to Assyrian vassalage under Ahaz. This policy averted interference in Judah when Sargon dispatched his troops to Ashdod, west of Jerusalem in 711 B.C. (Isa. 20:1).

In the meantime, Hezekiah concentrated on a construction defense program, organizing and equipping his army. To assure Jerusalem of an adequate water supply in case of a prolonged siege, Hezekiah constructed a tunnel connecting the Siloam pool with the spring of Gihon. Through 1,777 feet of solid rock, the Judean engineers channeled fresh water into the pool of Siloam, which was also constructed at this time. Ever since its discovery in 1880, when the inscription on it was deciphered, the Siloam tunnel has been an attraction for tourists. The wall of Jerusalem was also extended to enclose the Siloam pool.

Although Hezekiah did all in his power to prepare for an Assyrian invasion, he did not depend only upon human resources but publicly expressed his dependence upon God before his people, assembled in the city square, in these words: "With him is an arm of flesh; but with us is the LORD our God to help us and to fight our battles" (2 Chron. 32:8).

With the accession of Sennacherib to the Assyrian throne in 705, rebellions broke out in many parts of the Assyrian empire. In 701 Sennacherib marched his armies into Palestine, boasting in his own records that he conquered forty-six walled cities in the maritime plain. After exacting a large tribute from Hezekiah, the king of Assyria demanded the surrender of Jerusalem. Encouraged by Isaiah, Hezekiah placed his trust in God for deliverance. Before Sennacherib could fulfill his threat, he received word of a revolt in Babylon. Immediately he rushed back east, boasting that he had taken 200,000 prisoners but simply noting that Hezekiah had been shut up like a bird in a cage.

This successful resistance in 701 brought to Hezekiah the acclaim and recognition of the surrounding nations, expressed in abundant gifts (2 Chron. 32:23). Not least among those sending congratulations was Merodach-baladan of Babylon, who also had heard of Hezekiah's recovery from a severe illness. After Hezekiah displayed his wealth to the Babylonian embassy, the prophet Isaiah warned the king of Judah of impending judgment on Jerusalem, but tempered his warning by the assurance that he would have a period of peace during his reign.

Sennacherib did not conclude his efforts to suppress rebellions in the Tigris-Euphrates area until he destroyed Babylon in 689 B.C. Hearing about Tirhakah (2 Kings 19:9ff.), he directed his interests westward once more. This time he sent letters to Hezekiah with an ultimatum to surrender. Hezekiah, who had experienced a previous deliverance and since then had enjoyed over a decade of peace and prosperity, calmly but confidently spread these letters before the Lord as he prayed in the temple. Isaiah sent words of assurance. The Assyrian armies never reached Jerusalem, but were destroyed somewhere en route—possibly in the Arabian Desert. Sennacherib returned to Nineveh, where he was killed by two of his sons in 681 B.C.

Hezekiah, unlike a number of his predecessors, was buried in honor when he died in 686 B.C. Not only had he led his people in the greatest reformation in Judah's history, but he had also given religious leadership to many people from the northern tribes.

JOSIAH'S PREDECESSORS

Nearly half a century passed between the end of Hezekiah's reign and the enthronement of Josiah (686–640 B.C.). Manasseh, who had been made co-regent with his father in 696, reigned until 642. He was succeeded by his son Amon.

MANASSEH

Manasseh plunged Judah into its darkest era of idolatry by erecting altars to Baal and constructing idols comparable only to Ahab and Jezebel in the Northern Kingdom. Star and planetary worship was instituted. The Ammonite deity Moloch was acknowledged by the Hebrew king in the sacrifice of children in the Hinnom Valley. Astrology, divination, and occultism were officially sanctioned. In open defiance of God, altars for worshiping the host of heaven were placed in the courts of the temple, while graven images of Asherah, the wife of Baal, were placed in the temple itself. It is quite likely that tradition is correct in attributing the martyrdom of Isaiah to Manasseh, since he shed much innocent blood (2 Kings 21:16). Morally and religiously Judah reached a very low point under this wicked king.

During Manasseh's reign, Esarhaddon and Ashurbanipal extended Assyrian control down to Thebes in Egypt by 663 B.C. Although the date for Manasseh's captivity (2 Chron. 33:10-13) is not given, it is likely that he was taken to Babylon during the last decade of his reign. Being returned after his repentance, Manasseh probably had little time to reverse the idolatrous influence he had promoted throughout the kingdom during his earlier years.

AMON

Idolatry prevailed under Manasseh's son Amon. The early training of Amon had made a decidedly greater impact upon him than the belated period of reformation. Before two years of his reign had passed, Amon was slain by slaves in the palace. Although his reign was brief, his godless leadership provided opportunity for Judah to revert to terrible apostasy.

JOSIAH

National and international changes of great significance occurred during the thirty-one-year reign of Josiah. With the death of Ashurbanipal in 633 B.C. and the destruction of Nineveh in 612, the Assyrian empire gave way to the rising kingdoms of Media and Babylon. Josiah brought about the last great reformation before the destruction of Judah.

RELIGIOUS REFORMATION

As an eight-year-old boy, Josiah was suddenly elevated to the Davidic throne in Jerusalem after the death of his father. In all likelihood Josiah had been instructed by godly teachers and priests. When he was sixteen, he began to seek God earnestly. In four more years (628 B.C.), his devotion to God had crystallized to the point that he began a religious reformation. In 621 B.C. while the temple was being repaired, the Book of the Law was recovered, and the Passover was observed in a manner unprecedented in the history of Judah. Politically it was also safe to remove any religious practices associated with Assyria at this time since Assyrian influence was waning. Very likely Josiah continued to give religious leadership in leading his people back to God until the end of his reign.

HULDAH

When the Law was discovered in the temple, Huldah the prophetess was called in by the king. She warned the king of impending judgment and instructed him in his responsibilities to obey the Law. Since Manasseh had shed so much innocent blood, it is probable that he destroyed as many of the existing copies of the Law of Moses as he could find. Thus the contents of the Law were relatively unknown until this copy was made available to the king of Judah.

JEREMIAH

Jeremiah was called to the prophetic ministry in 627 B.C. Since Josiah had already begun his reform, it is reasonable to conclude that Jeremiah and Josiah worked hand in hand. Living in Anathoth, Jeremiah may not have been available or even acquainted with Josiah when the Book of the Law was found in 621. However, the first twenty chapters of Jeremiah may largely be related to the Josian era.

SUDDEN DEATH

The destruction of the Assyrian capital of Nineveh in 612 B.C. by the Medo-Babylonian coalition affected the entire Fertile Crescent. In a state of military preparedness, Josiah made his fatal mistake by rushing his armies up to Megiddo to stop Necho, king of Egypt, from aiding the remnant of the Assyrian army at Haran. Josiah was fatally wounded, and the Judean army was routed. Suddenly the national and international hopes of Judah vanished as the thirty-nine-year-old king was entombed in the city of David. After eighteen years of intimate association with Josiah, the great prophet is singled out by name in 2 Chronicles 35:25: "and Jeremiah lamented for Josiah."

THE LAST KINGS OF JUDAH

Rapid changes took place during the next quarter of a century, resulting in the destruction of Jerusalem. Although Assyria, which had dominated Palestine for more than a century, had fallen, the Babylonian kingdom emerged as the controlling power under which the kingdom of Judah was absorbed.

JEHOIAKIM—609—598 B.C.

Before Jehoahaz had ruled three months in Jerusalem, the king of Egypt returned from Carchemish, where he had halted the Babylonian advance, and placed Jehoiakim, another son of Josiah, on the Davidic throne. Jehoahaz was taken prisoner to Egypt and died there as predicted by Jeremiah (22:11, 12).

Jehoiakim was subject to Egypt until 605 B.C. when the Necho was defeated by the Babylonians in the battle of Carchemish. That summer the Babylonian armies advanced south and claimed treasures and hostages in Jerusalem, among whom were Daniel and his friends. By 598 B.C. Jehoiakim apparently maintained an anti-Babylonian policy so that Nebuchadnezzar marched his armies to Jerusalem. Jehoiakim seems to have been killed by marauding Chaldean bands supported by Moabites, Ammonites, and Syrians before the Babylonian forces reached Palestine.

Young Jehoiachin, son of Jehoiakim, ruled only three months. Realizing that it was futile to resist the Babylonian forces besieging Jerusalem, Jehoiachin surrendered to Nebuchadnezzar. This time the invaders stripped the temple and the royal treasuries and took the king, the queen mother, palace officials, executives, artisans, and community leaders captive. Not least among the thousands was Ezekiel. Zedekiah, the youngest son of Josiah, was made puppet king and left in charge of Judah.[1]

ZEDEKIAH—597—586 B.C.

Subject to the Babylonians, Zedekiah was able to maintain the kingdom of Judah for only eleven years. He was under constant pressure to join the Egyptians in a rebellion against the Babylonians. When Zedekiah yielded to the pro-Egyptian party, the Babylonian armies advanced to Jerusalem, besieging it in 588. After several years Jerusalem was conquered, the temple was reduced to ashes, and the capital of Judah was abandoned as its citizens were taken captive or dispersed. Zedekiah escaped but was captured at Jericho and taken to Riblah. After the execution of his sons, Zedekiah was blinded and taken in chains to Babylon.

JEREMIAH'S MINISTRY

Jeremiah served as a faithful messenger of God through the hectic decades that brought the kingdom of Judah to its doom. During Jehoiakim's reign, Jeremiah's scroll was burned by the king. When Jeremiah announced the destruction of the temple (Jer. 7, 26), the people would have executed him had it not been for Ahikam, a prominent political figure who came to defend him.

Throughout the last decade, Jeremiah constantly advised the vacillating king to be subservient to the Babylonian king. Being left with the lower classes of people, Jeremiah was subjected to persecution and frequent suffering as he warned the people of judgment to come, withstood the false prophets in Jerusalem, and advised the exiles by correspondence that they should not believe the false prophets who were active there, encouraging them in the hope of an immediate return to Jerusalem. Even though Jeremiah was imprisoned, thrown in a dungeon, and abandoned by his people, he was sustained by God to live with his people through the destruction of Jerusalem. At the end of a forty-year ministry, he witnessed the disintegration of the Davidic kingdom and the destruction of the Solomonic temple which had been the pride and glory of Israel for almost four centuries. The book of Lamentations may well express the reflections of Jeremiah as he saw the ruins of his beloved city of Jerusalem.

DISCUSSION QUESTIONS

1. Who were the participants in the Syro-Ephraimitic war?
2. What was Ahaz's attitude toward Isaiah?
3. What did Hezekiah do to reverse his wicked father's political and religious policies?
4. What preparation did Hezekiah make for defending his nation?
5. How did Isaiah help Hezekiah in 701 when Sennacherib demanded the surrender of Jerusalem?
6. Why did Sennacherib return so suddenly to Babylon in 701 B.C.?
7. How was Sennacherib defeated in his second attempt to subject Hezekiah?
8. What were the religious policies of Manasseh?

9. How did international developments aid Josiah in his religious reformation?

10. Why did Nebuchadnezzar destroy Jerusalem?

11. Evaluate the influence of the prophet Isaiah to illustrate the degree to which Christian statesmen are influencing world events today.

12. Using Josiah as a model, suggest present-day reforms that might result from the reading and applying of God's Word by the people of your community.

13. Summarize the ministry of Jeremiah during the last forty years of Judah's history. What is the Christian's responsibility toward governmental affairs?

14. List the most significant international events between 650–586 B.C. Discuss the relationship of these events to prophecy and to the violation of God's covenant with His chosen people (cf. Deut. 29, 30).

Chapter Twelve

BEYOND THE EXILE

LITTLE IS KNOWN ABOUT the conditions of the Jewish people who were taken into Babylonian exile. In the biblical narrative, the period from the destruction of Jerusalem in 586 B.C. to the return of the exiles beginning in 538 B.C. is passed in silence. The books of Ezra, Esther, and Nehemiah provide some insight into the activities of God's chosen people from the time of their return to the end of the Old Testament era, the days of Nehemiah and Malachi (ca. 450–400 B.C.).

Chronologically this material may be conveniently divided into four periods:

Jerusalem reestablished, ca. 539–515 B.C.	Ezra 1–6
Esther the queen, ca. 483 B.C.	Esther 1–10
Ezra the reformer, ca. 457 B.C.	Ezra 7–10
Nehemiah the governor, ca. 444 B.C.	Nehemiah 1–13

Jewish captivity had been foretold by Isaiah, Micah, Jeremiah, and other prophets for many generations. The exiles, conscious of the fact that their captivity came as God's judgment upon a sinful nation, experienced a deep sense of humiliation and anguish of soul.[1] The prophets likewise held out the promise of restoration. Noteworthy among the predictions were the messages by Jeremiah (25:11, 12; 29:10) that the captivity would be terminated in seventy years and the designation by Isaiah that Cyrus would be the shepherd used by God to allow the Jews to return (Isa. 44:28).

JERUSALEM REESTABLISHED

The first six chapters of Ezra provide a brief account of the experiences of the exiles who returned to rebuild the temple. Almost twenty-five years passed before they realized their hopes.

THE RETURN—EZRA 1–2

When Cyrus, king of Persia, conquered Babylon, he issued a decree that allowed the Jews to return to Jerusalem. He reversed the policy initiated by Tiglath-pileser of Assyria in 745 B.C. of deporting conquered peoples. Cyrus permitted displaced persons to return to their homelands.

Thousands of Jewish exiles prepared to leave Babylon. Loaded with vessels that Nebuchadnezzar had taken from the temple and with the approval and official support of King Cyrus, approximately 50,000 exiles successfully made the long trek to Jerusalem in 538 B.C. Outstanding among the eleven leaders mentioned were Zerubbabel, a grandson of Jehoiachin of the royal Davidic line, and Joshua (Jeshua), who served as the high priest officiating in religious matters.

SETTLEMENT AT JERUSALEM—EZRA 3–4

Upon arrival, the Jews immediately erected an altar and instituted worship, offering burnt offerings as prescribed by Moses (Exod. 29:38ff.). On the fifteenth day of the seventh month, they observed the Feast of Tabernacles (Lev. 23:34ff.). In the atmosphere of these celebrations and festivities, plans were made for the people to provide money and produce for the masons and carpenters who negotiated with the Phoenicians for materials to build the temple.

Construction was begun in the second month of the next year. Antiphonal singing and triumphant praise by the new generation accompanied the ceremony of laying the foundation of the temple. The older people who remembered the glory and beauty of the Solomonic temple wept bitterly and unashamedly. Before long, the people from Samaria expressed their interest in this building program. Denied participation, they responded with hostility and successfully hindered the work on the temple until 520 B.C.

THE NEW TEMPLE—EZRA 5–6

In the second year of Darius, the new ruler in Persia, the Jews were able to resume their building project. The prophets Haggai and Zechariah were instrumental in stirring up the people to a renewed effort. This time Tattenai and his associates were not only forbidden to interfere, but were under orders of Darius to allot royal revenue from the province of Syria to the Jews for the temple.

The temple was completed in five years (520–515 B.C.).[2] After the impressive dedication ceremonies, the priests and Levites instituted their regular services in the sanctuary as prescribed for them in the Law of Moses. Thus the hopes of the returning exiles were realized.

THE STORY OF ESTHER

The book of Esther relates the experiences of some of the Jews who remained in the land of their exile instead of returning to Jerusalem. Historically Esther is identified with the reign of Xerxes or Ahasuerus, king of Persia (485–465 B.C.). Although the name of God is not mentioned in this book, divine providence and supernatural care are apparent throughout.

JEWS AT THE PERSIAN COURT—ESTHER 1–2

When Xerxes suddenly ostracized Queen Vashti by his royal decree, a young Jewish orphan named Esther was crowned queen of Persia. Mordecai, a cousin who had formerly adopted Esther, was subsequently instrumental in uncovering a plot in which two guards conspired to take the king's life. Through Esther these plans were reported, and the culprits were hanged. In the official chronicle Mordecai was credited with saving the Persian ruler's life.

THREAT TO THE JEWISH PEOPLE—ESTHER 3–5

When Haman, a Persian official, was advanced in rank by the king, he was duly honored by everyone except Mordecai, who as a Jew refused to do obeisance. Seeking revenge, Haman planned the execution of the Jews, with the endorsement of the king.

Mordecai in the meantime alerted his people, who responded with fasting and mourning. Warning Esther that she possibly had come to the kingdom for such a time as this (Esther 4:14), Mordecai prevailed upon her to intercede before the king in behalf of the Jewish people. Consequently, she invited the king and Haman for dinner on two successive days, making her request known on the second engagement.

TRIUMPH OF THE JEWS—ESTHER 6–10

The night after the first dinner the king could not sleep. To pass the time, he requested to have the royal chronicles read to him, through which he learned that Mordecai had never been honored for saving the king's life. Upon inquiry by the king, Haman outlined the procedure for honoring a man whom the king wanted to honor, anticipating that he would be the recipient. Haman was shocked when he was ordered to honor

Mordecai, for whom he had in the meantime erected gallows of execution to be used on the day set for the destruction of the Jews.

At the second banquet Esther forthrightly identified Haman as the culprit. In consequence, Haman was hanged on the gallows he had prepared for Mordecai. The Jews were authorized to resist their enemies. In the fighting that broke out, thousands of non-Jews were slain. Peace was restored, and the Jews celebrated their deliverance. In commemoration of this deliverance, the Feast of Purim was observed annually.

EZRA THE REFORMER

The activities of Ezra himself are given in the last four chapters in the book bearing his name. He returned to Jerusalem in 457 B.C.

FROM BABYLONIA TO JERUSALEM—EZRA 7–8

Ezra was a ready scribe and student of the Law of Moses. In response to his appeal to Artaxerxes, Ezra was commissioned by this Persian king to lead a movement of Jews back to the province of Judah.

Elaborate preparation was made for this venture. Generous royal contributions, freewill offerings contributed by the exiles, and vessels for sacred use were given to Ezra for the Jerusalem temple. Provincial rulers beyond the Euphrates were ordered to supply Ezra with food and money lest the royal family incur the wrath of Israel's God. Ashamed to ask the king for police protection, Ezra assembled his people for prayer and fasting to appeal to God for divine aid as they embarked on the long and treacherous trek of nearly 1,000 miles to Jerusalem. Three and a half months later they arrived.

REFORMATION—EZRA 9–10

When Ezra learned that many of the Israelites—even civil and religious leaders in Judah—were guilty of intermarriage with heathen inhabitants he immediately took steps to correct these social evils. He called for a public assembly in the temple square and faced the congregation with the seriousness of their offense. After a three-month examination of the guilty parties, a sacrifice was made for a guilt offering with a solemn pledge by the offenders to annul their marriages.

NEHEMIAH THE GOVERNOR

Emerging as one of the most colorful figures in the postexilic era was Nehemiah, who came to Jerusalem in 444 B.C. He forfeited his own position in the Persian court to serve his people in rebuilding Jerusalem. The book bearing his name may be conveniently considered under the headings given below.

COMMISSIONED BY ARTAXERXES—NEHEMIAH 1:1–2:8

Serving as cupbearer to the Persian king, Nehemiah was greatly concerned about helping his people. After prayer and confession of the sins of his people, Nehemiah was able to make his request known when the king inquired about his personal welfare. In response, the king commissioned him to go to Jerusalem and serve as governor.

THE JERUSALEM MISSION—NEHEMIAH 2:9–6:19

Upon arrival, Nehemiah immediately toured Jerusalem by night to inspect the city and appraise the conditions. He organized the people, who responded enthusiastically in rebuilding the walls of the city. This sudden and intense activity aroused the opposition of the Arabs, the Ammonites, and the Ashdodites led by Geshem, Tobiah, and Sanballat. Nehemiah and his people not only prayed, but by an intensive, organized effort they guarded against attack and worked from dawn to dark to complete the walls.

Economically the people were hard pressed to pay their taxes and the interest and to support their families. Calling a public assembly, Nehemiah announced an economic policy canceling interest payments. Nehemiah himself set the example by not taking any governmental allowance in food and money during his twelve years of service.

Although the enemies of Nehemiah tried devious ways to ensnare him, they failed repeatedly. Praying that God might strengthen him to withstand these efforts and keeping constant vigil, he was able to counter every advance successfully. When the wall was completed in fifty-two days, the enemies lost face. Surrounding nations were duly impressed, realizing that God had favored Nehemiah. Thus the prestige of the Jewish state was established.

REFORMATION UNDER EZRA—NEHEMIAH 7–10

Nehemiah next turned his attention to setting up an organized guard system for the entire city. Some parts of Jerusalem were too sparsely settled to have enough people at all points on the wall. Consequently, he called for a registration of all the citizens in the province and recruited some for settlement inside the city.

Before Nehemiah had opportunity to complete his plans, the people gathered in Jerusalem for the religious festivities of the seventh month.

Nehemiah gave precedence to the reading of the Law, the observance of the Feast of Trumpets, the Day of Atonement, and the Feast of Tabernacles under the leadership of Ezra, the renowned teacher of the Law. After all these festivities and the repeated reading of the Law, the people responded with a pledge to keep the Law as given by Moses. Two laws were singled out for emphasis—intermarriage with the heathen and the keeping of the Sabbath. In a realistic and practical commitment supported by Nehemiah and led by Ezra, the temple ministry was restored.

NEHEMIAH'S PROGRAM AND POLICIES—NEHEMIAH 11–13

Nehemiah now resumed his registration and provided for adequate defense of the city wall by bringing more residents to Jerusalem. The dedication of the walls involved the entire province. Civil and religious leaders and all other participants were organized into two processions. Headed by Ezra and Nehemiah, one proceeded to the right, and the other to the left as they marched on the walls of the city. When the two companies met at the temple, a great service of thanksgiving took place, with music furnished by an orchestra and choirs. This extensive and joyous celebration and triumphant noise was heard afar.

In 432 B.C. Nehemiah made a trip back to Persia and then returned again to Jerusalem. Upon his return, he learned that numerous irregularities had prevailed in allowing strangers into the city and neglecting temple service. Boldly Nehemiah dealt with the offenders, expelling Tobiah the Ammonite and restoring the temple services with a prayer that God might remember his good deeds toward the temple and its staff.

Sabbath observance was next on the reform list. Warning the nobles that this was the sin that had precipitated Judah's captivity and the destruction of Jerusalem, Nehemiah ordered the gates of Jerusalem closed on the Sabbath, even forbidding the arrival of merchants on that day.

Nehemiah also dealt with the problem of mixed marriages. He warned the people that even Solomon had been led into sin through the foreign wives that were brought to Jerusalem. When the grandson of Eliashib, the high priest, married the daughter of Sanballat, the governor of Samaria, he was immediately expelled from Judah by Nehemiah. The account of Nehemiah concludes with the fitting words of his prayer, "Remember me, O my God, for good."

MALACHI'S PROPHECIES

The reforms of Nehemiah and Ezra are also reflected in the book of Malachi, whose ministry is usually dated during this period (ca. 450–400 B.C.). According to tradition preserved by Josephus, this prophet was the last of God's messengers before the long period of silence lasting approximately 400 years.

The messianic expectation is once more projected as the hope for those who fear God. Beginning with the assurance of ultimate victory through the seed of the woman in Genesis 3:15, the messianic promise had been unfolded in subsequent generations (cf. Gen. 12:3; 49:10; Exod. 3:15; Num. 24:17; 2 Sam. 7:16; 1 Chron. 17:14; Isa. 7:14; 9:6, 7; 28:16; Micah 5:2; and others). Malachi points to the terrible day of judgment that will be preceded by mercy in the coming of Elijah (3:1–4:5). In this message of predictive import, the name "Elijah" suggested a time of revival through a God-sent individual who appeared four centuries later as John the Baptist to prepare the way for the Messiah.

In this vivid way, Malachi reminds the godless that they should be afraid of the day of judgment. Those who revere God, however, are assured of God's eternal favor. God's curse rests upon the wicked, while God's blessing is bestowed upon the righteous.

CONCLUDING THE BIBLICAL RECORD OF THE OLD TESTAMENT

These three books, which are the main sources of information about the Jews after the destruction of Jerusalem in 586 B.C., conclude the biblical record of Old Testament times, leaving a long period of silence. Approximately four centuries later the New Testament opens with the birth of Christ.

DISCUSSION QUESTIONS

1. Who were the leaders of the exiles that returned to Judah?
2. What did they do immediately to establish worship upon arrival in Jerusalem?
3. What two prophets stimulated the Jews to a renewed effort to build the temple?
4. What feast was established as a result of the Jewish deliverance in the days of Esther?
5. What was Ezra's religious interest before returning to Jerusalem?

6. How did Ezra exemplify his concern for divine as well as human aid in helping his people?
7. What was the attitude of Nehemiah toward the plight of his people as reflected in his prayer in Nehemiah 1?
8. How did Nehemiah approach the king about his problem?
9. How did Nehemiah organize his efforts to rebuild the walls of Jerusalem?
10. What were the chief reforms of Nehemiah?
11. Compare the policies toward conquered nations by Assyria, Babylonia, and Persia. Trace the evidences of divine dealings with God's chosen people through these heathen nations.
12. List the qualities of leadership manifested by Nehemiah in facing the opposition by the people of Samaria during this period. What crucial events today test the leadership qualities of God's people?
13. Give a summarizing sentence identifying each of the seventeen books covered so far.
14. Trace the progressive revelation of the messianic promises.
15. List what you consider the most important events and their approximate dates covered so far in this study.

PART TWO:
JOB—MALACHI

PSALMS OF LAMENT
AND PRAISE

THE BOOK OF PSALMS is somewhat like a modern hymnbook in that it is a collection of songs and prayers written by several people over a long period of time. It describes the worshipers' response of praise because of God's power and love, expresses their hope based on God's promises for the future, and records their cries for God to rescue them from the troubles of life. This collection of songs is used by believers in their private devotions as well as in public worship.

Psalms were sung in the temple (Ps. 100:4—"Enter into his gates with thanksgiving, and into his courts with praise") and by the early church (Col. 3:16—"admonishing one another in psalms and hymns and spiritual songs, singing with grace in your hearts to the Lord"). When a psalm was sung ("Great is the LORD" from Ps. 48), the singer was testifying to God's greatness, the listener was hearing how God had worked in another person's life, and everyone was encouraged to trust in God's power. The psalms were filled with the emotions of fear and anguish because of persecution, as well as trust and love because of God's protection in the past. These prayers describe the close personal relationship that can exist between God and each one of us.

Many of the psalms were written to music. Thus the heading of Psalm 4 includes the direction, "for the choir director, (to be played) on stringed instruments," or the heading to Psalm 5 has "for the choir director, for flute accompaniment." Psalm 3 has the word *Selah* at the end of verses 2, 4, and 8. This word means "to lift up," but it is not clear whether this referred to increasing the volume of the instruments or to some sort of musical interlude. Several of the psalms encourage singing (Ps. 95:1, 2; 96:1, 2; 98:1, 4-6), and others promote the playing of instruments while people sing the praises of God (Ps. 98:5, 6; 108:1, 2; 150:3-5).

The psalms were arranged into five subdivisions or books (1–41; 42–72; 73–89; 90–106; 107–150). This order follows the fivefold division of the Pentateuch and may reflect the process of collecting these songs and prayers into Israel's hymnbook. Most of the psalms in the first two books were from David (3–41; 51–71), while many psalms in book three were written by Asaph (73–83). Songs of Ascent (120–134) and Hallelujah psalms (146–150) were grouped together in the fifth book. This suggests that the first two books may have been collected by David, the third and fourth by Solomon or Hezekiah, and the fifth by Ezra.

The earliest psalm of praise is attributed to Moses (Exod. 15), but it is not included in the book of Psalms. The headings suggest that Moses wrote one psalm (Ps. 90), that seventy-two psalms are related to David, that two psalms are by Solomon, and that a large group are attributed to the Levitical singers Asaph, Heman, Ethan, and Korah (1 Chron. 15:16-24; 25:1-8). David appointed these Levites to sing and play musical instruments at the temple worship services. Some psalms were written while the people of Israel were in exile by the rivers of Babylon (Ps. 137). In the New Testament, Peter claims that David wrote Psalms 16 and 110 (Acts 2:25-35), and Hebrews 4:7 connects him to Psalm 95.

HISTORICAL SETTING

Many of the psalms have two settings—the original historical experience of the author who wrote the psalm (David out on a hill taking care of his sheep) and the later setting of the psalm as it was sung in the temple in Jerusalem on a feast day. Some headings suggest the original historical situation that caused the author to write the psalm. Psalm 3 was connected to the events surrounding David fleeing from his rebellious son Absalom (see 2 Sam. 13:34–18:33). Psalm 18 fits the context of David fleeing from Saul (2 Sam. 21–22). Psalm 30 commemorates the dedication of the place where God's house would be built (2 Sam. 24), and Psalm 51 was David's prayer after his sin with Bathsheba (2 Sam. 11–12).

Other psalms contain no historical information in their heading about the situation of the author but have clues within the psalm itself. Psalm 45 is connected to a wedding, while 27:1-3 pictures the author surrounded by evildoers, adversaries, and a host of enemies.

The people who sang these songs many years later in the temple services or in the early church did not always know the situation of the original author. Nevertheless, they could identify with the feelings of hopelessness portrayed in these songs because they had experienced similar emotions in their own lives. Other psalms were primarily written to sing the praise of God in the temple or at a feast day. These psalms frequently deal with universal problems or common reasons for joy that affect people in all cultures.

CATEGORIZATION OF THE PSALMS

The psalms can be put into several different groups that have a similar topic, structure, or use. There are messianic psalms (Ps. 2; 110), wisdom psalms (Ps. 1; 73), royal psalms (Ps. 96–99), Zion songs (Ps. 46; 48), and historical psalms (Ps. 105; 106). The next chapter will look at many of these different kinds of psalms, but here the most popular types will be examined—the lament and the hymn of praise.

PSALMS OF LAMENT

People in Israel lamented and cried out to God for help for several reasons. Some psalms describe a situation in which the individual author or the whole nation is being attacked by some enemy. A city may seek for God's protection as an enemy army is marching against it (Ps. 44:4-16), or an individual might mourn his own personal situation such as David did when Saul had him trapped in a cave in the Judean desert (Ps. 142). At other times people lamented and confessed their sins (Ps. 51; 130), mourned because of a serious sickness (Ps. 6), or lamented the fact that they had been unjustly accused of some evil deed (Ps. 7; 17; 120).

When people lamented, they frequently wept, fasted, and put on sackcloth and ashes (see Joel 2:12-17). These were not casual requests for God's blessing, but serious prayers because they did not have modern medicine, a strong army or police force to maintain law and order, or the money to fight someone who had falsely accused them. Their only hope was to depend on God for mercy and protection. The book of Psalms includes six or seven community laments and about fifty individual laments.

Most laments have the same general structure (our prayers also tend to follow similar patterns), although there is a good deal of individual freedom within these broad patterns.[1] The lament structure usually includes:

1. *An invocation, a call for God to help.* This is frequently quite short. In Psalm 13 it is "How long wilt thou forget me, O LORD?" The invocation is a recognition that the lamenter is turning to God for help. Indeed, God is the only source of strength for those who are having difficulty.
2. *A lament or complaint.* In this section the worshiper describes the problem. Frequently, three issues are brought up: God is not pro-

tecting him, enemies are persecuting him, and he is in sorrow. In Psalm 13:1, 2 the worshiper complains about God: "How long wilt thou hide thy face from me?"; about the person's own situation: "How long shall I take counsel in my soul, having sorrow in my heart daily?"; and about the enemies: "How long shall mine enemy be exalted over me?"

These complaints were honest expressions of how the people felt. They did not hide their feelings of sorrow or disappointment (God already knew them anyway). Although they did not blame God, they did believe that God could solve their problems. They expressed their complaints because they believed their situation would change when God heard their prayers.

In modern prayers, people frequently do not spend much time describing their problems or telling God how they feel about these difficulties. These psalms encourage believers to be open with God, to tell Him exactly how they feel, not to hide behind some pious attitude.

3. *A petition or request for God's help.* This portion usually asks God to listen to the person's prayer and act to bring salvation or deliverance from the problems of life. In Psalm 13:3, 4 the petition is "Consider and hear me, O LORD my God: lighten mine eyes, lest I sleep the sleep of death; Lest mine enemy say, I have prevailed against him." Sometimes the petition includes the request that God would deliver from death, forgive sins, or defeat enemies. The request is an admission that we as believers are unable to solve all the problems of life in our own strength. By calling on God for help, we confess our dependence on God and by faith rest in His strong arms.

4. *Confession of trust or statement of confidence.* Even though believers may face great problems and feel very discouraged, the lament prayer is not a time to wallow in despair or depression. Once the petition is stated, the worshipers are to turn their attention from their problems to God, the solution to their petition. The confession of trust or statement of confidence is an expression of faith, an active looking forward to the fulfillment of the request. In Psalm 13:5 the psalmist proclaims, "But I have trusted in thy mercy; my heart shall rejoice in thy salvation." Because the person believes God can be trusted, there is confidence that God's salvation will bring great rejoicing in the coming days. As the hymn "Turn Your Eyes upon Jesus" says: "The things of this earth will grow strangely dim in the light of His glory and grace."

5. *A vow of praise.* Many laments end with a commitment that the believer will sing God's praise when He has answered this prayer. In Psalm 13:6 the worshiper promises: "I will sing unto the LORD, because he hath dealt bountifully with me." What began as a burdensome lament ends with a note of hope and victory, with the expectation of glorifying God and proclaiming His grace to others in song.

Some laments do not contain all these structural parts, and others may contain two sections of petition or two statements of confidence. Each prayer is an individual expression that follows a somewhat unique series of building blocks. The people were different, the situations were different, and their sense of hope or hopelessness varied based on the seriousness of the problem.

Regular reading or praying patterned on the psalms of lament will help us to pray with power and honesty. God is interested in our problems, and Hebrews 4:14-16 states that Jesus is anxiously waiting to intercede for us at the right hand of God the Father in heaven. Prayer is a testimony to the importance of a personal "talking" relationship with God, our belief in the transforming power of prayer, and our desire to experience the joy of having our prayers answered.

PSALMS OF PRAISE

Another large group of psalms are called hymns of praise. These fall into several subcategories according to the structure, topic, or reason for praising God. Some hymns declare God's praise for answering the lament of a believer (at the end of the lament the worshiper usually promises to praise God for the answer to the lament). Psalm 9 is this type of declarative or narrative hymn of praise.[2] God is praised (9:1-3, 7-11, 14) because the worshiper remembers how his enemies were destroyed by God (9:4-6, 12, 13, 15, 16).

A second group of hymns of ascent were sung as pilgrims or regular worshipers were coming to the temple. These psalms refer to the joy of seeing the city of Jerusalem and being in the temple to worship God (Ps. 122).

A major group of hymns proclaim the glory of God and list a series of reasons why God should receive praise. The structure of these descriptive hymns of praise is quite simple.[3]

1. A call to praise God.
2. Reasons for praising God.

This pattern may be partially or fully repeated in this simple formula. Psalm 100 is a well-known hymn that follows this pattern. It begins with a call to praise God in 100:1, 2: "Make a joyful noise unto the LORD, all ye lands. Serve the LORD with gladness: come before his presence with singing." This is followed with a reason for praising God in 100:3: "Know ye that the LORD he is God: it is he that hath made us, and not we ourselves; we are his people, and the sheep of his pasture." This pattern is repeated with another call to praise God in 100:4: "Enter into his gates with thanksgiving, and into his courts with praise: be thankful unto him, and bless his name," and a second reason for praising God in 100:5: "For the LORD is good; his mercy is everlasting; and his truth endureth to all generations."

Although the pattern is fairly simple, this brief psalm of praise contains a great deal of theology. The worshiper is recognizing the importance of coming to God's house to worship and praise God. This is not just a habit, the respectable thing to do, or an issue of obeying parents. Believers understand why God is praised: they have experienced His grace, and their hearts are full of motivation for thanksgiving. God created them, God considers them His special people, and He provides for their needs. He is good to them; He shows His love again and again; He is faithful in so many ways. He is worthy to be praised.

Sometime these declarative hymns of praise emphasize the call to praise God, as in Psalm 148:1-5a, 7-13a. It has only two very short sections (5b-6 and 13b-14) that give the reason why God should be praised. Other hymns have very brief calls to praise God (147:1a, 7, 12) but a very long list of reasons for praising Him (147:1b-6, 8-11, 13-20). These hymns fulfill one of the chief purposes for the existence of mankind on earth—the purpose of enjoying and glorifying God.

Since transportation was difficult in those days, people who lived a long way from Jerusalem were able to come to the temple and worship God only a few times each year. No wonder they were thrilled and excited about actually coming to the temple again. When the worshiper joined with the masses to sing the glory of God, it was an inspiring experience. As they sang through the hymn, they would be reminded of the many reasons they had to praise God. God had been good to them (by giving them good crops and plenty of food to eat). God had been faithful to them (by answering a prayer or by fulfilling a promise). God's love was very evident (by giving them good health or by giving them a new child in their family). God's grace was not ignored or taken for granted; it was celebrated to glorify Him and encourage others to put their trust in Him.

THEOLOGICAL SIGNIFICANCE OF THESE PSALMS

1. In times of difficulty believers can bring all their burdens to God, for He always hears and comforts those who come to Him.
2. The prayer for help should not just be centered on the problem or what is needed. It should also focus on God's ability to answer prayer, the believer's commitment to trust God, and the ultimate desire to glorify God for His grace and goodness.
3. God's house is a place of praise and thanksgiving. The joy of the Lord should fill the hearts and lips of those who have been blessed by God.
4. God is to be praised because He is God, we are His people, and He has provided for us.

DISCUSSION QUESTIONS

1. What can we learn about a psalm from its title?
2. What are some similarities and differences between the book of Psalms and our modern hymnbooks?
3. What is the common structure of the lament? How does this structure encourage the people lamenting to overcome the fear and the discouragement of their difficult situation?
4. List some reasons why people praise the Lord in the descriptive hymns of praise in Psalm 33, 111, 135, and 145.
5. Try writing and praying a simple prayer of lament based on a real problem you are facing (following the structure provided above) and also a basic hymn of praise that declares your own reasons for praising God. If you are musical, you might even set your hymn of praise to music.

SPECIAL THEMES
IN THE PSALMS

IN ADDITION TO THE lament and the hymn of praise examined in the last chapter, several other types of psalms emphasize special themes and have a unique structure or setting in Israeli life. These include historical psalms, imprecatory psalms, psalms of confession and penitence, wisdom psalms, royal psalms, and messianic psalms. Although these psalms are fewer in number, they contain many important theological ideas and reveal some significant aspects of Israeli worship.

HISTORICAL PSALMS

Historical psalms are different from other psalms in that they do not relate to a specific event in the life of a believer. Instead they review Israel's history in order to remind the listener of the nation's past sins, to praise God for His gracious deeds on their behalf, or to encourage the people to trust God because He has been faithful in the past.[1]

Psalm 78 is a catalog of God's wondrous deeds that parents taught their children so that the coming generation would have confidence in God, not forget His grace or commandments, and not be rebellious like their fathers (78:5-8). The first section (78:9-20) reviews God's miracles in Egypt, the crossing of the Red Sea, the cloud that led Israel through the wilderness, the giving of water from the rock, and the Israelites' rebellion when they did not have any water or meat to eat.

The second section (78:21-39) records God's anger at the people's unbelief, but also His gracious provision of manna (the bread of angels) and meat from the quails. This paragraph ends by returning to the theme of God's anger at the people's rebellion and unfaithfulness even after He provided for their physical needs.

The third section (78:40-53) focuses on how the people in the wilderness forgot God's power displayed in each of the plagues of Egypt.

The fourth section (78:54-72) summarizes the nation's entrance into the Promised Land and defeat of the Canaanites, but also the people's tendency to worship graven images. Because of the people's persistent sinfulness, God abandoned His tabernacle in Shiloh and later rejected the northern tribes of Israel. But God remained faithful to Judah, chose David to be their king, and instructed him to build a temple in Jerusalem. Throughout this time God guided the nation and cared for those He loved. This psalm and its themes are similar to other historical psalms (Ps. 105; 106; 135).

IMPRECATORY PSALMS

A number of psalms contain curses or imprecations against the enemies of God's people. Some of these curses are a small part of a lament (Ps. 139:19-22), while other curses take up the major portion of the psalm (Ps. 35; 69; 109). These psalms have caused a certain amount of uneasiness for Christians because they seem to be promoting a vengeful attitude, just the opposite of Jesus' command to love our enemies (Matt. 5:44). Although some believe that these statements are evil, sub-Christian, and a negative part of the old dispensation's ethics, a careful look at these expressions of righteous indignation suggests that they were not motivated by desires for sinful or personal revenge.

The curses in Psalm 109:6-20 reveal that the wicked have lied and made false accusations against the righteous (109:2-5). The believers ask that God would judge the wicked by taking their lives, leaving their children fatherless, taking their land, and cutting off their memory from the earth. This is the way that God Himself said He would righteously reward the wicked for their sinful deeds (109:6-20).

Elsewhere David cries out for God to slay the wicked because they speak against God and they take God's name in vain. David hates those who hate God; he hates them with great hatred (Ps. 139:19-22). But David is not speaking of personal vengeance, for in the very next verse he asks God to search him to see if there is any hurtful or vengeful thought in him (139:23, 24). It becomes clear that David is so identifying with God's hatred of sin that he cannot stand it any longer; he wants God to remove it.

The modern discomfort with these prayers may be more a commentary on present tendencies to downplay the seriousness of sin. Paul delivered to death and to Satan the man who continued in sin at Corinth (1 Cor. 5) and also cursed anyone who would preach another gospel other than the Gospel of Christ (Gal. 1:6-10). Possibly David and Paul were more in tune with God's hatred of sin than many realize. After all,

Scripture indicates that God will send some people to hell because of their sins.[2] Both Old and New Testaments encourage believers to love their neighbors (Lev. 19:18; Matt. 19:19), warn against personal vengeance (Deut. 32:35; Heb. 10:30), and teach us to hate and run from sin because God hates it.

PSALMS OF CONFESSION AND PENITENCE

A central characteristic of those who love God is their hatred of sin, their desire to turn from sinful attitudes and actions, and their willingness to confess their sin so that they can receive God's forgiveness. Although the Day of Atonement was a national day of humiliation and penitence so that the nation could be cleansed of its sins (Lev. 16), the believers in the Old Testament could acknowledge their sins and receive God's forgiveness at any time. Confessing sins was also closely associated with the presentation of the sin offering at the temple. It must be emphasized, however, that the act of offering a sacrifice was not the important element. The essential thing God was looking for was a broken spirit, the repentant heart of the sinner (Ps. 51:16, 17).

Many suggest that the prayers of confession in Psalms 51 and 32 were related to David's sinful sexual relationship with Bathsheba (note the heading of Ps. 51). In Psalm 51 David asks for God's grace and compassion. He wants God to blot out his sins and cleanse him from his iniquities (51:1, 2). David acknowledges that sexual relationships outside of marriage are sinful, that he did something that was evil in God's eyes, and that he deserves His judgment (51:3, 4). But David is turning from this evil way of life and asking God to purify him, to wash him clean, to create in him a clean heart (51:7-10). He does not want God to forsake him because of his sins; he wants God to restore joy to his life so that he can share what he has learned with others and warn them about making the same mistakes (51:11-13). Once God has forgiven him (because David has a humble heart, not because he has gone through the ritual of some sacrifice), David will praise God and sing for joy (51:14-17).

Psalm 32 is an illustration of David teaching others about his own experience. At first he tried to hide his sin, refused to call it sin, but his conscience weighed heavily upon him during sleepless nights (32:3, 4). Finally he confessed his sin and stopped trying to hide his guilt. Then God graciously forgave him (32:4, 5), and he enjoyed the blessedness of having his sins removed (32:1, 2). Because of this experience, David instructed the people in Israel to pray for forgiveness as soon as they committed a sin (32:6), not to be stubborn like a mule (32:9).

Continued sinfulness and an unrepentant attitude bring great sorrow, but confession of sins and trusting in God for forgiveness bring great joy (32:10, 11). Certainly David's admonition concerning the importance of confessing sins is in line with the New Testament message that God will be faithful and just and forgive our sins if we will confess them to Him (1 John 1:9).

WISDOM PSALMS

Although it is a little difficult to identify what a wisdom psalm is, most agree that there is a group of psalms that reflect the teachings of the wisdom books (Ps. 1; 37; 73; 112; 127; 128). Similarities of themes (prosperity or destruction, the righteous or the fool, the suffering of the righteous) and proverbial statements suggest that some of the psalmists had read wisdom writings and believed that their teaching could be used to instruct and encourage Israelite believers.[3]

Psalm 1 contrasts the life of the righteous (1:1-3) with that of the wicked (1:4, 5). The people who are blessed by God do not go to evil people for advice, do not spend their time doing what sinful people do, and do not mock or scoff at spiritual things. Instead they spend some of their time reading and studying God's Word. Because of this, God prospers what they do (1:1-3). The wicked do not act like the righteous; therefore, they will not stand when God brings His judgment on them (1:4, 5). The final comparison contrasts God's care for the righteous with the perishing of the wicked who are without God (1:6).

Psalm 73 is somewhat similar to the book of Job, for both wrestle with the difficult question of why the righteous person suffers and why so many wicked people seem to prosper (73:3-12). When it seems in vain to be pure, or when troubles seem senseless, the psalmist reminds the believer that the end of the wicked will not be happy (73:13-19). In times of trial, people must rest in the promise of God's presence with them (73:23), be assured of receiving their reward at a later time (73:24), get their eyes off their earthly desires, and cling to God for strength (73:25-28).

ROYAL PSALMS

Within this group of psalms are songs about or by an earthly king, as well as songs about the kingship of God. In the first group are Psalms 20, 21, 45, 72, 89, and 132. These psalms call on God to protect his anointed king in Jerusalem and give him victory in his wars against his enemies (Ps. 20). In response to God's deliverance from his enemies, the king is glad, trusts in God, and praises Him (Ps. 21). A song that was probably used at the wedding of one of Israel's kings is recorded in Psalm 45, and two psalms are about God's covenant with King David (see 2 Sam. 7:1-16)—Psalms 89 and 132.

Of equal or even greater importance are those psalms that celebrate the kingly rule of God Himself (Ps. 47; 93; 96-99). These are not enthronement psalms that accompanied an autumn festival in which God was made king, as some have suggested.[4]

In the theocracy established when Israel first became the people of God, it was understood that God was their ruler and king. This is why Gideon refused to become Israel's king (Judg. 8:23). The danger of having an earthly king was the temptation for him to rule instead of allowing God to be the supreme king (1 Sam. 8:4-7; 12:12-15).

The great King who is to be feared is God Himself (Ps. 47:2). He reigns over all the nations of the earth, and He is to be praised (47:6, 7). He is worshiped because He is King over all gods (95:3; 97:9), because He will judge all nations (96:9-13), and because He rules the earth with strength and justice (99:4). He is holy and an almighty King. Therefore, we should worship Him as our Master, Lord, and King of our lives.

MESSIANIC PSALMS

There are a number of problems associated with interpreting messianic psalms. Some people are very skeptical of messianic interpretations and deny that these psalms were prophetic of the coming of Jesus. They believe that these passages refer to David or to someone who lived in Old Testament times. Others accept the New Testament evidence that these refer to Jesus, but then read into the Old Testament passage information that was never understood until Jesus came.

It seems that a middle course between these extremes must be maintained. The interpreter must accept the witness of the New Testament that these refer to Jesus the Messiah, but one should explain these messianic psalms on the basis of what was revealed to David, not what was revealed hundreds of years later when the Gospels were written. Since the Davidic psalms say nothing about Jesus' virgin birth (it was revealed about 250 years later in Isa. 7:14), it appears that David did not know about this.

Psalms 2 and 110 are messianic psalms that predict that God will install His anointed Son as King in Zion (2:6). This King will rule the whole earth, and all people will submit to Him or be destroyed (2:8-12). This prophecy refers to the second coming of Christ when He will come in power to rule the earth and set up His kingdom. Psalm 110 reveals that the messianic King, who was David's Lord, will one day sit on the right hand of God and rule over the whole earth.

Some commentators disagree on how to understand some psalms that do not appear to be messianic in the Old Testament but are quoted in the New Testament. Some believe that there is a double fulfillment of these psalms, while others believe that there is a typological fulfillment. In all cases it is important that the student first try to figure out what these passages would have meant to David or other Israelite believers.

THEOLOGICAL SIGNIFICANCE OF THESE PSALMS

1. God is sovereignly involved in directing each believer's life.
2. In spite of human sinfulness, God graciously offers forgiveness to those who will repent.
3. God hates sin and will judge the sinner.
4. God's way of life has been revealed in His Word. The righteous person will wisely avoid sinful ways and follow God's way.
5. God is the King of this world. He reigns with all power and with perfect justice. In the end He will defeat every other power on earth, and all will praise Him.
6. At the end of time God will send the Messiah, who now sits at the right hand of God, to defeat the forces of evil and rule the whole earth.

DISCUSSION QUESTIONS

1. Why is it important to sing and read about God's great acts of grace and judgment in the past?
2. When would it be appropriate to pray an imprecatory prayer? What attitudes must the believer exhibit or avoid when praying such prayers?
3. List some wise sayings that you can apply to your life from Psalms 37, 73, 127, and 128.
4. Try to remember your last prayer of confession and then compare it to David's confession of sin in Psalm 51. Was your prayer as serious about the transformation of your heart as David's prayer was about his heart? How has the way you think and act changed in ways that would confirm your answer?
5. What are some areas of your life where God is Lord and Ruler? What does Romans 8:14-17 say about the struggle within us for control of our lives? What areas of your life would you like to see controlled by God's power and kingship? How does a person bring about this change?

Chapter Fifteen

WISDOM

THE CULTURAL SETTING OF the wisdom books is probably more important than the historical context in which they were written, for wisdom ideas were not tied to one particular time frame. They deal with life's basic issues (what is wise and foolish, suffering, raising children, the vanity of life without God, the need to fear God), which are faced in every age.

Some wisdom writings were constructive (Proverbs), providing instructions on how a person was to live successfully within the societal structure and within the moral order that God designed. Other wisdom writings raised questions about a person's ability to successfully understand and live within the social and moral order that existed (Ecclesiastes and Job). Both approaches recognized that God rules the world and that a right relationship with Him produces true wisdom.

Wisdom literature was popular in Egypt (Exod. 7:11; 1 Kings 4:30; Isa. 19:11, 12), Babylonia (Dan. 1:20; 4:6, 7), and Edom (Obad. 8; Job 2:11). Thus it is not surprising to find a section of the Bible devoted to wisdom.¹ It appears that the wise man Job was from the Edomite city of Uz (1:1). Solomon, Job, and pagan writers had a certain amount of wisdom that came from their natural limited human understanding of life, for God revealed Himself to all people in nature and conscience (Rom. 1–2).

Wisdom included the proper understanding of cultural and moral regulations as well as the proper relationship between mankind and the spiritual powers in the world. Of course the wisdom of the pagan gods was not in agreement with or as powerful as God's wisdom (Exod. 7–9; Dan. 2–5; 1 Cor. 1:18–2:16).

Biblical wisdom literature is also unique when compared to the books of Moses or the prophets, for wisdom is not directly related to the covenant relationship with Israel. Instead it deals with the question of God's just and ordered rule of the whole world.

JOB

God's Rule—Just or Unjust?

Although Job had many children and was a wealthy herdsman like some of the patriarchs in Genesis, this kind of lifestyle existed during the time of King David and was still common in the remote areas of the ancient Near East up until the nineteenth or twentieth century A.D. Since wisdom literature in Israel was associated with the life and times of Solomon and Hezekiah (1 Kings 3:3-14; 10:6, 7, 23-25; Prov 1:1; 25:1; Eccles. 1:1), many believe the book of Job came from that period.[2]

Outline of Job

Job's motives for serving God	1–3
Job guilty—or God unjust?	4–27
Where wisdom is found	28
Job's claim of innocence	29–31
Elihu's defense of God's justice	32–37
God's power and wisdom revealed	38:1–42:6
Job's restoration	42:7-17

The author of Job reveals information concerning the unseen spiritual battles that go on in this world. Since some of these events are a mystery to mankind, it is impossible for people to always understand the reason why God allows certain things to happen. This shows that reason cannot be the sole basis of a person's relationship with God. Although wisdom writings encourage a rational understanding of life, they recognize the limitations of human wisdom and call people to fear God and put their faith in Him.

JOB'S MOTIVES FOR SERVING GOD

Job was a righteous man who feared God and turned away from all evil (1:1, 8; 2:3). But the adversary of God and man thought that Job feared God only because He had blessed him with many children and great wealth. After God allowed Satan to test Job by taking his children and possessions, Job remained faithful to God because he believed that the God who freely gives also has the right to take away (1:20-22). In a second trial, God allowed Satan to afflict Job with a terrible skin disease. Still Job did not blame God, even though his wife suggested that he should curse God and die (2:9, 10).

JOB GUILTY—OR GOD UNJUST?

Job's three friends came to comfort and restore him. After an initial period of mourning and silence, the three adopted a pattern of alternating speeches. But sometimes the one speaking is not directly answering the charges of the preceding speaker. The series begins with Job lamenting that he was born and wishing that he were dead (3:1-26).

Eliphaz the Temanite (from an Edomite city) responded with three speeches (4–5; 15; 22). In the first he told Job to be strong, for he had encouraged others with similar advice. Job must put his confidence in God, who cares for the innocent and judges the wicked (4:3, 6-9). When people fall into sin, they should be happy when God reproves them. This is the way God works to redeem those in sin (5:17-20). This truth was the basic theological stance taken by Eliphaz and the other two friends throughout their dialogue with Job.

Eliphaz mocked Job's windy and unprofitable words (15:1-6) because Job rejected the wisdom of the traditional wise men and claimed to have some secret knowledge from God (15:7-13). Eliphaz knew that God judged the wicked (15:18-35); therefore, he reproved Job for claiming that he was innocent (20:1-20). He encouraged Job to repent so that God could restore him (22:21-30).

Bildad responded to Job three times (8; 18; 26) with a theological argument similar to that of Eliphaz. But it is clear that he had less sympathy in his voice. God is just and does not pervert justice; if Job would seek Him and repent, God would restore him (8:3-7, 20). Job must accept this traditional wisdom, for the wicked who forget God are like a plant with no water (8:8-15), but the righteous are like a plant with water (8:16-20). The fate of the wicked is trouble and eventually death (18:5-21).

Zophar's two speeches (11; 20) were caustic and very unsympathetic to Job's physical and mental trials. He coldly dismissed Job's statement that he was innocent. It sounded like boasting to him (11:3, 4). He thought that Job did not understand God's ways. If he would repent, God would restore him (11:7-15). Zophar totally rejected Job's observation that sometimes God does not judge the wicked (20:4-29).

In between these speeches Job lamented the anguish of his painful existence (7:3-8), questioned why God was attacking him (7:11-19), and rejected the advice of his worthless comforters (6:14-27). Job wanted to prove that he was right with God, but it was impossible to take God to court (9:1, 2, 14-16). How could he prove that God sometimes treats the wicked and the righteous the same way (9:22)? Unfortunately there was no judge to oversee this case or rule on Job's treatment (9:33-35). Job loathed his sickness so much (10:1-7) that he decided to go ahead with a court case against God (13:1-19).

First Job rejected his friends' traditional wisdom, because all true wisdom and power belong to God (12:1-6, 13-25). From that point on his speeches were directed to God. God had shattered his life while he was at peace, attacked him on every side, and made Job out to be His enemy (16:7-17). Job cried out for a heavenly witness or advocate to notice his plight (16:18-22), for his friends were useless comforters. Surely the righteous will be appalled at the way his friends and God have treated him (17:1-10; 19:1-12). People treated him like a social outcast, and his family, servants, and peers despised him (19:13-22). His hope was that an eternal record would be kept so that his Redeemer might justify him in the end (19:23-27).

The heart of Job's case was that God did not always bless the righteous and judge the wicked as his friends claimed. No, many wicked people were happy and prosperous (21:7-34; 24:1-17). Job wanted God to explain His execution of justice in this lawsuit and to tell Job why he, an innocent man, was suffering. Although God's power and wisdom are often beyond human understanding (26:5-14), Job needed an explanation. He was innocent (27:1-6), but he was judged. He needed something to counter the traditional wisdom viewpoint that God judges only the wicked. This implied that Job must be wicked (27:7-23).

WHERE WISDOM IS FOUND

The author of Job inserted a short poem about the difficulty of finding wisdom.[3] Although people have found precious stones and metal deep in the earth, where can they find wisdom? It is the most valuable thing, but it is hidden from mankind. Indeed, the only true source of wisdom is God.

JOB'S CLAIM OF INNOCENCE

The dialogue between Job and his friends ended in frustration for both sides. Job gave one final summary of his arguments to end his case. Formerly he was blessed by God, and he was a respected and honored man in society (29:1-25). But now he is mocked and dishonored in society and attacked by God (30:1-31). Yet he is innocent of a whole list of great and small sins (31:1-40). God must explain to him how this can be just.

ELIHU'S DEFENSE OF GOD'S JUSTICE

Although Elihu was not introduced at the beginning of the dialogue, he now speaks to justify God's action and refute Job's claims. After a long introduction to defend his right to speak (32:6-22), Elihu refuted Job's claim that God never answers people's inquiries. God spoke through visions, painful diseases, and a mediator who will deliver those who repent of their sins (33:13-28). By reaffirming the justice of God, Elihu refuted Job's claim that God was not dealing justly by treating everyone the same (34–35). Finally he described various aspects of the world that demonstrate God's sovereign rule. Some of these were so beyond human comprehension that it was preposterous for anyone to question anything God does (36–37).

GOD'S POWER AND WISDOM REVEALED

Finally the Lord answered Job in two speeches. First He challenged Job to teach Him about the measurements of the earth. It was God who created and controls the sea, the light, the underworld, and the weather through His power and wisdom (38:1-38). He also understands and controls the lion, deer, ox, ostrich, horse, and bird of prey (38:39–39:30). Can Job find some fault in God? No, he is silent in the presence of God's power and wisdom (40:1-5).

In God's second speech He challenges Job to teach Him about justice (40:6-14). But Job does not have the power or the wisdom even to bring the beasts Leviathan and Behemoth to justice, so how can he pretend to teach God, who made these beasts (40:15–41:34)? In response, Job admitted that he complained to God about things he really did not know about. Now that his eyes are opened to the mystery of God's glorious ways, he is humbled (42:1-5).

JOB'S RESTORATION

God also revealed that Job's friends were wrong and Job was correct. Job was not suffering for some great evil that he had committed. The three friends confessed their wrong, and Job prayed for them. Then God gave Job more children and blessed him with great riches.

THEOLOGICAL SIGNIFICANCE OF JOB

1. God may allow people to be tested so that they can demonstrate their dedication to God and His will for their lives.
2. It is an error to conclude that all sickness and trouble come because of sin. Sometimes the innocent suffer, and the wicked are not immediately judged.
3. Since people on earth cannot see the whole picture and have a very limited understanding of God's plans and wise purposes, they should not question God's justice.
4. Comforting the sufferer is not achieved by naive accusations, but by identifying with their grief and praying for God's mercy.

In the New Testament, James remembered the patience of Job during his long period of suffering and encouraged his readers to wait faithfully for God's compassion.

The mysterious and yet wise plan of God that governs the way He rules the world is treated at several points in the New Testament. Jesus told His disciples that a certain blind man was not blind because he or his parents had sinned. He was blind so that God's power could be displayed in Jesus; the affliction was not a punishment for sin (John 9:1-3).

ECCLESIASTES

Distinguishing between Vanity and the Good

This book's repeated statements about the vanity of life under the sun have frequently caused negative attitudes toward the value of Ecclesiastes. The book appears to be pessimistic, fatalistic, cynical, and without much spiritual significance. But this view ignores the numerous statements about what is good and enjoyable for mankind. People are to fear God and remember that every good thing that we have is a gift from God. Because of these two emphases (vanity and good), it is best to see the author as a realist who recognized that life was full of frustrating and vain situations. But he also realized that there are some values that give life meaning, and he encouraged the reader to be wise by knowing what has value and what is useless.

Outline of Ecclesiastes

Experience reveals much vanity in life	1:1–6:12
Much repetition is vain	1:1-11
Striving only brings vanity	1:12–2:26
No one can fully understand life or God	3:1–4:16
The vanity of hypocrisy and riches	5:1–6:12
Experience shows what is good	7:1–12:7
Things that are good and wise	7:1-29
It is good to enjoy life	8:1–9:9
Work, be wise, avoid foolishness	9:10–10:20
Remember your Creator and fear God	11:1–12:7

The preacher/teacher was a king in Jerusalem who was the son of David (1:1, 12). The only one who fits this description was Solomon. Was this a book written about Solomon, or did Solomon ever come to his senses and realize the vanity of his ways? Some suggest that he may have repented of his evil ways (1 Kings 11:1-11) when he was about to die, but the Bible never records anything about a revival at the end of his life.

EXPERIENCE REVEALS MUCH VANITY IN LIFE

What advantage do people gain from all their work? People profit about as much as the sun that goes round and round and is never done, about as much as the wind or the water that never finish their work. All this work seems to be in vain.

Constantly striving after wisdom is no answer, for that only increases one's grief (1:12-18). Striving after the pleasures of wine, possessions, more servants, gold, or beautiful music does not give lasting satisfaction (2:1-11). Although it is better to be wise, both the wise and the foolish die and are soon forgotten. Life and all its work sometimes seem futile, for who knows—maybe children will waste it all. The best thing to do is to enjoy whatever God has given. He will give wisdom and joy to the good person, but will take away what little the foolish person has to enjoy (2:24-26).

It is wise to recognize that there is a proper time for every experience of life—war and peace, birth and death (3:1-8). God has secretly arranged all these things so that people will fear Him. Although people cannot fully understand God's plan, they should rejoice, work hard, and see life as God's gift of grace (3:9-15). Life may seem unjust at times, but people are not much better at judging this than the beasts. God will judge every person's deeds, particularly people who oppress or who are selfish, over-competitive, or unteachable, or are workaholics (4:1-16). These characteristics lead to vanity, not wisdom.

It is vain to come hypocritically to the temple to worship God and say things that one does not really mean, for God knows what everyone is doing. All God requires is that one fear Him (5:1-7). Dependence on riches is also futile, for they will not satisfy and cannot be taken with one after death (5:10–6:9). It is best to just enjoy the things God has given. These are gifts from God, and He can give people the ability to be content with what they have (5:18–6:2).

EXPERIENCE SHOWS WHAT IS GOOD

Using some deep proverbs, Ecclesiastes suggests that it is good to think about the shortness of life, to listen to the wise person, to be patient, to not yearn for the good old days, and to be content with one's lot (7:1-14). Although it is hard to understand why the righteous sometimes suffer, the wise person will fear God and escape trouble by avoiding extremes. Wisdom gives a person some strength against the sinful tendencies that have affected everyone (7:19, 20).

Unfortunately there are very few wise people around, even though God originally made everyone righteous. One simple way to demonstrate wisdom is to be loyal and obedient to the laws and political rulers (8:1-9), though it is clear that governments do not always reward the deeds of the righteous (8:10-14). Although people may not understand why God allows these things, they can rest assured that every life is in God's hands (8:16-9:1). One day everyone will die, but before that day it is important that people be happy and enjoy life with their family, work hard at their responsibilities, and see wisdom as a great resource for a good life (9:2-18). Such behavior will help a person avoid foolish actions, such as falling in the pit that was dug to trap someone else (10:1-20).

People need to live by faith (11:1-6), rejoice, and think about God the Creator before old age sets in and they die (12:1-7). There is much vanity in life, so those who fear God and obey His commandments will learn wisdom from the people that God, the Good Shepherd, has put in their lives (12:8-14).

THEOLOGICAL SIGNIFICANCE OF ECCLESIASTES

1. People who are always striving after more wisdom, pleasure, or wealth will find futility, not true satisfaction.
2. Although people cannot fully understand God's plans, He is in control of all the aspects of each person's life.
3. People should enjoy the food, family, and work that God has given them—these are God's gifts.
4. Above all things, fear God and obey His commandments; be wise and walk circumspectly in this evil world.

DISCUSSION QUESTIONS

1. Why do people suffer? Give several suggestions from Job.
2. If you were one of Job's comforters and did not know about Job 1–3, what would you have said to Job?
3. What did Job learn when God spoke to him in 38–41? See 40:1-5 and 42:1-6.
4. Why does the book of Ecclesiastes compare so many things to striving after wind?
5. Compare Ecclesiastes 2:24-26, 3:12-14, 5:18-20, and 9:7-10 to Paul's admonitions in Philippians 4:11-13, 1 Timothy 6:6-11, and Hebrews 13:5-6.

Chapter Sixteen

INSTRUCTIONAL WISDOM

THE TITLES OF THE two books Proverbs and Song of Solomon are related to the period of Solomon, the son of David, who was king in Jerusalem about 970-930 B.C. (Prov. 1:1; 10:1; 25:1; Song of Sol. 1:1; 3:7, 9, 11; 8:11, 12). When Solomon became king, he asked God for wisdom so that he could lead the nation and accurately judge between what was right and wrong (1 Kings 3:6-12). God gave him a wise and discerning heart with more wisdom than anyone before him and anyone who would be born after him.

The Queen of Sheba testified to his wisdom (1 Kings 10:1-8), and, according to 1 Kings 4:32, Solomon spoke 3,000 proverbs and wrote 1,005 songs. This means that the entire content of Proverbs and the Song of Solomon is only a small percentage of his total writings. No one knows what the book looked like at the end of Solomon's life, but Proverbs 25:1 indicates that some of these sayings were not collected into the book of Proverbs until the time of Hezekiah. The introductions to chapters 30 and 31 reveal that sayings from Agur and King Lemuel were included within this collection. The dates and historical background of these men are unknown, but many would place them after the time of Hezekiah.

The Song of Solomon contains a series of songs that are also very difficult to date. These songs may have some distant connection with the wedding songs used by Arabs hundreds of years later in Syria, but this evidence relates more to the cultural background than to the date of the book. A better comparison might be the wedding song in Psalm 45. Since no direct evidence indicates that the songs in the Song of Solomon were originally sung at a wedding (the material after 5:1 took place after the wedding), it is wiser to simply view these songs as love poems and not assume that they were used at a wedding.[1] Some believe these songs were written about Solomon's wedding with his Shulammite bride, but not by Solomon himself.

Over the years there has been considerable debate over the meaning of this song. Many believe that it is an allegory of God's love for Israel and/or for the church. To others it is simply a literal story about married love. Actually it is both—a historical story with two themes of meaning. In one theme we learn about love, marriage, and sex; and the other theme demonstrates God's overwhelming love for His people.

Archeologists have found brief songs and proverbial statements among the writings of the Sumerians, Babylonians, and Egyptians.[2] Although songs and proverbial sayings were common among the uneducated, the upper class ideas discussed in these collections of proverbs suggest that they were used in the process of educating young men who would serve in the king's royal court (Prov. 14:35; 22:29; 23:1, 20). Of course, those who knew these proverbs probably taught these principles to people outside the court.

PROVERBS

The wisdom contained in the book of Proverbs is arranged in a variety of stylistic formulas: a) antithetical statements that contrast opposites— "The thoughts of the righteous are right; but the counsels of the wicked are deceit" (Prov. 12:5); b) comparisons that draw on nature—"As cold waters to a thirsty soul, so is good news from a far country" (Prov. 25:25); c) "better" comparisons that rank certain kinds of behavior as preferable—"It is better to dwell in the wilderness, than with a contentious and an angry woman" (Prov. 21:19); d) numerical sayings—"There be three things which are too wonderful for me, yea, four which I know not" (Prov. 30:18); e) admonitions concerning wise behavior—"Bow down thine ear, and hear the words of the wise, and apply thine heart unto my knowledge" (Prov. 22:17); f) prohibitions against foolish behavior—"Labor not to be rich; cease from thine own wisdom" (Prov. 23:4).

Although parts of the book of Proverbs are not as cohesively held together as some other sections, several units can be identified.

Outline of Proverbs

The purpose of Proverbs	1:1-6
Instructions to be wise	1:7–9:18
The proverbs of Solomon	10:1–22:16
Admonitions and warnings	22:17–24:34
Hezekiah's collection of proverbs	25:1–29:27
The words of Agur and Lemuel	30:1–31:9
The virtuous wife	31:10-31

Proverbs do not give absolute laws concerning what will happen, nor do they prophesy the outcome of certain behaviors. Proverbs draw on the experience of many people in order to instruct the young on how this world works. Certain character traits and actions bring good results and God's blessing, so a person would be wise to follow these. Other character traits and behavior patterns bring trouble and failure, so the wise will avoid these in order that their relationships with God and with other people will be just and righteous.

THE PURPOSE OF PROVERBS

The purpose of Proverbs was to give the reader wisdom, knowledge, and understanding, and encourage wise behavior, justice, honesty, prudence, and discretion. The person who wishes to be known for these characteristics will want to study this book often.

INSTRUCTIONS TO BE WISE

Wisdom is avoiding sinful companions (1:8-19), untrue speech (4:20-27), sexual immorality (5:1-23; 6:20-35; 7:1-27), laziness (6:6-11), and deceit (6:12-15). Instead people should fear God (1:7; 2:5; 3:7; 9:10), seek after the wisdom that God gives (2:6), trust in God with all their hearts (3:5), accept God's discipline (3:11, 12), honor God with their wealth (3:9), be just and honest in their dealings (2:7, 8), and freely give to those in need (3:27, 28). God created this world through His wisdom (3:19), put the mountains where they are, established the stars and planets in the heavens, set the boundaries for the oceans, and rejoiced over what He did (9:22-31). He knows how the world works and is sovereignly in control of it, so the wise person will fear Him and accept His guidelines for life.

THE PROVERBS OF SOLOMON

Although this section includes fewer topical groupings of verses, various themes are emphasized again and again in these antithetical sayings. God's sovereign control over the affairs of mankind is certain because He cares for the righteous when they are in trouble (10:3), He gives blessings and riches (10:6, 22), and He lengthens a person's life (10:27). God's eyes see everything that people do (15:3). He even knows their motives (16:2; 17:3; 21:2); therefore, He will destroy the house of the proud (15:25). Although people make plans for the future, it is God who answers their prayers and directs their steps according to His own purposes (16:1, 4, 9, 33; 19:21). Victory in war comes from God (21:31), and He will repay those who do evil (20:22).

The wise person will not act like the fool; he will avoid wickedness, slander, laziness, pride, deception, cruelty, and anger, and will fear God and walk in His ways so that his life will be long and blessed (14:2, 26, 27; 15:16, 33; 16:6; 19:23; 22:4). True wisdom brings people into a right theological relationship with God and a right social relationship with other people.

Admonitions and Warnings

This section, which has many similarities with the Egyptian *Admonitions of Amenemope*, is more like a series of laws rather than proverbs. Many paragraphs begin: "Do not . . ." and they warn not to oppress the poor (22:22), not to associate with hot-tempered people (22:24), not to concentrate on becoming rich (23:4), not to withhold discipline from a child (23:13), not to envy the life of the sinner (23:17; 24:1, 19) nor rejoice when the wicked fall (24:17). In most cases a reason is given to explain why such action is unwise (22:23—"For the LORD will plead their cause;" 24:18—"Lest the LORD see it and it displeases him").

The wise person will trust in God (22:19), desire to follow the way of wisdom (24:3-7), respect those who have authority (24:21), show no partiality in judgment (24:23), and work hard (24:30-34).

Hezekiah's Collection of Proverbs

The diverse proverbs collected by Hezekiah in this section are particularly well developed. "A word fitly spoken is like apples of gold in pictures of silver" (25:11). "If thine enemy be hungry, give him bread to eat; . . . For thou shalt heap coals of fire upon his head" (25:21, 22). "Answer a fool according to his folly, lest he be wise in his own conceit" (26:5). "As a dog returneth to his vomit, so a fool returneth to his folly" (26:11). These and many other rich comparisons provide a gold mine of practical advice for any person who truly wishes to be as wise as Solomon. Those who have eyes should read and be opened to the light.

The Words of Agur and Lemuel

The wise man Agur admits that he does not understand everything that God does (30:2-4), but he desires that God would teach him wisdom and keep him from deception (30:8-9). He then gives a series of numerical wisdom sayings related to the amazing behavior of people and animals (30:10-33). King Lemuel warns against the evils of drinking too much wine (31:1-9).

The Virtuous Wife

The last paragraph is an acrostic poem describing the virtue, diligence, skill, wisdom, piety, generosity, and inner beauty of a woman who is wise and fears the Lord. She is an excellent woman and a wonderful gift from God.

THEOLOGICAL SIGNIFICANCE OF PROVERBS

1. Fearing God is the first step to gaining wisdom.
2. God created this world and runs it according to His wise principles.
3. Foolish people reject God and His ways, but the wise trust Him and will enjoy His blessing.
4. God has set down guidelines to govern righteous interpersonal relationships between people. A wise person will learn them and follow them.

SONG OF SOLOMON

This book is like no other in the Old Testament. It is not a sermon like the prophetic texts, but a series of dialogues between a man and a woman, a chorus of the daughters of Jerusalem and a woman, and dialogues within dreams. Since Israel, the covenant, and God's activity with mankind are not key issues within these discussions, there were some early Jewish debates concerning its inclusion within the canon of Scripture.

Others were offended by its focus on what appears to be almost a lustful concentration on the beauty of the human body. Consequently, "more sanctified" interpretations were developed that saw this imagery as symbolic of the love between God and Israel, or for Christians, the love between Christ and the church. This led to exaggerated allegorical interpretations that were not connected to the historical or grammatical meaning of the text.

While most find only two main characters in this love story, some believe there is a love triangle within the book. Solomon was trying to woo a beautiful country girl, but she was in love with a plain shepherd boy from the country. The drama describes the tension that developed because of these conflicting loyalties.[3] Since the presence of the shepherd boy is not explicit in this story, this interpretation is not preferred.

In light of the important place that love has in the relationship between a man and a woman, it should not be too surprising to find a biblical discussion of this topic. Elsewhere Scripture condemns the perverse sexual relationships of the people of Sodom and Gomorrah (Gen. 19), has a long series of laws about purity and sexuality (Lev. 15; 18; 20), condemns David for his sin with Bathsheba (2 Sam. 11–12), abhors the prostitution that went on at Baal temples (1 Kings 14:24; 2 Kings

23:7), and warns young men to stay away from evil women (Prov. 7). In these songs there is a positive description of love and sexuality.

Outline of Song of Solomon

Mutual expressions of love	1:1–2:7
Meeting of the two in the country	2:8–3:5
The wedding procession and marriage	3:6–5:1
The bride's longing for her lover	5:2–6:9
Bridegroom's assurances of love	6:1–8:4
Final affirmations of love	8:5–14

A brief description of the events within each of these episodes will help clarify the movement of the action and the emphasis on expressing love for the beloved.

MUTUAL EXPRESSIONS OF LOVE

The woman desires to be with the king in his chambers (1:2, 3), but in all humility she does not see herself as beautiful (1:5-7). Solomon tells her how beautiful she is (1:9-10, 15). Then she thinks (1:12-14) and speaks about her admiration of Solomon and his house (1:16, 17). She still thinks she is just an average girl, like a common lily (2:1), but the great Solomon has caused her to be lovesick (2:3-6).

MEETING OF THE TWO IN THE COUNTRY

One day Solomon went to this young lady's country village and found her (1:8, 9). It is spring, and he calls her to come and spend some time with him (2:10-14). When he is gone, she dreams about him, goes looking for him at night, and finally finds her love (3:1-5). She cannot stand to be without him.

THE WEDDING PROCESSION AND MARRIAGE

A grand picture of the wedding procession with the king carried on a couch and with soldiers begins the preparations for the wedding day (3:6-11). Solomon praises his bride's outward appearance (4:1-6) and desires to go away with her to explore her love and the sexual pleasures of her garden (4:7-15). She accepts his love, and he enters her garden of love (4:16–5:1).

THE BRIDE'S LONGING FOR HER LOVER

After the wedding the bride misses her absent husband. In her dreams the lovers are living on different schedules and are separated from one another (5:2-7). She is desperate to find him, but he is gone. All she can do is sing a song of praise that expresses her deep love for her husband (5:10-16). Finally he returns to her garden of love (6:2, 3) and tells of his love for her (6:4-9).

THE BRIDEGROOM'S ASSURANCES OF LOVE

Solomon reassures his bride of her beauty and his deep love for her (7:1-10). She desires to take him away into the country (and away from business), maybe back to her home, so that they can better enjoy their love for one another (7:11–8:3).

FINAL AFFIRMATIONS OF LOVE

The couple goes away, and love is awakened near her home (8:5, 6). She describes the strength of the power of love and how precious it is (8:6, 7). Although she used to be a young, immature girl who was pure and did not know a man (8:8, 9), she has now found Solomon and willingly gives herself to him (8:10-12).

THEOLOGICAL SIGNIFICANCE OF SONG OF SOLOMON

1. Love expresses appreciation for the beauty (physical and mental) of the one loved and results in a powerful commitment of devotion and mutual fulfillment.
2. Love can be given, but not required or purchased.
3. Sexual purity before marriage is essential. Otherwise the unique bond of love within marriage will be weak.

DISCUSSION QUESTIONS

1. What do Proverbs 2–7 have to say about sexual behavior outside of the marriage relationship?
2. Using a concordance, look up the references in Proverbs for one of the following words—lazy/laziness, tongue, discipline, fear. List the references and then write a brief paragraph about this topic that you can share with someone else.
3. How does the fear of God affect a person's practical day-to-day life?
4. How would you define love? What are some characteristics of love in the Song of Solomon?
5. How can human love help us understand something of God's love for us? What should characterize our love for Him?
6. What are the various interpretations of Solomon's song?

Chapter Seventeen

UNDERSTANDING AND INTERPRETING THE PROPHETS

DIVERSITY AMONG THE PROPHETS

When most people speak of the prophets, they immediately think of individuals such as Isaiah or Daniel because they wrote some of the most important prophetic books of the Bible. These men were doubtless two key people God used to proclaim His Word. However, there were many other men and women in Israel who had the ability to speak prophetically but who did not write books (the names of some of these people are even unknown).

Because Moses had so much trouble with the people of Israel during their wilderness journeys, God encouraged him to share the burden with the seventy elders of Israel (Num. 11:10-17). After the seventy elders of Israel consecrated themselves to the Lord, God sent His Spirit upon them, and they prophesied. Since these men prophesied only this one time, they were not considered official prophets (11:24-25).

Some prophets such as Samuel, Jeremiah, and Ezekiel were also priests. Thus they filled two different functions in Israeli society. A few Levitical priests prophesied as they sang praise to God and played musical instruments in the temple (1 Chron. 25:1-5). Other prophets such as Gad and Nathan (who were sometimes called seers) had no official role in the temple but delivered God's Word from time to time and functioned as moral and political advisors to King David (2 Sam. 12:1-15; 24:11; 1 Chron. 21:9). A few prophets such as Elisha did miracles (2 Kings 4), but most did not have these powers. Some prophets worshiped together as a group or band of prophets at the time of Samuel (1 Sam. 10:5). Later the sons of the prophets who were in Bethel and Jericho at the time of Elisha lived and studied together (2 Kings 2:1-18). Most later writing prophets worked by themselves and made no reference to other prophets around them.

Miriam was the first woman to be a prophetess and a singer of God's praise (Exod. 15:20). Deborah was a prophetess and judge over Israel (Judg. 4:4), and Huldah was the prophetess who served Josiah and identified the book found in the temple as the Law of Moses (2 Kings 22:14-20).

These examples show that God used very different people from varied backgrounds to proclaim His words in many different contexts. This diversity was needed in order to allow God's Word to affect all aspects of society. But this diversity also caused some problems, for it became very difficult for some people to distinguish true prophets from false prophets.[1]

UNITY AMONG THE PROPHETS

The key factor identifying prophets was not their role or parental background or whether they wrote a prophetic book. The main issue was, did God fill these people with His Spirit and speak through them?

The Hebrew word *prophet* means to be God's spokesman, while words for *seer* refer to those who have insight into God's will. Although Baal prophets and other pagan diviners claimed to deliver the will of their gods (Jer. 23:13-22), they spoke out of their own imagination. The true prophets gave prophecies that were later fulfilled (Deut. 18:20-22); they were known for their moral character and hatred of sin (Mic. 3:8); they worshiped only the God of Israel (Deut. 13:1-5), and they were inspired with courage to declare God's message by the presence of the Holy Spirit within them (Mic. 3:8).

THE RECEPTION OF THE MESSAGE
BY THE PROPHETS

The prophets were messengers of God, delivering His words of judgment as well as His words of encouragement and hope. The method of receiving the divine message has always been partially hidden in mystery. Some prophets describe their "call" to the prophetic office as coming in a vision of God, with the Spirit coming to indwell them (Isa. 6; Ezek. 1-3), but most prophets never had a spectacular call experience.

The essential requirement for a prophet was the presence of God's Spirit and the reception of God's words. Through the Spirit's work in the minds and hearts of the prophets, they heard words and saw visions or dreams. The truth they received was molded and expressed in terms of the language and culture of that day and proclaimed to the people. The prophets' knowledge of Scripture, their cultural habits, and their personal styles of speech influenced how the words were said, but these did not change or corrupt the message. God revealed Himself to the prophets in ways they could understand so that they could communicate His truth in ways that made sense to the average Israelite.

THE DELIVERY OF THE PROPHETIC MESSAGE

Sometimes the prophets spoke their messages orally, but at other times they acted out a dramatic message because the stubborn people of Israel would no longer listen to what they said (Ezek. 4–5). Sometimes their original message was immediately written down on a tablet (Isa. 8:1; Hab. 2:2), but frequently their messages were not collected and written down on a scroll until some time later. Jeremiah 36:2 indicates that Jeremiah's messages from 627 to 605 B.C. were not written down until Baruch recorded them in 605 B.C. Many of the prophets chose to arrange their message in chronological order, but others (Jeremiah and Daniel) arranged parts of their books topically.

To make sure that the people of Israel understood that they were speaking for God, the prophets repeatedly began or ended their messages with phrases such as: "Thus says the LORD;" "declares the LORD;" "an oracle of the LORD;" "the LORD God came unto me and said." These statements assured the people that the prophets were not speaking their own words but the words of God. The declarations revealed the authority behind the prophets' words and encouraged the listeners to take seriously what was said.

The prophets Amos and Hosea delivered God's Word to the northern nation of Israel; Jonah gave a message of God's judgment to the foreign nation of Assyria; Daniel witnessed to Babylonian and Persian kings, but most of the writing prophets preached to the people of Judah. In almost every case God's deep and undeserved grace was evident. He not only warned these nations of His coming judgment but called them to repent of their sins so that they might escape His judgment. Even the pagan nations that were Israel's enemies were warned to repent.

THE MESSAGE OF THE PROPHETS

Since the prophets lived in different countries and delivered their messages over several hundred years, quite a variety of topics are discussed. Political, social, and religious situations varied, so new messages that fit the needs of each audience were given. Amos emphasized the social injustice in Israel, while Hosea focused primarily on God's hatred of Israel's worship of Baal. Obadiah condemned the Edomites for their pride and mistreatment of the Jews when the city of Jerusalem was destroyed, while Habakkuk questioned why God was allowing the wicked to prosper in Jerusalem and why He would use the wicked Babylonians to judge a more righteous nation. Each prophet was unique, but each had a message from God to deliver to a specific audience.

Their messages did have a common understanding of God and His character. The prophets consistently called all people to worship only the God of Israel. They repeatedly condemned sin and encouraged repentance. Their messages frequently reminded the Israelites of God's grace to His people when He brought them up from Egypt (Amos 2:9-11; 3:1, 2; 9:7), His deep love for them in making a covenant with them at Mt. Sinai (Jer. 11:1-13), and His demand that they should worship only Him (Jer. 10:1-16). If the people would acknowledge their sin, confess it to God, and turn away from their evil ways, God would bless them (Jer. 3:12-14; 4:1-4). If the people would not respond to God's grace and warning, the covenant curses would fall on the nation (Deut. 27–28), and they would be destroyed.

Although the prophets delivered many messages of doom and destruction, they also saw a future day of peace, righteousness, and blessing. God would forgive their sins and create a new heart in mankind (Ezek. 34:25-31) through the death of His servant (Isa. 53). He would give them a new covenant (Jer. 31:31-34). His Spirit would powerfully transform them (Joel 2:28, 29), and the land would produce abundantly (Amos 9:13-15). The righteous seed of David, the king of Israel, would reign as kings in Jerusalem (Isa. 9:1-7; Jer. 23:5-7). The evil nations of the earth will be judged, and God's dominion will be established as authority is given to the heavenly Son of Man (Dan. 7:9-14). Then the nations will come to Jerusalem to hear God teach His law, and war will end forever (Isa. 2:1-4). A new heaven and earth will come into existence (Isa. 65:17), and the departed spirits of the dead will come to life (Isa. 25:8; Dan. 12:1, 2).[2]

Through these messages the prophets hoped to persuade the people of Israel and Judah to turn from their selfish ways and dedicate their lives to God's service. Although the pagan people in Nineveh responded to Jonah's message, and the postexilic community responded to the challenge from Haggai and Zechariah to rebuild the temple in Jerusalem, most prophets never record any kind of positive response. Their hearers were without excuse because they heard the word of truth, but in their depraved state they refused to submit to the will of God.

THE INTERPRETATION OF PROPHECY

Frequently different interpretations of prophetic texts are found in commentaries and theology books because the meaning of some verses is not clearly spelled out. Some of the problems relate to the language of these books. The poetic nature of many prophecies and the use of symbolic language make interpretation difficult. Problems can also arise when the reader is not aware of the historical situation surrounding the prophet's message. Finally, differences of opinion exist because people come to the text with different theological assumptions, particularly as it relates to the eschatological fulfillment of prophecy related to the Messiah and the establishment of God's kingdom.

Sound principles of interpretation are needed in order to guard against being led astray by false doctrine or wild speculation. The primary goal is to understand what God communicated through each prophet. This goal is accomplished through historical and grammatical research into the meaning of the text. In-depth research will require knowledge of the Hebrew language and extensive understanding of Israel's history. Fortunately, many good translations of the Hebrew Bible and many commentaries, study Bibles, and concordances are now available to help the average person clarify difficult passages.[3]

When studying a prophetic book, begin by reading through the whole book at once (this probably will not be possible for some of the longer books). Reading the entire book will provide a basic understanding of the thrust of the book and prevent wrong conclusions based on an incomplete knowledge of what was said. From this reading, and with the help of study resources, a general understanding of the historical background should begin to emerge. Was the prophet preaching in Israel or Judah? Who was the king at this time (usually this is given in the first verses of each book)? What were the prevailing political, social, and religious conditions during this period?

Next divide the book into topical sections in order to get an outline of the prophet's messages. What problems did the prophet preach about? Trace the argument of the prophet as he attempts to convince people to accept God's Word and act upon it. How do these shorter messages fit together to make up the whole book? Which messages relate to the present situation of the people to whom the prophet delivered his message, and which refer to things that will happen in the future?

Now study individual passages in more detail. The difficult poetry or symbolism in a verse can be compared in two different translations, or the meaning of a word can be examined by using a concordance to do a word study. Words that symbolize ideas foreign to our culture are especially difficult. For example, *shepherd* is a symbol of kingship (2 Sam. 5:2; Ezek. 34); *cows of Bashan* refers to the rich women of Samaria who are "bossy" and extremely rich (Amos 4:1, 2); *singing hills* are a picture of joy (Isa. 44:23).

Some of the most difficult passages are those that prophesy future events. Ahijah's prophecy to Jeroboam, which was accompanied by the tearing of a garment into twelve pieces (1 Kings 11:29-32), was literally fulfilled a short time later when the twelve tribes of Israel were divided into two nations (1 Kings 12:15-20). The prophet Ahijah knew what would happen, but he did not give any of the details of the situation or the exact date. In a similar manner, Isaiah told Hezekiah that God would deliver him from the Assyrian king Sennacherib (1 Kings 19:20-34), but he did not say when or how this would happen.

Like these examples, most prophecies do not give all the details of exactly what will happen or the date when God will accomplish what He has promised. The person of faith needs to know what God will do, but faith always involves trusting in Him for many things that are unseen and unknown.

With messianic prophecies, the interpreter needs to be careful not to read New Testament fulfillment back into the Old Testament. Although the prophet Isaiah knew that the Messiah would be born of a virgin (Isa. 7:14), he did not know where He would be born or how this would happen. God revealed to Micah that the Messiah would be born in Bethlehem (Mic. 5:2), but the prophet never said anything about the census that would bring Mary and Joseph from Nazareth to Bethlehem.

Even more problematic are attempts to fit Old Testament passages into the tribulation and millennial texts of the New Testament. Since God never said anything to any of the Old Testament prophets about the difference between heaven and the millennium (the distinction is only mentioned in Revelation 20), it is very difficult to know whether a prophetic text is referring to a heavenly time period when the new heaven and the new earth will exist or whether it is referring to what the book of Revelation calls the millennium. Since what would happen was far more important than when, the believers had to trust God to fulfill His Word. Jesus said that we and the angels do not need to know the dates that God has set (Acts 1:7; Matt. 24:36). Nevertheless, Scripture is not totally without a chronological ordering of events, for a careful comparative study of prophecy shows that the Messiah's tribulation would come before His glorification (Isa. 53), and a similar pattern exists at the end of time.

These prophecies are a source of hope for the future and a warning to be ready for the day of the Lord. They encourage believers to trust in God's sovereign plan for this world in spite of the evil, war, persecution, and natural disasters that will become worse and worse in the future. Old Testament prophecies give basic information about what God will do in the future, but for a fuller and more complete revelation on these topics, believers should also read Jesus' words in Matthew 24, Paul's words in 2 Thessalonians 2, and John's words in the book of Revelation. Although many of "the words are closed up and sealed till the time of the end. . . . Blessed is he that waiteth . . ." (Dan. 12:9, 12).

THEOLOGICAL SIGNIFICANCE OF THE PROPHETS

1. God revealed His will to the prophets through the gift of His Holy Spirit.
2. God's message was faithfully communicated by the prophets in words that were meaningful and applicable to those who heard.
3. God progressively (not all at once) revealed information about the future.
4. God's future plans are sure, but the dates when they will come to pass are known only to Him.
5. God's kingdom will be established; therefore, the believer has hope and looks forward to worshiping at the throne of God.

DISCUSSION QUESTIONS

1. What are some of the advantages and disadvantages of having so much diversity among the prophets? How does diversity among believers today help spread God's Word?
2. What was the basic prophetic understanding of: a) God; b) sin; c) repentance; d) judgment? How much do these differ from the New Testament understanding of these issues?
3. List some reasons why people differ in their understanding of prophecy. Write your interpretation of Isaiah 4:2 and then compare it with another person's interpretation. Did you come to different conclusions? If so, explain why.
4. What books do you have that help you discover the historical and grammatical meaning of a verse? What books might give you more information?
5. What regular step-by-step method do you use when studying a book of the Bible? Which steps are the easiest, and which are the most difficult?

Chapter Eighteen

EARLY PROPHETS
FROM ISRAEL

SHORTLY AFTER THE DEATH OF Solomon (931 B.C., see 1 Kings 11–12), the powerful kingdom David had established was split into the two nations of Israel (the ten northern tribes) and Judah (the two southern tribes). Jeroboam I, the new king of the northern nation of Israel, set up his own government and army, built a new temple at Bethel (near the southern border) and at Dan (near the northern border), and put non-Levitical priests in charge of the worship of the two golden calves in these temples. These idols were supposed to represent the God who brought them up from the land of Egypt (1 Kings 12:25-33), but the calves were soon confused with the Canaanite god Baal, the god of fertility and rain, who was also pictured as a bull calf. Before long the Israelites were fully involved with the pagan cult of Baalism. Although God raised up the prophets Elijah and Elisha to defeat and destroy this religion during the time of Ahab and Jezebel (1 Kings 16:29–18:46; 2 Kings 1), Baalism was still deceiving the people of Israel years later when Amos and Hosea were preaching in Israel.

Because of the northern nation's sinfulness, God was angry with them and sent the Syrian kings Hazael and Ben-Hadad to defeat them (2 Kings 13:2-3). In the midst of this oppression, the Israelites cried out to God for mercy. As Jonah prophesied, God had compassion on them and sent the Assyrians to defeat the Syrians (2 Kings 13:4, 22, 23; 14:25). With this enemy defeated, Israel was able to become powerful and quite prosperous under the leadership of Jeroboam II (793–753 B.C.). Amos, who prophesied during this prosperous period, saw this wealth as the source of a false sense of security (6:1-7) and condemned those who added to their riches by oppressing the poor (Amos 2:6-8; 3:10; 5:10-12). Hosea's ministry continued after Jeroboam's reign, when a series of weak kings ruled Israel with tyranny (2 Kings 15). Their ineffectiveness allowed the strong Assyrian king Tiglath-pileser III to make Israel his vassal

(2 Kings 15:19, 29; 16:9). The northern nation of Israel was finally taken into Assyrian captivity in 722/721 B.C., a few years after Hosea's prophecy.

JONAH

The Great Compassion of God

The prophet Jonah had two prophetic messages to deliver to two different nations—Israel and Assyria. Scripture says very little about his prophecies concerning Israel and does not record his exact words. Scripture says that he spoke the Word of God early in the reign of Jeroboam II to promise military victories for Israel (2 Kings 14:25). Jonah's prophecy was fulfilled during Jeroboam's reign, but the Israelites did not continue to serve God once they were delivered from their enemies.

The book of Jonah describes the prophet's ministry to the Assyrians in Nineveh early in the reign of Jeroboam II.

Outline of Jonah

God's compassion on Jonah	1:1–2:10
Jonah rejects God's commission	1:1-16
Jonah turns to God for salvation	1:17–2:10
God's compassion on Nineveh	3:1–4:11
Nineveh turns to God for salvation	3:1-9
Jonah rejects God's mercy on Nineveh	3:10–4:11

This book is unique when compared to other prophetic books, for it contains only one short statement from Jonah's preaching (3:4). The book shows that the prophets were real people who were not always perfect. They sometimes struggled with the responsibility of telling others about God's hatred of sin. Jonah learned the hard way that God does not want anyone to perish; He wants everyone to know the truth and repent (1 Tim. 2:4; 2 Pet. 3:9).

GOD'S COMPASSION ON JONAH

After receiving God's commission to go to the great Assyrian capital of Nineveh, Jonah chose to reject God's calling for his life. Foolishly Jonah thought he could hide from God (1:3), avoid the problems he might encounter by preaching in the violent pagan city of Nineveh, and ensure God's destruction of the Assyrians by not warning them of God's impending judgment (4:2). After he boarded a ship going to Tarshish, God did not reject Jonah but brought him to the place where he willingly chose to serve God in Nineveh (3:3). After a storm and the casting of lots, Jonah admitted his guilt and accepted the punishment of certain death in the sea. In compassion God calmed the sea for the pagan sailors (1:15) and sent a large fish to swallow Jonah, rescuing him from drowning (1:17). Immediately the pagan sailors feared God and worshiped Him while Jonah prayed for God's help in the belly of the fish (2:1, 7). Jonah, who did not want God to be compassionate to the undeserving Assyrians in Nineveh, recognized that God's undeserved compassion had been given to him (2:9). Thus he obeyed God's second call (3:1).

GOD'S COMPASSION ON NINEVEH

Jonah boldly proclaimed the message of destruction in the streets of Nineveh (3:4).[1] To his surprise, the king and people of Nineveh believed God and in humility repented of their violent ways and sought God's mercy (3:5-9). God, in His sovereign freedom, had compassion on Nineveh and did not destroy it.

Ironically, Jonah rejected God's redemptive work in Nineveh and became angry with God (4:1-2).[2] Although Jonah selfishly had compassion on the plant that gave him shade in the hot desert outside the city of Nineveh, he did not want God to be merciful to the people in Nineveh. This account shows the depth of God's love and the danger of a shallow human love for unbelievers.

THEOLOGICAL SIGNIFICANCE OF JONAH

1. This story reveals that God uses believers to carry out His plan to spread the news of God's hatred of sin and to tell of His grace to those who repent and turn to Him in faith.
2. Although God's messengers may reject His will, God does not abandon His plans. Through God's control of events, His servants will experience His discipline in order to bring them to obedience.
3. Since no one can hide from God, each person must faithfully do God's will and share the message that God has given to him or her.
4. Limiting God's compassion to His covenant people is a great misunderstanding of God's love and will lead to a great misunderstanding of His will for the believer.

Jesus taught from the book of Jonah in Matthew 12:38-41. He compared the three days that Jonah spent in the fish to the three days He would spend in the earth after His death. He also said that the repentant people of Nineveh would condemn the Pharisees who rejected Jesus' message, a message even greater than Jonah's.

AMOS

God's Intent to Destroy Israel

Amos made his living as a fruit grower and a manager of shepherds[3] in the small village of Tekoa about six miles south of Bethlehem (1:1). God instructed him to go to the northern nation of Israel and warn them that God would spare His judgment no longer (7:8, 14, 15). Although Amos had not been trained in the prophetic schools of his day, he courageously withstood the condemnation of the high priest at the temple at Bethel (7:10-17) and the unbelief of his audience. Because God had spoken to him, he knew it was his responsibility to share the message (3:8).

His prophecy was given two years before a major earthquake (ca. 760 B.C.). Uzziah, king in Judah, and Jeroboam II, king of Israel, were at the height of their military power at this time, and a rich upper class was ruling the nation through violence and oppression. The people were going through their religious rituals at the temple at Bethel, but their hearts were not turned toward God (4:6-13). Amos announced the unthinkable: God would destroy His own chosen people, the northern nation of Israel.

Outline of Amos

War oracles against the nations	1:1–2:16
Oracles against six foreign nations	1:3–2:3
Oracles against Judah and Israel	2:4-16
Confirmation of God's judgment on Israel	3:1–6:14
Reasons for God's judgment	3:1–4:13
Laments because of Israel's false hopes	5:1–6:14
Visions and exhortations about Israel's end	7:1–9:15
Five visions of God's destruction	7:1–9:10
God's restoration after judgment	9:11-15

Amos's skill as a preacher is demonstrated in his blunt castigation of those who were getting rich through oppression, his mockery of those who were not truly worshiping God, and his laments for those who were blindly trusting in false promises. His illustrations are those of a country shepherd (2:13—a wagon with grain on it; 3:12—a shepherd rescuing a lamb from a lion; 9:9—a sieve to separate grain), but his knowledge of world history (1:3–2:3) and his biting sarcasm show that he was very knowledgeable about what was really going on in his world.

WAR ORACLES AGAINST THE NATIONS

When troops would go to war, frequently a prophet or priest would be consulted to ask God's blessing and determine if God would give them victory (Judg. 20:18, 26-28). Traditionally these prophecies would reveal that God would destroy their enemies and give them victory. This would give the soldiers confidence to fight. In chapters 1 and 2 Amos's prophecy follows this same pattern (possibly given before a major battle). He describes the terrible inhumanity (killing pregnant women—1:13) that characterized the nations around Israel and assures them that God would destroy these nations because of their sins (1:3–2:3). But instead of ending his prophecy with news of salvation for Israel, Amos surprised his audience by announcing that Israel was worse than the other nations and would be destroyed too. The wealthy and powerful in Israel were selling the poor into slavery for small debts and sexually abusing their servants (2:6-8). They forgot that God hates oppression and had delivered them from the slavery of Egypt years ago (2:9, 10). None of them should become a slave again.

CONFIRMATION OF GOD'S JUDGMENT ON ISRAEL

Most Israelites rejected Amos's prophecy. They were the chosen people of God; they had been redeemed from Egypt; God loved them (3:1, 2). But Amos claimed that the privilege of election carried the responsibility of faithful obedience and not God's automatic blessing. It is only logical: If a lion roars, it is attacking its prey; if a nation sins, it will be judged by God (3:3-7). God's message through Amos was God's roar; He was about to attack Israel, His prey (3:8).

What was their sin? Violence, ignoring the difference between right and wrong (3:9, 10), oppression of the poor (4:1), and half-hearted worship at their temples (4:4, 5). In spite of God's chastening, they never turned to God in true repentance (4:4-11); therefore, they must prepare to meet an angry God (4:12).

Amos saw the future judgment and lamented the destruction of the nation (5:1-3, 16, 17). If they would only seek God and be just in their relationships with others, they would live (5:4, 14, 15). Since God hated their worship (5:21), which included false Assyrian gods (5:26),[4] the day of the Lord would be a day of darkness, not salvation (5:18-20). Amos lamented the false sense of security that wealth gave the rich (6:1-7). They would all die.

Amos received five visions that pictured the coming destruction of Israel. In the first two, Amos pleaded for God's mercy on Israel (7:1-6). Surprisingly, God was compassionate and delayed the judgment, even though the Israelites did not repent. In the final three visions (7:7-9; 8:1-3; 9:1-4) God revealed that He would spare Israel no longer. He would remove the temple at Bethel and bring an end to the reign of Jeroboam II. No one would be able to escape His judgment. Although some thought that God's punishment would never touch them (9:10), Amos revealed that every sinner in Israel would die.

Amaziah, the high priest at the temple at Bethel, accused Amos of treason and told him to go earn his living prophesying back home in Judah (7:10-13). Amos refused Amaziah's advice because God had sent him to speak His Word in Israel (7:14-16).

The book ends with a final message about the nation's restoration long after its judgment (9:11-15). God's promises would be fulfilled. The kingdom of David would exist again. The land would be unbelievably fruitful and filled with Jews and Gentiles who call on God's name.

THEOLOGICAL SIGNIFICANCE OF AMOS

1. All people, Jews and Gentiles, will be held accountable for their sins. God hates violence and oppression of the weak.
2. Privilege carries responsibility. God's people will be judged if they take His grace for granted and fail to follow Him.
3. If there is no turning to God, no meeting with Him, "worship" is mere ritual, hypocrisy that God hates.
4. Riches and power can bring a false sense of material security and make one think there is no need to trust God for the future. A false trust in God's promises can give a false sense of spiritual security and cause a person to think there is no need to repent.
5. When God speaks, His servants cannot be quiet. Warnings of God's judgment must be given, even when opposed.

In Acts 15:16-18, James used the promise of restoration in Amos 9:11-15 to remind the Jewish members of the early church that God wanted the Gentiles to be part of the church. This opened the door for Paul's missionary efforts among the Gentiles.

HOSEA

No Knowledge of God, No Love, No Truth

Hosea's ministry (755-25 B.C.) began shortly after the time of Amos and continued almost until Israel was taken captive by the Assyrians in 722/21 B.C. Hosea was born in Israel and married Gomer before the end of the prosperous reign of Jeroboam II (1:1-4). In the years that followed, he saw anarchy, war, economic weakness (5:8, 9; 8:1), and heavy taxation by the Assyrians (2 Kings 15:19, 29). Although his ministry ended before the fall of Israel, his prophecies warned of the approaching destruction of the nation.

Outline of Hosea

Adultery in Israel and Hosea's family	1:1–3:5
Covenant lawsuit against Israel for adultery	4:1–14:9
There is no knowledge of God	4:1–6:6
There is no steadfast love for God	6:7–11:11
There is no truth in Israel	11:12–14:9

Hosea uses the marriage relationship as an analogy to describe the love relationship between God and His covenant people. This analogy explains God's agony over Israel's unfaithfulness to their covenant relationship. After describing the tragedy of his own marriage (1–3), Hosea reports on God's divorce case against Israel. His covenant lawsuit contains a series of: a) accusations, b) announcements of punishment, and c) offers of hope. The first two are expected parts of a divorce lawsuit, but God's consistent offer of hope at the end of each section demonstrates the great love God has for His sinful people.

ADULTERY IN ISRAEL AND HOSEA'S FAMILY

In order to teach Hosea and the Israelites the seriousness of the nation's sins and the depth of God's love for His covenant people, God had Hosea marry a prostitute to symbolize God's relationship with the sinful Israelites (1:2). After some time Gomer was unfaithful to Hosea (the third child probably was not Hosea's, contrast 1:3 and 1:6), just as Israel was unfaithful to God. Accusations of adultery were brought against Gomer (2:1, 5), and Israel was charged with the adultery of worshiping the Canaanite fertility god Baal (2:8-13).

In spite of this terrible sin, Hosea loved Gomer again, and God loved Israel again (3:1). On account of God's love, those who were not His people would one day become His people (1:9; 2:23), and His kingdom would be established under a Davidic king (3:5). Through this experience Hosea came to understand the nature of giving undeserved love. He began to see how God felt when the Israelites were unfaithful to their covenant relationship with Him.

COVENANT LAWSUIT AGAINST ISRAEL FOR ADULTERY

God brought three charges against Israel: There is no knowledge of God, no steadfast love, and no truth. The reason the people had no knowledge of God is that the priests in Israel forgot God's Word (4:6; 5:4) and ignored His instructions (4:10). Instead they became drunk and had sex with prostitutes at the Baal temples (4:11-14). Because of this God would judge the priests (5:1, 2) and bring war on the nation (5:8, 14). At the end of this section God made the surprising offer to heal the people if they would seek Him and desire to know Him (5:15–6:3).

The second accusation is that the people had transgressed God's covenant, murdered (6:7-9), raised up wicked kings (7:5-7; 8:3), made political alliances with pagan nations (7:8, 11; 8:8-10), and worshiped the golden calves (8:5, 6). Each of these accusations shows that Israel had no steadfast love for God. Although God loved them and brought them up from Egypt, they rejected His love (11:1-4). God must discipline them, but because of His deep love He would not give them up. One day they would respond to Him and return to Him (11:8-11).

The third charge is that the nation was full of deception and lies like Jacob their father; there was no truth in them (11:12–12:4). Their worship of Baal was a deception, for there is no other God but the Lord (13:1-4). Although the nation would soon be destroyed, Hosea called the people to return to God and receive His forgiveness and healing (14:1-4).

THEOLOGICAL SIGNIFICANCE OF HOSEA

1. Sin is not a minor thing to God; it is a betrayal of a love commitment, a prostitution of love to something other than God.
2. In spite of the horribleness of sin, God's love is deeper. He will forgive and heal those who seek and love Him.
3. The difficult circumstances of life can be used by God to strengthen us so that God is glorified through our weakness.
4. A real experiential knowledge of God and His Word, a consistent love for God, and truthfulness are central factors of a personal relationship with God.

The New Testament, like Hosea, uses the marriage relationship to describe a person's covenant relationship to God (Eph. 5:22-33). Paul and Peter use Hosea 1:10 and 2:23 to demonstrate that God's grace in redeeming the Gentiles was a fulfillment of His plan to make those who were not His people, His people (Rom. 9:25, 26; 1 Pet. 2:10). Jesus quoted Hosea 6:6 to explain that God desires steadfast love rather than sacrifices (Matt. 9:13; 12:7).

DISCUSSION QUESTIONS

1. How do the sovereignty of God and the free will of mankind work together in the story of Jonah?
2. What was wrong with Jonah's understanding of God?
3. What does Amos 1 say about the accountability of the heathen?
4. Does God condemn riches in Amos, or is it the use of wealth?
5. What did Hosea learn about God through his marriage?

Chapter Nineteen

EARLY PROPHETS
FROM JUDAH

AFTER THE DEATH OF Solomon (931 B.C.) and the division of Israel into two nations (see 1 Kings 11-12), the southern nation of Judah suffered under the leadership of a series of kings. These rulers did not love God the way King David had. Rehoboam built idols and altars to Baal and allowed cultic prostitution to thrive in Judah (1 Kings 14:22-24). Both kings Asa and Jehoshaphat attempted to eliminate Baalism (1 Kings 15:11-14; 2 Chron. 17:1-6), but this false religion was still flourishing in Judah during the prophetic ministry of Micah and Isaiah because King Ahaz and King Manasseh encouraged it (2 Kings 16; 21; Isa. 7).

Micah and Isaiah lived through four different time periods, under four quite different kings of Judah. When Isaiah first began to prophesy, Uzziah (called Azariah in 2 Kings 15:1-7) was the powerful and prosperous king of Judah. God blessed all that he did, but later he became very proud and was struck with leprosy (2 Chron. 26:3-21). Isaiah condemned the proud (Isa. 2:11-19) and Judah's preoccupation with wealth (Isa. 3:16-26).

When the wicked King Ahaz came to power in Judah (2 Kings 16), he worshiped foreign gods and refused to trust God for help. Therefore, God allowed the Assyrian king, Tiglath-pileser III, to make Judah his vassal, as Isaiah and Micah had prophesied (Mic. 1:12-16; Isa. 7). Ahaz's son, the godly King Hezekiah, removed the idols from Judah and rebelled against the Assyrians. Judah was hopelessly outnumbered, but Hezekiah put his total trust in God. In response, God sent an angel to destroy the Assyrian army and deliver the nation (Isa. 36, 37; 2 Kings 18, 19).

In spite of Hezekiah's great love for God, his son Manasseh began to reintroduce Baalism into the nation (2 Kings 21). The righteous were persecuted, and social relationships were undermined by distrust among relatives and violence against the weak (Mic. 7:1-6). Micah and Isaiah brought messages of hope to the people of Judah during these dark days. God would not abandon His people, and one day He would restore His kingdom.

MICAH

God Coming for You

Micah was from Moresheth-gath, a Judean city near the old Philistine stronghold of Lachish. He proclaimed most of his prophetic messages in the capital city of Jerusalem. He began his ministry before the fall of Samaria in 722/21 B.C. and received new messages from God until the early years of Manasseh.

The prophet's messages can be divided into three major sections. Each section begins with warnings of judgment and ends with a message of salvation and hope.

Outline of Micah

God will come with great power	1:1–2:13
He will judge Israel and Judah	1:1-16
Reasons for God's judgment	2:1-11
God will gather a remnant	2:12-13
New leadership will come to Jerusalem	3:1–5:15
God will remove evil leaders	3:1-12
Zion will have a new leader	4:1–5:15
The people must come to God	6:1–7:20
Coming with proper worship	6:1-16
Coming with hope, not despair	7:1-20

Some of these messages are divine judgment speeches (3:1-4), while others are oracles of salvation about the Messiah and the establishment of God's kingdom (4:1–5:5). There is a lament concerning the terrible conditions in Judah (7:1-7), as well as a covenant lawsuit against Judah (6:1-16).

GOD WILL COME WITH GREAT POWER

Early in Micah's ministry (before 722/21 B.C.), he saw a glorious theophany of God coming forth in power from a temple in heaven (1:2-4). God was coming to destroy the idols, false temples, and the capital city of Samaria in Israel. Micah also saw and lamented the coming destruction of Judah (1:8-16). Using the names of towns to create puns, he warned that Aphrah would roll in the "dust" (10), the "deceptive" Achzib would be deceived (14), and calamity from God would fall on Jerusalem. Why would this happen? Because the powerful landlords in Judah coveted and stole property from the poor (2:1-4, 9), because the people thought God was patient and would never punish them (2:6, 7), and because the nation followed drunken false prophets (2:11).

In spite of this sure and severe judgment, God would not reject the righteous remnant of Judah. One day He would gather them together; their king would lead them to freedom (2:12, 13).

New Leadership Would Come to Jerusalem

In order to transform Judah, God needed to remove the evil leadership in Judah (Ahaz and other high officials in government). Those who were ruling unjustly by savagely mistreating others would be treated in a similar manner by their enemies (3:1-4, 9, 10). Money-hungry prophets and priests were more concerned with their profits than with giving spiritual direction from God. Unlike Micah they were not filled with God's Spirit, so they foolishly taught that God would never judge Judah. They refused to boldly condemn the people for their sins (3:5-8, 11).

In the last days new leadership would come to Jerusalem, and God Himself will reign as king over Zion (4:1, 7). At that time the poor and weak, as well as foreigners from all the nations, will come to Jerusalem to be instructed by God (4:2, 6, 7). All war will end, and prosperity will fill the earth (4:3-5). Although the nation would first go through the excruciating pain of exile in Babylon (4:9-11), a new and powerful ruler (the Messiah) would be born in Bethlehem (5:2). He would bring peace to all the world, restore the remnant of Judah, and remove all those earthly things (military might, strong cities, false gods, and false prophets) that people put their trust in (5:4-15).

The People Must Come to God

During the final years of Hezekiah, Manasseh began to introduce his pagan ways into the nation. Micah declared God's covenant lawsuit[1] against Judah because they forgot that God had delivered them from Egypt and had reversed the curse of Balaam (6:1-4). They thought that they could please God by going through the ritual of many sacrifices, but God requires that people act justly, love kindness, and walk humbly with Him (6:6-8). God would destroy these unjust, violent, and deceptive people (6:9-16).

Living during the early years of Manasseh was depressing even for a prophet of God. Micah lamented because it seemed that the godly people had perished, violence was everywhere, and no one could be trusted

(7:1-6). But suddenly he remembered that God is a God of salvation. He hears and answers prayer (7:7, 8). Although some mocked Micah (7:10), he remained confident that the people of Judah would one day return and rebuild Jerusalem after their exile (7:11, 12). God would shepherd them back to their land just as He did when they came out of Egypt (7:14-17). Remembering this, he praised God, for God's unchanging love brings forgiveness of sins, and His everlasting compassion knows no end (7:18-20).

THEOLOGICAL SIGNIFICANCE OF MICAH

1. God will bring judgment on those who do not rule with justice.
2. Teachers who presume on God's patience or think that God will never judge sin are not filled with the Spirit of the Lord.
3. Empty ritual is useless. God wants His people to have humble hearts and behavior that is just and kind to others.
4. It is possible to have hope in the midst of oppression and violence if we trust in God and His promises.
5. The Messiah was born in Bethlehem as Micah had predicted (Matt. 2:3-6), and one day He will reign as king over all the earth. All war will end, and people from all nations will worship Him.

ISAIAH

Judgment and Redemption from the Holy One

Isaiah's earliest prophecies were given near the end of the reign of Uzziah (ca. 750 B.C.) and continued until the beginning of Manasseh's co-regency with Hezekiah (ca. 690 B.C.), paralleling most of Micah's ministry. Isaiah was married and had at least two children (7:3; 8:3). He lived in Jerusalem, and from time to time he spoke to the kings of Judah (Isa. 7; 39). He delivered prophecies of judgment and salvation about Judah, as well as many foreign nations (Isa. 13–27). He is best known for his messianic prophecies about both a king and a suffering servant (Isa. 9; 53). His writings are infiltrated with his sense of the holiness of God because his life was forever changed once he saw the glory of God, the almighty King sitting on His throne (Isa. 6). Isaiah's messages are organized into major blocks.

Outline of Isaiah

The exaltation of God humbles man's pride	1–6
The Prince of Peace will end Judah's wars	7–12

God's sovereign plan for the nations	13–27
Trusting God or military might	28–39
The incomparable God will bring deliverance	40–48
The suffering Servant will bring salvation	49–55
God's final restoration and judgment	56–66

Isaiah was a gifted preacher who used elaborate illustrations (Judah is a vineyard in chapter 5) and interesting figures of speech (Judah's kings are called the rulers of Sodom in 1:10). His messages were bold declarations of the power of God to save people from sin and to deliver kings from stronger political rulers. He called the nation to trust God because there is no other God. God will establish His kingdom forever, he declared.

THE EXALTATION OF GOD HUMBLES MAN'S PRIDE

Isaiah called the rebellious people of Judah who had suffered military disaster to repent, act justly, and cease offering meaningless ritual in the temple (1:1-20). God would remove the nation's oppressive leaders and the proud, rich women who lived during the prosperous reign of Uzziah (3:1–4:1). He would destroy His precious vineyard that produced no good fruit (5:1-7). Then in the last days God will humble all proud people when His glory is revealed on earth (2:2, 3, 10-17). Jerusalem will be transformed, the Branch of God (the Messiah) will be there, sins will be removed, and Jerusalem will be holy (4:2-6).

In the year Uzziah died, Isaiah saw a vision of the glory of the holy King of kings sitting upon His throne in the temple. Isaiah humbled himself, was forgiven, and sent by God to harden the hearts of those who refused to listen to God (6:1-13).[2]

THE PRINCE OF PEACE WILL END JUDAH'S WARS

During the reign of the wicked King Ahaz, Judah was attacked by Syria and Israel. Ahaz refused to trust in God for deliverance (7:1-19). Instead the king sought help from Assyria—even though God foretold the demise of Israel and Syria (8:1-7; 9:8–10:4) and the arrogant Assyrians (10:5-19). In this hopeless situation God offered hope and peace through Immanuel,[3] the son born to the virgin (7:14); through the great Light, the Prince of Peace who would rule forever on the throne of David (9:1-7; see Matt. 4:13-16); and through the shoot or branch who was filled with God's Spirit (11:1-9). These promises will cause people to trust in the God of their salvation and thank Him (12:1-6).

GOD'S SOVEREIGN PLAN FOR THE NATIONS

Because the nations became quite proud of their riches and military might (13:11, 19; 16:6; 23:9), Isaiah's war oracles against the nations prophesied the fall of Babylon, Assyria, Philistia, Moab, Syria, Egypt, Edom, Arabia, and Tyre (13–23). On the day of the Lord, these nations would be destroyed when the wrath of God burned against them (13:6-13). No one can frustrate this plan or God's plan to establish Judah back in its land (14:1-3; 16:5). Surprisingly, we read that many Gentiles from Egypt and Assyria would respond to God and become part of the people of God (19:19-25). Isaiah's words encouraged those Jews who were uncertain about their future. The pagan nations were not to be feared. God's plan for the world will be fulfilled.

These events would foreshadow the final day of judgment when God will destroy everything on the earth with fire. Because of wickedness, God will punish men, kings, and proud cities (24:1-22). At that time He will reign with His people in Zion and be exalted. Death and tears will end, and all will sing for joy at the lavish banquet of God. The dead will be brought to life; joy and salvation will cover the earth (25:1–26:19).

TRUSTING GOD OR MILITARY MIGHT

Isaiah moves from God's final plans for the earth to the time just before Israel fell in 722/21 B.C. He contrasted the drunken, unteachable leaders of Israel (kings, priests, and prophets) with God, who rules with perfect justice and gives true instruction to the remnant of the nation (28:1-29). They would be destroyed, as would Judah, who did not learn from Israel's mistakes. Their prophets would deceive them. The people would give lip service to God, but their hearts would be far from Him (29:9-14), as evidenced by the leaders' tendency to depend on Egypt for security from the Assyrians (30:1-4; 31:1-3). These leaders did not want to trust in God or the prophet's words (30:9-12).

Isaiah condemned this worthless trust in the flesh. God desired to teach Judah, bless them with prosperity, and deliver them from the Assyrians, but they must first trust Him (30:18–31:9). To encourage this faith, Isaiah reminded the people that one day their righteous messianic King would come and remove their blindness (32:1-8). He called the complacent women to mourn the coming danger (32:9-14), and he prophesied the exaltation of God when the fierce Assyrians would be destroyed by Judah's King (33:1-24). Edom and all God's enemies would face God's wrath (34:1-15), but joy would be in Jerusalem when the ransomed returned to dwell in Zion (35:1-10).

Hezekiah accepted this message and placed his total trust in God when the Assyrian army surrounded the city of Jerusalem (36:1-22). Although human reason suggested that Hezekiah should surrender, he and Isaiah went to the temple and prayed that God would defeat the Assyrians, thus declaring His glory to all the nations (37:14-20). God answered this prayer, and an angel killed 185,000 Assyrian troops that night (37:36). Because of Hezekiah's righteous prayer to God, his life was lengthened by fifteen years (38:1-22). In spite of his earlier faith, Hezekiah later made an alliance with the Babylonians rather than trusting God totally (39:1-8).

THE INCOMPARABLE GOD WILL BRING DELIVERANCE

Although these chapters are not dated, they were probably given in the last days of Hezekiah when his wicked son Manasseh began to rule. Through these prophecies God encouraged the faithful remnant to maintain their trust in God, for He would deliver them from future exile in Babylon. Comfort is promised because God is coming with power to rule His people (40:1-11). Since no nation or foreign god has even a fraction of the power of God, they need not be feared (40:12-26). Though the people were confused and blind to the power of God, there was hope in the Lord (40:27; 41:10; 42:18-20). If God's people will wait and trust in Him, they will never lack strength (40:27-31).

God disputed the claims of other pagan nations and their gods. Their gods can do nothing; they are just nicely carved pieces of wood that some man made (41:5-7, 21-24; 44:9-20). The Babylonian gods Bel (called Marduk by the Babylonians) and Nebo would fall and Babylon would also (46:1–47:15). There is no other God beside the God of Judah. He is the first and the last, the Holy One, the Creator, the Savior and King (41:4; 43:10-15; 44:6-8; 48:12). He knows all about the former things that happened in ancient history and has planned out the future for His people (43:18-21).

After Judah went into exile, God would raise up a powerful king who would defeat many nations. That king, Cyrus, would allow the Jews to return home from Babylon and enable Jerusalem and God's temple to be rebuilt (41:1-4; 44:24–45:7; 48:20; see the fulfillment in Ezra 1:1-6). This message shows that God still loves them, for He chose them to be His servants. They will be God's witnesses to declare His glory among the nations.

THE SUFFERING SERVANT WILL BRING SALVATION

Isaiah drew a contrast between the Jews who were God's disobedient servants (42:19) and another Servant that was chosen by God to establish justice and righteousness on the earth (42:1-4). Although He will toil in vain among His own people, in the end He will be a light to the nations so that God's salvation may reach to the ends of the earth (42:6; 49:4, 6). At first He will be despised and humiliated (46:7; 50:6); His face will be disfigured; He will willingly die for the sins of others (52:14; 53:3-8). In the midst of this He will look to God for help, and God will raise Him from the dead and greatly exalt Him (50:7-10; 52:13; 53:12). He will be a guilt offering to God to bear the sins of the world even though He was sinless (53:9-11). This exalted suffering Servant is the messianic King, the Jesus of the New Testament (Mark 10:33, 34; John 10:17, 18; Acts 8:32-35).[4]

God not only promised to save His people from their sins, but He encouraged them to seek the Lord, pay attention to the Law, and enjoy His deliverance (51:1-3). Their exile would soon be over. He would restore His faithful remnant to Zion, and it would be like a beautiful garden. Then the people would break forth into singing, proclaiming, "Thy God reigneth," when God delivers Jerusalem (52:1-10). The barren and rejected city of Jerusalem would overflow with people and joy because of God's everlasting love for His people (54:1-8). If they will only seek the Lord and forsake their wicked ways, God will pardon their sins (55:6-8). Although His marvelous ways are far beyond human understanding, His word will be accomplished according to the everlasting covenant with David (55:1-13).

GOD'S FINAL RESTORATION AND JUDGMENT

The ethics of God's new restored kingdom will be characterized by justice, the proper observance of the Sabbath (56:1-8), humble fasting that delights in God and reaches out to the needs of the oppressed (58:1-12), and a turning from the iniquities that separated people from God (59:1-3). When the glory of the Lord will rise as a light of salvation for His people, the nations will come to Jerusalem to worship and give gifts to Him (60:1-9). God will change their sorrows into joy, their deserts into gardens, their ruins into rebuilt cities. The nation will be called Zion of the Holy One of Israel, my delight is in her, the holy people (62:1-12). The Servant will proclaim the acceptable day of the Lord, freedom from prison, a day of joy and praise for all who mourn (61:1-3). These events will also include a final day of judgment on Edom and all the nations, for God's fierce wrath will trample down all who reject Him (63:1-7).

The prophecies of Isaiah end with a prayer of praise to God for His lovingkindness in saving them from past affliction, a confession of sin and rebellion against the Holy Spirit, and a petition that God would again reveal His power and glory to His people and not be angry with them anymore (63:7–64:12). God answered this prayer with a promise to reveal Himself to all those who seek Him and turn from sinfulness. He promised to act on behalf of His faithful servants by pouring out His blessings on this new heaven and earth that He will create (65:1-25). In the end, all the wicked will dwell in a place of eternal fire where the worms do not die, but all the rest of the nations will see the glory of God, and all will bow down before Him (66:18-24).

THEOLOGICAL SIGNIFICANCE OF ISAIAH

1. God hates pride and loves the humble. Pride will be destroyed, and God alone will be exalted.
2. God is sovereignly in control of all the nations of the earth. He uses some nations as instruments in His hand to punish other nations. God delivers nations that put their total trust in Him rather than in alliances or military power.
3. God will send His Immanuel, the Prince of Peace, the messianic King on David's throne, to deliver God's people and establish His kingdom of prosperity, peace, and joy.
4. God is the first and the last, the Creator, Savior, and Holy One of Israel, and yet He cares for His own. All the power of the nations is like nothing before Him.
5. The suffering Servant paid the penalty for the sins of the world through His death and exaltation. He is a light to all nations, and through Him many Jews and Gentiles will be holy and enjoy the glorious kingdom of God.

DISCUSSION QUESTIONS

1. What are some of the characteristics of a true prophet (Mic. 3:8) and the false prophets in Micah's day?
2. Why was Micah so discouraged (Mic. 7:1-6)? How did focusing on God's power help him overcome his depression?
3. What factors caused Isaiah (Isa. 6) to be willing to go wherever God sent him? Did Isaiah expect to win many converts?
4. What evidence in Isaiah 19, 45, 49, 60, and 66 suggests that God's missionary purpose was to win people of all nations?
5. How does the New Testament relate the prophecies of Isaiah 7:14, 9:1-7, 49:6, 52:13–53:12, and 61:1-3 to the life of Jesus?

Chapter Twenty

LATE PREEXILIC
PROPHETS

THE EVENTS THAT LED to the destruction of Judah in 587/86 B.C. and its exile in Babylon were directly related to the nation's inept political leadership and its religious apostasy. Manasseh did not trust God but submitted to the powerful Assyrians and rebuilt the idols and pagan places of worship Hezekiah had destroyed (2 Kings 21). Later Josiah (640–609 B.C.) began to seek the Lord in his eighth year (632 B.C.), tore down some pagan altars in his twelfth year, and carried out a great revival in his eighteenth year when the Law of Moses was discovered in the temple (2 Chron. 34, 35).

When the Assyrians were defeated at Nineveh (612 B.C.), Egypt took control of Judah. A few years later (605 B.C.) Babylon defeated Egypt and took Jewish captives to Babylon. More captives went to Babylon when the evil kings Jehoiakim and his son Jehoiachin returned to the pagan ways of Manasseh and were defeated at Jerusalem in 597 B.C. (2 Kings 23:36–24:17). The last king of Judah, Zedekiah, followed this same pattern of idolatry, and eventually the Babylonians returned to destroy the temple and all of Jerusalem. Nebuchadnezzar took all but the very old and injured away into Babylonian captivity (2 Kings 24:18–25:12).

Jeremiah served as God's prophet to Judah with Zephaniah during the reign of the righteous King Josiah, with Habakkuk during the reign of the wicked King Jehoiakim, and with Joel during the reign of Zedekiah, the last king of Judah. A few years after Zedekiah came to the throne (597 B.C.), he rebelled against Nebuchadnezzar.

It was this rebellion that prompted the Babylonians to lay siege to Jerusalem again, and in 587/86 B.C. the city and temple were burned (2 Kings 24:18–25:21). Some Jews fled to the nearby country of Edom to escape from the war, others died in the fighting, but most of those left were taken into captivity in Babylon. Nebuchadnezzar made

Gedaliah the new governor of the people left in Judah, but soon he was killed. The remaining Jews fled to Egypt (Jer. 40–44).

NAHUM

God's Wrath on Nineveh

Nahum came from the Judean village of Elkosh to preach a message of encouragement to Josiah and the people of Judah. Although God was gracious to the Assyrians after they responded positively to the preaching of Jonah over 150 years earlier, before long they went back to their old ways. The Assyrians, whose capital was Nineveh, oppressed Judah and many other countries. Many righteous people began to wonder if God would ever destroy the Assyrians as Isaiah prophesied (Isa. 10:5-34). God revealed to Nahum that He still was an all-powerful God who executes judgment against evil and is good to those who trust Him. These prophecies encouraged Josiah not to submit to the Assyrians but to move forward with his political and religious reforms.

Outline of Nahum

God's judgment of Nineveh	1:1–2:2
God's wrath and goodness	1:1-8
Wrath on Nineveh, peace to Judah	1:9–2:2
The destruction of Nineveh	2:3-13
Reasons for Nineveh's inevitable doom	3:1-19

The vividness of Nahum's description of the battle for Nineveh and his knowledge of the geography of the rivers flowing beside and through the city suggest that the prophet was very aware of the military tactics of his time. But the essence of his message was not based as much on his knowledge of Assyria as on his knowledge of the character of God.

GOD'S JUDGMENT OF NINEVEH

Nahum began his prophecy with a poem that reminded his listeners of God's wrath, His power, and His goodness (1:1-8). It is impossible to understand God's ways apart from a knowledge of His character. He is a holy God who requires holy living. Although He is slow to anger, He will not leave His enemies unpunished. He is also a God of great power. Not even the mountains can stand when His wrath is poured out like fire. This power will also protect those who trust in God in times of trouble (1:7, 8).

These theological truths apply directly to Judah's situation. God's power will bring a complete end to the Assyrian enemies of God (1:9-11). Though they are very strong, God is stronger and will bring an army to destroy their reputations and their idols (1:14; 2:1). Judah will then be free, peace will come, and Judah will again celebrate and worship God (1:13, 15).

THE DESTRUCTION OF NINEVEH

The siege and capture of Nineveh, the Assyrian capital, is described in brilliant pictures. Speeding chariots, clashing swords, terrified red-dressed soldiers, tumbling walls near the river, looting of the palace riches, fleeing troops, and weeping women are part of the battle scene. Although the Assyrians roared around the ancient Near East like a vicious lion, God would cut off their strength and military might (2:11-13).

This prophecy would have seemed very unlikely in Nahum's day because the Assyrian king Ashurbanipal was the most powerful of all the Assyrian kings. History and archeological excavations suggest that the city did fall in 612 B.C. and that its defeat was partially due to a flood, just as Nahum predicted (2:6, 8).[1]

REASONS FOR NINEVEH'S INEVITABLE DOOM

To encourage faith in those who heard this prophecy, God explained why He was erasing Nineveh from the map. It was a violent and bloody city, and they killed innocent people by the thousands in their military conquests (3:1-4). Because of this, God would disgrace them, throw filth in their faces, and totally devastate the city. Though many thought Nineveh was impregnable, it would be defeated just like the impregnable Egyptian city of Thebes, which the Assyrians defeated in 663 B.C. (3:8-12).

Nahum ends his prophecy by taunting the Assyrians (3:14-19). He mockingly encourages them to draw some water (with the flood, that was the last thing they needed), to fortify the wall with some new bricks (it was too late to do this after the wall had fallen), and to multiply themselves like grasshoppers (but grasshoppers just hide or fly away). When people hear about the fall of Nineveh, they will rejoice and clap their hands.

THEOLOGICAL SIGNIFICANCE OF NAHUM

1. God sovereignly rules the nations of this world. Some will receive His wrath, but He will be good to those who trust Him.
2. Military power and riches will not deliver a sinful nation from the power of God's destruction. No nation is indestructible.

3. God was gracious to the Assyrians when Jonah preached to them, but Nahum indicates that God's patience lasts only so long.

The apostle Paul saw that the joy at the announcement of the good news of peace in Nahum's day (1:15) was similar to the joy when the good news of Christ was proclaimed in his day (Rom. 10:15).

ZEPHANIAH

The Day of the Lord

The prophet Zephaniah lived before the major reform of King Josiah (621 B.C.), when idolatry, violence, and false prophets still existed (1:1-6; 3:1-4) in Judah. The reference to a "remnant of Baal" in 1:4 may suggest that Josiah had made some initial attempts to remove Baalism from Jerusalem (628 B.C.) but that the task was not complete. If this prophecy is dated about 625 B.C., Josiah would have just declared independence from Assyria (627 B.C.) and was in need of encouragement in his religious reforms. The prophet warns about the coming day of the Lord.

Outline of Zephaniah

God's judgment on the day of the Lord	1:1-18
Repent before the day of the Lord	2:1–3:8
Restoration and joy on the day of the Lord	3:9-20

The idea of the day of the Lord comes from the belief that God is a divine warrior who fights holy wars against His enemies. When He comes in power to defeat the wicked, He also delivers His own people. The day of the Lord is a day of victory and joy for those who love God, but a day of destruction for unbelievers.[2]

GOD'S JUDGMENT ON THE DAY OF THE LORD

Zephaniah warned that God would come and devastate the earth, removing man, beasts, birds, and fish. This judgment was particularly aimed at Judah, because some people were still worshiping the Canaanite god Baal, bowing down to the Ammonite god Milcom (or Molech), and praying to Assyrian astral deities (1:4, 5; cf. Jer. 8:2; 19:13). People were rejecting the reform movement of Josiah, refusing to turn to God, and continuing in the pagan worship introduced earlier by Manasseh.

Zephaniah claimed that the day of the Lord was not just a divine punishment that applied to the pagans who worshiped idols. God's wrath would soon fall on all who refused to follow Him, even the Jews. God would slaughter them like a sacrifice, both the royal princes who had accepted foreign customs and the violent criminals who deceived and stole (1:7-9). Every part of Jerusalem would be affected, even the rich part of town (1:10-13).

To show how serious the danger was, Zephaniah reminded his listeners of the horribleness of the day of the Lord (1:14-18). It would be a day when tough soldiers would cry, when people would walk around aimlessly like blind people, when rich people would not be able to buy security. Wrath, distress, destruction, and blood would be everywhere. It would be like hell on earth.

Repent Before the Day of the Lord

The good news was that it was possible for Judah to avoid the judgment side of the day of the Lord. Zephaniah exhorted the people to gather at the temple and repent before the anger of the Lord fell on them (2:1-3). If they humbled themselves, sought God's face, and followed His ways, God might be gracious to them.

God revealed a second reason why they should repent. The Philistines, Moabites, Ammonites, and arrogant Assyrians would be defeated, and the faithful remnant of the Jews would receive their land (2:4-15). Eventually all people will bow before Judah's God (2:11), so why would anyone from Judah want to worship worthless pagan gods and be destroyed like the heathen? Although God hoped that Judah would fear Him and follow His ways (3:7), they did not trust God because their political and religious leaders profaned the temple and preached that God would never judge them (3:1-5).

Restoration and Joy on the Day of the Lord

If the people would repent, then they would be a part of the righteous remnant from all over the world that had purified lips, forgiven sins, humble attitudes, and holy lives (3:9-13). These people would rejoice because God their King would dwell in their midst (3:14, 15). God would also rejoice over His people who were weak and oppressed, but now were gathered together and blessed.

THEOLOGICAL SIGNIFICANCE OF ZEPHANIAH

1. No sinner, no matter what nationality or religion, can avoid the wrath of God's judgment on the day of the Lord.

2. Those who repent and humble themselves will be purified and have the blessing of enjoying God's presence forever.

HABAKKUK

Resolving Questions About God's Justice

The prophet Habakkuk prophesied after the fall of Nineveh in 612 B.C. but before the surprising rise of the Babylonian kingdom under Nebuchadnezzar in 605 B.C. This places Habakkuk in Judah around 607 B.C. during the reign of the wicked king Jehoiakim (2 Kings 23:34–24:17). Because Habakkuk's final prayer was set to music for singing in the temple (3:1, 19), some believe the prophet may have also served as a Levitical singer in the temple (1 Chron. 25:1-8).[3] His book is organized by his three prayers.

Outline of Habakkuk

A prayer for God's justice in Judah	1:1-11
A prayer questioning God's justice	1:12–2:20
A prayer for mercy in a time of difficulty	3:1-19

Habakkuk struggled with some of the same problems that Job did. Neither man doubted the power or holiness of God, but neither understood how a God of justice could allow certain things to happen. Both received a new vision of God and both trusted God's wisdom in spite of very difficult situations.

A Prayer for God's Justice in Judah

The early years of Jehoiakim's reign were full of violence, strife, wickedness, injustice, and the oppression of the righteous (1:1-4). In his prayer Habakkuk questions why God allowed this evil to go unpunished and why He did not save the righteous who served God so faithfully during the reign of Josiah.

God's answer revealed that He would demonstrate His justice in a surprising way (1:5-11). The state of Babylon would amazingly rise to power and invade Judah, violently bringing about the justice Habakkuk desired by killing the violent people in Judah. No one would be able to stop this fierce military machine; it would be as fast as a leopard. It would mock the power of Judah's puny king and crush him.

A PRAYER QUESTIONING GOD'S JUSTICE

Though God's reply answered Habakkuk's original question, this divine plan raised even greater questions. How could the holy everlasting divine Rock who promised to protect His people (1:12) give His approval to the wicked Babylonians by allowing them to destroy the more righteous nation of Judah (1:13)?

Habakkuk waited, and God gave a twofold answer that the prophet was to record on a tablet so that all could see it (2:1-3). First, the righteous person must live by faith in God in times of difficulty (2:4). Since God's mysterious ways are often beyond human understanding, Habakkuk must trust God. Second, God indicated that the proud Babylonians who looted nations with violence, who thrived on drunkenness and worshiped idols of stone were not receiving God's approval (2:4-19). They would be cut off, and violence would overtake them, for one day the glory of the Lord will fill the earth (2:14).

A PRAYER FOR MERCY IN A TIME OF DIFFICULTY

Habakkuk was assured by God's answer, but that did not remove the difficulty of going through the terrible wars with Babylon. He pleaded that God would be merciful while pouring out His wrath (3:2). The prophet's faith was strengthened as he remembered the glorious power of God in the past. Nothing could stand before His anger when He marched through the earth to save His people (3:12, 13). Realizing the power of God, Habakkuk trembled at the thought of the upcoming destruction. Yet his heart rejoiced, and the load on him was removed as he placed his life in the strong hands of God (3:17-19).

THEOLOGICAL SIGNIFICANCE OF HABAKKUK

1. God's ways are sometimes mysterious, but they are guided by His character. Justice on earth does not mean that the innocent will never suffer, but God will be with those who suffer.
2. The just shall live by faith. God's power and past mercy give strength to face present difficulties with joy.

The New Testament writers used Habakkuk's statement that the just shall live by faith (Rom. 1:17; Gal. 3:11; Heb. 10:37) not through works. Abraham (Gen. 15:6) and Habakkuk (2:4) make it very clear that no one can work his or her way into heaven. Salvation is solely by grace through faith (Eph. 2:8-10).

JOEL

The Day of the Lord—Near and in the Future

Joel prophesied shortly before the fall of Jerusalem in 587/86 B.C. People from Judah had been taken into captivity in Babylon in 605 and 597 B.C. (3:1-3), but the temple in Jerusalem had not yet been destroyed (2:16, 17). Around 590 B.C., Joel taught that the severe grasshopper plague was a warning from God that the day of the Lord, the final day of Judah, was very near.

Outline of Joel

Repent because of the present day of the Lord	1:1–2:17
Lament because of the locust	1:1-20
Repent because military destruction is near	2:1-17
Grace and wrath on the future day of the Lord	2:18–3:21
Restoration and the Spirit	2:18-32
Judgment of the nations	3:1-17
Blessings on Judah	3:18-21

It is difficult to determine whether the description of the army of locusts in 2:1-17 is to be understood literally, a position that seems to make chapter 2 a repetition of chapter 1, or if 2:1-17 is a description of the coming Babylonian army, using the imagery of grasshoppers. Since the locusts in chapter 1 have already come and those in 2 will come in the near future, chapter 2 probably refers to the Babylonian army.[4]

REPENT BECAUSE OF THE PRESENT DAY OF THE LORD

A very unusual event happened, something that fathers would tell their sons about for years. Judah had an unbelievable infestation of grasshoppers. They were everywhere and eating everything in sight. Everyone was weeping because there would be no wine, no figs, no grain for offerings at the temple, no harvest for the farmers, and no fruit on the trees (1:4-12).

Joel did not interpret this plague as a freak of nature but as a warning from God. He encouraged the priests to call the people together at the temple, start a fast in sackcloth, and cry out to God for help (1:13, 14). They should lament because when there was no grain in the barns and no water in the rivers, it was a sure sign that the day of the Lord was very near (1:17-20).

Joel pictured this day of the Lord as a great military invasion, similar to an invasion of grasshoppers (2:1-17). These creatures would invade the land by the thousands, and nothing would be able to stop them. In the great and awesome day of the Lord, Judah would be destroyed (fulfilled in 587/86 B.C.). The only hope was for the people to gather at the temple (2:14-17), return to God, weep, and fast. God might be patient a little longer and gracious even though the people did not deserve it (2:12-13).

GRACE AND WRATH ON THE FUTURE DAY OF THE LORD

Joel balances his warning of judgment in the near future with words of hope for the final day of the Lord. The locust plague will be reversed on that day because the locusts and northern army of Babylonians will be gone (2:20, 25); abundant grain will be in the fields. There will be joy and no more shame. God will pour out His Spirit on all flesh in a new way, and whoever calls on the name of the Lord will be saved (2:28-32). Judah will be restored from captivity, and the nations will be judged (3:1-8).

God will sit as judge over all the nations on that final day of the Lord (3:9-14). Then all will know that He alone is God, for He will dwell in Zion, and it will be a holy place (3:17, 21).

THEOLOGICAL SIGNIFICANCE OF JOEL

1. The only way to avoid the judgment of God is to repent with all your heart and trust in God's mercy.
2. On the final day of the Lord, God will judge the wicked and bless the righteous with His presence.

Peter taught that Joel's prophecy of the outpouring of the Spirit on all flesh (Acts 2:17-21; Joel 2:28-32) began to be fulfilled at Pentecost. Paul taught that it was necessary to call on the name of the Lord to be saved (Rom. 10:13; Joel 2:32).

JEREMIAH

Overcoming Deception and Persecution

Jeremiah was from a priestly family that lived in Anathoth, a city of Benjamin just four miles northeast of Jerusalem (1:1). Jeremiah suffered great persecution at the hand of Judah's last two kings, and his own extended family tried to kill him (11:18-23). He struggled with why God was making him go through such bitter experiences. He cried out in frustration with several laments (12:1-6; 15:10-21; 18:19-23; 20:1-13).

Through all these hardships Jeremiah came to realize that nothing was too difficult for God to accomplish (32:17, 18).

Outline of Jeremiah

Prophecies and prayers of Jeremiah	1–20
Early calls for repentance	1–9
Exhortations and laments	10–20
Warnings concerning the fall of Jerusalem	21–29
Promises of hope and restoration	30–33
The final days of Jerusalem	34–45
Exile in Egypt	40–45
God's judgment on the foreign nations	46–51
Historical account of Jerusalem's fall	52

Of all the prophets, Jeremiah was the most open about his own personal struggles with his calling to preach, his difficulty with false prophets who deceived the people with words of peace (28, 29), and his frustration over the beatings and imprisonment that he endured (20:1-6; 37:1–38:28). His prayers reveal his disappointment with the nation's unwillingness to repent and his agony over the deceptive ways of the nation (7:1-15; 8:18–9:1). In spite of this, Jeremiah had a deep love for his people, even though they were full of idolatry and about to be destroyed.

PROPHECIES AND PRAYERS OF JEREMIAH

Jeremiah was chosen to be God's prophet before his birth. Although he did not feel adequate for the responsibility of speaking God's positive and negative words (1:6-10), God strengthened him and promised to make him as secure as a fortified city against those who would oppose him (1:17-19).

In his early preaching during the reign of Josiah, Jeremiah contrasted the nation's original love for God and special holy relationship to God (2:2, 3) with their present ignorance of God's law, their rampant Baalism, and their deceptive belief that they had done nothing wrong (2:4-37). He challenged them to admit their sins and return to God so that He could establish the messianic kingdom in Jerusalem (3:11-18; 4:1-4).

The people claimed to know the way of the Lord, and they thought that they were wise. But they did not act justly or speak truthfully, so God could not pardon their sins (5:1-9; 8:4-9). They did not fear the Lord because the false prophets deceived the people with promises of peace (5:11-13, 20-24, 30-31; 6:13-15; 8:10-12).

The people were also deceived by their temple worship. They thought that if they came to the temple, everything would be all right.[1] But God required that they amend their ways and stop oppressing the poor, stealing, swearing falsely, and offering sacrifices to Baal (7:1-10). They needed to boast in the Lord rather than in their riches or might (9:23, 24). If they did not change, God would destroy them and the temple (7:14, 15). This prospect brought great sorrow to Jeremiah. He mourned because there seemed to be no healing available for Jerusalem (8:18–9:1; 10:19-25).

Later in the reign of King Jehoiakim (609–597 B.C.), Jeremiah castigated the people for their worship of pieces of wood with golden chains (10:1-5). These idols were a deception and could not walk or talk. God is the King of all nations, a living God, the Creator, and the inheritance of the Jews. These idols are stupid, a delusion, a mockery of the truth (10:6-16). By worshiping them, the people had broken their covenant relationship with God (11:1-13). Therefore, God forsook them and hated His beloved people and was forced to destroy their land (12:6-13). In tears Jeremiah confessed the nation's sins and pleaded for God's mercy (14:7-22), but the time of judgment had come, and God refused to listen to Jeremiah's prayers (14:11; 15:1).

When Jeremiah prophesied the fall of Jerusalem, persecution came his way. After some men from Anathoth tried to kill him, he lamented his vulnerable position (11:18-23), complained about the prosperity of the wicked (12:1-6), and rejected his miserable prophetic calling (15:10-18). God corrected Jeremiah and challenged him to be strong (12:5) and repent of his complaining so that God could again use him as His prophet (15:19-21). Later when Jeremiah was beaten and put in stocks, he cried out to the Lord in agony because he could no longer endure all the mockery and violence against him (20:7-11). It almost seemed to him that God had deceived him when He called him; he suggested that it would have been better if he had never been born (20:7, 14-18).

During this time Jeremiah acted out several symbolic lessons. The worthless loincloth represented the worthless state of Judah (13:1-11). The absence of weeping at the death of Jeremiah's friends showed what would happen when Judah fell (16:1-9). The potter's forming of a vessel was similar to God's sovereign control over the nation (18:1-12), and the breaking of the pottery symbolized God's breaking of His people (19:1-13).

WARNINGS CONCERNING THE FALL OF JERUSALEM

Most of the narrative describes Jeremiah's dealings with King Jehoiakim or Zedekiah rather than being a series of sermons preached by Jeremiah. The prophet told Zedekiah that God would destroy Jerusalem and that the only way to survive was to surrender to the Babylonians (21:1-10). The kings of Judah did not rule with justice. Instead they shed innocent blood and refused to follow God. Therefore, God was determined to destroy them if there was no repentance (22:1–23:2). The righteous remnant (the good figs) would come from those who went into exile (24:1-10). After seventy years some would return to the land (25:12; 29:10). Then God would shepherd His people and send the messianic King from the line of David to rule them with justice (23:3-8).

God would also remove the deceptive prophets who claimed that the Lord had spoken to them (23:9-40). Some of them tried to kill Jeremiah when he predicted the destruction of the temple (26:1-19), and later Hananiah and other exilic prophets contradicted Jeremiah's prophecy that the exile would last seventy years (28–29).

PROMISES OF HOPE AND RESTORATION

Jeremiah's words of hope were given near the end of Zedekiah's reign while the city of Jerusalem was under siege by the Babylonians, and the people had given up all hope of survival (32:1). When all human strength was gone (30:5-7), God wanted to assure the nation that through His power He would destroy Babylon and restore Judah after their exile (30:8-11). For now there would be no healing for the incurable wound that God was inflicting on them (30:12-15).

In the future God would restore Judah to health, rebuild her cities, and fill the nation with joy (30:17-22). In His lovingkindness God would restore His covenant with them; it would be an everlasting new covenant written on their hearts (31:1-3, 31-37).

Jeremiah believed God's promises that the nation would return to the land. He knew that nothing was too difficult for God; therefore, in faith he purchased some property in Anathoth from his uncle (32:6-17). Since God created the earth and controls everyone on it, it is possible to believe that God could cleanse the sins of Judah, restore people and joy to the land, set the messianic branch from the line of David on the throne, and reestablish worship in the temple (33:1-22).

THE FINAL DAYS OF JERUSALEM

The armies of Nebuchadnezzar surrounded the city of Jerusalem (34:1), and there seemed to be little hope. At this time the people made a covenant with God in the temple to release their Jewish slaves, possibly hoping that God might have mercy on them (34:8-16). A short time later when an Egyptian army came up to Palestine, the Babylonian army left Jerusalem to fight them (37:5-11). When the wealthy Jews saw this, they immediately forced the slaves they had freed back into slavery, in spite of the oath they swore to God (34:11). God was very angry with the people because they did not honor or obey God like the Rechabites (35). The people and kings had been wayward ever since Jehioakim burned the scroll that contained the Word of the Lord (36).

Since Jeremiah consistently and faithfully announced God's judgment on Judah, he was falsely accused of treason, beaten, put in prison (37), and later thrown into a well to die. Jeremiah soon sank into the mud up to his armpits, but a godly Ethiopian servant of the king and thirty men pulled him out with ropes (38:1-13). Finally enemy troops entered the city and killed many government officials, blinded Zedekiah, and destroyed the walls and the houses in the city (39:1-10). In God's grace Jeremiah and the Ethiopian servant of the king were treated kindly because they trusted God (39:11-18).

EXILE IN EGYPT

Nebuchadnezzar appointed Gedaliah as the new governor over the Jews left in Judah and the people who had fled into Edom and Moab before the Babylonians attacked Jerusalem. Before long, Ishmael killed Gedaliah and slaughtered eighty innocent men (40:13–41:3).

Fearing the reprisal of the Babylonians, the remainder of the people went to Bethlehem in order to flee to Egypt (41:16-18). Before they left for Egypt, they decided to have Jeremiah pray to see if this was God's will. They swore to do whatever the Lord said, but when Jeremiah told them that God would curse them if they went to Egypt or richly bless them if they trusted God and stayed in Judah, they thought he was lying (40:1–41:3). Consequently, God sent a curse on all of them except Baruch (45:1-5) because they disobeyed God's word, went to Egypt, and offered sacrifices to Egyptian gods (43:8–44:30).

GOD'S JUDGMENTS ON THE FOREIGN NATIONS

Although Judah was destroyed, God was not trying to teach the people that the foreign nations around them were free of judgment. Judah had a special relationship with God and was held more accountable, but every person in every nation is responsible for his or her own actions. Judah should put her trust in God, not in any of these nations. God would defeat the powerful armies of the Egyptians with the army of Babylon (46), an overflowing flood of troops would devastate Philistia (47), and catastrophic destruction would bring the proud land of Moab to weeping (48). Ammon, Edom, Syria, Kedar, and Elam would suffer similar destinies when God's sovereign rule took control of their lands (49). Jeremiah also sent a message with Seriah to the people in Babylon. Even the great nation Babylon would fall (50–51). Then God would return a remnant to Judah (50:28-34).

HISTORICAL ACCOUNT OF JERUSALEM'S FALL

The book of Jeremiah ends with a description of the final battle for Jerusalem, a record of the vessels the Babylonians took from the temple, and a note about a Babylonian act of mercy to the Judean King Jehoiachin after thirty-seven years of exile.

THEOLOGICAL SIGNIFICANCE OF JEREMIAH

1. God strengthens those He calls and gives them His words.
2. When people are deceived by false preaching or the belief that they know what God can or cannot say, when they put false trust in religious places or observances, then judgment is near.
3. Those who are godly may suffer great persecution, but they must not bow to public, religious, or official pressure. The pressures of ministry may sometimes make one want to quit, but an honest taking of these issues to God in prayer will bring peace.
4. Believers should weep, not rejoice, over God's judgment of the wicked and intercede for God's mercy.
5. God is sovereignly in control of all things. He can destroy strong nations as well as forgive and restore His people from captivity and weakness. Truly, nothing is too difficult for God.

The description of the new covenant in 31:31-34 is identified with Jesus' death (Heb. 8:7-13; 9:15) since He was the mediator of the new covenant. At the Last Supper Jesus instituted the Communion service and referred to it as a symbol of the new covenant (Luke 22:20; 1 Cor. 11:25).

LAMENTATIONS

God as the Source of Both the Good and the Bad

This book contains five funeral songs that express the people's grief over the fall of Judah and the destruction of the dearly loved city of Jerusalem. Most believe that Jeremiah wrote these songs in 586 B.C., shortly after the Babylonian army desolated and burned Jerusalem.[2] The songs describe the horrible devastation and cruelty that the author saw. They acknowledge that sin brought God's judgment and look beyond the present agony to see a God of faithfulness and mercy who is able to restore the nation.

Outline of Lamentations

Grief over the destruction of Jerusalem	1
The day of God's anger for sin	2
A prayer for God's compassion	3
The siege of Jerusalem	4
A plea for God's restoration	5

These poems (except chapter 5) are skillfully written in acrostic form, with each verse beginning with the next letter of the Hebrew alphabet.[3] The poems are somewhat repetitive, but each has a unique way of mourning the enormous loss and shame that the people felt. Interestingly, the songs do not blame God for this calamity but see Him as the just punisher of their sins.

GRIEF OVER THE DESTRUCTION OF JERUSALEM

In this section Judah weeps bitterly because she has become a slave to a foreign nation. The Jews grieve that there will be no worship in Zion, no rulers, priests, or people. They have sinned against God, and He has abandoned them to their enemies. They plead with God to see the defilement of the temple, to reach out His hand and comfort them in their time of distress, and to punish their enemies.

THE DAY OF GOD'S ANGER FOR SIN

God's fierce anger did not spare Judah. The Divine Warrior threw down its defenses, shot His arrows, and sent forth His fire against the temple. He destroyed walls, gates, and palaces. Prophets, elders, virgins, and mothers sat in sackcloth and ashes. Her false prophets gave empty visions, and her enemies sneered and laughed. Oh, that God would look and see the weeping, the death, the barbarity, the pain of enduring the anger of God.

A Prayer for God's Compassion

After recognizing that everything that has happened was part of God's plan to punish His people, the lamenter turns to God for hope. Great is God's faithfulness; He is a savior to those who seek Him. Once justice is served, God will have compassion if His people will turn to Him. Then they will not fear, for God will redeem them and judge their enemies.

The Siege of Jerusalem

Although Jerusalem had been a place of beauty, once the siege began, everything changed. Gold was gone, people were cruel, the rich were poor, the white linen of the priest became as black as soot, and some people even ate their children. Fire spread through Zion because the people's uncleanness caused God to abandon them. Enemies came to destroy, and Edom rejoiced.

A Plea for God's Restoration

The final song describes the people's lack of freedom in their desperate situation. They had no bread, their women were ravished, and they had no joy because of their sins. The song ends with a strong affirmation of God's eternal rule over all mankind. Since that is true, they can be assured of restoration.

THEOLOGICAL SIGNIFICANCE OF LAMENTATIONS

1. It is a fearful and terrible thing to fall into the hands of an angry God. God's wrath justly punishes the sinner.
2. In the midst of trials or divine punishment, there is hope in the faithfulness of God if one repents and seeks His mercy.

OBADIAH

Pride Goes before a Fall

Obadiah lived through the final devastating Babylonian war on Judah (587/86 B.C.) and saw how the Edomites took advantage of the people of Judah. His prophecies were given to encourage the disillusioned Jews, who wondered why God did not punish the Edomites for their wicked ways.

Outline of Obadiah

Edom would be judged for its pride	1:1-9
Edom's violence against Jerusalem	1:10-14
The day of the Lord for Edom	1:15-21

A further description of how Edom took advantage of the Jews in Jerusalem when the city was destroyed is found in Ezekiel 25, 35, 36, and Psalm 137. Not only did the Edomites mock when Judah fell, but they robbed and killed fleeing Jews, tried to make Judah part of their territory, and spoke arrogantly about God.

EDOM WOULD BE JUDGED FOR ITS PRIDE

Edom was very proud because it was easy to defend. To get to the capital, one had to go through a narrow crack between mountains (fifteen feet wide at points) and then up some fairly steep slopes (1:3, 4). Since a major trade route went through the nation, it became very wealthy (1:5) and had many allies (1:7), but God would take all this away when He punished Edom.

EDOM'S VIOLENCE AGAINST JERUSALEM

A second reason why Edom would be punished was her violence against Jerusalem when it was destroyed by the Babylonians. The Edomites did not help their neighbors. Rather they gloated over Judah's misfortune, helped themselves to whatever the Babylonians did not take, and robbed those who fled to Edom for protection.

THE DAY OF THE LORD FOR EDOM

The day of the Lord's destruction of Edom was near. Judah would again be holy to God, and the Jews would return to inhabit the land (1:17, 19-21), but God would destroy Edom and all its people.

THEOLOGICAL SIGNIFICANCE OF OBADIAH

1. Pride in military security, wealth, alliance, or wisdom will not save but will be the source of one's downfall.
2. Gloating over or taking advantage of the misfortunes of others will bring the judgment of God.

DISCUSSION QUESTIONS

1. How can God be a God of both wrath and goodness?
2. Is it appropriate for believers to question the justice of God? How can one overcome doubt in difficult times?
3. Describe the day of the Lord for the righteous in Zephaniah 3:9-20.
4. How does Joel help to reveal the nature of true repentance?

5. Identify God's promises to Jeremiah when he was first called into ministry (Jer. 1). Did he know there would be opposition?
6. In what ways were the people of Judah deceived? How did Jeremiah attempt to transform their understanding?
7. Describe the different ways Jeremiah reacted to persecution in 11:18-23, 15:15-21, 26:1-19, and 38:1-23.
8. What are some similarities and differences between the new covenant (Jer. 31:31-37) and the old one under Moses?
9. How does the faithfulness of God give hope in the midst of great sorrow in Lamentations 3?
10. How does the national pride in Edom compare with the pride of countries today?

Chapter Twenty-One

EXILIC PROPHET

Ezekiel

PEOPLE FROM JUDAH WERE taken into exile in Babylon on three occasions. In 605 B.C., the fourth year of Jehoiakim, Nebuchadnezzar took a small group of Jews to Babylon (including Daniel and his three friends; see Dan. 1:1, 2) after his defeat of the Egyptians at Carchemish. A few years later Jehoiakim rebelled against Nebuchadnezzar; consequently, the Babylonians attacked Jerusalem and took King Jehoiachin (Jehoiakim had died) and over 10,000 more captives into exile in 597 B.C. (including Ezekiel; see 2 Kings 23:36–24:17; Ezek. 1:2). Zedekiah became the new ruler, but after a few years he also rebelled against Nebuchadnezzar. Jerusalem suffered another attack and was finally destroyed in 587/86 B.C. (2 Kings 24:18–25:21). While Jeremiah proclaimed God's Word in Judah during these difficult days, Ezekiel was prophesying to the Jews in Babylonian exile.

Very little is known about the conditions in exile from the book of Ezekiel. This is because Ezekiel was describing to the exiles in Babylon what was happening back in Judah. It seems as though the Babylonians did not persecute Ezekiel for his religion, nor did they enslave him. From time to time the elders of Israel gathered together at Ezekiel's house where he would share another Word from the Lord (8:1; 14:1; 20:1).

Ezekiel was born during the time of King Josiah (640–609 B.C.). He was married (24:15-18), but there is no indication that he and his wife had any children. He was from a priestly family and was twenty-five years old when he was deported to Babylon. At age thirty he received God's call to be a prophet in a vision of the glory of God near the Chebar canal in Babylon (1:1-3). At that time he was filled with the Spirit of God and became dumb, unable to speak except when God opened his mouth (2:1, 2; 3:24-27). Ezekiel performed several dramatic sign messages and had a number of visions about what was going on in Jerusalem while he was in Babylon. Some of his messages of judgment counteracted the optimistic messages of the false prophets who thought that Jerusalem would never be destroyed (4–24). Other messages gave hope to the discouraged exiles after the final destruction of Jerusalem (34–48).

Outline of Ezekiel

Ezekiel's call to prophesy	1–3
God's judgment on Judah	4–24
Signs and messages of Zion's fall	4–7
The glory of God leaves the temple	8–11
Judah's sins will bring destruction	12–24
Oracles of judgment against the nation	25–32
The restoration of Judah	33–48
Hope of restoration and rebirth	33–37
Victory over Gog and Magog	38–39
God's glory in the new temple	40–48

When God spoke to Ezekiel, He frequently used the title "son of man." The name indicated Ezekiel's humanity, which stood in stark contrast to the glory of God. Ezekiel was very aware of the complete holiness and purity of the glorious God he saw in his vision, and very much aware of the terrible sinful acts of the people of Judah. He was God's watchman to warn the nation of God's judgment if they did not repent of their sins.

EZEKIEL'S CALL TO PROPHESY

Most of the Jews in exile with Ezekiel thought that God was located in the temple in Jerusalem, so it was quite a surprise to hear that the glory of God was with His people in exile and had appeared to Ezekiel. Ezekiel saw a brilliant display of the total otherness of God's splendor. God was on a throne in the midst of a fiery expanse that was moved by winged, four-faced heavenly creatures and a series of wheels (1:4-28).[1]

After Ezekiel humbled himself in worship, God commissioned him to be a prophet to the stubborn people in exile, not to some faraway pagan nation that spoke an unintelligible language. Ezekiel was not to fear opposition (they would be like scorpions—2:6) or to be discouraged by their unwillingness to respond positively (2:3-7). He was to declare the Word of God on the scroll that he swallowed. If he did not give God's words of warning, God would hold Ezekiel accountable. If he gave the warning, and the people refused to listen, then they would be accountable (3:17-21).

GOD'S JUDGMENT ON JUDAH

Although most of the people in exile did not believe that God would ever allow Jerusalem to be destroyed, Ezekiel used symbolic acts and messages of destruction to convince them that God would destroy the nation because of its terrible sins. Ezekiel built a scale model of Jerusalem under military attack (4:1-3) and then lay on his side and ate unclean food to illustrate the terrible conditions in Jerusalem during its siege (4:4-17). The fate of the people was represented by his hair; some were killed by the sword, while others were scattered into many nations (5:1-17). The day of the Lord was near for Jerusalem because their arrogance, abominations, and violence had brought God's wrath on them (7:1-27). When this day happened, they would know that He is God.

A year after his call, Ezekiel received another vision of the glory of God in the temple at Jerusalem (10:1-21). Many exiles in Babylon believed that Jerusalem would never be destroyed because God Almighty lived in the temple, but in his vision Ezekiel saw the glory of God leave the temple and Jerusalem (9:3; 10:19; 11:22-25). God left because the seventy elders of Judah were worshiping idols in the temple area and in a cellar under the temple (8:5-18). God marked the righteous with a sign, but the wicked were killed and the temple destroyed (9:1-11).[2] The only hope for Judah was for God to remove their sins and give them a new heart (11:14-21).

Ezekiel rejected the false view that God's judgment was a long way off (12:21-28). He condemned the false prophets who misled the people by whitewashing over Judah's sins, saying there would be peace for Jerusalem (13:1-23). To the contrary, if the people did not repent and put away their iniquity, not even the prayers of men of God such as Noah, Daniel, or Job could change God's determination to destroy Judah (14:1-23).

In an allegory, Ezekiel compared Judah to a young girl that God cared for and married. But the bride ignored her husband and loved others (foreign customs, idols, her own beauty). Therefore God would judge His adulterous wife, for Judah was worse than her evil sister, the northern nation of Israel, and even worse than Sodom and Gomorrah (16:1-59). This allegory is similar to Ezekiel's parable of the two evil sisters, Oholah (Samaria) and Oholibah (Jerusalem) in chapter 23.

In another allegory, Ezekiel described how a great eagle (Nebuchadnezzar—17:3, 12) would control Palestine even though another great eagle (an Egyptian king—17:7, 17) would attempt to help Judah. Soon the lion (Judah) would have one of her cubs (King

Jehoiachin) captured and taken to Babylon (19:1-9). Soon the vine (Judah) would have one of its branches (kings) plucked (19:10-14). Jerusalem would be like a pot over a hot fire, and the people would be the meat cooking in it (24:3-5). A final ominous sign was the death of Ezekiel's wife, the desire of his eyes, whom he was not to mourn (24:15-20). God would also destroy His temple, the desire of the people's eyes, and they would be so devastated that they would not be able to mourn (24:20-24). Then they would know that the Lord truly is God.

Although the exile of Judah was sure, one day God would graciously take a tender twig (the Messiah) from the tree and exalt Him (17:22-24). The people would no longer profane God's holy name. Then He would accept them and gather them from exile. Then they would understand that God had dealt with them as they deserved (20:39-44).

Throughout all of this section Ezekiel demonstrated that the nation would pay for its sins. Some in exile thought that they were suffering for their fathers' sins, not their own (18:2). They accused God of being unfair (18:29), but God said that each person would suffer for the sins he or she committed (18:4-20).

ORACLES OF JUDGMENT ON THE NATIONS

After a series of brief oracles predicting God's judgment on Ammon, Moab, Edom, and Philistia (25), Ezekiel described God's punishment of the proud and wealthy city of Tyre (27). Ezekiel mockingly lamented this proud king who thought he was a god (28:2, 6, 11-15), for God would have Nebuchadnezzar destroy him and his wealthy city (26; 28:16-19).[3]

Egypt was also very proud of its rich delta area that was likened to the Garden of Eden (29:1-9; 31:1-9). That spot would become a desert when the Babylonians came and destroyed the cities (29:9–30:26). Ezekiel mockingly lamented the pharaoh's death (32:1-8) and pictured Egypt's entrance into Sheol to join the other nations that lay there in shame (32:21-32).

THE RESTORATION OF JUDAH

The beginning of Ezekiel's messages of hope and the end of his dumbness coincided with the news that the Babylonians had finally captured the city of Jerusalem (33:21, 22). This event demoralized those in exile and exposed their false hopes. They began to wonder if there was any hope of returning to Judah and if God would ever fulfill His promises to Abraham and David.

In this new situation Ezekiel was reminded that he was still God's watchman to the exiles (33:1-16). But his message was now a word of hope, because sometime after their judgment God would shepherd His people and gather them together back in the land of Judah. He would make His servant David their messianic prince, restore His covenant of peace with them, give them a new heart, cleanse their iniquity, and bless them with prosperity (34:1-31; 36:22-38; 37:15-28). Then they would know that the Lord is God.

God would defeat Judah's enemies, including Edom (a symbol of the rest of the nations), which arrogantly rejoiced when Judah fell and tried to take her land (35:1–36:15). He would also destroy Gog and Magog to sanctify His name, so that all the nations of the earth would recognize that He alone is God (38–39).

The final eight chapters (40–48) contain an unusually detailed description of the measurements for a gigantic temple that would be the center for the restored nation's worship. For the priest Ezekiel, this was a very important aspect of returning to a right relationship with God. The return of the glory of God to this temple was of utmost importance to the completion of God's work (43:1-5). Levitical priests from the family of Zadok would minister in the temple, and a prince would rule the people (43:18–44:31). The nation would celebrate its festival at the temple (46) located in the city called "The LORD is there" (48:35). The land would again be divided among the tribes, and there would be a freshwater river running from Jerusalem through the Dead Sea and beyond (45:1-8; 47–48).

THEOLOGICAL SIGNIFICANCE OF EZEKIEL

1. A fresh vision of the splendor of God's glory causes one to bow down, worship, and willingly obey the Word of God.
2. Believers are God's watchmen, called to warn sinners of God's judgment if they do not repent. A watchman who fails to warn will be held accountable by God.
3. God will destroy His own people and their places of worship if they no longer recognize Him or faithfully worship Him.
4. God controls all the nations of the world and will destroy the proud who try to play God.
5. God is just, and every person will be held responsible for his or her own sins.

6. God will keep His promises, cleanse His people's sins, restore them to their land, give them a new heart and covenant, renew true worship, and raise up their Messiah.

The New Testament writers show evidence that they had read the book of Ezekiel. John's description of the glory of God in Revelation 4:1-11 sounds very close to Ezekiel 1, and his swallowing of a scroll in Revelation 10:8-11 is similar to Ezekiel's experience. Jesus and Paul accepted Ezekiel's view of the responsibility of a watchman (Matt. 10:5-15; Acts 18:6; 20:26). Gog and Magog are mentioned again in Revelation 20:8, and the new Jerusalem is part of John's vision (Rev. 21:10, 12, 16, 22).

DISCUSSION QUESTIONS

1. Is the modern picture of God consistent with Ezekiel's vision, or has God sometimes become revisualized or modernized to fit our ideas or wishes?
2. How can God be both the all-powerful, holy Ruler of the world and our loving Father?
3. How did Ezekiel correct the people's misunderstanding concerning the possible destruction of the temple, their misunderstanding that they were paying for their fathers' sins, and their doubts about the future fulfillment of God's promises?
4. Is God unconditionally committed to a people or nation that rejects Him? Why or why not?
5. Read some commentaries on Ezekiel and find two or three different ways that people have understood the restoration of the temple in Ezekiel 40–48.
6. How did God's action prove that He is God?

Chapter Twenty-Two

EXILIC PROPHET

Daniel

NEBUCHADNEZZAR ROSE TO power in 605 B.C., the year he defeated Egypt, expanding the small nation of Babylon into a world empire. After this battle he went to Jerusalem and took Daniel and his friends into captivity (Dan. 1:1).[1] Nebuchadnezzar returned in 597 B.C. to defeat the Judean king Jehoiachin and take more captives into exile (including Ezekiel). After Zedekiah rebelled, the Babylonian king attacked and totally destroyed Judah in 587/86 B.C. (2 Kings 24–25).

Nebuchadnezzar was followed by three relatively weak kings who had short reigns. The last king was Nabonidus (556–539 B.C.), a worshiper of the moon god Sin rather than Marduk. When he spent a number of years away from the capital, he put Belshazzar in charge (Dan. 5).

In 539 B.C. Cyrus, the king of Persia, defeated the Babylonians and established a decree that allowed the Jews to return to Jerusalem (Ezra 1:1-6). About 50,000 Jews returned, but the old man Daniel and many others remained behind in Babylon.

Daniel and his three friends were Hebrews from the educated upper class and royal families of Judah (1:3). God preserved His people in captivity through the influence of Daniel, who served as one of the top government officials for about seventy years. Although there were some difficult trials along the way, such as being thrown into the lions' den, Daniel had a good reputation (5:11-16) and maintained his high position even after the Persians defeated the Babylonians.

Daniel's book contains a description of his relationships with government officials and a series of visions about how God rules over all the nations of the earth.

Outline of Daniel

God's kingdom will destroy all others	2:1-49
God delivers Daniel's friends from the furnace	3:1-30
God rules over kings and all mankind	4:1-37
God brings Babylon to an end	5:1-31
God delivers Daniel from the lions	6:1-28
God's care for His persecuted people	7:1-12:13
Persecuted saints receive the kingdom	7:1-8:27
Prayer to forgive and restore Israel	9:1-27
Times of war and distress	10:1-12:13

Two literary characteristics make the book of Daniel somewhat unique. Daniel 1:1–2:4a and chapters 8–12 were written in Hebrew like most of the rest of the Old Testament, but 2:4b–7:28 were written in Aramaic, the international language used to conduct political and economic business in that day. This suggests that Daniel wanted parts of his book to be read by people who did not speak Hebrew.

A second distinctive is the apocalyptic imagery of strange beasts and plants, symbolic numbers and colors, and detailed predictions about battles and persecution in the future. Although other prophets (especially Zechariah) used symbolism, the visions in Daniel are closer to the apocalyptic imagery in the New Testament book of Revelation than any of the other prophets. When this strange imagery was not interpreted by Daniel, he probably did not think that that symbol was essential to the overall meaning of the message.

Therefore, great care must be taken when modern interpreters attempt to explain what Daniel did not interpret. Even the great and wise prophet Daniel could not understand all the imagery unless it was interpreted by God or an angel (7:16; 8:27; 12:8, 9).

GOD'S RULE OVER THE GENTILE NATIONS

Daniel and his three friends—Shadrach, Meshach, and Abednego—were chosen to enter a three-year educational program in the Babylonian language and its extensive wisdom, religious, and historical literature. Only the best-looking and most intelligent young men were brought into this government-sponsored training program for work in the king's court (1:4, 5). Daniel and his friends believed that the king's food and wine would defile them (it may have been consecrated to a pagan god), so they diplomatically requested meals of vegetables and water for a ten-day trial. God honored the dedication of these young men and miraculously gave them good health and more wisdom than the other students and ten times more wisdom than Babylon's wise men (1:17-21).

In the second year of his reign, Nebuchadnezzar had a disturbing dream of a great statue that was destroyed by a rock. The magicians and wise men of Babylon admitted defeat, saying they could not tell the king his dream because a god had not revealed it to them (2:11). Nebuchadnezzar decided to kill the wise men, including Daniel and his friends. After these young men prayed for God's mercy, He revealed the dream and interpretation to Daniel (2:12-19). Daniel praised God because He has all wisdom and power, and He reveals His mysteries to mankind (2:20-23).

Daniel witnessed to the king, revealing that God had told him that the statue's head of gold was Nebuchadnezzar (2:28, 36-38). The other parts of the statue referred to later weaker kingdoms, and the final kingdom was the everlasting kingdom of God (2:44, 45). Because he could interpret the dream, Daniel and his God were honored, and his three friends were given new jobs.

Later Nebuchadnezzar made a statue (probably of himself) and required all political officials to bow down to it to demonstrate their loyalty to him (3:1-5). Shadrach, Meshach, and Abednego believed that God could deliver them from any harm, so they refused to bow down before the image and were thrown into a blazing furnace. An angelic being from God delivered them unharmed, and Nebuchadnezzar was again forced to recognize the power of God (3:24-30).

In spite of this witness to Nebuchadnezzar, he was a very proud man. Finally he was humbled by God and challenged to recognize that the Lord is the ruler over all mankind (4:17, 25, 32). The king's dream of the destruction of a great tree was fulfilled (4:10-27), and he was humbled and became like a beast (4:28-33). When he was restored to his throne, the king praised, exalted, and honored God, confessing that He is all powerful, true, and just when He humbles the proud and raises up the lowly (4:34-37).

Later while King Nabonidus was away from Babylon, Belshazzar sponsored a great banquet in spite of the fact that the city was at war (5:1-4). At this drunken party, the gold and silver cups from the temple in Jerusalem were desecrated in toasts of praise to the Babylonian gods. In the middle of the party a hand appeared and wrote a message on the palace wall (5:5). No one could read the message except Daniel. It said that God had numbered and weighed Babylon, but found that it did not measure up to His requirements. Therefore God would divide it among the Medes and the Persians (5:25-28).

This prophecy was fulfilled that very night in 539 B.C., for the besieging Medo-Persians broke through and captured Babylon, destroying its power (5:30, 31). The fall of Babylon fulfilled the prophecies of Isaiah (13, 14) and Jeremiah (50, 51) that were given many years earlier.

When the Persians took over the Babylonian empire, they reorganized their vast territory into 120 states (satrapies), with three central commissioners in charge (6:1, 2). Daniel was greatly respected by the new king and the most skilled of his officials; therefore, the others tried to find fault with Daniel.[2] Finally they got the king to pass a law that forbade requesting anything from anyone or any god except the king (6:7). When Daniel prayed to God according to his usual custom, he was arrested and thrown into the lions' den. God miraculously delivered him by sending an angel and closing the mouths of the lions (6:22). The king rejoiced that Daniel was saved and had the prophet's enemies thrown into a den of hungry lions.

GOD'S CARE FOR HIS PERSECUTED PEOPLE

The second half of the book contains more visions of God's sovereign control of the nations, but these messages focus on how God would protect His people in the midst of some very severe persecution. Earlier in the Babylonian reign of Belshazzar, Daniel had a dream (which was very similar to Nebuchadnezzar's dream in chapter 2) about four beasts coming from the sea (7:1-8). In this case none of the kings or nations is identified because the focus is entirely on the last beast. The last animal was particularly violent and boastful, but finally the Ancient of Days, God Almighty, judged these beasts and gave eternal dominion over all the kingdoms of the earth to the Son of Man (the Messiah) so that all people would serve Him forever (7:9-14).

This vision was comforting because it gave assurance that God's saints would inherit the kingdom of God (7:18, 27), but it was also very disturbing because it revealed that God's people would go through severe persecution when the last beast and the little horn ruled (7:8, 19-25). This small horn is frequently identified with the Antichrist of Revelation 13 and 17.

Two years later Daniel had a similar dream about fighting between a ram, a male goat, and a horn (8:1-8). The ram was interpreted as Medo-Persia (8:20), and the goat represented Greece (8:21), but the violent small horn is not identified. He was some future ruler (8:17, 19) who would boast, try to make himself equal to God, and severely persecute the holy people of God for a limited period of time (8:9-14, 23-26). Finally he would be defeated by God (8:25). Although this horn is similar to the earlier horn, it is frequently identified with the Greek ruler Antiochus Epiphanes, who persecuted and killed many Jews around 165 B.C.[3]

Later in the Persian period, the eighty-year-old Daniel was reading in Jeremiah (25:11, 12; 29:10) that God would return the people to Jerusalem in seventy years (9:1, 2). Suddenly he realized that he had come in 605 B.C. and that it was now 538 B.C., only a few years before the exiles were to return. Daniel fasted and prayed, confessing the nation's sins and recognizing the justice of God in sending them into exile. Then he asked God to turn away His anger and return them to Jerusalem (9:3-19).

God told Daniel through the angel Gabriel that it would be seventy weeks of years before God would remove all sin, bring in everlasting righteousness, anoint the holy temple, and fulfill all prophecy (9:24). During this period, Jerusalem would be rebuilt, the anointed Messiah would come and be cut off, and then the city of Jerusalem would be destroyed, and the people would undergo great persecution and war (9:25, 26). In the middle of the last week of years all worship at the temple would be halted. But by the end of that week, the one who desolated and persecuted the people of God would be defeated.[4] Daniel was extremely alarmed by the description of the war and persecution introduced in chapters 7–9.

The final three chapters expand on these themes in order to help future generations to prepare for these trials and to strengthen them with the hope that one day God will reward the faithful with eternal life and the wicked with eternal disgrace (12:1-3).

After three weeks of fasting and praying, Daniel saw a vision of future events from the angel Michael. This report gave Daniel some insight into the unseen spiritual battles going on in his world, for Michael was delayed because of a battle with the evil powers controlling Persia (10:1-13, 20, 21). The angel revealed that there would be four more Persian kings, and then the Greeks would defeat Persia and control all the ancient Near Eastern world (11:1, 2).

This prophecy was fulfilled about 200 years later when Alexander the Great defeated the Persians around 331 B.C. His kingdom was later divided into four kingdoms that fought against each other and invaded Palestine, the Beautiful Land. In the midst of these wars a very evil ruler (probably Antiochus Epiphanes) desecrated the temple in Jerusalem, killed many Jews, magnified himself above God, and spoke blasphemies against God (11:29-39).

At the end of time, the Antichrist will act like this earlier ruler, for he also will blaspheme God (11:36-45). Although this will be the worst persecution that the world has ever known, all the faithful dead have hope because their names are written in God's book of life. They will be resurrected to eternal life, while the wicked will suffer God's judgment

(12:1, 2). Daniel faithfully wrote down these visions even though he did not totally understand what they meant or know exactly when these events would take place (12:5-9).

THEOLOGICAL SIGNIFICANCE OF DANIEL

1. All wisdom comes from God. He reveals His wisdom to His faithful servants in order to bring glory to Himself.
2. All power to control individuals and nations rests with God. He raises up whomever he wishes and humbles the proud to demonstrate His power and bring people to submission to Him.
3. Although God's saints have and will suffer great persecution, God will eventually deliver them and give them His eternal kingdom, which will be ruled by the Son of Man.

The New Testament contains several references to the book of Daniel. When Jesus was talking about events at the end of time, he reminded his hearers of the persecutions that would happen when the abomination of desolation would be put in the temple at Jerusalem (Matt. 24:15, using Dan. 9:27; 12:11). Revelation 13 refers to several beasts coming out of the sea and focuses on the last one who would blaspheme God and make war against the saints (Dan. 7). Revelation 14 demonstrates that God will judge the beast and deliver the kingdom over to the Son of Man, who will come on a cloud (Dan. 7:9-14). Jesus also described the Son of Man (Matt. 24:30; 25:31-46), who would come in His glory, judge the wicked, and raise the righteous dead to life everlasting and the wicked dead to eternal punishment (Dan. 12:1, 2).

DISCUSSION QUESTIONS

1. Compare and contrast the wisdom of Daniel and the Babylonian wise men in Daniel 1 and 2.
2. How were Daniel (chapter 6) and his three friends (chapter 3) examples to those saints who would suffer severe persecution in the future?
3. What was Nebuchadnezzar's and Belshazzar's central sin (chapters 4 and 5)? What was God trying to teach them?
4. How did Daniel's knowledge of Leviticus 26, 1 Kings 8, and Jeremiah 25 influence his prayer in chapter 9?
5. What warnings about interpreting prophecy are provided in 2 Peter 1:20, 21? What does 1 Peter 1:10-12 tell us about what the prophets knew and what they did not know?

Chapter Twenty-Three

POSTEXILIC
PROPHETS

CYRUS, THE KING OF Persia, defeated Babylon in 539 B.C. and decreed that the Hebrews in captivity could return to Palestine and rebuild the temple (Ezra 1:1-3). About 50,000 Jews returned around 538 B.C. under the leadership of the governor Zerubbabel and the high priest Jeshua/Joshua (Ezra 1:11; 2:64-66). Once they returned, the people rebuilt the altar and began to lay the foundation of the temple (Ezra 3:3, 8-10). But when the people who were living in the land tried to join in the rebuilding, Zerubbabel and Jeshua refused to cooperate. In response, the people threatened the Jews and caused the work on the temple to stop (Ezra 4:1-5).

About sixteen years later (520 B.C.), in the second year of the reign of Persia's King Darius, God raised up Haggai and Zechariah to challenge the people to start work on the temple again (Ezra 4:24–5:2; Hag. 1:1; Zech. 1:1). The temple was finished four years later, in 516 B.C. (Ezra 6:15).

Later, in 458 B.C., during the reign of the Persian King Artaxerxes, Ezra came to Jerusalem and carried out a religious reform because many people had intermarried with foreigners who worshiped other gods (Ezra 7:1-10; 9:1–10:15). A few years passed, and then in 445 B.C. Nehemiah came to Jerusalem to help rebuild the city walls (Neh. 2:1; 6:15). Before long Ezra led another revival because people were intermarrying with foreigners again (Neh. 8:1–10:31). About twenty-five years after this (420 B.C.), God raised up Malachi to bring the nation back to Himself because they no longer feared God or lived according to His ways.

HAGGAI

Setting Priorities

The rebuilding of the temple was of major concern to the Jews when they first returned to Jerusalem. But they were continually frustrated on every side by local and Persian authorities, and the reconstruction project floundered. Haggai's messages indicate that the people also suffered from an imbalance in their spiritual priorities.

Outline of Haggai

Glorify God and build the temple	1:1-15
Comparing the glory of the temple	2:1-9
Holiness precedes blessing	2:10-19
God's work will be accomplished	2:20-23

Haggai was a great motivator. Although he had official government policy, circumstances, economic conditions, and widespread spiritual apathy against him, he was able to overcome these negatives by focusing on the nation's priorities.

GLORIFY GOD AND BUILD THE TEMPLE

After years of frustration over not being able to rebuild the temple, most people in Judah just gave up on the idea. They did not have enough money to complete such an expensive project because God sent a drought on their land (1:6, 9-11). What income they had, they spent on building nice homes for themselves.[1] Everything pointed to the conclusion that it was not the appropriate time to finish the work (1:4). Haggai challenged these conclusions and set up the higher priorities of doing what God desires and what glorifies Him (1:8). The people revered God, obeyed what He said, and began to work on the temple because they believed that God was with them (1:12-15).

COMPARING THE GLORY OF THE TEMPLE

After working on the temple for two months, the people saw clearly that the new building would be much smaller than Solomon's temple and without gold on the walls, floor, and furniture (2:3; cf. 1 Kings 6:14-36). Many thought that this temple was an embarrassment, not worth the effort. But was exterior beauty what the temple was all about? Haggai challenged the people to set higher priorities, for God's Spirit would strengthen them. He still controls all the nations on the earth, and He owns all the gold in the world (2:4-8). Yet God gave this new temple great glory when Cyrus paid for the full cost of construction (Ezra 6:8-10).

HOLINESS PRECEDES BLESSING

Two illustrations from the priestly regulations suggest that holiness was not gained by just being in the temple or coming into contact with something holy (2:10-13). Haggai saw that the people were defiled and needed holiness, not just a series of ritualistic observances in the new temple. Once holiness was their priority, they would receive God's blessing (2:14-19).

GOD'S WORK WILL BE ACCOMPLISHED

Finally Haggai promised the new governor Zerubbabel that God would be with him, would control all the surrounding nations that threatened him, and choose him (a Davidic descendent who would wear the king's ring) to be a sign of God's continuing work to bring about His kingdom on earth (2:20-23).

THEOLOGICAL SIGNIFICANCE OF HAGGAI

1. In spite of opposition or negative circumstances, the believer must always give priority to what pleases and glorifies God.
2. Comparisons often lead to discouragement, but God's promises and power give strength to overcome all problems.
3. God is less concerned about external ritual than He is about internal holiness.

ZECHARIAH

God's Restoration of Zion

The prophet Zechariah was probably from a priestly family (Neh. 12:4, 16), and he, along with Haggai, played a key role in challenging those who returned from Babylonian captivity to rebuild the temple (Ezra 4:24–5:5). Although the first eight chapters that encouraged the building of the temple are dated around 520–518 B.C., chapters 9–14 have no dates and are more concerned with the time when God will establish His messianic kingdom. Because of these differences, it is possible that God gave these rather apocalyptic messages in 9–14 a good number of years after the temple was rebuilt.

Outline of Zechariah

Visions to encourage building the temple	1–6
Call to repentance	1:1-6
Visions of restoration of Jerusalem	1:7–2:13
Visions of empowered leaders	3:1–6:15
The question of fasting	7–8
Burdens concerning the future of Israel	9–14
The rejection of the good shepherd	9:1–11:17
The acceptance of the good shepherd	12:1–14:21

Zechariah provided messages of hope for the leaders and a community of believers who were powerless because of their own sinfulness. They were discouraged because it seemed that God was not restoring their nation. To solve these problems, sin must be removed, God's shepherd must be accepted, and then God could establish His kingdom.

VISIONS TO ENCOURAGE BUILDING THE TEMPLE

Before Zechariah presented his visions to the people, he called them to repentance (1:1-6). Since God was angry with His people because of their sin, any possible future hope depended on their willingness to return to Him. Fortunately, the people repented (1:6).

God gave a series of visions to encourage the people about the restoration of Jerusalem. God was watching over Jerusalem (symbolized by His angels on horses in 1:10, 11) and would destroy their enemies (symbolized by the horns—1:15, 18-21; 2:8). Jerusalem would be so large that the people returning to it would not fit within its walls. It would be filled with joy, God's presence, and people from many nations (1:16, 17; 2:1-7).[2]

The leaders also were encouraged. Joshua the high priest was defended, cleansed, and promised free access to God's throne of grace through prayer. God's eyes would be on the stones of the temple, and it would be completed (3:1-10). Through Zerubbabel and Joshua (symbolized by the two olive trees), God's Spirit would turn mountains into plains and see to it that the top stone on the temple would soon be in place (4:1-14). God's curse on sin (symbolized by the woman) would be removed (5:1-11), and He would sovereignly control the four corners of the earth (6:1-8). God's promise to send the branch (the Messiah) was memorialized by a crown of jewels put on Joshua, for the Messiah will have both priestly and kingly functions (6:9-14).

THE QUESTION OF FASTING

Some people from the city of Bethel came to Zechariah to find out if they had to continue the fasts that commemorated the burning of the temple in Jerusalem in the fifth month (Jer. 52:12, 13), for the new temple was now built. Zechariah questioned whether they were really fasting for God or for themselves. Then God challenged them to give priority to practicing justice and compassion and to avoid being stubborn like their fathers (7:8-12). If they obeyed, God would restore Jerusalem, give them peace, and make Israel a blessing among the nations (8:1-13). God would turn their past fasts into joyous feasts (8:19).

BURDENS CONCERNING THE FUTURE OF ISRAEL

The first burdensome message from Zechariah (9–11) described God's judgment of Tyre and Philistia (9:1-7) and His restoration of His people (9:8–11:3). Restoration would include the coming of Israel's humble King (the Messiah) on a donkey, the renewal of God's covenant relationship with His people, the giving of rain, the removal of all idolatry and false prophecy, and the strengthening of His people. But Israel would reject this King. They would follow the evil shepherd who brings destruction, and the Good Shepherd would be sold for thirty pieces of silver (11:4–17).

The second burdensome message (12–14) described God's deliverance of Judah in a great war against God's people by all the nations of the earth (12:1-9). When God saves Israel and destroys the nations, then the people will recognize the one they pierced, reject their false leaders, mourn their sins, and be cleansed (12:10–13:6). During a final attack on Jerusalem, when many will be killed, God Himself will stand on the Mount of Olives and rescue His people (13:7–14:5). Then He will reign as king over the whole earth and destroy all who refuse to worship Him as the King of kings (14:9-21).

THEOLOGICAL SIGNIFICANCE OF ZECHARIAH

1. The only way to avoid God's anger is to repent of sins.
2. One day God will judge the wicked among the nations, bring the righteous from the nations to join His people, and dwell among His joyful people.
3. God's work will be accomplished through His Spirit, not by human might, earthly wisdom, or military power.
4. The ritual of fasting is useless if it is not a fast unto God.
5. Although many rejected the Good Shepherd, through a tremendous demonstration of God's power and grace, one day a multitude of Jews and Gentiles will recognize Him as King of kings and worship Him.

The New Testament showed that Jesus was the humble King who brought salvation, though He rode on a donkey (Zech. 9:9 and Matt. 21:5). Jesus identified Himself as the Good Shepherd (Zech. 11:4-14 and John 10:14), and He was sold for thirty pieces of silver (Zech. 11:12 and Matt. 26:15). John 19:37 recognizes that the one who was pierced (Zech. 12:10) was Jesus at the cross. Revelation 22:5 talks about a time when there will no longer be any night (see Zech. 14:6, 7), and Revelation 22:1, 2 refers to the river running out of Jerusalem (Zech. 14:8).

MALACHI

Honoring God

The prophet Malachi proclaimed God's Word about 100 years after Haggai and Zechariah. The walls of Jerusalem were now up, so the city had good security. Since the rebuilding of the temple had happened so long ago, many were not very excited about their worship there. The priests were no longer teaching the people about sacrificial regulations. Many were twisting Ezra's command to divorce foreign wives into permission to divorce their Hebrew wives. Some even questioned if there was any value in serving God. Malachi addressed these issues using a dialogue format, which included a series of questions and answers.

Outline of Malachi

Disputation about God's love for Israel	1:1-5
Disputation about honoring God in worship	1:6-14
Disputation against the priests	2:1-9
Disputation on marriage and divorce	2:10-16
Disputation on God's justice	2:17–3:6
Disputation on tithing	3:7-12
Disputation on the value of serving God	3:13–4:6

The prophet Malachi believed that there was one essential factor behind the various ethical and worship problems that the people faced. They did not think of God as the great sovereign King who should be feared; therefore, they did not live according to His covenant instructions.

DISPUTATION ABOUT GOD'S LOVE FOR ISRAEL

Some of the Jews in Jerusalem questioned whether God really loved them. But proof of God's love is evident in His choice to give His blessings to Jacob rather than to Esau (Gen. 25:25, 26). God's recent judgment of the Edomite descendents of Esau showed that He did not waver from His plan. Malachi reminded these people that one day God will be glorified around the world, thus encouraging their recommitment to Him.

DISPUTATION ABOUT HONORING GOD IN WORSHIP

God compared Himself to a father and a master but noted that He did not receive the honor appropriate to such positions. Some questioned this accusation. How did they dishonor God? By offering blind and lame sacrifices that even their own governor would not accept, came the reply. It would be better to close the temple rather than continue such hypocrisy. People needed to remember that God is a great King, and His name will be feared among the nations.

DISPUTATION AGAINST THE PRIESTS

God was not worshiped properly because the priests did not act in godly ways—honoring God, giving the people true instruction in God's law, walking in righteousness and peace, or turning people from wickedness. Because they corrupted the Levitical covenant, God would despise and curse them; He would spread the intestinal refuse from the sacrificial animals all over their faces and defile them.

DISPUTATION ON MARRIAGE AND DIVORCE

The Jewish family was defined by its relationship to one father, Abraham, and one God, the God of Israel. But many Hebrews were destroying the traditional family—some by marrying foreign wives and others by divorcing their Hebrew wives. This profaned the people's worship of God at the temple and made it impossible for Him to accept their sacrifices. God hates divorce; certainly those who have the Holy Spirit in them would not do this.

DISPUTATION ON GOD'S JUSTICE

Things were so bad that some actually questioned the justice of God, suggesting that God delights in those who do evil. But God would demonstrate His justice on the earth when He sent His messenger to prepare the way for the coming of the messenger of the covenant (the Messiah).³ He would purify the Levites and remove the wicked who do not fear God, so that His people would once again present pleasing offerings to God. God is just; His character and His promises do not change.

DISPUTATION ON TITHING

God asked the people to repent, but they did not seem to know what to repent about. God revealed that they were not tithing. If they would stop robbing God, He would end the plague He had sent to destroy their crops, and He would pour out a blessing so large that they would not have room to store their produce.

DISPUTATION ON THE VALUE OF SERVING GOD

Finally God accused some arrogant people who began to think that it was vain to serve God or to repent. They were so mixed up that they called the proud the blessed ones and the wicked the strong ones. In response those who feared God encouraged one another by remembering that God has a book that includes the names of those who honor Him. Those faithful people are God's special possessions, as precious as an only son. In the great day of the Lord, God will distinguish between the wicked and the righteous who serve Him. His burning fire will destroy the arrogant evildoers and give joy and healing to those who fear Him. It pays to remember what God revealed through Moses in the past and what God will do on the day of the Lord when He sends Elijah to restore the nation.

THEOLOGICAL SIGNIFICANCE OF MALACHI

1. God's love and justice do not change. His election and the final judgment on the day of the Lord demonstrate His character.
2. Honoring God, the great King, is not accomplished through hypocritical worship. God deserves our best.
3. God hates divorce and intermarriage with pagans. These acts destroy the family and make worship unacceptable.
4. The teacher/preacher who does not fear God, give true instruction from God's Word, walk in uprightness, and turn people from evil will not receive God's blessing.
5. God does distinguish between the righteous and the wicked; therefore, it is worthwhile to fear and serve God.

In the New Testament book of Romans (9:13) Paul used Malachi 1:2, 3—"I loved Jacob, and I hated Esau"—to show that God's purposes were fulfilled by His election of individuals. The messenger who would prepare the way of the Lord in Malachi 3:1 and Elijah in Malachi 4:5 was identified as John the Baptist by Jesus in Matthew 11:9, 10, 14.

DISCUSSION QUESTIONS AND ACTIVITIES

1. What were the three priorities that Haggai emphasized?
2. Why do comparisons often cause discouragement?
3. How did Zechariah encourage the leaders of his day?
4. What prophecies in Zechariah 9–14 relate to the life of Jesus?
5. If people truly honor God, how will this affect their family life, their worship, and their tithing?
6. Why is it worthwhile to fear and serve God?

Old Testament Chronology

DATES	BIBLE EVENTS	CONTEMPORARY CULTURES
Period of Beginnings	Genesis 1–11	Prehistorical era
Ca. 2000 B.C.	The Patriarchs Abraham	Patriarchal narratives reflect culture of
to	Isaac	Mesopotamia and Egypt
	Jacob	
Ca. 1800 B.C.	Joseph	
to		
Ca. 1400 B.C.	Israelites reside in Egypt	Egypt enslaves Israelites
to	Moses	Palestine occupied
	Joshua	Various nations oppress
	The Judges	Israel
Ca. 1100 B.C.		
	Samuel	
to	Saul	
	David	
Ca. 931 B.C.	Solomon	Surrounding nations
	The Divided Kingdom	defeated by Israel

	South	*North*	
	Rehoboam	Jeroboam I	
Ca. 875 B.C.	Jehoshaphat	Ahab	Syrian Kingdom 931–732
Ca. 790 B.C.	Uzziah	Jeroboam II	
732 B.C.			Fall of Syria
722 B.C.		Fall of Samaria	
716 B.C.	Hezekiah		
640 B.C.	Josiah		Assyrian domination of Palestine 745–650
586 B.C.	Fall of Jerusalem		
539 B.C.	Return of the Jews		Babylonian supremacy 625–539
520–515 B.C.	Second Temple Haggai Zechariah		Medo-Persian rule 539–331
457 B.C.	Ezra		
444 B.C.	Nehemiah Malachi		

Ca. is a contraction of "circa" meaning "approximately."

The Divided Kingdom Era
931–586 B.C.

Date	NORTHERN KINGDOM (Israel) Kings	Prophets	SOUTHERN KINGDOM (Judah) Kings	FOREIGN KINGS
931	Jeroboam Dynasty		Rehoboam	Rezon[1]
	Jeroboam	Ahijah	Shemaiah	Abijam	
			Iddo		
	Nadab			Asa	
909	Baasha Dynasty			Azariah	
	Baasha			Hanani	
		Jehu			
	Elah				
	Zimri (7 days)				
885	Omri Dynasty				
	Omri (Tibni)	Elijah		Jehoshaphat	Benhadad[1]
	Ahab	Micaiah	Eliezer		
	Ahaziah	Elisha		Jehoram	Shalmaneser III[2]
	Joram		Jehoiada	Ahaziah	
841	Jehu Dynasty				
	Jehu			Athaliah	Hazael[1]
	Jehoahaz		Zechariah	Joash	
	Jehoash	*Jonah*		Amaziah	Benhadad II[1]
	Jeroboam II	*Amos*		Azariah	
		Hosea			
	Zechariah				
752	Last Kings			Jotham	Shalmaneser IV[2]
	Shallum		*Isaiah*		
	Menaham				Tiglath-pileser III[2]
	Pekahiah			Ahaz	Rezin[1]
	Pekah	Oded			Shalmaneser V[2]
	Hoshea				
722	FALL OF		*Micah*		Sargon II[2]
	SAMARIA			Hezekiah	Sennacherib[3]
				Manasseh	Esarhaddon[2]
			*Nahum**		Ashurbanipal[2]
				Amon	
640			*Zephaniah**		
			Jeremiah	Josiah	
			Huldah		
			*Habakkuk**		
			*Joel**	Jehoahaz	Nabopolassar[3]
				Jehoiakim	Nebuchadnezzar[3]
			Daniel	Jehoiachin	
			Ezekiel	Zedekiah	
586			FALL OF JERUSALEM	

Notes: Writing prophets are indicated in *italics*.
Obadiah,* Haggai, Zechariah, and Malachi ministered after the Fall of Jerusalem.
*Approximate time   [1]Syria   [2]Assyria   [3]Babylonia

NOTES

2 THE PATRIARCHS

1. For a more extensive study of Abraham, Isaac, and Jacob, see Charles Pfeiffer, *The Patriarchal* Age (Grand Rapids: Baker Book House, 1961).
2. For a discussion of this chapter, see Samuel J. Schultz, *The Old Testament Speaks* (New York: Harper & Row, 1970), p. 39.

3 GOD'S HOLY NATION

1. Three Hebrew words are used adverting to Pharaoh's attitude, denoting an intensification of a condition already existing. Cf. Joseph P. Free, *Archaeology and Bible History* (Wheaton, IL: Scripture Press, 1976), pp. 93, 94.
2. For a fuller description of the religion of Israel in its contrast to contemporary heathen practice, see Samuel J. Schultz, *The Old Testament Speaks* (New York: Harper & Row, 1970), pp. 57-74.

4 LOOKING FORWARD TO CANAAN

1. For a detailed analysis, see A. A. MacRae, "Numbers," in the *New Bible Commentary* (Grand Rapids: Eerdmans, 1953), pp. 162-194.
2. Korah's family did not perish. His descendants occupy an honored place in subsequent history. Samuel ranks perhaps next to Moses as a great prophet. Heman, a grandson of Samuel, was an outstanding singer in David's time. A number of psalms are designated as "for the sons of Korah."

5 POSSESSING THE PROMISED LAND

1. George Ernest Wright and Floyd V. Filson, eds., *Westminster Historical Atlas of the Bible* (Philadelphia: Westminster Press, 1956), p. 34.
2. For a discussion of the possibility that the city of Bethel was included in this conquest, see Samuel J. Schultz, *The Old Testament Speaks* (New York: Harper & Row, 1970), p. 97.
3. For various views and interpretations of this miracle of Joshua's long day, see Bernard Ramm, *The Christian View of Science and Scripture* (Grand Rapids: Eerdmans, 1955), pp. 156-161.
4. For a discussion of the chronology for this period, see Schultz, *The Old Testament Speaks*, pp. 103-105.

8 THE SOLOMONIC KINGDOM

1. For a fuller description of the temple and its furnishings, see Samuel J. Schultz, *The Old Testament Speaks* (New York: Harper & Row, 1970), pp. 144-147.

2. Nelson Glueck, *The Other Side of the Jordan* (New Haven, Yale Station: American Schools of Oriental Research, 1940), p. 94.

10 THE KINGDOM OF JUDAH: REHOBOAM—JOTHAM

1. For a chronological description of the kings of Israel and Judah, see the chart "Old Testament Kings and Prophets" by John Whitcomb (Winona Lake, IN: Grace Theological Seminary), rev. 1962.

2. In this study the son of Jehoshaphat is designated by the name Jehoram, and the son of Ahab is designated as Joram, even though the two are used interchangeably in Scripture.

3. For a more extensive treatment of these developments, see Samuel J. Schultz, *The Old Testament Speaks* (New York: Harper & Row, 1970), pp. 203-205.

11 THE KINGDOM OF JUDAH: AHAZ—ZEDEKIAH

1. Note the alternate names for these last kings:
   Jehoahaz—Shallum Jehoiachin—Coniah or Jeconiah
   Jehoiakim—Eliakim Zedekiah—Mattaniah

12 BEYOND THE EXILE

1. Historical evidence seems to be lacking to support the idea that the Jewish captives were mistreated physically or suppressed in their civic and religious activities during the days of Babylonian supremacy. Cf. Charles Francis Whitley, *The Exilic Age* (London: Westminster Press, 1957), p. 79.

2. The events of the book of Haggai took place during this time.

13 PSALMS OF LAMENT AND PRAISE

1. Claus Westermann, *The Psalms: Structure, Content and Message* (Minneapolis: Augsburg, 1980), pp. 29-45.

2. Ibid., pp. 71-80.

3. Ibid., pp. 81-92.

14 SPECIAL THEMES IN THE PSALMS

1. Herbert Carl Leupold, *Exposition of the Psalms* (Grand Rapids: Baker Book House, 1969), pp. 561, 562.

2. C. S. Lewis, *Reflections on the Psalms* (1961), p. 31, suggests that the psalmists took right and wrong more seriously. They also knew the difference between the two.

3. William. S. LaSor, David A. Hubbard, and Frederick W. Bush, *Old Testament Survey* (Grand Rapids: Eerdmans, 1982), pp. 522, 523.

4. Sigmund Mowinckel, *The Psalms in Israel's Worship* (Nashville: Abingdon, 1962), strongly supported this theory on the basis of Babylonian rituals. There is no evidence that the Israelites had such a ritual, and if they did, it would certainly have been quite different from the pagan religion in Babylon.

15 WISDOM

1. *The Ancient Near East*, ed. James Pritchard (Princeton, NJ: Princeton University Press, 1969), includes a series of wisdom texts that archeologists have found in Egypt and Babylonia. It is interesting to note that they treat some of the same basic concerns found in the Bible, but solutions were sometimes quite different.

2. John E. Hartley, "Job," *International Standard Bible Encyclopedia*, Vol. 2 (Grand Rapids: Eerdmans, 1982), pp. 1065, 1066.

3. It is not very clear who is speaking this beautiful poem in chapter 28. It hardly seems consistent with Job's speeches. Note that the next chapter introduces Job, implying that he was not speaking in chapter 28. Francis I. Andersen, *Job* (Downers Grove, IL: InterVarsity Press, 1976), concludes that the poem was written by the author/editor of the book.

16 INSTRUCTIONAL WISDOM

1. G. Lloyd Carr, *The Song of Solomon* (Downers Grove, IL: InterVarsity, 1984), pp. 26-32, discusses various approaches to interpreting the Song of Solomon.

2. G. Lloyd Carr, "The Love Poetry Genre in the Old Testament and the Ancient Near East," *The Journal of the Evangelical Theological Society* 25 (1982), pp. 489-498.

3. Franz Delitzsch, *Commentary on the Song of Songs and Ecclesiastes* (London: T. & T. Clark, 1985).

17 UNDERSTANDING AND INTERPRETING THE PROPHETS

1. Gary V. Smith, "Prophecy, False," *International Standard Bible Encyclopedia*, Vol. 3 (Grand Rapids: Eerdmans, 1986), pp. 984-986.

2. Smith, "Prophet, Prophecy," ibid., pp. 997-1001.

3. Two texts that give many helpful guidelines for those wishing to develop good interpretive skills are Walter C. Kaiser, *Toward an Exegetical Theology* (Grand Rapids: Baker Book House, 1981) and Henry A. Virkler, *Hermeneutics: Principle and Processes of Biblical Interpretation* (Grand Rapids: Baker Book House, 1981).

18 EARLY PROPHETS FROM ISRAEL

1. For information on the history, archeological discoveries, and a map of the city of Nineveh, see D. W. Wiseman, "Nineveh," *The Illustrated Bible Dictionary*, Vol. 2 (Leicester: InterVarsity Press, 1980), pp. 1089-1092.

2. Edwin Good, *Irony in the Bible* (Philadelphia: Westminster Press, 1965), pp. 39-55, discusses a number of ironic features in Jonah.

3. Peter C. Craigie, "Amos the NOQED in Light of Ugaritic," *Studies in Religion* 11 (1982), pp. 29-33, shows that the term "shepherd" in 1:1 refers to a manager of shepherds.

4. G. V. Smith, *Amos: A Commentary* (Grand Rapids: Eerdmans, 1989), pp. 188, 189, believes Sakkut refers to the Assyrian worship of the god associated with the planet Saturn. This god was considered a king and called Ninurta in some texts.

19 EARLY PROPHETS FROM JUDAH

1. H. B. Huffmon, "The Covenant Lawsuit in the Prophets," *Journal of Biblical Literature* 78 (1959), pp. 285-295.
2. Jesus quoted these verses (Matt. 13:14-17), realizing that one of the purposes of His ministry was to harden the hearts of unbelievers. This does not deny people's free choice to repent, but if they repeatedly refuse to repent, God may give them over to their depraved minds and harden their hearts (Rom. 1:18-32).
3. Because of the context (7:15-17) some believe that this prophecy was fulfilled when a virgin of Ahaz's day gave birth to a child by natural means. Others believe there was a double fulfillment, one in Ahaz's day and one when Christ was born. Some think that 7:14 refers only to Jesus' birth. Isaiah 7:15-17 refers to the time it takes a child to know what is right and wrong (possibly three years) as a measure for when the Assyrians would control Ahaz and Judah.
4. The first two chapters in Harold H. Rowley, *The Servant of the Lord and Other Essays in the Old Testament* (London: Nelson, 1952), survey various ways people have interpreted this passage.

20 LATE PREEXILIC PROPHETS

1. C. J. Gadd, *The Fall of Nineveh* (London: British Museum, 1923), pp. 25-30, and H. W. F. Saggs, "Nahum and the Fall of Nineveh," *Journal of Theological Studies* 20 (1969), pp. 220-225, discuss these issues.
2. M. Weiss, "The Origin of the Day of the Yahweh Reconsidered," *Hebrew Union College Annual* 37 (1966), pp. 29-72, discusses various possible ways of interpreting the Day of the Lord.
3. Ralph L. Smith, *Micah-Malachi* (Waco: Word, 1984), p. 93, but this is only an educated guess.
4. Douglas Stuart, *Hosea-Jonah* (Waco: Word, 1987), pp. 232-234.
5. Thomas Overholt, *Threat of Falsehood* (Naperville, IL: Allenson, 1970).
6. Roland K. Harrison, *Jeremiah and Lamentations* (Downers Grove, IL: InterVarsity Press, 1973), p. 197.
7. Norman K. Gottwald, *Studies in the Book of Lamentations* (London: SCM, 1954), pp. 23-32.

21 EXILIC PROPHET—EZEKIEL

1. John B. Taylor, *Ezekiel* (Downers Grove, IL: InterVarsity Press, 1969), pp. 54-59, gives a more detailed description of what Ezekiel saw.
2. Some have suggested that the man in linen in 9:1 was Gabriel or the angel of the Lord, but the text gives no identification.

3. Some believe that the description of the king of Tyre is a picture of the fall of Satan, but the main emphasis is on the historical person who was the king of Tyre. Since the king claimed to be perfect and a god, he was clearly controlled by the lies of Satan and the false mythologies of Tyre's religion.

22 EXILIC PROPHET—DANIEL

1. The apparent inconsistency between Daniel's reference to his going into captivity in the third year of Jehoiakim (Dan. 1:1) after the battle at Carchemish and Jeremiah's association of this event with the fourth year of Jehoiakim is based on either the use of two different calendars (the new year could begin in April or October depending on whether one is using the religious or civil calendar) or the Babylonian practice of not counting the first year of a king's reign as year one, since he had not yet ruled for a year. Leon J. Wood, *A Commentary on Daniel* (Grand Rapids: Zondervan, 1973), pp. 25-27.

2. See John F. Walvoord, *Daniel: The Key to Prophetic Revelation* (Chicago: Moody, 1971), pp. 132, 133, for a discussion of the identification of Persia's King Darius, mentioned in 5:31, 6:1, 9:1, and 11:1. Many think this may be the name of one of the Persian generals; others consider it just another name for Cyrus.

3. Wood, *Commentary on Daniel*, pp. 214, 215.

4. Daniel 9:24-27 is a key passage where millennialists and amillennialists differ. The first group believes these verses are describing events at the end of time just before the millennium. The second group believes these verses are describing events around the time of Christ's first coming and death. See Walvoord, *Daniel: The Key to Prophetic Revelation*, pp. 216-237, for a discussion of some of these differences.

23 POSTEXILIC PROPHETS

1. Pieter A. Verhoef, *The Book of Haggai and Malachi* (Grand Rapids: Eerdmans, 1987), p. 58, believes their houses were furnished with wood paneling on their inner walls, a fairly expensive look usually associated with a king's palace (1 Kings 6:15; Jer. 22:14).

2. Joyce Baldwin, *Haggai, Zechariah, Malachi* (Downers Grove, IL: InterVarsity Press, 1972), p. 109, believes the "me" who was sent against the nation in 2:8 refers to the prophet, but it is likely that the "me" in 2:8 and 2:11 is a reference to the Messiah.

3. Verhoef, *The Book of Haggai and Malachi*, pp. 287-296, sees these verses as eschatological judgments, but part of this prophecy was fulfilled in the first coming of Jesus and part will be fulfilled in His second coming.

BIBLIOGRAPHY

CHAPTER 1

Davis, John J. *Paradise to Prison: Studies in Genesis*. Grand Rapids: Baker Book House, 1975.

Keil, Carl F., and Delitzsh, Franz. "The Pentateuch." In *Commentary on the Old Testament in Ten Volumes*. Vol. 1. Grand Rapids: William B. Eerdmans Publishing Co., 1982.

Kidner, Derek. *Genesis*. The Tyndale Old Testament Commentaries. Downers Grove, IL: InterVarsity Press, 1968.

Morris, Henry M. *The Biblical Basis of Modern Science*. Grand Rapids: Baker Book House, 1984.

Phillips, John. *Exploring Genesis*. Chicago: Moody Press, 1980.

Schultz, Samuel J. *The Old Testament Speaks*. New York: Harper & Row, 1970.

Walton, John. *Chronological Charts of the Old Testament*. Grand Rapids: Zondervan Publishing, 1977.

CHAPTER 2

Ahronia, Yohanan, and Avi-Yonah, Michael. *The Macmillan Bible Atlas*. New York: Macmillan Publishing Co., 1977.

Albright, William F. *The Archaeology of Palestine*. Clouster, MA: Peter Smith Publisher, 1960.

Beitzel, Barry J. *The Moody Atlas of Bible Lands*. Chicago: Moody Press, 1985.

Edersheim, Alfred. *Old Testament Bible History*. Grand Rapids: William B. Eerdmans Publishing Co., 1972.

Finegan, Jack. *Light from the Ancient Past*. 2nd ed. Princeton, NJ: Princeton University Press, 1959.

Harrison, Roland K. *Old Testament Times*. Grand Rapids: William B. Eerdmans Publishing Co., 1970.

Vos, Howard F. *Archeology in Bible Lands*. Chicago: Moody Press, 1977.

CHAPTER 3

Cole, R. Alan. *Exodus: An Introduction and Commentary*. The Tyndale Old Testament Commentaries. Downers Grove, IL: InterVarsity Press, 1973.

Davis, John J. *Moses and the Gods of Egypt*. Grand Rapids: Baker Book House, 1971.

Goldberg, Louis. *Leviticus: A Study Guide Commentary.* Grand Rapids: Zondervan Publishing, 1980.

Harrison, Roland K. and Wiseman, J. D. *Leviticus: An Introduction and Commentary.* The Tyndale Old Testament Commentaries. Downers Grove, IL: InterVarsity Press, 1980.

Keil, Carl F., and Delitzsh, Franz. "Exodus." In *Commentary on the Old Testament in Ten Volumes.* Vol. 1. Grand Rapids: William B. Eerdmans Publishing Co., 1982.

Schultz, Samuel J. *Leviticus.* Everyman's Bible Commentary. Chicago: Moody Press, 1983.

Wenham, Gordon J. *The Book of Leviticus.* The New International Commentary of the Old Testament. Grand Rapids: William B. Eerdmans Publishing Co., 1979.

Youngblood, Ronald F. *Exodus.* Everyman's Bible Commentary. Chicago: Moody Press, 1983.

CHAPTER 4

Jensen, Irving. *Numbers: Journey to God's Rest-Land.* Everyman's Bible Commentary. Chicago: Moody Press, 1968.

Keil, Carl F., and Delitzsh, Franz. "Numbers." In *Commentary on the Old Testament in Ten Volumes.* Vol. 1. Grand Rapids: William B. Eerdmans Publishing Co., 1982.

Noordtzu, A. *Numbers: Bible Student's Commentary.* Grand Rapids: Zondervan Publishing, 1983.

Pfeiffer, Charles F. *The Bible Atlas.* Rev. ed. Nashville: Broadman Press, 1973.

Schultz, Samuel J. *Deuteronomy: The Gospel of Moses.* Everyman's Bible Commentary. Chicago: Moody Press, 1979.

Thompson, John A. *Deuteronomy: An Introduction and Commentary.* The Tyndale Old Testament Commentaries. Downers Grove, IL: InterVarsity Press, 1975.

CHAPTER 5

Atkinson, David. *The Message of Ruth: The Wings of Refuge.* Downers Grove, IL: InterVarsity Press, 1983.

Barber, Cyril J. *Ruth: An Expositional Commentary.* Chicago: Moody Press, 1983.

Campbell, Donald K. *No Time for Neutrality.* Wheaton, IL: Victor Books, 1981.

Cundall, Arthur E., and Morris, Leon. *Judges and Ruth.* The Tyndale Old Testament Commentaries. Downers Grove, IL: InterVarsity Press, 1968.

Davis, John J. *Conquest and Crisis: Studies in Joshua, Judges and Ruth.* Winona Lake, IN: BMH Books, 1969.

_____ and Whitcomb, John C., Jr. *A History of Israel: From Conquest to Exile.* Grand Rapids: Baker Book House, 1980.

Enns, Paul P. *Judges.* Bible Study Commentary. Grand Rapids: Zondervan Publishing, 1982.

_____. *Ruth.* Bible Study Commentary. Grand Rapids: Zondervan Publishing, 1982.

Garstang, John. *Joshua–Judges.* Grand Rapids: Kregel Publications, 1978.

Jensen, Irving L. *Joshua: Rest-Land Won.* Everyman's Bible Commentary. Chicago: Moody Press, 1966.

Lewis, Arthur. *Judges and Ruth.* Everyman's Bible Commentary. Chicago: Moody Press, 1979.

Soggin, J. Alberto. *Judges: A Commentary.* Old Testament Library. Philadelphia: Westminster Press, 1981.

Wood, Leon. *Distressing Days of the Judges.* Grand Rapids: Zondervan Publishing, 1982.

Woudstra, Martin H. *The Book of Judges.* The New International Commentary of the Old Testament. Grand Rapids: William B. Eerdmans Publishing Co., 1981.

CHAPTER 6

Crockett, William Day. *A Harmony of the Books of Samuel, Kings, and Chronicles.* Grand Rapids: Baker Book House, 1951.

Jorden, Paul J., and Streeter, Carole S. *A Man's Man Called by God.* Wheaton, IL: Victor Books, 1980.

Keil, Carl F., and Delitzsh, Franz. "The Books of Samuel." In *Commentary on the Old Testament in Ten Volumes.* Vol. 2. Grand Rapids: William B. Eerdmans Publishing Co., 1982.

Laney, J. Carl. *First and Second Samuel.* Everyman's Bible Commentary. Chicago: Moody Press, 1982.

Wood, Leon J. *Israel's United Monarchy.* Grand Rapids: Baker Book House, 1980.

CHAPTER 7

Ackroyd, Peter R. *The Second Book of Samuel.* New York: Cambridge University Press, 1977.

Coggins, R. J. *The First and Second Book of the Chronicles.* New York: Cambridge University Press, 1976.

Keil, Carl F. "The Books of the Chronicles." In *Commentary on the Old Testament in Ten Volumes.* Vol. 3. Grand Rapids: William B. Eerdmans Publishing Co., 1982.

Sailhamer, John. *First and Second Chronicles.* Everyman's Bible Commentary. Chicago: Moody Press, 1983.

Williamson, Hugh G. M. *1 and 2 Chronicles.* The New Century Bible Commentary. Grand Rapids: William B. Eerdmans Publishing Co., 1982.

CHAPTER 8

Hubbard, David A. "Solomon." In *The New Bible Dictionary.* Ed. J. D. Douglas. Grand Rapids: William B. Eerdmans Publishing Co., 1962.

Keil, Carl F. "The Books of Kings." In *Commentary on the Old Testament in Ten Volumes.* Vol. 3. Grand Rapids: William B. Eerdmans Publishing Co., 1982.

McNeely, Richard I. *First and Second Kings.* Everyman's Bible Commentary. Chicago: Moody Press, 1978.

CHAPTER 9

Thiele, Edwin R. *A Chronology of the Hebrew Kings.* Grand Rapids: Zondervan Publishing, 1977.

Wright, George E. *Biblical Archaeology.* Philadelphia: Westminster Press, 1963.

CHAPTER 10

Payne, J. Barton. *Encyclopedia of Biblical Prophecy.* New York: Harper & Row, 1973.

CHAPTER 11

Harrison, Roland K. *Jeremiah and Lamentations.* Downers Grove, IL: InterVarsity Press, 1973.

CHAPTER 12

Baldwin, Joyce G. *Esther.* The Tyndale Old Testament Commentaries. Downers Grove, IL: InterVarsity Press, 1984.

Barber, Cyril J. *Nehemiah and the Dynamics of Effective Leadership.* Neptune, NJ: Loizeaux Brothers, 1980.

Fenhsam, F. Charles. *The Books of Ezra and Nehemiah.* The New International Commentary on the Old Testament. Grand Rapids: William B. Eerdmans Publishing Co., 1983.

Keil, Carl F. "Esther." In *Commentary on the Old Testament in Ten Volumes.* Vol. 3. Grand Rapids: William B. Eerdmans Publishing Co., 1982.

Laney, J. Carl. *Ezra/Nehemiah.* Everyman's Bible Commentary. Chicago: Moody Press, 1982.

Whitcomb, John C., Jr. *Esther: Triumph of God's Sovereignty*. Everyman's Bible Commentary. Chicago: Moody Press, 1979.

CHAPTERS 13 AND 14

Craigie, Peter C. *Psalms 1-50*. Word Biblical Commentary. Waco: Word Books, 1983.

Leupold, Herbert C. *Exposition of Psalms*. Grand Rapids: Baker Book House, 1969.

CHAPTER 15

Anderson, Francis I. *Job*. Tyndale Old Testament Commentaries. Downers Grove, IL: InterVarsity Press, 1976.

Hartley, John E. *The Book of Job*. New International Commentary on the Old Testament. Grand Rapids: William B. Eerdmans, 1988.

Kaiser, Walter C. *Ecclesiastes: Total Life*. Chicago: Moody Press, 1979.

Kidner, Derek. *A Time to Mourn and a Time to Dance*. Downers Grove, IL: InterVarsity Press, 1976.

CHAPTER 16

Carr, G. Lloyd. *Song of Solomon*. Tyndale Old Testament Commentaries. Downers Grove, IL: InterVarsity Press, 1984.

Glickman, S. Craig. *A Song for Lovers*. Downers Grove, IL: InterVarsity Press, 1976.

Kidner, Derek. *The Proverbs*. Old Testament Commentaries. Downers Grove, IL: InterVarsity Press, 1964.

Segraves, D. L. *Ancient Wisdom for Today's World*. Hazelwood, MO: Word Aflame Press, 1990.

CHAPTER 17

Boice, James M. *The Minor Prophets*. 2 Vols. Grand Rapids: Zondervan Publishing, 1983-86.

Gaebelein, Frank E., ed. *The Expositor's Bible Commentary*. Vol. 7. Grand Rapids: Zondervan Publishing, 1986.

CHAPTER 18

Hubbard, David A. *Joel and Amos*. Tyndale Old Testament Commentaries. Downers Grove, IL: InterVarsity Press, 1989.

CHAPTER 19

Leupold, Herbert C. *Exposition of Isaiah*. 2 Vols. Grand Rapids: Baker Book House, 1968-71.

Ridderbos, Jan. *Isaiah*. Bible Student's Commentary. Grand Rapids: Zondervan Publishing, 1985.

CHAPTER 20

Baker, David W. *Nahum, Habakkuk, Zephaniah*. Tyndale Old Testament Commentaries. Downers Grove, IL: InterVarsity Press, 1988.

Harrison, Roland K. *Jeremiah and Lamentations*. Tyndale Old Testament Commentaries. Downers Grove, IL: InterVarsity Press, 1973.

Stedman, Ray C. *Expository Studies on Jeremiah: Death of a Nation*. Waco: Word Books, 1976.

CHAPTER 21

Ellison, Henry L. *Ezekiel: The Man and His Message*. Grand Rapids: William B. Eerdmans, 1956.

Taylor, John B. *Ezekiel*. Tyndale Old Testament Commentaries. Downers Grove, IL: InterVarsity Press, 1969.

CHAPTER 22

Baldwin, Joyce G. *Daniel*. Tyndale Old Testament Commentaries. Downers Grove, IL: InterVarsity Press, 1978.

Walvoord, John F. *Daniel: The Key to Prophetic Revelation*. Chicago: Moody Press, 1971.

CHAPTER 23

Baldwin, Joyce G. *Haggai, Zechariah, Malachi*. Tyndale Old Testament Commentaries. Downers Grove, IL: InterVarsity Press, 1978.

Kaiser, Walter C. *Malachi: God's Unchanging Love*. Grand Rapids: Baker Book House, 1984.

BOOK THREE:
EXPLORING THE
NEW TESTAMENT

WALTER M. DUNNETT

CONTENTS

PREFACE

"TELL ME, SIR," the sincere young woman inquired anxiously of the preacher, "what is the Bible all about?" After serious thought the preacher replied, "My girl, the Bible is all about Jesus."

That, essentially, is the message of the New Testament. It is all about Jesus. From the story of the humble birth in Bethlehem as recorded in the Gospels, to the scene of the glorious exaltation as King of Kings and Lord of Lords depicted in the book of Revelation, the subject is the same. At the beginning of this study of the New Testament, the student will do well to look for the Lord Jesus Christ and His teachings.

Before a study of the books of the New Testament is undertaken in systematic fashion, two preliminary matters of great importance must be considered. The New Testament has a background which, when properly considered, will help to illuminate the books themselves. Chapter 1, therefore, deals with the three most important areas of this setting: the Hebrew, the Greek, and the Roman. Following this treatment, the chapter presents an overview, or "bird's-eye view," of the whole New Testament. This approach, sometimes called the "synthetic," is vital to acquaint the student with the major divisions or parts of the New Testament and the unity of the whole.

Having completed chapter 1, you, the student, are ready to investigate each book separately. Chapters 2 through 12 consider the respective writers and their writings—the purpose, outline, main content, and leading features.

The attention of the reader is called to the application activities at the end of each chapter and the bibliography at the end of the book. These serve at least a dual purpose: (1) they provide opportunity for you to carry on your studies in a more detailed and intensive manner whenever you wish to do so, and (2) they provide information regarding matters that could be given only passing mention. You will find that the discussion questions at the end of the chapters will be valuable for testing your grasp of the materials you have studied.

Thanks are due to Moody Press, Chicago, for their kind permission given to use materials from my book, *An Outline of New Testament Survey*. The outlines, charts, and one quotation in chapter 11 have been taken from that work.

On, then, to study. May it be done in the spirit of 2 Timothy 2:15 and result in the enrichment of the life of all who undertake the task at hand.

Walter M. Dunnett

Chapter One

BACKGROUND AND COMPOSITION OF THE NEW TESTAMENT

THE WORLD OF THE New Testament was a busy and exciting one. All roads led to Rome; the Caesars held sway across most of the inhabited earth; and in a tiny town of Palestine One was born who was to change the world! Following the time of Christ on earth, the Christian Church emerged, beginning as a small band of men and women, then growing to a great multitude of people. The books of the New Testament were written to instruct local congregations of believers and to inform them of the life and teachings of Christ.

But these events did not come about suddenly. They were the result of preparation—and that by God Himself! "But when the fulness of the time was come, God sent forth his Son" (Gal. 4:4). In the years that preceded the coming of Christ, God had been active in the lives of men and in the affairs of the nations. Many had a part in this pre-Christian era. Among the three most important contributors were the Hebrews and their religion, the Greeks and their language, and the Romans and their social and political organization.

THE HEBREW PREPARATION

Chosen by God as "a kingdom of priests, and an holy nation" (Ex. 19:6), the people of Israel were in a position of privilege. They were to be the messengers of the Lord to the nations around them. But they failed! Because of almost continuous disobedience and the gross sin of idolatry, God's judgment fell with finality upon them in the year 587 B.C., and the nation was carried away captive by Nebuchadnezzar into the land of Babylon.

From this center of captivity they were progressively scattered across the ancient world. This crucial event, called The Great Dispersion, left its effects upon the Hebrew people. But as they went, and wherever they went, many of them let it be known that they were worshipers of the one true God, Jehovah. Two emphases in particular, monotheism (the belief in only one God) and the Law of God, stood out in the midst of pagan societies.

In later years, when Christ was born and the apostolic proclamations went forth, the way had been prepared. The words, the ideas, the message itself was not entirely new. And not only had people heard the message, they had read it too. The Hebrew Old Testament was translated into Greek in the city of Alexandria in Egypt between the years 250-150 B.C. As Greek was then the common language of the world, this translation, called the Septuagint (meaning "the Seventy"), made the Old Testament teachings available to all who could read.

Sometime during the second century B.C., the major sects (or parties) among the Jews seem to have had their origin. As one reads the historical books of the New Testament (Matthew through Acts), the names of the Pharisees and the Sadducees often appear. The Pharisees were the larger of the two groups and were predominantly the students and teachers of the Old Testament, while the Sadducees were the powerful political leaders, including the high priests and leading officials of the Jerusalem Sanhedrin (composed of seventy people plus the high priest).

One is impressed with the orthodox character of the Pharisees. They firmly maintained the sacred character of the entire Old Testament, taught belief in the resurrection and the judgment of the last day, and affirmed the existence of angels and spirits. These tenets the Sadducees denied (Acts 23:6-8). Yet it was the former group that most often came under the condemnation of the Lord Jesus in His teaching—not because they failed to be orthodox, but because they emphasized the unimportant and neglected the weightier elements of the Law (Matt. 23:23, 24).

THE GREEK PREPARATION

One language and one world! That was the ambition of young Alexander, the son of King Philip of Macedon more than three hundred years before the birth of Christ. His ambition was largely realized between the years 334–323 B.C. Sweeping across the ancient world, like lightning across the sky, Alexander soon conquered much of the land. To cement his victories, he established the Greek language as the *lingua franca*, the common tongue, and the Greek culture as the pattern of thought and life. Although his vast empire quickly disintegrated after his premature death, the results of that empire were long-standing.

How did these fourth-century happenings relate to the coming of

Christianity and the New Testament? A matchless vehicle of expression for the Christian message was provided. The apostolic preaching was done largely in Greek; and the New Testament books were written in Greek, the common language of the world. Using the vocabulary of their day, the writers filled the words with new and significant meaning designed to convey the message of spiritual life to their readers. Such important terms as *Christ, redeem, ransom, church, wisdom*, and *word* illustrate this.

THE ROMAN PREPARATION

Above all else Rome was noted for her insistence upon law and order. The world was organized into a great empire extending from the western end of the Mediterranean Sea to the Euphrates River in the Near East. By means of provinces and districts closely supervised by local governors, the empire was efficiently administered.

In the providence of God, the Romans prepared the world for the coming of Christianity in a number of ways.

First, the emphasis on law and order, backed by superior military might, made possible the days of peace during the reign of Caesar Augustus. It was during these days, says Luke the historian, that Mary brought forth her firstborn son (Luke 2:1-7) in the tiny village of Bethlehem in the Roman province of Judea.

Second, the Roman system of roads contributed greatly to the measure of ease and safety by which travelers could make their way back and forth across the empire. These roads were well paved, well drained, and usually patrolled. Paul traveled on such important roads as the Egnatian Way across Achaia and Macedonia and the Appian Way leading to Rome.

A third important factor, though negative in character, was the marked degeneration of morality and religion, and the deep longing for redemption found among the peoples of the Mediterranean Basin. They had lost faith in the ancient gods. The state religions were too formal and rigid to satisfy personal longings. The current philosophies of the day, likewise, lacked in real vigor and failed to appeal to the common man. Both in the East and the West, so-called mystery cults arose to offer personal salvation, fellowship with the gods, and the observance of secret rites.

Into this scene came Christianity proclaiming salvation, forgiveness, and peace. Centered in the historical incidents of the life, death, and resurrection of Jesus Christ, Christianity supplied the answer to man's spiritual need and moral void.

FIRST-CENTURY PALESTINE

The principal ruling family in Palestine in the years that saw the dawn of the Christian era was the Herodian dynasty. Herod the Great was appointed by the Romans as the king of the Jews, reigning from 37 to 4 B.C. His rule was marked by intrigue and bloodshed, including the incident recorded in Matthew 2, called "the slaughter of the infants."

Of the sons of Herod the most noted in the gospel records was Herod Antipas who ruled from 4 B.C. to A.D. 39 as Tetrarch of Galilee and Perea. It was this Herod whom John the Baptist accused of wrongfully marrying Herodias, costing John his life (Matt. 14:1-12). Jesus called Herod "that fox" (Luke 13:32), and it was he who was involved in the trial of Christ in Jerusalem (Luke 23:7-12).

Herod Agrippa I, the son of Aristobulus and grandson of Herod the Great, succeeded Antipas and ruled over Galilee, Samaria, and Judea. His reign, from A.D. 37–44, was cut short by his sudden death. Acts 12 records his murder of James the son of Zebedee and the imprisonment of Peter together with a cryptic account of Herod's death (v. 21-23).

The last of the family to reign was Herod Agrippa II (A.D. 50-100). He appears in Acts 25 and 26 in conjunction with the trial of Paul before Festus in Caesarea. He, along with Festus, rendered a verdict of acquittal (26:31, 32).

Among the Roman procurators of Judea in the first century, Pontius Pilate (A.D. 26–36) is most notable as far as the New Testament record is concerned. Because of his share in the trial of Christ and his condemnation of the Lord after repeatedly rendering the verdict of "not guilty" (John 18:38–19:6), Pilate had attained unusual notoriety in history. Shortly after the death of Christ, he was deposed by Tiberius for an attack on the Samaritans and was ordered to appear before the emperor (A.D. 36). What actually happened to Pilate after this is uncertain.

Amid these political circumstances, the Jews were ruled directly by their own high priest and his cohorts in the Great Sanhedrin in Jerusalem. Three of these high priests are mentioned in the New Testament. Annas, the high priest emeritus, was the father-in-law to Caiaphas, the ruling high priest at the time of the trial of Christ (John 18:13); Ananias appears in Acts 23:2.

The religious life of the Jews was centered in the temple in Jerusalem. This structure, called Herod's Temple, was in process of completion during the time of Christ (cf. John 2:20). It had as its antecedents the temples of Solomon and Zerubbabel and was the symbol of their religious hopes and aspirations. From near and far the people came to worship, offer sacrifices, and observe the religious festivals of Judaism, especially the feasts of Passover, Pentecost, and Tabernacles.

Side by side with the temple in the religious life of Judaism was the synagogue. Especially to all those at a distance from Jerusalem, the synagogue was a substitute for the temple. There were a number of synagogues even in Jerusalem. They were primarily places of instruction and prayer for the Jews and Gentile adherents of the Jewish faith. The Scripture was read, commented on, and at various places in the service prayers were offered. Both Jesus and the early Christians frequented the synagogue (Luke 4:16-30; Acts 13:14ff.; 26:11).

To the Jew, the Old Testament was the book of God. God was One, the Law was the revelation of His will, and life was under His jurisdiction. There was an air of expectancy that God would intervene and save His people (Luke 2:25). So it was when Christ was born, He came into a world prepared—"in the fulness of the time." The New Testament complements the Old Testament, carrying on and completing the record of God's revelation, and clarifying to the Jew, the Gentile, and the Church of God the eternal truths of the living God.

COMPOSITION OF THE NEW TESTAMENT

The New Testament contains twenty-seven books that may be classified into three major groups based on their literary characteristics.

Chronological Division

Many scholars hold James to be the earliest book of the New Testament, written about A.D. 45.[1] Aside from the question of the place of James, it is practically certain that some of Paul's letters represent the first written records of the early church. Galatians is regarded by some to have been written as early as A.D. 47/48. The Thessalonian Epistles are from the early ministry of Paul the missionary, written from Corinth before or during the time of Gallio (cf. Acts 18:12-17; 1 Thess. 3:1-10), which would mean A.D. 50 or 51. These early writings give an insight into the character of the Christian message and Christians themselves. Especially important in this regard are passages such as Galatians 1:6–2:21; 6:11-17; 1 Thessalonians 1:2-10; 2:13-16; and 2 Thessalonians 2:1-12; 3:6-15.

In contrast to these writings, those of John the apostle constitute the last of the books to be written. According to tradition, as well as indications in the books themselves, John's works reflect problems being faced by the Church near the end of the first century. His major writings deal mainly with aspects of salvation: the Gospel—the nature of salvation; the first epistle—the assurance of salvation; and the Revelation—the consummation of salvation.

Literary Division

While the literary divisions of the New Testament do not follow a chronological scheme, they do reflect the logical order of God's program. First, the Gospels and Acts constitute the basic history necessary for a proper understanding and appreciation of the later works. The life of Christ and the origin of the Church is foundational. The story of the founder is required before one regards the superstructure that was erected. The Church is "built upon the foundation of the apostles and prophets, Jesus Christ himself being the chief corner stone" (Eph. 2:20).

Matthew—The introduction to "Jesus Christ, the King of the Jews." Herein is recorded the fulfillment of many of the Old Testament prophecies with the coming of the Messiah. The teaching of Christ is emphasized.

Mark—The picture of Jesus as the "Servant of the Lord." He is busy about His Father's work; thus Mark emphasizes the activity, especially the redemptive activity, of Christ.

Luke—The portrait of Jesus as "the Son of Man," the perfect representative of humanity. His life was given "to seek and to save that which was lost" (19:10). The sympathy and graciousness of Christ are emphasized.

John—The presentation of Jesus as the "the Son of God," the eternal Word who came to reveal God to man. This Gospel emphasizes the relation of Christ to those around Him—the personal contacts that changed the lives of those who met Him. By the true realization of His divine Sonship, eternal life was received.

A Harmony of the Ministry of Jesus

Gospel	The Period of Preparation	The Period of Public Ministry		The Period of Suffering	The Period of Triumph
		Opening	Closing		
Matthew	1:1–4:16	4:17–16:20	16:21–26:2	26:3–27:66	28:1-20
Mark	1:1-13	1:14–8:30	8:31–13:37	14:1–15:47	16:1-20
Luke	1:1–4:13	4:14–9:21	9:22–21:38	22:1–23:56	24:1-53
John	1:1-34	1:35–6:71	7:1–12:50	13:1–19:42	20:1–21:25

Acts—The continuation of Luke's Gospel, presenting the risen Christ working through His apostles who had been empowered by the Holy

Spirit. The origin of the Church, the Body of Christ, and its expansion "unto the uttermost part of the earth" is the theme of this first church history.

Second, the New Testament Epistles give the interpretation of the person and work of Christ and apply His teachings to the lives of believers. The majority of these letters, at least thirteen, were penned by the apostle Paul. Most of them are written in letter form. Of the twenty-one, all have names attached to them except Hebrews and the three Epistles of John.

Nine of the Pauline writings were sent to churches, four to individuals. Most of them deal with problem situations then existing in the churches (Ephesians seems to be an exception). Some are very personal in tone (Philippians and 2 Corinthians); others appear to have a more formal, almost thesis-like style, and in their main features (excluding the usual personal introduction and conclusion) show a rather businesslike tone. Romans would probably be the outstanding example of this type. Further, the letters of Paul show great variety in content and also combine doctrinal and practical components in good balance.

The remaining epistles, while varied in authorship, may be conveniently grouped under two main headings. Some deal primarily with the problem of suffering (Hebrews, James, and 1 Peter), while the rest treat the problem of false teaching (2 Peter, 1, 2, and 3 John, and Jude). Both problems became increasingly serious as the first century progressed. Persecution came first from Jewish opponents and later (after A.D. 64) from the Roman government. Christ had warned His followers of the rise of false Christs and false prophets (Matt. 24:24), and Paul had said much the same thing to the elders of the Ephesian church (Acts 20:29, 30). By the time John wrote his letters, the Gnostics (teachers who claimed to possess a superior philosophical-religious type of knowledge) were plaguing the Church. John's epistles were an answer to that error.

Finally, there is the well-known prophetical writing in the New Testament, the Revelation (or Apocalypse, the unveiling) of Jesus Christ. Like the prophecy of Daniel in the Old Testament, this book deals, for the most part, with the judgments of God in the last days upon "those that dwell upon the earth." In Revelation the climax of redemption is portrayed. The earlier word of Paul, that God's purpose was "to sum up all things in Christ" (Eph. 1:10 ASV), is realized as John writes, "The kingdoms of this world are become *the kingdoms* of our Lord, and of his Christ; and he shall reign for ever and ever" (Rev. 11:15).

And so the New Testament has come to us. "God, who at sundry times and in divers manners spake in time past unto the fathers by the prophets, hath in these last days spoken unto us by *his* Son" (Heb.1:1, 2).

DISCUSSION QUESTIONS

1. Discuss the significant contributors and their contributions leading to the coming of Christ and the writing of the New Testament.
2. In what important ways did the Jewish Dispersion prepare the way for Christianity?
3. How did the Greek language and culture relate to Christianity?
4. In what ways did the Roman Empire contribute to the rise and spread of Christianity?
5. Distinguish between the Pharisees and the Sadducees. Which group is more prominent in the Gospels?
6. Name the three literary divisions of the New Testament and list the books included in each division.
7. Compare John's dealing with the subject of salvation in his Gospel, the first epistle, and the Revelation.
8. How do the Gospels and the Acts lay the foundation for the remaining New Testament writings?
9. In what ways do the Epistles deal with the life and teachings of Christ?
10. How does the book of Revelation present Christ?

APPLICATION ACTIVITIES

1. To get a clearer view of Christ in the New Testament, prepare a simple chart to use throughout the class sessions, listing the various aspects of His character and work. For example:

Portraits of Christ

His Character	*His Work*
Model Sufferer, Luke 23:34	Savior, Luke 2:11
Sinless One, Luke 4	Teacher, Matthew 5

2. As the class sessions develop, list specific qualities in Christ's life desirable in your own life.
3. Refer to several good Bible commentaries or dictionaries for further background studies in preparation for a deeper understanding of the New Testament. In commentaries, background information is generally given prior to verse-by-verse comments.

Chapter Two

THE SYNOPTIC
GOSPELS

Matthew, Mark, Luke

THE FIRST THREE GOSPELS are called the Synoptic Gospels because they "see together" or have the same point of view with regard to the life of Christ. They present the life of Christ in a way that complements the picture given in the Gospel of John.

The approach to the subject here will be twofold: first, we will consider the distinctive features of each Gospel; second, we will look at the common features of the three Gospels. That is to say, what are the characteristics that cause each book to differ from the others and what are the common characteristics found in all three books?

THE GOSPEL OF MATTHEW

Author

Matthew, one of the original disciples of Christ, wrote the first book in the New Testament. He was first named Levi and worked as a publican collecting taxes in Palestine until he was called to follow Jesus (9:9, 10; Mark 2:14, 15).

Purpose and Content

Matthew addressed his Gospel primarily to Jewish readers and presented Jesus as the Messiah, the King of the Jews. This is seen in such passages as His genealogy (1:1-17); the visit of the Magi (2:1-12); His entry into Jerusalem (21:5); the judgment of the nations (25:31-46); and, in common with the other Gospels, the superscription over the Cross (27:37). In addition to these statements, there is much in this first Gospel concerning "the kingdom of heaven." This expression is used by Matthew alone.

This book also serves as the bridge between the Old and the New

Testaments. It links together the prophecies of the coming Messiah with the fulfillment of prophecy in the person of the Lord Jesus. Matthew often alludes to or quotes from the prophets and connects their words with his subject. Of particular importance are such passages as 1:22, 23; 2:15, 17, 18, 23; 4:14, 16; 8:17; 12:17, 21; 21:4, 5; 26:54, 56; 27:9. It is as though Matthew first notes the Old Testament which says, "He is coming," then presents his own message which says, "He is here!"

The Discourses of Christ

The prominence of the discourses of Christ is easily observed in this Gospel. Matthew's pattern, as may be seen clearly in the outline of the book, is to include narrative material about Christ, followed by an important discourse. There are five in the book, one in each of the five major divisions:

1. The Sermon on the Mount (5:1–7:29)
2. The Commission to the Twelve (10:1-42)
3. The Parables of the Kingdom (13:1-53)
4. The Meaning of Greatness and Forgiveness (18:1-35)
5. The Olivet Discourse (24:1–25:46)

In one way or another, each of these discourses relates to the claims that the King makes upon those who would share in His kingdom.

Outline

In the light of the dominant theme of this Gospel, then, the following outline will aid the student's progress through the book. The clue to Matthew's structure is given by the fivefold repetition of the expression "when Jesus had finished [or *ended* or *made an end of*]" (7:28; 11:1; 13:53; 19:1; 26:1). This phrase marks the end of each major division of the Gospel. Together with the introduction (1:1–4:11) and the two concluding sections (26:3–28:15; 28:16-20), these five divisions form the complete record.

The introduction of the King	1:1–4:11
The demands of the King	4:12–7:29
The deeds of the King	8:1–11:1
The program of the King	11:2–13:53
The destiny of the King	13:54–19:2
The problems of the King	19:3–26:2
The death and resurrection of the King	26:3–28:15
The final commission by the King	28:16-20

THE GOSPEL OF MARK

Author

In contrast to Matthew, Mark was not one of the original disciples of Christ. He was, however, a native of Jerusalem (Acts 12:12), a companion of Simon Peter (1 Peter 5:13), and the cousin of Barnabas (Col. 4:10) who, in turn, was a close associate of Paul and the Jerusalem apostles. His relationship to the apostles was, therefore, close enough to render him familiar with the life of Christ and the activities of the early Christian group.

In A.D. 112, Papias cited Mark as "the interpreter of Peter." A comparison of Peter's sermon in Acts 10:34-43 with Mark's Gospel shows the former to be an outline of the life of Jesus that Mark has given in much greater detail.

Purpose and Content

Mark addressed his Gospel primarily to Roman readers and presented Jesus as the Worker, the Servant of Jehovah. (According to tradition, Mark wrote his record of the life of Christ in Rome.) The chief characteristic of Christ in this book is His activity, the mark of a good servant. The Greek word *eutheos*, translated variously as "straightway," "immediately," "anon," or "forthwith," appears forty-two times in the book. This message made a natural appeal to the busy, practical Roman reader.

According to the amount of space Mark allots to it, the most important activity of Christ was His death and resurrection. About three-eighths of the entire book is devoted to the narrative of the Passion Week (the last week of the life of Christ, 11:1–16:18). In the story, this is the most striking feature and shows clearly what aspect of Christ's life was considered by the Gospel writers to be of supreme concern.

Outline

In keeping with the theme of the activity of Christ, the outline treats His life as a series of tours as He carried on His ministry. The result is that one is impressed with the continual busyness of the Servant of Jehovah.

Introduction	1:1
Preparatory events	1:2-13
First tour of Galilee—Miracles and parables	1:14–4:34
Tour of Decapoli	4:35–5:43
Second tour of Galilee	6:1-29
Retreat to the desert	6:30-52

Third tour of Galilee	6:53–7:23
Tour of the north country	7:24–9:29
First announcement of passion	8:31
Fourth tour of Galilee	9:30-50
Second announcement of passion	9:31
Tour of Perea and Judea	10:1-52
Third announcement of passion	10:33
Ministry in Jerusalem	11:1–13:37
The passion and resurrection	14:1–16:20

THE GOSPEL OF LUKE

Author

According to the New Testament, Luke was a physician (Col. 4:14), a companion of Paul (Philem. 24), and the writer of a two-volume history of the life of Christ and the early church (Luke and Acts). His Gospel has long been the favorite of Christian and non-Christian readers alike because of its sublime presentation of a spotless life. Luke, as Mark, was not among the original disciples of Christ.

Purpose and Content

Luke addressed his Gospel primarily to Greek (or non-Jewish) readers and presented Jesus as the Son of Man, the ideal human being. As the Greeks had long sought after the "perfect man," Luke's work was designed to fulfill that quest. Some of the most important passages are the account of the birth of Christ (1:26-38; 2:8-20); the testimony of God to His Son (3:21, 22); the announcement of Jesus as the Anointed One (4:16-24); and the mission of the Son of Man (19:10). Together with these passages one should consider Luke's emphasis on the prayers of Jesus; His matchless parables (10:30-37; 15:1-32; 18:9-14); the human interest features (10:38-42; 19:1-10; 24:13-35) where the Lord deals graciously yet firmly with interesting people; and the prominence of the Holy Spirit in the life of Christ (1:35; 3:22; 4:1, 18).

A further illustration of the outreach of this book is the repetition of phrases having relation to humanity. From first to last, Luke shows that the gospel (God's Good News) is meant for all men (2:10, 14, 31, 32; 3:6; 9:56; 10:33; 17:16; 19:10; 24:47).

Outline

The outline is based upon the concept of Christ as "the Son of Man." Luke portrays Him as carrying on a full ministry among the peoples of Palestine with a view to the extension of that ministry to the regions beyond (24:47; cf. Acts 1:8).

Prologue—The purpose stated	1:1-4
The preparation of the Son of Man	1:5–4:13
The Galilean ministry of the Son of Man	4:14–9:50
The Perean ministry of the Son of Man	9:51–18:30
The Jerusalem ministry of the Son of Man	18:31–21:38
The passion ministry of the Son of Man	22:1–23:56
The resurrection ministry of the Son of Man	24:1-53

CHARACTERISTICS COMMON TO THE GOSPELS

While each Gospel has its distinctive emphasis, a number of great events or areas are common to them all. This fact has made these among the best-known teachings and events of Christ's ministry:

Announcement of the Savior by John the Baptist (Matt. 3; Mark 1; Luke 3)

Baptism of the Savior (Matt. 3; Mark 1; Luke 3)

Temptation of the Savior (Matt. 4; Mark 1; Luke 4)

Teachings and Miracles of the Savior (the major portion of each Gospel)

Transfiguration of the Savior (Matt. 17; Mark 9; Luke 9)

Trial, Death, and Burial of the Savior (Matt. 26, 27; Mark 14, 15; Luke 22, 23)

Resurrection of the Savior (Matt. 28; Mark 16; Luke 24)

OTHER SPECIAL FEATURES

In addition, the narrative of Christ's birth and certain events in His life are given in detail

Unusual Nature of Christ's Birth

Emphasis is placed upon the unusual nature of Christ's birth—it was prophesied in the Old Testament, announced by an angel to Joseph and Mary, and brought about by the operation of the Holy Spirit (Matt. 1, 2; Luke 1, 2).

The Parables of Christ

The teachings and miracles of Christ occupy the major portion of the Gospel records. Distinctive in His teachings was the frequent use of parables. A parable is a story or situation in the human realm which is employed as a means of illustrating or defending some spiritual principle. In these three Gospels at least thirty separate parables are found, plus many other short, axiomatic statements that are parabolic in nature.

Among the most notable of these are the parables of the kingdom in Matthew 13 and the parables of the lost things in Luke 15.

The Kingdom

One of the most important areas of our Lord's teaching was concerned with the kingdom. The two expressions, "the kingdom of heaven" and "the kingdom of God," occur often, although the former is limited to Matthew. God's kingdom is essentially "His rule over His creation." It is first of all, a spiritual reality. "The kingdom of God cometh not with observation . . . for, behold, the kingdom of God is within you" (Luke 17:20, 21). The kingdom is in the hearts of believers, but it is also a visible reality. The Son of Man "shall come in his glory . . . and before him shall be gathered all nations" (Matt. 25:31, 32). At this time He shall appear and rule over the earth, a theme so prevalent in the prophets (cf. Isa. 11:1-10; Zech.13:1-6; Mal. 4:1-3). When the kingdom was announced by John the Baptist (Matt. 3:1-3) and by the Lord Jesus (Mark 1:14, 15), the spiritual aspect was prominent. In the coming of "the Day of the Lord" at the close of this age, the visible aspect will be evidenced. Thus God's program will be fulfilled, all things will be summed up in Christ, and ultimately God will be all in all.

The Miracles

Alongside His teachings, the miracles of Christ formed an important part of His ministry. They were both evidences of His messiahship and occasions for bringing needy people to a realization of a greater need than physical necessities—that of spiritual need. In proportion to its length, more miracles are found in Mark than in Matthew and Luke—at least twenty individual situations. This is quite in keeping with Mark, the Gospel of the busy Servant. When the Lord formally announces Himself as God's Anointed at the outset of His public ministry (Luke 4:16-21), He included these two aspects of His commission: the proclamation of the Gospel and the working of miracles. When He had thus announced Himself, He added, "This day is this Scripture fulfilled in your ears" (v. 21). Both His words and His works were means of revealing God to men. This was the function of the Son (Matt. 11:27).

DISCUSSION QUESTIONS

1. What is meant by the "Synoptic Gospels?"
2. To whom was each of the Synoptic Gospels written and for what purpose?
3. Summarize the distinctive content of each book.

4. Give at least one important biographical fact about each of the writers of these three Gospels. Illustrate by a Scripture reference for each.
5. Discuss the unique position of the book of Matthew as linking the Old and New Testaments.
6. State the five major discourses of Christ in the book of Matthew.
7. How is the activity of Christ made prominent in Mark?
8. In Luke's Gospel, what are some ways in which Jesus is portrayed as the Son of Man?
9. What common characteristics are found in all three books?
10. What are the distinctive characteristics of each book?

APPLICATION ACTIVITIES

1. Prepare your own outline of each Synoptic Gospel.
2. For a fuller comprehension of the Synoptic Gospels, prepare a simply-diagramed chart showing the important features of each, such as main theme, persons, parables, miracles, and teachings.
3. From your study in Activity #2, note the progression of opposition against Christ. Where did this opposition begin? Where did it end? What type of people were usually the instigators of opposition? What were the issues?
4. Summarize Christ's prophetic teachings presented in His Olivet Discourse.

Chapter Three

GOSPEL OF JOHN

Author

According to the persistent tradition of the Church since the early second century, the fourth Gospel was written by John the apostle, son of Zebedee and brother of James. As one of the Twelve, he was close to Jesus. He is usually identified with the beloved disciple who appears anonymously a number of times in this book (13:23; 18:15, 16; 19:26, 27).

Purpose and Content

John clearly states his purpose for writing this Gospel (20:30, 31), placing emphasis upon three important words: *signs, believe,* and *life.* A good understanding of these terms, together with their use in the Gospel, allows one to gain a working knowledge of the book's content.

Signs

The word *signs* is John's term for the miracles of Jesus.[1] By it he means to impress the reader with the meaning of the miracle and especially with the revelation of who Jesus really is. Taken together, the signs are meant to show that Jesus is "the Christ, the Son of God."

Out of the many signs which Jesus did, John selected seven to demonstrate the nature of Christ. Each of them has a particular message.

1. Water changed into wine—Jesus' power over *quality*
2. The nobleman's son healed—Jesus' power over *distance*
3. The impotent man healed—Jesus' power over *time*
4. The five thousand fed—Jesus' power over *quantity*
5. Walking on the water—Jesus' power over *natural law*
6. The blind man healed—Jesus' power over *helplessness*
7. Lazarus raised from the dead—Jesus' power over *death*

Of the seven signs, five are found only in John's Gospel. The feeding of the five thousand is the only miracle recorded by all the writers; the walking on the water appears also in Matthew and Mark.

BELIEVE

One of the most frequent words in the book, *believe,* appears at least ninety-eight times. It always occurs in the verb form (*believe*), never the noun form (*belief*). This continually gives the impression of action, of something happening. John is teaching the meaning of believing in Jesus not so much by definition as by illustration. The word is used to indicate the response of people to Jesus. If they believed on Him, they became His followers; if they did not believe, they became His opponents. At any rate, once having met Him, they could not remain neutral.

Along with the word *believe,* John employs a number of synonyms to make his meaning clear. Some of these are *receive* (1:12), *drink* (4:14), *come* (6:35), *eat* (6:51), and *enter* (10:9). All these words, used in the routine of daily life, become full with meaning when applied to the spiritual relationship of men and women to Christ. Believing on Him is like receiving a gift, drinking refreshing water, entering by a door into a sheepfold. The need is met, the thirst is quenched, the hunger is satiated.

LIFE

This term expresses the result of believing in Christ. To receive life is to become a child of God by being born into His family. It is the divine nature imparted to the believer. The Lord Jesus said to the Pharisee, Nicodemus: "Except a man be born again, he cannot see the kingdom of God" (3:3). This life is described as eternal in quality (3:15) and is, therefore, the opposite of the state of spiritual death, which means to perish (3:16).

In addition, there will be a manifestation of this gift in the one who receives it. The Holy Spirit, who is the agent of regeneration, will be as rivers of living water flowing from within the one who has drunk of the water of life (7:37-39). Thus the life is imparted to others around the believer, as dry ground is refreshed by a stream.

Thus, John has stated his purpose. In writing the story of Christ, he has sought to bring his readers face to face with this person who by His words and His works confronts men and women with a great decision. From first to last Christ is described as deity (1:1; 20:28). Yet He has come in human form (1:14) so that He might give Himself to bring life to those who sit in the shadow of death (12:23, 24). Not only did Christ die, but He rose again (chap. 20). As the living Lord, He calls forth the devotion and loyalty of His followers (21:15-19).

Outline

Christ's Teachings

Having gained a general idea of what John has done in writing his Gospel, let us consider the teachings of the Lord Jesus. What does He teach and how does He impart these truths to the people?

THE RELATIONSHIP BETWEEN THE SIGNS AND HIS TEACHING

The signs were occasions for Jesus' teaching, so that one may expect to find this order followed in the book.

In chapter 5, Jesus healed the infirm man beside the pool of Bethesda in Jerusalem. Following the sign, the Jews challenged His right to do such a thing on the Sabbath Day (5:16). This called forth His claims of equality with God in nature (5:17, 18), in power (5:21), and in authority (5:26, 27). To substantiate these claims, He called upon certain witnesses including John the Baptist (5:33), His own works (5:36), the Father (5:37), the Scriptures (5:39), and Moses (5:46).

In chapter 6, Jesus was faced with the task of feeding more than five thousand hungry people. After His disciple Philip had failed to provide a solution to the problem, Andrew brought a boy to Jesus with his lunch of five barley loaves and two fishes (6:9). Using these, Jesus fed the people and thus met their physical need (6:12). When the crowd returned the following day, obviously looking for another free meal, the Lord admonished them to "labour not for the meat which perisheth" (6:27). Then He taught them of their spiritual need and declared, "I am the bread of life" (6:35). A lengthy discourse followed in which He drew a contrast between "the flesh" and "the spirit" (6:63). He uncovered the shortcomings in their understanding of spiritual realities.

They held improper motives (6:26). In coming to Him only for physical bread, they had missed the meaning of the sign. They employed improper methods (6:28), failing to do the works of God. They retained an improper conception of their religious heritage (6:30, 31), placing Christ on the same level as Moses. They evidenced an improper desire in asking for this bread (6:34). For when He explained what it meant "to eat the living bread," they murmured, they strove one with another (6:52), and, finally, many who followed Him turned away (6:66).

In addition to these two outstanding examples, the sign of chapter 9 is an admirable illustration of His claim, "I am the light of the world" (8:12; 9:5), and the sign of chapter 11 makes clear His claim, "I am the resurrection and the life" (11:25).

The Seven "I am's"

The Lord Jesus makes claims for Himself by means of the "I am" phrases in this Gospel. Although some of these have been referred to in passing, the complete list should be carefully observed by the reader:
1. "I am the bread of life" (6:35)
2. "I am the light of the world" (8:12; 9:5)
3. "I am the door" (10:7, 9)
4. "I am the good shepherd" (10:11)
5. "I am the resurrection and the life" (11:25)
6. "I am the way, the truth, and the life" (14:6)
7. "I am the true vine" (15:1)

Aside from the graphic figures Christ employed to describe Himself, the striking thing about these claims is their exclusive nature. In the Greek, "I am" is an emphatic grammatical construction. The Lord states to the Jews, "Verily, verily, I say unto you, before Abraham was, I am" (8:58). He thus took upon Himself the title of deity from their Old Testament Scriptures, for this was the title by which God revealed Himself to Moses (Ex. 3:14). The alternative to eating "the bread of life" is death; if one refuses "the light," he remains in darkness. He is "the only way;" no one comes to God except by Him. He is the "true vine," not an imitation.

The Personal Interview

Of great importance in communicating his message is John's use of personal interviews. Again and again, people are brought into contact with Jesus. They are never the same again. Either they believe and follow Him, or they turn away in unbelief. While there are many such situations in the book, the main examples include:

Andrew—Though Andrew was not as well-known as his brother Simon Peter, he possessed noteworthy qualities. Andrew, having believed in Jesus for himself, became a personal worker. He is always seen bringing someone else to Jesus. First, his brother, Simon; then a lad; then the Greek visitors in Jerusalem (1:35-42; 6:8, 9; 12:20-22).

Simon Peter—When Peter met Jesus, the prophecy of his new name (meaning a change in character) was given. He was Simon (meaning unstable); he would become Cephas (meaning "a stone;" 1:42). Along with this he was ready to confess his faith in Jesus as "the Son of the living God" (6:68, 69). Although he was overconfident, leading to his temporary denial of his Lord (13:36-38; 18:15-18, 25-27), he was graciously restored and recommissioned to follow Christ anew and feed His sheep (21:15-22).

Nicodemus—Although Nicodemus was a man thoroughly trained in the Old Testament truths, he had not experienced the new birth; he did not have a realization of the messiahship of Jesus. The Lord explained for Nicodemus how He himself fulfilled the Old Testament type of the serpent in the wilderness, and how as God's Son He was sent to be the Savior of all who would believe in Him (3:1ff.). That Nicodemus came to true belief seems to be indicated by the incidents that follow in the book (7:50, 51; 19:39-42).

Using the same approach, the following people in John's Gospel are worthy of study:

Philip (1:43-46; 6:5-7; 14:8-12)

The woman of Samaria (4:1-42)

The blind man (chap. 9)

Martha and Mary (11:1-46)

Thomas—In him is seen the culmination of belief in John's Gospel with his confession of the deity of Christ—"my Lord and my God" (11:16; 14:5-7; 20:24-28).

Pilate—He is the outstanding example of unbelief in the Gospel (18:28–19:16), along with Judas Iscariot (6:70, 71; 13:21-30; 18:1-15).

UPPER ROOM DISCOURSE

Attention should be given to the unique discourse of this Gospel found in chapters 13–16, commonly called the Upper Room Discourse. Bishop B. F. Westcott calculated that 92 percent of the material in John was unique and that, consequently, only 8 percent was material held in common with the Synoptic Gospels. Of John's unique material, this section is the most outstanding unit in the book. After His public ministry was concluded (at the end of chap. 12), Jesus met privately with His disciples and told them of two important things that were soon to happen. First, His departure was near. He was going away; they could not come with Him at this point. Eventually, however, He would return to receive them into the Father's house. Second, the Holy Spirit would be sent to take His place. He would not leave the disciples alone (literally "orphans," 14:18, NASB). He would send "another Comforter," one "just like Himself." The Holy Spirit would indwell them (14:17), teach them (14:26), empower them to witness (15:26, 27), and guide them into all the truth (16:13).

Prologue and Epilogue

Finally, notice the opening and closing sections of the book, the prologue (1:1-18) and the epilogue (21:1-25). The former contains the message of the entire Gospel. In the prologue, John introduces: (1) The chief character of the book—*the Word*. The Word is God, the Creator, the Giver of Life, the One manifest in flesh, and the Revealer of the Father. (2) The chief vocabulary terms of the book—*life, light, darkness, witness, believe, truth*. (3) The chief plot of the book—conflict. Notice the words used to illustrate spiritual conflict: light vs. darkness; received him not vs. received him; physical birth vs. spiritual birth; law vs. grace and truth. This conflict continues throughout the book until it culminates in the cross and the resurrection.

The epilogue furnishes an appropriate climax to the Gospel. It teaches the logical result of believing in Jesus. True believers will follow Jesus and thus give expression to their faith in service (21:19). Peter learned that believing in Jesus did not only eventuate in the spoken word of confession, but in the life of dedicated service.

DISCUSSION QUESTIONS

1. Define and show the importance of each of the three words: *signs, believe, life*.
2. What is the striking feature about the "I am" claims of Christ? Illustrate this from Scripture.
3. What two important messages were communicated in the Upper Room Discourse?
4. What is the contribution of the prologue to the message of John?
5. What does the epilogue of the book emphasize?

APPLICATION ACTIVITIES

1. Trace the Scriptures in John that reveal Christ's deity.
2. List and summarize the passages in John referring to the Holy Spirit.
3. In John's Gospel, list Christ's various titles and their significance.
4. Using the chart idea suggested in chapter 2, activity #2, trace events in Christ's life as recorded in John's Gospel. What is the significance of John's writing of events that are not included in the other three Gospels?

Chapter Four

BOOK OF ACTS

THIS IS THE SECOND volume of Luke's history of Christianity. Without the book of Acts, many details of the life of the early church would be missing. Of the first thirty years we would know only what could be pieced together from the New Testament Epistles.

From the book of Acts itself we discover that Luke, the author, was a companion of Paul and an eyewitness to many of the events about which he writes. This evidence appears in the so-called "we sections" of the text, that is, places where Luke includes himself in the story by the use of the first person plural pronoun (16:10-17; 20:5–21:18; 27:1–28:16). Besides Luke's firsthand experiences, he also had occasions for personal interviews. Paul was able to tell him of his Gentile ministry; the leaders at Jerusalem proved to be valuable resources concerning the Jerusalem church; and Philip in Caesarea gave him access to the data of Philip's Samaritan ministry.

Purpose

Why did Luke write the book of Acts? What were the chief motives behind his work? Consider the following:

THE HISTORICAL MOTIVE

This is the most obvious one, of course. Acts is a continuation of the narrative begun in the Gospel of Luke (Luke 1:1-4; cf. Acts 1:1-5). The books are addressed to the same individual, Theophilus. They are linked together by the phrase, "the former treatise." One concerns what "Jesus began both to do and teach," while the other records the continuation of that ministry by "the apostles whom he had chosen."

Again, compare Luke 24:44-53 with Acts 1:6-11. Both passages speak of the coming of the Holy Spirit, of the disciples as witnesses, and of the ascension of the Lord Jesus into heaven.

Luke, therefore, gives his readers the history of the first sixty or sixty-five years of Christianity. About thirty years were included in each of his two works. It is the story of the Good News of salvation, beginning in a manger in Bethlehem and extending to the very hub of the Empire, of Rome itself (cf. Phil. 4:22). The narrative opens with the witness of the shepherds in the fields of Judea and terminates with the salutations of saints in Caesar's household.

THE DOCTRINAL MOTIVE

As in his Gospel, Luke's chief doctrinal emphasis here is upon the person and work of the Holy Spirit. In fact, the explicit references to the Spirit in Acts occur with great frequency (Acts 1-11; 13, 15, 16, 19, 20, 21, and 28). The Lord Jesus, in His last recorded utterance prior to the Ascension, promised the disciples that "ye shall receive power, after that the Holy Ghost is come upon you." The fulfillment of that promise is clearly seen in the Acts. The Holy Spirit was the motivating power in the apostles' witness and work for Christ. The Spirit filled them again and again (cf. 2:4; 4:8, 31; 6:5; 7:55; 9:17; 11:24; 13:9). In situations where discipline (5:3, 4), wisdom (6:3), or guidance (16:6, 7) was required, the Holy Spirit operated in the believers. By His coming, differing groups were united into that one great company, the Church (the Jews, chap. 2; the Samaritans, chap. 8; the Gentiles, chap. 10; some disciples of John, chap. 19).

THE APOLOGETIC MOTIVE

In one sense, the book of Acts is simply a defense of Christianity. That believers need to defend (1 Peter 3:15; Phil. 1:17-18) and contend for the faith is clear (Jude 3). Luke shows to the world that in the first generation, the Church was never the object of official persecution at the hands of the Roman government—the Jews, often; but the Romans, never. This is a remarkable record which, at that particular time when Paul had appealed to Caesar for a fair trial, needed to be clearly stated.

In each contact between the apostles and officials of the Roman government, they were either accepted or ignored but never persecuted. A number of these situations are recorded by Luke:

1. Paul and Barnabas before Sergius Paulus, the proconsul at Cyrus— he "believed" (Acts 13).

2. Paul and Silas in Philippi—The Roman jailer was saved, and the magistrates of this Roman colony apologized for the unjust treatment accorded the missionaries because of the false charges of the Jews (Acts 16).

3. Paul before Gallio, the proconsul of Achaia—He "cared for none of these things" (i.e., problems of Jewish law, Acts 18); Gallio was indifferent.

4. Paul in Ephesus—The Asiarchs (Acts 19:31) were friends of Paul; the town clerk restored order, thereby rescuing the missionaries from possible violence.

5. Paul safeguarded by Claudius Lysias, the Roman captain of the castle Antonia in Jerusalem (Acts 21, 22).

6. Paul before Felix in Caesarea—He often called for and listened to Paul speak (Acts 24).

7. Paul before Festus in Caesarea—He considered Paul innocent of the charges against him by the Jews (Acts 25).

When persecution against the apostles and the Church does appear in Acts, it is at the hands of the Jews—either the Sanhedrin or groups such as those who follow Paul in his journeys (cf. chaps. 4, 5, 7, 8, 16, 17, 18) and the silversmiths of Ephesus (Acts 19).

THE BIOGRAPHICAL MOTIVE

Of the many interesting and important persons who appear in Acts, Peter and Paul are those to whom Luke gives a place of prominence. His record is concentrated largely upon their activities. Peter occupies the major portion of chapters 1–12; Paul of chapters 13–28.

It might be said that the first generation of the Church was the story of these two. The Jerusalem church was led by Peter for the first few years of its existence. Even the early probing into surrounding areas, such as Samaria (chap. 8) and Caesarea (chap. 10), were to one degree or another the work of Peter. The ministry of the gospel in the Gentile lands, from Syria to Rome itself, was mainly carried on by Paul. In the great provinces of Galatia, Macedonia, Achaia, and Asia, he founded churches and established them in their newfound faith.

Working alongside Peter and Paul were a number of other notable individuals: Stephen (chaps. 6, 7); Philip the evangelist (chap. 8); Barnabas (chaps. 4, 9, 11, 13-15); John Mark (chaps. 12, 13, 15); Silas (chaps.15-17); Timothy (chaps. 16, 17); Aquila and Priscilla (chap. 18); Apollos (chaps. 18, 19). Some of these and others as well also appear in Paul's epistles, where they are described as his fellow workers.

In giving this record, then, Luke has made it clear which people were actively responsible for the growth and expansion of the Church. Thus the epistles are illuminated for us by his biographical portraits.

Outline

The key verse of Acts (1:8) provides a basis for the outline of the book. As the Lord Jesus spoke of the future ministry to be accomplished by His followers, consequent upon the coming of the Holy Spirit, He stressed two things: (1) persons and (2) places. "Ye shall be witnesses unto me"—that is the personnel of the mission. "In Jerusalem, and in all Judea, and in Samaria, and unto the uttermost part of the earth"—that is the geography of the mission. The main divisions of the outline reveal the primary locations; the subpoints indicate the chief persons in each place.

Introduction—Apostolic commission given	1:1-11
The Gospel in Jerusalem—Origins	1:12–8:3
The ministry of Peter	1:12–5:42
The ministry of Stephen	6:1–8:3
The Gospel in Samaria and Judea—Transition	8:4–11:18
The ministry of Philip	8:4-40
The ministry of Saul begun	9:1-31
The ministry of Peter concluded	9:32–11:18
The Gospel in the uttermost part—Expansion	11:19–21:14
The ministry of Barnabas	11:19–12:25
The ministry of Paul the apostle	13:1–21:14
The first journey	13:1–14:28
The Jerusalem Council	15:1-35
The second journey	15:36–18:22
The third journey	18:23–21:14
The Gospel in Caesarea and Rome—Imprisonment	21:15–28:29
Paul taken prisoner in Jerusalem	21:15–23:10
Paul as a prisoner in Caesarea	23:11–26:32
Paul as a prisoner in Rome	27:1–28:29
Conclusion—Apostolic commission fulfilled	28:30, 31

The Gospel in Jerusalem

In the first section of Acts, it is Peter who plays a part in a variety of situations. He assumes the leadership after the Ascension of the Lord and is instrumental in bringing about the election of Matthias after Judas Iscariot's suicide. Peter preaches the notable sermon on the Day of Pentecost resulting in the salvation of three thousand persons. He and John heal the lame man at the temple gate and subsequently defend their act and preaching before the Jewish Sanhedrin. It is Peter who condemns Ananias and Sapphira for their plot to deceive the church and leads the congregation in the choice of the seven to supervise the distribution of goods to the widows.

One thing that is outstanding throughout this narrative is the spirit of unity that prevailed among the Christians. Notice carefully the references that illustrate this condition, especially the first prayer meeting (1:14); the preparation for Pentecost (2:1); the sharing of goods and consistent witness (2:43-47; 4:23-31); the prayer for boldness (4:23-31); the daily ministry of the Word (5:41, 42).

Near the end of the opening unit, Stephen is featured as a mighty and fearless defender of the faith. While he loses his life, becoming the first martyr of the Church, his influence endures. This is especially important in the case of one of the spectators at his martyrdom, a young man named Saul (7:58), who later is brought to Christ and becomes Paul the apostle. At this point, however, he sets out to persecute the believers and forces them all, except the apostles, to flee from Jerusalem.

The Gospel in Judea and Samaria

The second major section of the book concerns the work of the Church in the regions of Judea and Samaria, just to the north of Jerusalem. Philip the evangelist, one of the seven chosen in chapter 6, went to Samaria, and the result was most gratifying. Many believed his message concerning Christ. When the church in Jerusalem heard the news, Peter and John were sent to confirm them in their newfound faith (Acts 8:15-17). Philip departed to the south, near Gaza, and led the Ethiopian treasurer to Christ. Peter went on toward the seacoast, eventually coming to the home of Cornelius, the Roman centurion in Caesarea, and had the joy of witnessing the salvation of Cornelius and those of his household. With the reception of the Holy Spirit, these Gentile believers were recognized as sharing in the fellowship of the Church with the Jews (chap. 2) and the Samaritans (chap. 8).

During this period of history, the conversion of Saul occurs (chap. 9). That Luke attaches great importance to this event is evidenced by his three long accounts of the incident (cf. chaps. 9, 22, 26). With Paul's conversion, the chief persecutor of the Church is changed into her most prominent defender and preacher.

The Gospel to the Uttermost

The third and most lengthy unit of Acts is mainly the record of the development and expansion of the Gentile ministry led by Paul and his fellow workers.[1] Going back to the record of Saul's persecution of the church in Jerusalem (cf. 11:19 with 8:1-4), Luke first traces the progress of the Gospel from the home base to the Syrian city of Antioch. Here the narrative resumes with the dispatching of Barnabas to establish the new believers in that important city. Antioch, ranked as the third city of the Empire (after Rome and Alexandria), became the home base for missionary work among the Gentiles. After Barnabas went to Tarsus and brought Saul back with him, the two worked together in the church until it was thriving. It was here that believers were first called Christians (11:26). Then, following a brief trip to Jerusalem to deliver needed goods to the famine-stricken Christians, these two men were called by the Holy Spirit to a new and larger work—and the missionary journeys of Paul began.

"The Missionary Journeys of Paul" chart in the back of the book will make clear the particulars of Paul's ventures.

The Journeys of Paul

The initial journey was concentrated primarily in the province of Galatia (chaps. 13-15); the second in the province of Macedonia and Achaia (chaps. 16-18); the third in the province of Asia (chaps. 19-20).[2] In these places, Paul spent most of his time in population centers—cities like Antioch of Pisidia, Philippi, Thessalonica, Corinth, and Ephesus. Once the evangelization of these cities had been completed, the Gospel radiated to the surrounding country (cf. 1 Thess. 1:8).

Paul found himself in a variety of situations and audiences. On occasion the missionary was in the Jewish synagogue (as in Pisidian Antioch, Thessalonica, Athens, Corinth, and Ephesus); or before the leaders of the city (as in Athens); or in prison (as in Philippi). When preaching to a Jewish audience, Paul used the Old Testament Scriptures as a basis for his message (as in Antioch and Thessalonica); whereas in addressing pagan, or at least non-Jewish groups, he generally began with their natural surroundings (as in Lystra and Athens). His usual approach was to preach first to the Jews of the region, if they were to be found; then to the Gentiles.

Paul's ministry in these areas, covering a period of about ten years, resulted in the establishment of a chain of churches all along the Mediterranean shores. As he wrote to the Roman Christians, he recalled that "from Jerusalem, and round about unto Illyricum, I have fully preached the gospel of Christ" (Rom. 15:19). This period of his labors was terminated with the final visit to Jerusalem which resulted in his arrest (on a false charge by some Asian Jews) and his consequent imprisonments in both Caesarea and Rome.

The final section of Acts is the record of Paul's experiences while a prisoner. He makes his defense before a Jewish mob and the Jewish leaders in Jerusalem (chaps. 22, 23), before Felix, Festus, and Herod Agrippa II in Caesarea (chaps. 24–26), and finally is taken to Rome amid many harrowing experiences, including shipwreck (chap. 27, 28). Here, in his own rented house, though constantly chained to a guard,

Paul is free to carry on his preaching and teaching. No wonder "they of Caesar's household" heard and received the Good News of salvation.

Relationship of Acts to the Gospels and the Epistles

Before closing this study, the character of Acts as a central book in the New Testament should be noted. It is the bridge between the Gospels and the Epistles and therefore has close ties to each of these writings.

First, it continues and, in one sense, completes the narrative begun in the Gospels. The earthly life of Christ is followed by the ministry of His apostles.

Second, it shows the fulfillment of our Lord's prophecy of the Church (Matt. 16:18) and prepares the way for the expounding of this subject in the Epistles. Many questions are answered regarding the circumstances of the Church's beginning, early leaders, and growth into a universal fellowship.

Third, Acts gives the background for several of Paul's epistles, relating the details concerning the founding of the churches to which the letters were subsequently written.

Galatians—Antioch, Iconium, Lystra, and Derbe (Acts 13:14–14:28)

Philippians—Philippi (Acts 16:11-40)

1 and 2 Thessalonians—Thessalonica (Acts 17:1-9)

1 and 2 Corinthians—Corinth (Acts 18:1-16)

Ephesians—Ephesus (Acts 19:1-41; 20:17-35; cf. also 1 and 2 Timothy)

By reading these chapters before reading the respective epistles, light is cast on the nature of the cities, the people, and the problems faced by Paul.

Fourth, the book of Acts illustrates in the active life of the church many of the principles enunciated in the Epistles. Such matters as organization, discipline, witnessing, evangelism, and teaching are clearly mirrored in the narratives of Acts. Especially prominent is the stress upon the necessity of the work of the Holy Spirit. The early church not only taught this truth but experienced it as well.

DISCUSSION QUESTIONS

1. List Luke's four motives for writing Acts. Show how each is reflected within the narrative.
2. What is the key verse of Acts? In what ways does it provide the framework for the rest of the book?

3. Summarize in your own words the account of the proclamation of the Gospel in Jerusalem (Acts 1:12–8:3).
4. Summarize in your words the account of the proclamation of the Gospel in Judea and Samaria (Acts 8:4–11:18).
5. In what provinces were each of Paul's three missionary journeys centered?
6. Name the two most prominent individuals associated with Paul in each of the three missionary journeys.
7. What is the relationship of the book of Acts to the Gospels and the Epistles?

APPLICATION ACTIVITIES

1. List some of the problems of the early church. How were these solved? Relate these to the present-day church.
2. Appraise the various ministries or some of the outstanding personalities in the book of Acts—especially Stephen, Peter, Philip, and Paul. Observe the influence of the Holy Spirit in each man's life. Compare your observations with your study of the various aspects of Christ's life.
3. List ways that your church can enrich and expand its ministry in various fields of Christian activity. Use the book of Acts as your guide book.
4. For better appreciation of New Testament faith and practice, prepare your own comprehensive outline of the book of Acts.

Chapter Five

PAULINE EPISTLES

1 and 2 Thessalonians

AS A LETTER WRITER and as a man, Paul has no superior in the history of the Church. His life story is one of the most amazing in the history of mankind, and people of all ages since the beginning of the Christian era have, in one way or another, been indebted to him. Before giving attention to the written legacy he has left, the main details of his life must be considered.

The best insights into Paul's life come from his own pen and are to be found in several of the Epistles, particularly Philippians, Galatians, and the Corinthian letters. In addition, the three accounts of Paul's conversion experience and the record of his activities and witness recorded in the book of Acts give valuable information.

BACKGROUND OF PAUL

Paul was first and foremost a Jew. This is the main factor in understanding his character and activities. He was born of Jewish parentage in the city of Tarsus, in the province of Cilicia, and was thus known for many years as Saul of Tarsus. According to his own testimony he was a Pharisee, as his father had been before him (Acts 23:6); he spoke the Aramaic tongue ("a Hebrew of the Hebrews"); and he was taught the trade of tentmaking in his youth (Acts 18:3). Further, Paul was of the tribe of Benjamin (Phil. 3:5). Historically, the Benjamites were fighters, and Paul seems to give evidence of an abundance of zeal in all his endeavors, especially in the persecution of the Church (Gal. 1:13). At an early age he went to Jerusalem, and according to his recorded testimony in Acts, studied under the noted Rabban Gamaliel I, a leading teacher of the School of Hillel (22:3).[1] From Paul's own words in Galatians, we learn that he had "profited in the Jews' religion" beyond many of his fellows, "being more exceedingly zealous of the traditions of my fathers" (1:14).

The beginning of Saul's furious campaign to exterminate the Church coincided with the murder of Stephen (Acts 7:58–8:3). Not only did he persecute "both men and women" in Jerusalem, but, with letters of arrest from the high priest (Joseph Caiaphas), he went to other cities as well to carry on his work (Acts 26:10, 11). It was on one such mission that Saul of Tarsus met Jesus and was dramatically converted.

Saul was a Greek by culture. Not only was he reared in one of the leading centers of Greek learning, but he shows an acquaintance with the Greek mind. As an intelligent scholar, Saul knew many of the commonly used sayings taken from classical and contemporary writers (Acts 17:28; Titus 1:12). He also had a world outlook. Unlike the man of provincial demeanor, Paul could write, "I am made all things to all *men*, that I may by all means save some" (1 Cor. 9:22). Thus, by his background, he was suited to stand before the Gentiles proclaiming Jesus' name.

Further, Saul was a Roman citizen. When questioned about his status by the Roman captain in Jerusalem who had informed his prisoner that he had purchased the coveted citizenship with "a great sum," Paul replied with pride, "But I was actually born *a citizen*" (Acts 22:28 NASB). He had appealed to his citizenship rights earlier in Philippi to gain proper respect from the local magistrates (Acts 16:37-39). This status allowed a number of valuable rights such as the right to a proper trial before condemnation and punishment, the right to appeal to Caesar for justice (cf. Acts 25:11, 12) and, in event of the death penalty, execution by decapitation rather than crucifixion.

CONVERSION OF PAUL

One day it happened! The thing that Saul could never have imagined would happen to him occurred with revolutionary effects. He had denied the Christian claim that Jesus was the Messiah, the Son of God. Further, he did not believe that Christ had risen from the dead as Stephen had proclaimed when he cried, "Behold, I see the heavens opened, and the Son of man standing on the right hand of God" (Acts 7:56). "Liar!" the mob cried and stoned him. Saul stood by "consenting unto his death." But when the Lord Jesus spoke to Saul on the day of the great experience outside Damascus, Saul knew that Stephen had been right and he had been wrong. Jesus was alive after all! And further, He must be the Son of God. Thus, in the synagogues of Damascus, Saul proclaimed Christ as Savior.

To explain exactly what happened to Saul is difficult. But there can be little doubt, from Paul's own testimony, that the change in his life was due to a personal encounter with Christ and a new relationship to Him

(Gal. 2:20; Phil. 3:7ff.; 2 Cor. 5:14-19). While the experience was sudden and dramatic, the effects were enduring. The impact must have necessitated great psychological and intellectual readjustments. This may well account for the period spent in Arabia and Damascus before his first visit to Jerusalem (Gal. 1:16-19). Then he went back to his home territory, and for a period of eight to ten years little is known of his activities.[2]

Paul leaves us in no doubt, however, that Christ had both appointed him an apostle and revealed the Gospel to him, so that he "might preach him among the heathen" (see especially Gal. 1:1-20).

MINISTRY OF PAUL

Paul's missionary labors begin with the invitation of Barnabas to join Paul at Syrian Antioch. For the next twenty years or so Paul carried on a vast ministry.

Background

Beginning in Antioch (Acts 11:25, 26) Paul later evangelized the provinces of Galatia, Macedonia, Achaia, and Asia, besides many smaller areas as well. He founded, established, and organized churches in all these areas.

Together with Barnabas, Peter, James, and other leaders of the Church, Paul had a major part in resolving the problem of the basis of Gentile salvation and the matters of fellowship between Jew and Gentile (cf. Acts 15:1-35; Gal. 2:1-10). Paul's wide outlook and genuine concern that the Gospel might reach out to all the world triumphed over the narrower perspective and more limited concern of the Jerusalem apostles. He had truly caught the vision of his Lord that the message should go out to all nations.

His Written Ministry

At least thirteen samples of Paul's correspondence have been preserved, and he doubtless wrote many others that did not survive.[3] His written ministry shows great diversity, and yet the letters may be naturally grouped under four basic headings, each reflecting a common emphasis. An attempt is also made to indicate an approximate chronological sequence, though any sense of finality here is impossible.

The Eschatological Letters: 1 and 2 Thessalonians (date: about A.D. 50–51)—These epistles emphasize the doctrine of the last things and are especially concerned with the Second Coming of Christ and the implications of that event in the present life of the believer.

The Soteriological Letters: 1 and 2 Corinthians, Galatians, and Romans (date: about A.D. 55–58)[4]—Various aspects of the doctrine of salvation are delineated in this class of letters. The Corinthian Epistles stress the application of salvation to the life of the Church; Romans and Galatians discuss the doctrine of justification and its outward expression in Christian living.

The Christological Letters: Colossians, Philemon, Ephesians, and Philippians (date: about A.D. 60–62)—Often called the Prison Epistles, as they were written (according to tradition as well as internal evidences) from Paul's prison in Rome (Acts 28:30, 31), these letters present the doctrine of Christ in a distinct manner. They contain great passages that highlight the person and work of Christ in a definitive fashion (Col. 1:14-22; 2:3, 9-15; Philem. 15-20; Eph. 1:7-12; Phil. 2:5-11).

The Ecclesiological Letters: 1 Timothy, Titus, and 2 Timothy (date: about A.D. 63–67)—The doctrine of the (local) church is the main theme of these last three letters of Paul, often called the Pastoral Epistles. They deal primarily with the responsibilities of the leaders of the churches. The letters contain detailed instructions regarding the officers, administration, and activities of the church. The last days of Paul are reflected in the closing chapter of 2 Timothy.

1 THESSALONIANS

On his second missionary journey, Paul arrived in Thessalonica, the capital of Macedonia (Acts 17:1-9). Things went well for the missionaries (Silas and Timothy were Paul's companions at this point) until jealous Jews raised a cry against them, charging them with acts "contrary to the decrees of Caesar, saying that there is another king, *one* Jesus" (17:7). Thus they were driven from the city. When Paul arrived later in Corinth (Acts 18), he wrote the letters to the troubled Thessalonican Christians, who had themselves become the objects of persecution since Paul's departure (1 Thess. 2:14). In lieu of a personal visit (1 Thess. 2:17, 18), the apostle expresses his thanks to God for the news brought by Timothy of the firm stand of the believers (1 Thess. 3:6-10).

Outline

Salutation	1:1
Thanksgiving	1:2-10
The Pauline ministry defended	2:1–3:13
The Christian walk delineated	4:1–5:24
Conclusion	5:25-28

Purpose and Content

The Thessalonian epistles are the only letters of Paul that do not contain an official title of the writer, simply his name (and Silvanus and Timothy) at the beginning. He writes, it would seem, as a personal friend and spiritual adviser to his spiritual children who find themselves beset by afflictions and tribulations. They are perplexed as to why such things should happen to them. Does God care? To encourage them Paul reminds them how he himself was shamefully treated when he came into their city (2:1, 2), and that he had "told you before that we should suffer tribulation" (3:4). All such things are part of the purpose of God.

Since the apostle had departed, some of their number had died. What was to be their attitude toward death? Pagan religion from which they had turned (1:9) held little hope for the afterlife; rather, it was a place of darkness and fear. Would they ever see their loved ones again? On the authority of "the word of the Lord" (4:15), Paul assures them that the dead and living saints shall be one day reunited and "caught up together . . . in the clouds, to meet the Lord in the air" (4:17). This was a word of comfort, indeed. But, on the other hand, the Second Advent called for vigilance as well (5:6). Here is the application of the doctrine to the everyday life of the Christian.

In this letter Paul closes every chapter with some teaching regarding the return of the Lord. In 1:10, the believer is "to wait for [God's] Son from heaven." Paul reminds his readers that they will be his "glory and joy" at the coming of the Lord (2:19, 20). In 3:13, it is the desire of the apostle that the Christians be established "unblameable in holiness before God, even our Father, at the coming of our Lord Jesus Christ with all his saints." A major section follows in 4:13-18, where Paul informs his readers of the reunion of the dead and living saints at the descent of the Lord from heaven, and the entrance into eternal bliss with Him. Finally, 5:23 pictures the believer "preserved blameless unto the coming of our Lord Jesus Christ."[5]

2 THESSALONIANS

Outline

Salutation	1:1, 2
Anticipation of the Day of the Lord	1:3-12
Description of the Day of the Lord	2:1-17
Exhortation to prayer and proper conduct	
in view of Day of the Lord	3:1-16
Conclusion	3:17, 18

Purpose and Content

Between the time of the writing of the two letters, a new problem had arisen. Apparently someone had caused concern on the part of the believers with regard to their relation to "the Day of the Lord." Paul wrote that they "be not soon shaken in mind, or be troubled, neither by spirit, nor by word, nor by letter as from us, as that the day of Christ is at hand" (2:2).

Why was it that the idea of "the Day of the Lord" should disrupt their peace of mind? Probably because the aspect of this event most prominent in their thinking was that of tribulation, judgment, and destruction. Such a portrayal occurs in many of the related Old Testament passages from which the concept comes (Joel 1:15–2:11; Obad. 15, 16; Zeph. 1:14-18; Zech.14:1-8). It was to be a time that would strike terror into the hearts of men. The Thessalonians had begun to wonder whether they also might fall victim to the Day of Judgment.

It would not be proper to say that there is a simple solution to such a complex problem. The chronological relationships of eschatological events is not always made clear. To be more precise, would these believers find themselves caught in the precarious days of "the great tribulation" that was to come upon the earth? Or, would the Lord take them away before the judgment dawned?

First, Paul said there are certain things which must occur before the full force of God's eschatological judgment will be manifested. There will be apostasy from true religion (2:3); there will be the appearance of the "man of sin" (2:3); and, finally, there will be the removal of a present restrainer (2:6, 7). These will be definite indications of the approaching day of reckoning.

Second, the believers are to be awake and aware of conditions about them and strengthen themselves in their faith (1 Thess. 5:4-8; 2 Thess. 2:15). Thus they will be fortified for any crisis.

Third, and most vital of all, Paul assures the Christians that God is in control. He is working out His purpose, and they are kept within His hand (1 Thess. 5:9, 10, 23, 24; 2 Thess. 1:11, 12; 2:13, 14). This is the ultimate assurance the believer has. The Second Advent not only brings judgment, but blessing also. The prophets had spoken of this aspect with regard to Israel (Joel 2:28-32; Mic. 4:1-5; Zeph. 3:9-20; Mal. 4:2, 3). Paul now informs his readers that they will be with the Lord and share in His victory over His enemies (1:7-10).

Again, as in the first letter, the apostle closes with a number of practical exhortations, especially dealing with the need for honest toil among the Christians. Some of them, thinking that the Lord was to come at once, had ceased working and were becoming a drag upon the rest of the community. An almost certain solution to that problem is given by Paul in 3:10, as he says, "If any would not work, neither should he eat." This is at once a good combination of Christian teaching and common sense. All are to work together while they wait together for the great day of Christ's appearing.

DISCUSSION QUESTIONS

1. What three national cultures affected Paul's life?
2. Show the influence of these varied backgrounds upon Paul's life and ministry.
3. How did Paul's conversion affect his life and teaching?
4. Name four basic categories into which Paul's writings fall and name the books in each.
5. State the doctrine primarily emphasized in each category.
6. What was Paul's experience in Thessalonica on his second missionary journey (Acts 17:1-9)?
7. Name two major problems dealt with by Paul in 1 Thessalonians.
8. With what subject does each chapter of the first epistle close?
9. What doctrinal problem, which arose among believers between the writing of the two Thessalonian Epistles, influenced the content of the second epistle?

APPLICATION ACTIVITIES

1. To assist you in mastering the basic content of the Thessalonian letters, prepare your own outline of these two books.
2. List the passages in Thessalonians relating to Christ's Second Coming in the chronological order of events.
3. With the aid of a topical index, examine other Scripture portions to determine the manner of Christ's Second Coming.
4. List several qualities that are admirable about Paul's life, indicating which impress you most.
5. What features of Paul's conversion are characteristic of all conversions? In what ways was his conversion unique?
6. To assist you in deepening your dedication to the lordship of Christ, list specific ways and means to live in light of His coming. Use the Thessalonian Epistles as a basis for your list.

Chapter Six

PAULINE EPISTLES

1 and 2 Corinthians

ACCORDING TO THE previous classification of Paul's Epistles, these letters are to be considered primarily soteriological, since they deal largely with the subject of salvation. Together with Galatians and Romans, they form the heart of the Pauline writings. Even the radical critics, who have often rejected many of Paul's writings as authentic works, usually have accepted these letters as genuine. The core of Paul's preaching—faith in Christ and dedication to Him—is written large in all of them. His favorite expression, "in Christ," describing the new relationship of the regenerated individual to his Savior and Lord, occurs again and again.

This correspondence emerges from the third missionary journey of Paul (cf. Acts 18:23–21:14). First Corinthians was written from Ephesus (1 Cor. 16:7-9), while 2 Corinthians likely came from Macedonia (see 2 Cor. 2:12, 13; 7:3-7).

1 CORINTHIANS

Background

Paul first visited Corinth on his second journey (Acts 18:1-17). While waiting for Silas and Timothy to come from Macedonia and rejoin him in Corinth, Paul met Aquila and Priscilla and, finding them to be tentmakers as he was, lived with them while carrying on his preaching.

Upon the arrival of his companions, carrying with them news of conditions to the north (in Thessalonica and Berea), Paul reemphasized his proclamation "that Jesus was the Christ" (i.e., Messiah). This brought about the usual reaction from the Jews, and Paul henceforth concentrated on the Gentile ministry in Corinth (Acts 18:6). Before long a number of people became Christians, even including Crispus the ruler of the synagogue. For a period of at least eighteen months Paul continued a systematic teaching program among them.

The event that apparently led to the departure of the apostle from the city was his appearance before Gallio, the proconsul of Achaia, whose residence was in Corinth. As Gallio listened to the arguments of Paul's Jewish accusers, he manifested a calm indifference. This was because it concerned matters of Jewish law, not Roman law, and his courtroom was not the place for religious disputes. It should be said that Gallio's indifference was in reality a blessing, for it diverted the actions of the Jews and set Paul free to continue his work.

While in Ephesus on his third journey (Acts 19:1-41), some of the household of Chloe brought tidings to Paul that things were not well in Corinth (1 Cor. 1:11). In addition, a letter had been sent by the Corinthian church containing a number of problems to which they wished answers from the apostle (1 Cor. 7:1; 8:1; 12:1; 15:12; 16:1). To reply to these and related matters, Paul wrote this first epistle.

Outline

Introduction	1:1-9
Reply to reports from Chloe	1:10–6:20
Reply to the letter from Corinth	7:1–16:9
Conclusion	16:10-24

Purpose and Content

The central concept of the letter is that redemption must be applied to everyday situations. The believer is to remember that the new life in Christ calls for a new way of living. The appeal being made is to the relationship of the Holy Spirit to the believer (3:16, 17; 6:11, 19, 20).

It will help to emphasize these commands if one recalls the character of the city of Corinth. In the first century it was noted for its wickedness and immorality, highlighted by the corrupt, sensual worship of Aphrodite, the Greek goddess of love. Her temple, including a thousand religious prostitutes, stood in manifest contrast to the believer as "the temple of the Holy Spirit" and His demand for righteousness.

In the first section of the letter (chaps. 1–6), most of Paul's teaching deals with the problem of authority in the church. The Corinthian believers had been divided by various religious loyalties. Some had appealed to Paul, the leading exponent of the doctrine of justification by faith and of the liberty of the Christian from the bondage of law and the founder of this church. Others sided with Apollos, the learned teacher from Alexandria, filled with the knowledge of the Scriptures. He had followed Paul in his visit to Corinth (Acts 18:24–19:1). There were still others who held that Peter, one of the original disciples of the Lord, with his great love for Christ and his studied concern for the principles of the law of the Lord, was a worthy leader. And finally, there were those who looked with pious disapproval at such discord and exclaimed, "We simply follow Christ!" These last were indeed the worst of all, for they set themselves up above their brethren and sought to keep Christ all to themselves. Paul's crisp answer to all such disputes is given in 3:1-9. Along with his answer Paul calls upon them to gain true spiritual insight and to remember that they are responsible to God—both in the present and one day at the judgment seat (2:1-16; 3:10-23).

Paul dealt with two other matters in this section: sexual immorality (5:1-13; 6:12-20) and lawsuits (6:1-11). In addition, he rebuked the church for not handling these matters themselves. The former is dealt with by a severe judgment that resulted in the eventual reclaiming of the offender (5:3-5). The latter problem should be cared for, taught Paul, by the church, not in heathen courts. Lawsuits, in fact, are in themselves "a fault among you" (6:7). The final appeal is to maintain the unity and purity of the body of Christ.

In the second section of the letter (chaps. 7–16), a number of varied problems appear. The majority of the content, however, relates to the matter of spiritual relationships, either of believers to one another (chaps. 7–10) or to situations within the ministries of the church (chaps. 11–14). When dealing with the problems of marital relationships, Paul commands that the sanctity of marriage is to be maintained by those contemplating marriage, in the case of a divided household, and by unmarried women. A spiritual basis is in evidence throughout the discussion.

When the problems of conscience are being faced, Paul sets forth a number of guiding principles.[1] First, nothing is permitted to remain in one's life if it causes another Christian to stumble (8:9, 13). Second, the preaching of the Gospel is not to be hindered, rather aided (9:12, 22). Third, all things are to be done "to the glory of God" (10:31).

The ministry of women in the church and the proper conditions for observing the Lord's Supper are discussed in chapter 11. The nature and use of spiritual gifts is the burden of Paul in chapters 12–14. These gifts are to be exercised in love (chap. 13), and all things are to "be done decently and in order" (14:40). This is necessary because all believers are members of one body (12:12-30). Therefore, if the unity of the body is to be maintained, and if the work is to go forward, proper use of spiritual gifts is required.

Only in chapter 15 is a purely doctrinal issue discussed. This is the classic passage in the New Testament on the subject of the resurrection of the body. First, Christ's resurrection is described (v. 1-19). Then, Paul applies this great truth (v. 20-58). Because Christ came out of the grave, so shall all men in God's own time (v. 22). Paul describes the resurrection of the body. It shall be "a spiritual body" (v. 44), that is, characterized by spiritual rather than natural life. Even like our Lord's resurrected body, however, it will be a recognizable form. The great hope of the believer's resurrection is described in verses 50-58 (cf. 1 Thess. 4:13-18).

In closing this lengthy epistle, Paul reminds the Corinthians, as he has done in the Galatian churches, of the collection he is receiving for the needy saints in Jerusalem. That which they give is to be given regularly, voluntarily, and proportionately (16:1, 2).

2 CORINTHIANS

Purpose

One of the most personal of Paul's letters, 2 Corinthians is, for the most part, a defense of Paul's ministry (chaps. 1–7) and his apostleship (chap. 10–13). Chapters 8 and 9 consist of an added plea to fulfill their ministry of giving and a pointed reminder that they have been somewhat negligent in the fulfillment of their stewardship.

Outline

Salutation	1:1, 2
Problems of the Christian ministry	1:3–7:16
Problems of Christian giving	8:1–9:15
Problems of a Christian minister	10:1–13:10
Conclusion	13:11-14

Background

After having sent the first epistle to the Corinthian church, Paul waited at Ephesus for their response. He then went north to Troas to meet Titus, but when Titus did not appear, Paul continued into Macedonia (2:12, 13). When the two did meet, Paul wrote concerning the Corinthian church that he was comforted by the report of "your earnest desire, your mourning, your fervent mind toward me" (7:7). The news, however, was not all favorable. A vocal element in the church was protesting against the authority of the apostle. Apparently a group of Jewish opponents (11:2) were discounting the reality of Paul's faith in Christ and the genuineness of his ministry (10:2) and were despising his person (10:10). While there had been repentance on the part of some in the church (2:1-11), the unrepentant group continued to press hard upon Paul. Thus Paul bares his inmost feelings here in a way not seen in any other existing letter that he wrote.

Characteristic Features

Amid the multitude of personal references, Paul has given to the church in this letter many enduring doctrinal affirmations. Notice especially the leading references to the character and workings of God (1:3, 4; 2:14; 4:5, 6; 5:18-21; 6:14-18; 9:7-15), the contrast between the old and new covenants (chap. 3), the future state (5:1-10), the ministry of reconciliation (5:14-21), and Christian stewardship of money (chaps. 8, 9).

DISCUSSION QUESTIONS

1. Illustrate from these Corinthian Epistles the reasons it may be said that they form the heart of the Pauline writings.
2. Briefly summarize Paul's experiences in Corinth prior to writing 1 Corinthians.
3. What was the immediate occasion for Paul's writing 1 Corinthians?
4. What is the central concept of 1 Corinthians and how can it be fulfilled?
5. Illustrate from Paul's dealing with any three problems in the Corinthian church how Paul's solutions are applicable today.
6. Summarize the teaching of 1 Corinthians 15 concerning the resurrection.
7. What was Paul's major purpose in writing 2 Corinthians?
8. Briefly summarize the background of 2 Corinthians.
9. List several important doctrinal emphases in 2 Corinthians.

APPLICATION ACTIVITIES

1. Select a number of passages that might serve as maxims for a day (e.g., We are ambassadors for Christ). Some find spiritual help from listing a Scriptural maxim at the top of each day's "to do" list.
2. Prepare a list with Scripture references of key doctrinal truths found in the Corinthian Epistles.
3. Discuss to what extent the ways Paul defended himself in 2 Corinthians 10-13 are applicable today.
4. List your significant roles in family and church life (e.g., husband, father, son, church member, and other). Under these headings list Scriptures from the Corinthian Epistles that state guiding principles for these specific roles.[4]

Chapter Seven

PAULINE EPISTLES

Galatians and Romans

THESE BOOKS EMPHASIZE the salvation found in the Corinthian Epistles. Galatians is a sturdy defense of the doctrine that "a man is not justified by the works of the law but by the faith of Jesus Christ" (2:16). In no other writing has Paul so forcibly established the genuineness of his apostolic commission and his message.

GALATIANS

Background

The questions of the date and destination of this letter, as well as the place of writing, are difficult to answer with any certainty. It may well have been the earliest of Paul's writings, penned soon after his first missionary journey upon his return to Syrian Antioch. Thus, it would be dated about A.D. 48/49. But the Epistle has also been placed later by some (as late as A.D. 58, Lightfoot). Even the late date, of course, would still presuppose the lapse of a relatively short period of time after the founding of the Galatian churches.

While the letter is addressed to the churches of Galatia, the matter of destination is problematic due to the first-century meaning of the name itself. That is, "Galatia" could be understood in more than one way. This territory, located in eastern Asia Minor, was settled by the Gauls in the third century B.C. and took its name from these invaders. Eventually, after the Romans came into control of the area, the territory was enlarged. An area to the south was included with the northern section, and the whole new province was called Galatia. When Paul wrote the letter, then, was he addressing people in North Galatia or South Galatia? Most of the older commentators favor the former view; the majority of recent writers favor the latter view. Whichever is accepted, the message of Galatians remains unaffected.

Outline

In examining the structure of the book, one may discern logical steps in Paul's argument. Once he has set the stage for what he has to say (1:1-10), he immediately plunges in to defend his position—that justification before God comes by faith and not by works and that Christ has set us free from the bondage of the law.

Introduction	1:1-10
The autobiographical argument—The Gospel revealed	1:11–2:21
Direct revelation of the Gospel	1:11-24
Apostolic confirmation of the Gospel	2:1-10
Personal application of the Gospel	2:11-21
The doctrinal argument—The Gospel prophesied	3:1–4:31
The personal appeal	3:1-5
The experience of Abraham	3:6-14
The promise and the Law	3:15-22
The nature of sonship	3:23–4:7
The danger of defection	4:8-20
The lesson by allegory	4:21-31
The practical argument—The Gospel applied	5:1–6:10
Conclusion	6:11-18

Purpose and Content

One cannot help but observe that there is no familiar and friendly introduction to this letter as is common in Paul's Epistles. Paul states his business and gets into the details of the argument at once. Paul is amazed that these Christian congregations are wavering so soon in their loyalty to Christ and himself. He roundly condemns those who "pervert the gospel of Christ" (1:6, 7) and calls down the curse of God upon them (1:8, 9).

First, Paul himself has received his Gospel from Christ (1:11, 12). It has not been communicated to him by others; they have only concurred with him in his message and ministry (1:16–2:10). Therefore, on the basis of his own well established experience, he claims that his message is genuine.[1]

Second, the Gospel is not a new thing; it was taught in the Old Testament (3:8). Abraham is the great example of justification by faith in God. As he came into this relationship long before the Law was given, the Law did not justify him—neither can it justify anyone (3:9-14). Paul elaborates this principle by contrasting the "child" with the "son" (3:23–4:7) and drawing upon the story of Abraham's two sons to teach the same truth allegorically (4:21-31).

Third, the Gospel works in personal experience (5:1). When applied, the Gospel gives the individual freedom from bondage to sin, victory over the flesh (the old nature within), and the ability to show forth works of righteousness. All this is set within the framework of the work of the Holy Spirit in the believer's life. "If we live by the Spirit, let us also walk in the Spirit" (5:25).

Thus, in Galatians, probably the earliest of Paul's writings, appears a powerful presentation of the nature of justification. The response of faith on the part of the sinner not only brings him right standing with God, but brings into his life the dynamic of the Spirit to do the work of God.

ROMANS

At the center of "the good tidings of great joy" that were spoken to the shepherds of Bethlehem was a Savior, One who would redeem His people. This subject of redemption is defined and developed by Paul in his letter to the Romans, the most orderly and detailed treatment of salvation in the New Testament.

Background

For many years the apostle had wanted to visit the Christians in Rome (15:23), desiring to establish them in the faith (1:11). While Paul had been heretofore hindered, he stood ready "to preach the gospel to you that are at Rome also" (1:13-15). On his third missionary journey, shortly before leaving Corinth (Acts 20:1-3), Paul wrote this letter in lieu of a visit, and sent it, apparently, by the hand of Phoebe of Cenchrae (16:1, 2). Soon afterward he was arrested in Jerusalem (Acts 21:27ff.). Thus, as it turned out, he did arrive in Rome, but not as a free man (Acts 28:16).

Outline

The theme of the letter is redemption (3:24). Throughout the book Paul carefully develops five aspects of the subject of redemption.

Introduction	1:1-17
Sin—The need for redemption	1:18–3:20
Gentile sin	1:18–2:16
Jewish sin	2:17–3:8
Universal sin	3:9-20
Justification—The provision of redemption	3:21–5:21
Sanctification—The effect of redemption	6:1–8:39
The union with Christ	6:1-23
The conflict of natures	7:1-25
The victory by the Spirit	8:1-39

Purpose and Content

Paul's introductory words combine many remarks of a personal and a theological nature (1:1-17). He tells a good deal about himself. He is a bondservant of Christ, yet an apostle (1:1). His commission is to the nations (1:5). He is a man of prayer (1:9, 10), an earnest worker (1:13-15), and unashamed of the message he proclaims (1:16). Along with this, he describes the Gospel as being prophesied in the Old Testament (1:2), centered in the Son of God (1:3), "dynamite" that brings salvation to those who believe it (1:16), and a revelation of God's righteousness to the faithful ones (1:17).

The first major division of the epistle (1:18–3:20) delineates the sinful condition of man and demonstrates the universal need for redemption. Common to the descriptions of various classes of persons is a picture of spiritual and moral degeneration. Indeed, the former leads to the latter.

Man has turned away from God and fallen into idolatry (1:21-23); thus "God gave them up" (1:24, 26, 28). Some have condemned their fellowmen, but they are in reality worthy of condemnation themselves (2:1-3), for they practice the same things. God "will render to every man according to his deeds" (2:6). Gentiles, without the written law of the Jews, have the voice of conscience within (2:14, 15). With all his privileges, the Jew himself has not maintained his spiritual life, and the name of God is blasphemed among the Gentiles because of Jewish failure (2:24, 25). The final verdict declares the guilt of all before the righteousness of God. By works "shall no flesh be justified in his sight" (3:20).

Then the provision of God is declared (3:21–5:21). Justification is the answer—and it is "by faith of Jesus Christ unto all and upon all them that believe" (3:22). God is able to maintain His own righteousness and yet declare the sinner righteous because of the redeeming work of Christ (3:24-26). To illustrate the principle of justification by faith, Paul draws upon the example of Abraham (as he had done earlier in Galatians), showing that Abraham's acceptance preceded both the institution of circumcision and the giving of the Law; thus it was by his faith alone that he was declared righteous (4:10-13). Having been justified, the sinner is able to realize some of the benefits (5:1-11) that accrue from the work of the Lord Jesus (5:12-21).

Next, the logical effect of redemption is discussed (6:1–8:39). The implications of the new relationship with God are far-reaching. A new life (6:11) and a new loyalty (6:12-14) should be manifested. Despite the constant demands of the old nature to dominate (7:24), there is victory through the work of the Holy Spirit (chap. 8). He empowers (8:16) and intercedes (8:26). Surely the Lord's promise is true, "My grace is sufficient for thee" (2 Cor. 12:9).

Following this, Paul makes clear the universal nature of the message (9:1–11:36). It is to both Jew and Gentile. Though God may have set aside His people Israel, He has not cast them off (11:1). He is sovereign and is only working out His purpose of redemption (9:19-32). There is yet a day of restoration and blessing for Israel (11:25-32). In the present day, the Gospel goes out to all and "whosoever shall call upon the name of the Lord shall be saved" (10:13).

In the last major division of the letter, Paul describes the outworking of redemption (12:1–15:13). Beginning with a plea for complete dedication to the Lord (12:1, 2),[2] Paul goes on to show the varied responsibilities and relationships of the Christian. The Christian is to evaluate himself sanely in the light of the grace of God; to fulfill his ministry within the church (12:3-8); and to have proper relationships to other individuals (12:9-21), to government (13:1-7), to society (13:8-14), and to Christians who differ from him in personal scruples (14:1–15:13).

The concluding words are largely personal in nature, consisting of the hopes and plans of the apostle, especially with reference to his visit to Rome, and a list of greetings to friends and fellow workers in the church (15:14–16:27).

DISCUSSION QUESTIONS

1. What significant doctrine does Galatians clearly defend?
2. State the basic claims presented by Paul in Galatians as to the genuineness of his message.
3. What was the occasion of Paul's writing the Epistle to the Romans?
4. What Old Testament character does Paul use in Romans and Galatians to illustrate justification by faith? What is the significance of the time this character appeared in Old Testament sequence?
5. According to Galatians 5:1-24 and Romans 6–8, how does a Christian live a spiritual life?

6. How can a man be justified by God (Rom. 3:21–5:21)?
7. Referring to the outline and Scripture divisions of the book of Romans, summarize briefly Israel's past, present, and future.
8. State some of the main responsibilities the Christian has in doing the will of God (Romans 12–15).

APPLICATION ACTIVITIES

1. For a better comprehension of Romans and Galatians, expand the outlines given in this text.
2. Utilizing your Bible concordance or index, contrast the use of the words *law* and *grace* or *faith* and *works* in the Bible.
3. In a panel discussion, consider ways in which Christian liberties are sometimes abused, and suggest remedies.
4. Using verses only from the book of Romans, outline the steps leading to salvation.
5. Referring to interpretive news periodicals such as *Newsweek* and *Time*, trace significant developments in contemporary history that appear to be fulfillment of prophecy concerning the Jews. Why should the Christian be alert to these?

Chapter Eight

PAULINE EPISTLES

Colossians, Philemon, Ephesians, Philippians

A MISFORTUNE OR A BLESSING? How is Paul's imprisonment to be viewed? Would it have been better for all concerned if Paul had remained a free man and able to carry on his missionary travels? Or did God direct Paul into such a situation as this? Possibly the question may never be settled to the satisfaction of all, but this point is clear: the period that Paul spent in the Roman prison (Acts 28:30, 31) was one of the richest of his career. It provided him an entrance into the household of the emperor (Phil. 1:13; 4:22) and brought forth the Prison Epistles—the most profound and Christ-exalting examples of Paul's written works.

Each of these letters contains references to Paul's situation. In Colossians 1:24 and 4:18, he speaks of his "sufferings" and his "bonds." Philemon 1, 9, and 10 refer to him as a prisoner and one in bonds. Again, in Ephesians 3:1, 4:1, and 6:20, Paul makes mention of being a prisoner and "in a chain." Finally, Philippians 1:12, 13 calls attention to his bonds and the presence of the whole praetorian guard. Given this evidence, the place of Paul's imprisonment has been traditionally held to have been Rome.

COLOSSIANS

Here is one of two epistles written by Paul to churches he had not personally founded. It seems likely that during his lengthy stay at Ephesus (Acts 19) the message of Christ had been taken to Colossae by one of his fellow workers. He describes Epaphras, a Colossian Christian serving with Paul (4:12), as "our dear fellow servant, who is for you a faithful minister of Christ; who also declared unto us your love in the Spirit" (1:7, 8).

Background
Colossae did not rank with Ephesus in either size or importance. It was an inland city, lying beside the Lycus River, near Laodicea and Hierapolis

(cf. 4:13). Located on the main commercial thoroughfare between East and West, the city was influenced by contrasting ideologies. These influences seem to be reflected in the epistle as Paul writes to describe the person of Christ (cf. 1:14-20) and to correct the current errors relating to redemption and the pattern of Christian living (2:8–3:4).

The name usually given to the false teaching in this city is the Colossian heresy. This heresy apparently consisted of a mixture of Jewish and Gnostic ideas, combined to create a threat to the Gospel of Christ. The unsound teaching sought to reduce Christianity to a legal system and to obscure the person and work of Christ. Paul attacks the errors at Colossae by a clear presentation of counter truths. The key verse is 1:18—"that in all *things* he might have the preeminence."

Outline

Salutation	1:1, 2
The prayer of thanksgiving	1:3-8
The prayer of intercession	1:9-14
The supremacy of Christ	1:15-23
Paul's desire for the saints	1:24–2:7
Paul's exhortations to the saints	2:8–4:6
Paul's representatives to Colossae	4:7-9
Greetings	4:10-17
Conclusion	4:18

Comparison with Ephesians

As one reads this epistle, he or she may be impressed with its likeness to Ephesians. Indeed, the two may be called the twin epistles of the New Testament. They are most nearly alike in their presentation of Christ and His body, the Church. In Colossians, Christ is "the head of the body" (1:18); in Ephesians, it is "the church, which is his body" (1:22, 23). The development in Colossians, then, concentrates on the exalted position of Christ; in Ephesians, upon the nature of the Church.

Another notable likeness is the section dealing with the application of the Gospel to practical affairs. Both epistles describe the old man and new man together with the evidences of each (Col. 3:9, 10; Eph. 4:22-24). Also, each contains commands to the various members of the household to fulfill their rightful functions (Col. 3:18–4:1; Eph. 5:22–6:9).

Purpose and Content

The key passages telling of Christ are to be found in 1:15-23 and 2:8–3:4. In the first, Christ is described as preeminent in at least four distinct relationships: to God (1:15); to created things (1:16, 17); to the Church

(1:18); and to the work of redemption (1:19-23). This discussion is preliminary and necessary to expose the heresy described in chapter 2. The presentation of the superiority of Christ is the answer to all such errors. This is Paul's basic approach in the section that follows.

In reading 2:8–3:5, the main characteristics of this false teaching seem to be:

1. Rationalistic philosophy that denied revelation (2:8).

2. Legalistic religion that was seriously endangering the concept of Christian liberty (2:16).

3. Voluntary humility and worship of angels, based on a superior knowledge (2:18).

The responses Paul gives to each of these aspects of false teaching are as follows (in corresponding order):

1. Christ is the fullness of God, and the One in whom the Christian is "made full" (2:9).

2. Christ is the reality, the fulfillment of the types and shadows of ceremonial religion (2:17). In Him, these types are done away.

3. Christ is the Head (2:19). If He is not given His proper place, things will come in that are in reality useless for spiritual life (2:23).

Finally, Paul shows the implications of these teachings. A new kind of life, a new way of living is demanded (3:5-17). The person in whom the Word of Christ "dwells" richly will give evidence of this new life (3:16, 17). Paul emphasizes especially domestic relationships:

Wives—be in subjection to your husbands (3:18)

Husbands—love your wives (3:19)

Children—obey your parents (3:20)

Fathers—do not provoke your children (3:21)

Servants—obey your masters; you really serve Christ (3:22-25)

Masters—treat your servants justly (4:1)

Thus, Christ is not only to be preeminent in one's doctrine but in his duties as well.

PHILEMON

Background

Along with constituting a part of the New Testament canon, this brief epistle is a prime example of Paul's personal correspondence. It is a letter written by one Christian to another, asking that a favor be granted because of their mutual relationship to Christ and to each other. It is a masterful example of the tactful approach to a delicate and difficult situation. The letter was sent along with the letter to the Colossians to Philemon, in whose house the Colossian church met.

Outline

Salutation	1-3
The prayer for Philemon's ministry	4-7
The petition for Onesimus's restoration	8-21
The prospect of Paul's visit	22
Conclusion	23-25

Purpose

Within the framework of Christology, Paul here illustrates the principle of forgiveness and restoration on the basis of substitution. He asks that Onesimus, the slave who is worthy of punishment, be forgiven by his master and received back "not now as a servant, but above a servant, a brother beloved" (16).

Paul beseeches and offers to pay any debt that stands due to Philemon (18, 19). Thus the doctrine of imputation is illustrated. The merit of one person is reckoned to the account of another.[1]

EPHESIANS

Background

Ephesus, in the first century A.D., called herself the first city of Asia. Although the ancient city of Pergamum (cf. Rev. 2:12), just to the north, was still the official capital of the province, Ephesus had risen rapidly in stature. An important center commercially, intellectually, and religiously, she boasted one of the seven wonders of the ancient world: the ornate, glistening temple of Diana, the great goddess of the Ephesians (cf. Acts 19:23ff.).

The history of the Ephesian church may be traced in some detail through the New Testament. Paul founded and established the church as was recorded in Acts 19 and 20. Having received the apostle's teaching for over two years, the church was well grounded in the faith. The Ephesian Epistle reflects the spiritual capacity of this church (notice especially Eph. 1:3-14). Further, the letter warns against the conflict with evil spirits (6:10ff.), which were a menace in this city (cf. Acts 19:11-17).

The letters to Timothy, who was left in Ephesus by Paul to carry on the work (1 Tim. 1:3ff.), show the next stage in the history. False teachers had begun to trouble the believers, and Paul sends instructions regarding sound teaching and the proper organization of the church. In Revelation 2:1-7, the last chapter is written concerning this church in the

New Testament. It is a sad word—she has left her "first love" for Christ (2:4). When she did not repent of her condition, as church history shows, she was removed—her lampstand no longer shone as a witness in Ephesus.

Outline

The central theme of the epistle is the Church as the body of Christ. Paul has given a sublime presentation of this truth from the very inception of the Church to its witness within the world and its conflict against the forces of evil.

Salutation	1:1, 2
The Church in the purpose of God	1:3-14
The Church and the power of God	1:15–2:10
The Church as the household of God	2:11-22
The Church as the revelation of God	3:1-13
The Church and the fullness of God	3:14-21
The Church and the standards of God	4:1–6:9
The Church and the armor of God	6:10-20
Conclusion	6:21-24

Purpose and Content

The letter is addressed to believers, described as "the saints" and "the faithful." One emphasizes the believer's position in Christ, the other his character before God.

In the first part of the epistle (1:3-14) Paul concisely describes the origin of the Church, here in its universal aspect, in the purpose of God. He highlights such important themes as election (1:4), predestination (1:5, 11), adoption (1:5), redemption (1:7), purpose (1:9, 10), and the sealing with the Holy Spirit (1:13), culminating in the final possession of the Church by God (1:14).[2]

By God's power the Church has been called into being (1:15–2:10) and is described as a great household, consisting of both Jew and Gentile (2:11-22), sharing alike in the riches of God's inheritance (3:1-13). God dwells within the Church, which has been built upon a solid foundation and is being made up of many parts, each having its own place in the structure (2:19-22).

The two concepts of "walk" and "warfare" are characteristic of the practical division of the book (4:1–6:24). While the word *walk*, denoting one's manner of life, appears twice in the early chapters (2:2, 10), it is more common in the last part (4:1, 17; 5:2, 8, 15). The Christian is to "walk worthy," "walk not as other Gentiles," "walk in love," "walk as children of light," and "walk circumspectly." He is to walk in keeping with his position as a member of the body of Christ (cf. 1 John 2:5, 6).

The exhortations to the members of the household are generally lengthier than in the Colossian letter. In Ephesians, Paul gives much attention to the husband-wife relationship, using it as an illustration of Christ and the Church (5:32).[3] An abbreviated comparison of the two passages should make apparent the leading features of each:

Ref.	Ephesians	Ref.	Colossians
5:22-24	*Wives:* be subject to your own husbands	3:18	*Wives:* be subject to your husbands
5:25-31	*Husbands:* love your wives; notice Christ's example	3:19	*Husbands:* love your wives; do not be bitter against them
6:1-3	*Children:* obey your parents; it is God's command	3:20	*Children:* obey your parents; this is the right thing to do
6:4	*Fathers:* provoke not your children, but nurture them	3:21	*Fathers:* provoke not your children, lest they be discouraged
6:5-8	*Servants:* be obedient to your masters; serve the Lord	3:22-25	*Servants:* be obedient to your masters; work heartily, as unto the Lord
6:9	*Masters:* serve the Lord; forbear threatening; you have a Master in heaven	4:1	*Masters:* render just and equal dues to your servants; you have a Master in heaven

In closing the Epistle to the Ephesians, the apostle deals with the Christian's warfare (literally, wrestling or hand-to-hand combat) against the spiritual forces of darkness (6:10-20). The Christian's provision against this foe is the whole armor of God. Using it will enable the Christian "to stand against the wiles of the devil" (v. 11).[4] Paul describes the various pieces of the armor and their function.

Thus, while the Christian finds himself "in the heavenly places" (1:3, 10, 20; 2:6; 3:10; 6:12), he is also to avail himself of all God's provisions and give careful heed to all His demands for his life and warfare upon the earth.

PHILIPPIANS

"Rejoice in the Lord always: *and* again I say, Rejoice" (4:4). This note characterizes the Philippian letter. A proper appreciation of Paul's great faith in God makes joy seem a natural expression in spite of adverse circumstances.

Background

The city of Philippi was the starting point for the preaching of the Gospel in Europe. Paul sailed from Troas, following the Macedonian vision (Acts 16:9), "assuredly gathering that the Lord had called us for to preach the gospel unto them" (Acts 16:10). He arrived in a city that had an illustrious history. It was on this site that, in 42 B.C., the famous battle was fought between Octavian and Antony against Brutus and Cassius. Following the battle, the status of a Roman colony was conferred upon the city by the victorious Octavian. Thus it came to be modeled after the imperial city of Rome. The people were proud of their rights of citizenship (Acts 16:20, 21). Through the city ran the famous Via Egnatia, the trade route between East and West.

When Paul, Silas, Timothy, and Luke arrived here, they preached first to a group of women gathered for prayer near the river (Acts 16:13). These, among them Lydia and her family, later constituted the nucleus of the church in the city. Soon, however, trouble arose. When Paul and Silas expelled a demon from a slave girl, her masters, seeing their gain from her services was gone (Acts 16:19), had the two imprisoned on a false charge. But an earthquake during the night liberated them from prison, their jailer became a Christian (Acts 16:34), and their appeal to their Roman citizenship freed them from further punishment (cf. Acts 16:22-24, 38-40). Years later, at the time of the writing of this letter, Paul was a prisoner again! This time, due to false accusations also, he had been sent to Rome in chains. Yet he penned an epistle that radiates joy and speaks often of the good tidings, the Gospel of Christ. This is a demonstration of his testimony, "For to me to live is Christ" (Phil. 1:21).

Outline

As the epistle is composed of many personal matters, the structure is not as clear-cut as many of Paul's other writings. The underlying theme, however, is the Gospel, and the key words are *joy* and *rejoice*.

Salutation	1:1, 2
Thanksgiving and prayer for the saints	1:3-11
Paul and his circumstances	1:12-26
Believers and their conduct	1:27-30
Christ and His example—Humility	2:1-18
Timothy and Epaphroditus and their concern	2:19-30
Paul and his example—Maturity	3:1–4:1
Exhortations and appreciation	4:2-20
Conclusion	4:21-23

Purpose and Content

Viewing the major features of the letter, one is readily able to see that the chief hortatory sections deal with the concepts of unity through humility (2:1-18) and maturity in Christ (3:1–4:1). A number of specific applications of this maturity are given in 4:2-20.

The main personal sections concern Paul himself (1:12-26; 3:4-14; 4:10-20) and two of his fellow workers, Timothy and Epaphroditus (2:19-30). The leading doctrinal passage concerns the incarnation and exaltation of Christ (2:5-11). In every kind of situation, Christ is exalted: in Paul's own sufferings (1:12-26); in the Christian's personal life (2:1-5); in Paul's own desires and ambitions (3:7-14); and in his realization of true serenity (4:10-18).

By His own example, Christ has shown the way of acceptance with God. The lowly place precedes the exalted position. Though the qualities of deity were resident within Him (2:6), Christ willingly relinquished His prerogatives to accomplish the work of the Cross (2:7, 8). Thus, God exalted Him to the supreme place over every creature; to Him every knee must bow (2:9-11). This is the Christ whom Paul desires to know in daily experience (3:10), and the One whom we await from heaven "Who shall change our vile body . . . like unto his glorious body" (3:20, 21).

DISCUSSION QUESTIONS

1. Why are Colossians, Philemon, Ephesians, and Philippians called Prison Epistles?
2. What was the Colossian heresy?
3. List several reasons for calling Colossians and Ephesians the twin epistles of the New Testament.
4. In the book of Colossians, Paul deals with what major domestic relationships?
5. How is the doctrine of imputation illustrated in the book of Philemon?
6. Briefly trace the history of the Ephesian church as portrayed in the New Testament.
7. What is the central theme of the book of Ephesians?
8. Name at least three of Paul's experiences in Philippi prior to his writing the Philippian Epistle.
9. Why was it possible for Paul to have the major theme that he had in his letter to the Philippians in spite of his experiences?

APPLICATION ACTIVITIES

1. In each of the epistles studied in this chapter, find one or more significant indications of Paul's attitude during the days of his imprisonment.
2. Utilizing key phrases from these four epistles, draw a word portrait of Christ. -OR- Expand the chart you prepared in chapter 1, activity #1.
3. Trace specific scriptural commands and guiding principles that apply directly to your various roles in life. -OR- Expand the chart begun in chapter 6, activity #4.
4. For personal enrichment, trace and summarize the use of the words "in Christ" as found in Ephesians and Colossians.
5. Prepare your own outline for one or more of the epistles covered in this chapter.

Chapter Nine

PAULINE EPISTLES

1 Timothy, Titus, 2 Timothy

THE LAST GROUP OF epistles in the Pauline collection have been named the Pastoral Epistles because of their emphasis on the personal responsibilities and the public functions of the pastor (literally, shepherd) of the local church. Written to two of Paul's closest companions, Timothy and Titus, these are the latest of Paul's letters, usually dated near the end of his life, about A.D. 63-67. Especially in 2 Timothy Paul seems to anticipate the end (cf. 4:6).

Although scholars are divided on the matter of the authorship of these books, the three letters are here assumed to be Pauline.[1] They reflect Paul's life between the time of his imprisonment mentioned in Acts and his death some years later.

I TIMOTHY

Background

Apparently converted under the preaching of Paul on his first mission to Galatia, Timothy enters the pages of the New Testament in Acts 16:1ff. As Paul made a return journey into the same territory, he found Timothy, likely in Lystra. Timothy is called by the apostle "*my* own son in the faith" (1 Tim. 1:2) and "*my* dearly beloved son" (2 Tim.1:2). Having been reared by his mother, a Jewess (although his father was a Greek, Acts 16:1, 3), Timothy knew the Old Testament Scriptures from his childhood (2 Tim. 3:14, 15) and now, being converted to Christianity, was "well reported of by the brethren that were at Lystra and Iconium" (Acts 16:2).

Timothy accompanied Paul from this time onward, being left later in Ephesus to straighten out the affairs of the church, particularly some doctrinal difficulties, and to oversee its organization and deportment (cf. 1 Tim. 1:3ff.; 3:1-14; 4:6-16). When Paul wrote to him from Rome, he asked Timothy to come soon to visit him, bringing John Mark with him and also some personal belongings (2 Tim. 4:9, 11, 13). We do not know whether Timothy arrived before Paul's death.

From the contents of these letters, as well as scattered references in other epistles, Timothy may be pictured as a faithful, diligent worker, dear to Paul's heart (cf. Phil. 2:19, 20). The fact that the great apostle entrusted Timothy with the responsibility of a leading church, bears testimony to Paul's confidence in his companion. It may also be concluded that Timothy needed occasional prodding and encouragement by Paul, possibly due to a natural timidity (cf. 2 Tim. 1:6, 7; 1 Tim. 4:12-16). As a "man of God" (1 Tim. 6:11), he was exhorted to emulate his Lord "who before Pontius Pilate witnessed a good confession" (6:13) and to "keep that which is committed to thy trust" (6:20).

Purpose

The letter has a double aspect. One is the emphasis upon Timothy as a person—he has certain responsibilities to fulfill as a minister of the Lord and as an exemplary individual. The other is the emphasis upon his official responsibilities—he is to see that the church is properly taught, organized, and administered. The former aspect is seen particularly in 1:3-7, 18-20; 4:6-16; 5:1ff.; 6:11-21; the latter particularly in chapters 2, 3, 5, and 6:1-10. As might be expected, there is not a hard and fast line between the two. Personal and official responsibilities cannot logically be separated.

Outline

Salutation	1:1, 2
Charge to Timothy	1:3-20
Exhortations for church order—Prayer and worship	2:1-15
Requirements for church officers—Elders and deacons	3:1-13
Parenthesis	3:14-16
Instructions for church activities	4:1–6:21a
Conclusion	6:21b

Basic Features

As more will be said about Timothy himself in the second letter, special attention is given here to the basic features of church organization and administration.

First, the ideal church should be characterized by proper prayer life (chap. 2). Regulations for the objects of prayer are first given (v. 1-4), then for the respective functions of men and women in the church (v. 8-15). Emphasis is upon the proper attitudes in prayer and service, rather than upon outward appearances. Men are assigned the place of official teachers and administrators.

Second, the ideal church should be characterized by proper organization (3:1-13). The requirements for elders, deacons, and the women (deaconesses?) are enumerated in this passage. They relate both to the moral and spiritual qualities of the person desiring an office, and to the functions he is expected to perform. The first-century church held high standards, indeed.

Third, the ideal church should be characterized by proper administration of its various affairs (5:1–6:10). Emphasis is placed here first upon the care for and the responsibilities of widows (5:3-16). If a widow is aged and desolate, let the church care for her. If she has children or grandchildren, let them care for her. If she is a young widow, Paul recommends remarriage and rearing of a family. Following this, instructions are given regarding the work of the elders (5:17-25), the servants (6:1, 2), and the teachers (6:3-10). Each is to discharge his responsibilities knowing that he is answerable to the Lord.

TITUS

Background

Like Timothy, Titus also appears to have been led to Christ by Paul. The apostle calls him "*mine own son* after the common faith" (Titus 1:4). He was a Greek, possibly from Syrian Antioch. When Paul and Barnabas went from Antioch to Jerusalem to discuss their ministry with the leaders of the church there, Titus accompanied them (Gal. 2:1-3). He is presented as an example of a Gentile become Christian without the necessity of Jewish circumcision. Titus thus illustrates the principle of which Paul speaks in Galatians 2:16.

Strange as it may seem, the name of Titus does not appear in the book of Acts. Of all the major companions of the apostle Paul, only Titus and Luke are not mentioned there by name, although Luke is included anonymously in the "we sections."

The chief picture which we gain of Titus, aside from the references in the epistle that bears his name, is found in 2 Corinthians. He seems to have been the kind of person we today call a troubleshooter, thus he was sent by Paul into difficult situations to attempt a solution. Paul rejoices, as he writes to the Corinthians, in that he was comforted by the return of Titus from Corinth because the apostle's hopes for the church seem to have been justified. Apparently Titus had been successful in smoothing the troubled waters (2 Cor. 7:6-10, 13-16). He had been sent to see about the promised contribution for the Jerusalem church. Having been lax in fulfilling this ministry, the Corinthians were urged by Paul to demonstrate to his fellow workers "the proof of your love, and of our boasting on your behalf" (cf. 2 Cor. 8:6, 16, 17, 23, 24).

We see in the Epistle to Titus that Paul had left his companion in the island of Crete to "set in order the things that were wanting, and ordain elders in every city" (1:5). As in the case of Timothy in Ephesus, Titus was given the responsibility of organizing and administering the affairs of these churches, together with carrying on a sound program of teaching. His last appearance in the New Testament is in 2 Timothy 4:10 where he has left Rome and gone to Dalmatia, apparently to represent Paul once again.

The epistle itself has as its theme "sound doctrine" (cf. 1:9; 2:1, 7, 8). Proper understanding of the truth should eventuate in good works (cf. 1:16; 2:7, 14; 3:1, 8, 14). The good works are not the basis of salvation (3:5) but are to be the evidence of it (3:8).

Outline

Salutation	1:1-4
Paul's instructions to Titus	1:5–3:11
Regarding the churches	1:5-16
Regarding individuals	2:1-15
Regarding the world	3:1-8
Regarding heresies	3:9-11
Personal notes	3:12-14
Conclusion	3:15

Purpose and Content

It appears that the chief problem in Crete came from false teachers, mainly "of the circumcision" (i.e., Jewish), who are described by Paul as "unruly and vain talkers and deceivers" (1:10). They were teaching "Jewish fables" (1:14) and introducing "foolish questions, and genealogies, and contentions, and strivings about the law" (3:9). Along with this was the moral laxity of the Cretans (1:12, 13) and the careless demeanor of some of the members of the church (2:2, 3, 10; 3:2). To counteract such vanities, Paul urges upon Titus the need for sound doctrine, emphasizing that the Word of God is the basis for the Christian life (cf. 1:3; 2:5, 10). When this teaching is properly received, good works should result.

The doctrine of God is also prominent in the epistle. Several of the references relate to the Father (1:1, 3, 4; 2:10; 3:4); others to the Son (1:4; 2:13; 3:6); and to the Holy Spirit (3:5).

The doctrine of salvation is central in 2:11-14 and 3:4-7. The grace of

God not only saves, but also instructs the believer and gives him the blessed hope. Those who have been redeemed are to show a change in character (v. 14). Notice, too, the four important words describing God's character in relation to salvation: "kindness," "love" (3:4), "mercy" (3:5), and "grace" (3:7).

As compared with 1 Timothy, the instructions regarding church officers are more brief in Titus. Here only the elder (or bishop) is described; the deacons are not mentioned. Once again the need for men of high spiritual and moral qualities is stressed. They must be both exemplary in character and capable in their functions. "In all things shewing thyself a pattern of good works . . . that they may adorn the doctrine of God our Saviour in all things" (2:7a, 10b).

2 TIMOTHY

Background

At the time of the writing of this letter, Paul was awaiting execution. According to tradition, he was imprisoned in the Mamertine dungeon in Rome, under circumstances much less favorable than those of Acts 28:30. He seems to expect death rather than release (4:6; contrast Phil. 1:19; Philem. 22).

Purpose and Content

Thus these are the final recorded words of Paul in the New Testament. With special interest we look into these pages for thoughts of the great apostle as he faces the end of his life and ministry. As he faces death alone, except for the companionship of Luke the physician (4:11), Paul's chief concern is for the welfare of Timothy and the success of his work in Ephesus. The leading exhortations that appear throughout the letter are worthy of careful attention:

"Stir up the gift of God, which is in thee." (1:6)

"Be not thou therefore ashamed . . . but be thou partaker of the afflictions." (1:8)

"Hold fast the form of sound words." (1:13)

"That good thing which was committed unto thee keep by the Holy Ghost." (1:14)

"The things that thou hast heard of me among many witnesses, the same commit thou to faithful men." (2:2)

"Of these things put *them* in remembrance." (2:14)

"Study to shew thyself approved unto God." (2:15)

"Flee also youthful lusts." (2:22)

"Continue thou in the things which thou hast learned." (3:14)

"Preach the word." (4:2)

"Watch thou in all things . . . make full proof of thy ministry." (4:5)

These constitute the major thrust of the epistle. It is a letter of personal counsel.

Outline

Salutation	1:1, 2
Thanksgiving for Timothy	1:3-18
Exhortations to Timothy	2:1-26
Warnings to Timothy	3:1-17
The final charge to Timothy	4:1-8
Personal instructions to Timothy	4:9-21
Conclusion	4:22

Characteristic Features

Brief consideration should be given to two or three of the outstanding passages in the epistle. Chapter 2 is characterized by the seven metaphors used to describe the believer. Paul, by the use of these varied figures of speech, makes clear to Timothy the differing facets of the Christian's ministry and the responsibility connected with each.

As a *child,* he is to be strong and active. (v. 1, 2)

As a *soldier,* he is to suffer hardship and also please his superior. (v. 3, 4)

As an *athlete,* he is to obey the rules of the game. (v. 5)

As a *husbandman* (farmer), he is to labor and thus have full participation in the results. (v. 6)

As a *workman,* he is to be diligent, rightly handling the Word of God. (v. 15)

As a *vessel,* he is to be honorable, ready for the Master's use. (v. 21)

As a *servant,* he is to be gentle and helpful. (v. 24, 25)

In 3:14-17 one of the classic passages on the nature of the Scriptures appears. The nature of the Scriptures (the written Word) is divine; they are "inspired of God." God has "breathed them out" to men; the result is His Word communicated faithfully. They are able to (1) enlighten one unto salvation (v. 15) and (2) thoroughly equip the man of God (v. 17).

The letter ends with a series of personal remarks, including the request that Timothy visit Paul soon (4:9), before the winter season if possible (4:21). While in his prison cell Paul wanted his cloak for warmth and his books for study. To the very end of his life Paul remained active and alert. "I have fought a good fight, I have finished my course, I have kept the faith: henceforth there is laid up for me a crown of righteousness, which the Lord, the righteous judge, shall give me at that day" (4:7, 8).

DISCUSSION QUESTIONS

1. Why are these epistles called the Pastoral Epistles? Illustrate your answer with references from the letters.
2. What was Timothy's family and spiritual background prior to his joining Paul in ministry?
3. Describe the characteristics of Timothy as a Christian worker.
4. How did Paul show his confidence in Timothy?
5. What three basic features should characterize the church according to 1 Timothy?
6. In what ways did Titus demonstrate his abilities as a problem solver?
7. What is the theme of the book of Titus?
8. In what ways were false teachers causing problems in Crete?
9. State several of the leading exhortations of Paul to Timothy as found in 2 Timothy.
10. List several of the metaphors Paul uses in 2 Timothy to describe the believer.

APPLICATION ACTIVITIES

1. Compile some maxims for Christians as found in 2 Timothy. -OR- Expand your list of maxims prepared for chapter 6, activity #1.
2. As you see the picture of Paul in 2 Timothy just before his death, what facts impress you most?
3. Prepare a list of standards for church leaders, based on these Pastoral Epistles and applicable for today's situations.
4. Describe the dangers facing the church in Paul's day in present-day terminology and as though affecting your own church.
5. To develop your ability to summarize Bible truths, prepare your own outline for each of these three books.

Chapter Ten

THE CHURCH AND SUFFERING

James, Hebrews, 1 Peter

THERE WERE PERIODS DURING the first century when the church, in one place or another, felt the pangs of suffering and hardship. These trials came from various sources and, to some extent, for different reasons. Nevertheless, they were equally distressing, and the Christians were at times perplexed as to the purpose of all these things in their experience.

If James is rightly dated at about A.D. 45, and thus the earliest book in the New Testament, it reflects trial in the church not long after the time of its inception (Acts 2). It describes trials from without (1:2) and within (1:13-15), recalls suffering as seen in earlier days by the prophets and Job (5:10, 11), and exhorts the suffering person to pray (5:13). The book, apparently meant for Jewish converts of the Dispersion (1:1), is really a treatise on the faith that endures in the face of all types of obstacles.

Hebrews, also written to Jewish converts, makes references to the sufferings of believers. Written at a later date than James (probably shortly before A.D. 70), it is an exhortation to Christians to press forward, to endure, even in the face of serious pressures (cf. 12:3ff.). Whether or not it was written in or near Rome, it reflects the serious conditions existing at that time, near the end of the reign of Nero.

First Peter, to a much greater degree, is also concerned with this problem. The word *suffering* occurs seventeen times, being used both of the sufferings of Christ and His people. The problem is particularly reflected in 4:12-19. By this time (about A.D. 63-65) the pressure of Nero's persecution of the Roman Christians may have been felt in some of the provinces as well (cf. 1:1) or at least the threat was present. Thus, Peter writes to give hope by furnishing a proper perspective (cf. 1:6-9).

JAMES

Unquestionably James is one of the most down-to-earth books in the New Testament. The writer is dealing with everyday affairs, covering such matters as one's speech, business ventures, the respect of persons, disagreements between Christian brethren, relations between employers and employees, and a number of other things. These are problems that touch our lives continually. The teaching of James, then, is designed to show the ways in which one's faith in God is not only tested to determine its genuineness, but applied to every area of human life.

Authorship

The writer of the book identifies himself as "James, a servant of God and of the Lord Jesus Christ" (1:1). As a number of men by this same name appear in the New Testament, brief consideration should be given to the problem. James, the son of Zebedee and the brother of John, was among the original disciples of the Lord Jesus. He was beheaded, however, by Herod Agrippa I (Acts 12:1, 2) before the year A.D. 44, and thus would not play a part in the history of the Jerusalem church during the time under consideration. James the son of Alphaeus was also one of Jesus' disciples (Matt. 10:3), but is not otherwise referred to in the narrative. Another of our Lord's disciples, Judas (not Iscariot), had a father whose name was James (Luke 6:16). But the only prominent figure by this name who continued through this period is the man called by Paul, "James, the Lord's brother" (Gal. 1:19). He appears in the Gospels as one of the four brothers of Christ (Matt. 13:55) and was, during Christ's ministry, an unbeliever (John 7:5). He is seen, however, as a believer in the Jerusalem prayer meeting (Acts 1:14; cf. 1 Cor. 15:7). Upon Peter's departure from Jerusalem, he assumes the leadership of the church there (Acts 12:17). A comparison of Galatians 2:9 with Acts 15:13-29 marks James as one of the pillars of the church. His final appearance in the New Testament is in Acts 21:18. According to tradition, James was martyred by the Jews in Jerusalem in A.D. 62.

Traditionally, this last of the four individuals has been known as the writer of the epistle bearing his name. He was a very devout man, deeply concerned about the careful regulation of the life of one who professed to believe in God. Known also as a man of prayer, he urged the same exercise upon his readers (cf. 5:16-18). His outlook is much the same as that found in the teaching of our Lord. Especially notable is the close similarity between this epistle and the Sermon on the Mount (Matt. 5-7).

What is faith? That is the question James attempts to answer. It is neither an academic nor an irrelevant inquiry. It is one that pierces to the depths of one's heart and to the center of his workaday world.

Outline

Introduction	1:1
The test of faith	1:2-27
The nature of faith	2:1–3:12
The works of faith	3:13–4:17
The application of faith	4:13–5:20

Purpose and Content

Surely it is worthy of notice that in an epistle dealing much with testing and suffering the opening words include "all joy" (1:2). Joy is a result of life with God. There are over four hundred instances of vocabulary relating to biblical joy. Joy comes from God and furthers the Christian's sanctification, especially during trials.

The chief purpose of trial is that it might bring about endurance (the literal meaning of "patience" in this passage) and completeness (1:3, 4). The word *temptation* (or trial) here has reference to outward pressures that bear hard upon the Christian. They are there by God's permission, designed to test (or prove) his faith and, when overcome, hold promise of reward (1:12). There is also the temptation that arises from within (1:13-15), due to man's own sinful nature, which does not come from God.

True faith is productive. This is due to its vital character—that which is alive is active. James discusses this important facet of truth under the subject of "faith and works" (2:14-26). The key statement is found in 2:14—"What *doth it* profit, my brethren, though a man say he hath faith, and have not works? can faith save him?" The expression "that faith" (ASV) has reference, not to faith in general, but a particular kind of faith, namely that which does not produce anything. James is saying if a man's life is barren of good works, we can only conclude that there is no genuine faith in God present. From the human point of view, then, faith must be shown to be known.

While this passage has often been set over against Paul's teaching about faith in Romans 4, the two really complement, rather than contradict, each other. In Romans, God knew that Abraham's faith was genuine because he looked on his heart; in James, men only knew Abraham's faith was genuine when they saw his good works as evidence. It seems that Paul himself puts the two elements together when he writes of faith working through love (Gal. 5:6).

James goes on from this point to show the relevance of all this to the life of one who professes to have faith in Christ. His injunctions such as on the use of the tongue (chap. 3), on business plans (chap. 4), and on prayer (chap. 5) are of a most practical nature.

HEBREWS

Theme

The central plea of this epistle is for the believer to "go on unto perfection" (6:1), not to digress or turn back to his former ways. On the one hand, solemn warnings are interspersed throughout the letter showing the danger of neglect, unbelief, immaturity, and apostasy. One is not to turn away from the truth and the privileges of the Gospel. On the other hand, the superiority of Christ is emphasized to a degree not found in any other book in the New Testament. He stands above men, angels, and ceremonies—He is the final revelation of God (1:2) and the mediator of a new and better covenant (8:6).

Authorship

One of the outstanding questions attached to Hebrews is the matter of authorship. The name of the author is absent from the letter, and all attempts to give a final answer have fallen short. Since about the fourth century the name of Paul has often been associated with it. One may point to the similarities with Paul's known epistles, such as the reference to Timothy (13:23); the request for prayer (13:18, 19; cf. Phil. 2:23, 24); the use of the phrase "the just shall live by faith" (10:38; cf. Rom. 1:17; Gal. 3:11), together with the great emphasis on the subject of faith.

Due to other features of the epistle, however, many have suggested other authors. The general style of the writing and the approach to the subject are not characteristically Pauline. The constant use of the Septuagint (the Greek version of the Old Testament) in quotations, the polished grammar, the view of the Law as "a shadow" (10:1) rather than "a curse" (Gal. 3:13), look away from Pauline authorship. Thus the names of Barnabas, Luke, and Apollos have all been suggested by scholars in early or later times. Usually such discussions end with the use of the famous statement by Origen of Alexandria (third century): "Who it was that wrote the epistle, God alone knows certainly."

Despite the uncertainty as to the human author, the grandeur of the epistle remains unmarred. It is a matchless presentation of the glories of Christ, the Redeemer, High Priest, and Changeless One (cf. 1:3; 2:17; 4:14-16; 7:25; 10:11-13; 13:8). The superiority of Christ and of the life of faith constitute the dual theme of the book.

Outline

Purpose and Content

The opening statement of the epistle gathers the whole of the biblical revelation. God has spoken in the prophets—the Old Testament; and He has spoken in (His) Son—the New Testament. The very height of revelation came in the One who is also described as (1) Heir, (2) Creator, (3) Deity, (4) Preserver, and (5) Redeemer (1:2, 3). Now He resides at "the right hand of the throne of the Majesty in the heavens" as our High Priest (8:1).

Thus Christ appears as superior to the angels, for He is their Creator (1:4–2:18); to Moses and Joshua, for He is the Master over the servant (3:1–4:13); to Aaron and his successors, for He is the Great High Priest overshadowing the lesser priests (4:14–7:28). The New Covenant, of which Christ is mediator, is superior to the Old (8:1-13), and His sacrifice is superior to the ceremonial offerings of bulls and goats (9:1–10:18).[1]

The second major division (10:9–13:25) concerns faith as the superior way of life. Chapters 11 and 12 are especially outstanding here. The former shows in what ways the faith of the saints of the Old Testament was tested; the latter shows why our faith is tested. The "heroes of faith" showed what it meant to walk with God, to live and die in dependence on His promises. Christ is the greatest example of all—"the author and finisher of *our* faith" (12:2). We are to consider Him (12:3) and learn that God, in permitting trials and in chastising us, is dealing "with [us] as with sons" (12:7) to bring us to maturity and, ultimately, perfection.

Along with the two major emphases of the epistle are included the warning sections. While expositors differ as to precise interpretations, none fail to recognize the serious nature of these words. All the warnings could well be summed up in the words of 12:25, "See that ye refuse not him (God) that speaketh."[2]

Generally speaking, the warnings grow more severe and more climactic as the letter proceeds. The first warns of neglect (2:1-4); the last cautions against absolute refusal to heed what God has spoken (12:25-29). In terms of descriptive language, the two most harsh may well be those of 5:11–6:20 and 10:26-31. The one who "fell away" cannot be renewed to repentance; the one who "sins willfully" after knowing the truth is left without any sacrifice for sins.[3] The antidote to such perils is given in the exhortations of the book. There are thirteen expressions in all, urging the believer to grow in faith and to press forward instead of going backward in his spiritual experience (4:1, 11, 14, 16; 6:1; 10:22, 23, 24; 12:1 twice, 28; 13:13, 15).

I PETER

Background

Written to "the strangers who scattered throughout Pontus, Galatia, Cappadocia, Asia, and Bithynia" (1:1), the first Epistle of Peter gives a ray of hope in the darkness to those suffering affliction and persecution. The word *suffering* is used ten times with reference to the lot of the Christian (2:19, 20; 3:14, 17; 4:1, 13, 15, 19; 5:9, 10).[4] In addition the word *temptation* or *trial* occurs in two crucial passages—1:6 and 4:12, respectively. What is the Christian to do and think in the face of such conditions? Peter's answer is given by his use of the word *hope,* found in 1:3, 13, 21; 3:5, 15, and by the assurance that God has a very definite purpose in permitting these difficulties in our lives.

Author

The name Peter is one already familiar to the reader of the historical books of the New Testament. He played a major part in the earthly ministry of our Lord and was the leader of the Jerusalem church in the first twelve chapters of Acts. A fisherman of Bethsaida, close to the Sea of Galilee in northern Palestine (John 1:44), Peter was the older brother of Andrew. He was first brought to Jesus by his brother (John 1:40-42), and it was prophesied by the Lord at that time that the old, unstable Simon would one day be the new, rock-like Peter. Peter was called from his fishing boat to become a fisher of men (Mark 1:16-18; Luke 5:1-11). Finally, in Mark 3:13-16, he was called and chosen as one of the Twelve to accompany the Lord and to carry on an evangelistic ministry. As one of the inner circle, together with James and John, he accompanied Christ at a number of important events: the raising of Jairus's daughter (Luke 8:54); the Transfiguration scene (Luke 9:28); and on the crucifixion eve in the Garden of Gethsemane (Matt. 26:37). Being overconfident regarding his undying loyalty to his Lord, Peter soon denied Him (John 13:36-38; 18:15-27), but was afterward graciously restored to fellowship and commissioned to follow and serve Christ once again (1 Cor. 15:5; John 21:15-19). As the leader of the early church in Jerusalem, Peter appears as a fearless preacher, defender, and administrator. That he did learn his lesson is evident from the reading of this letter. It abounds with references to faithfulness, the care of a shepherd for the sheep, and the responsibilities of the Christian toward his Lord and his fellow Christians. Thus, out of a full life, Peter, now an old man, writes to believers who are beset by trials and sufferings. He had found the Lord sufficient; now he exhorts these people to cast all their anxieties upon Him because He cares for them (5:7).

Outline

Salutation	1:1, 2
Perspective and suffering	1:3–2:10
Pressure and suffering	2:11–4:6
Service and suffering	4:7-11
Witness and suffering	4:12-19
Personal attitudes and suffering	5:1-11
Conclusion	5:12-14

Purpose and Content

The Christian life is never described as a bed of roses. In fact, Peter states, amid the sufferings that were then present, "For even hereunto were ye called: because Christ also suffered for us, leaving us an example, that ye should follow in his steps" (2:21). For what reasons are such things permitted by the Lord? They are meant to prove our faith that we may "be found unto praise and honour and glory at the appearing of Jesus Christ" (1:7). It is actually a privilege to "suffer for righteousness' sake" (3:14); our Lord has suffered on this account (2:21; 4:1). Partaking of Christ's sufferings will result in rejoicing at His coming (4:13). There is suffering that is "according to the will of God," which is meant to bring a committal of our souls "in well doing, as unto a faithful Creator" (4:19). That is to say, God knows what He is doing. We are to continue to do well despite our circumstances. We have been called as God's children to share His glory. He Himself shall "make you perfect, stablish, strengthen, settle *you*" (5:10).

Countering this emphasis is the note of hope.[5] What comfort this affords to the Christian. God has begotten us "unto a living hope" (1:3), and has reserved an inheritance for us in heaven (1:4), and is guarding us in view of that day (1:5). Our hope is on the grace of God and on God Himself (1:13, 21; 3:5). Even as He raised Christ from the dead, so we also shall be caught up to glory. The hope within us, being laid hold of by faith, becomes so real that people around us inquire concerning it (3:15). Thus the very hardships we face become opportunities for witnessing for Christ.

Peter's use of the imperative mood of the verb in his epistle is noteworthy, together with participles used in the sense of commands. By such devices he has attempted to impress upon his readers that living for God makes real demands upon us. This positive injunction is to guide us and form us unto the day of Christ's appearing.[6] It is an application of Christ's word in the second Gospel, "Thou shalt love the Lord thy God with all thy heart, and with all thy soul, and with all thy mind, and with all thy strength . . . (and) thou shalt love thy neighbour as thyself" (Mark 12:30, 31). We show our love by obeying His commands (cf. 1 Pet. 1:22).

DISCUSSION QUESTIONS

1. On what important subject is James a treatise?
2. According to James, what are some aspects of daily living that should be affected by our faith?
3. Give a brief background of the probable writer of the book of James.
4. Compare and show the relationship of James's teaching on faith with Paul's teaching on the subject in Romans 4.

5. In what ways is the book of Hebrews similar to Paul's known epistles?
6. What is the dual theme of the book of Hebrews?
7. To whom is Christ considered superior in the book of Hebrews?
8. Briefly summarize the ministry of Peter prior to Christ's death.
9. Summarize Peter's teaching concerning suffering as found in 1 Peter.

APPLICATION ACTIVITIES

1. Compare and contrast the lives of Peter and James.
2. What important lessons should be learned from the warnings of Hebrews?
3. List some practical problems found in most Christians' lives that are answered in these epistles. Indicate where each answer is found.
4. To understand more fully the differences between "law" and "grace" or "faith" and "works," expand activity #2 of chapter 7 by indicating specific contrasts between them in the book of Hebrews.
5. Prepare a summary of the character and ministry of Christ as presented in the book of Hebrews. -OR- Expand your chart prepared for chapter 1, activity #1.
6. List the characteristics of today's true Christian as portrayed in these epistles.

Chapter Eleven

THE CHURCH AND FALSE TEACHING

2 Peter, Jude, and 1—3 John

THE LAST FIVE New Testament Epistles, three of them containing only one brief chapter each, are linked together by their common concern with false teaching in the realm of Christian doctrine and ethics. Second Peter and Jude warn against those who scorn the authority of the Lord and His Word. Like false teachers in the Old Testament, they will taste the judgment of God coming upon them. The three letters ascribed to John, though like Hebrews in their anonymity, are written against the malignant influence of Gnosticism, which at this date (late first century) was beginning to show itself as a system of teaching. Professing to possess superior, mystic knowledge leading to salvation, the teaching of the Gnostics set forth strange views of Christ and the nature of creation. John calls it the "*spirit* of antichrist" (1 John 4:1-3).

2 PETER

Authorship

The early church was slow in acknowledging 2 Peter to be on the same level with the other books that came to compose the New Testament canon. A number of contrasts with 1 Peter are readily noticed, such as the lack of specific address (as in 1 Pet. 1:1), the rough grammatical character and style of writing, and in addition, the striking similarities of language between chapter 2 and the Epistle of Jude. Yet it should be remembered that the book was recognized as canonical by the Council of Laodicea in A.D. 363 and the Council of Carthage in A.D. 397.

    The internal evidence for Petrine authorship is much more definite. The writer calls himself "Simon Peter, a servant and apostle of Jesus Christ" (1:1). The name Simon (or Simeon) is reminiscent of Peter's original name (cf. John 1:42; Acts 15:14). There are many autobiographical references in the letter. The author recalls the Transfiguration experience (1:16-18; cf. Mark 9:2-8). He uses a fisherman's word, *enticing,* in 2:14, 18 (ASV). In 3:1, he makes reference to this letter as "this second epistle" he had written to these readers. Further, he is one with his readers in having obtained similarly precious faith.

Theme

The key word of the epistle is *knowledge,* which occurs twelve times in its various forms (1:2, 3, 5, 6, 8, 16, 20; 2:20, 21; 3:3, 17, 18). In a letter that aims to combat false teaching, the knowledge of the truth is the key idea. Together with this, Peter stresses the importance of remembering certain things (1:12, 13; 3:1) and shows the danger of forgetting important truths (1:9; 3:8). Thus, throughout the letter, the teachings of the Word of God are represented as true and normative for the Christian life.

Outline

Introduction	1:1, 2
Knowledge and the Christian life	1:3-11
Knowledge and the Word of God	1:12-21
Knowledge and the false teaching	2:1-22
Knowledge and the Second Coming	3:1-13
Conclusion—Steadfastness and growth	3:14-18

Purpose and Content

God has made full provision for the spiritual life of the believer (1:3). Thus, the believer's responsibility is to avail himself of the divine resources so that he will be neither "barren nor unfruitful in the knowledge of our Lord Jesus Christ" (1:8). This is Peter's opening thought in the epistle, and by means of these statements he prepares the way for his main arguments.

First, the Word of God given by the Holy Spirit (1:20, 21) is that to which we should give heed (1:19). Because its source is divine, its message is authoritative. It should be stressed that the chief thrust of the statement in 1:20, 21 is regarding the origin, not the meaning, of Scripture. It came not "by the will of man" but "by the Holy Ghost."

Second, the path taken by the false teachers, who deny "the Lord that bought them," leads toward certain judgment (2:1) and "the latter end is worse with them than the beginning" (2:20). Those who follow them can expect nothing better. The sure judgment of God upon the sinners of the Old Testament (2:4, 5, 6, 15) is a solemn warning to all.

Third, the Second Coming of Christ will be God's vindication of His name and purpose, and "the day of the Lord" will be the day of judgment for the scoffers of the world (chap. 3). Those who deny the reality of this event forget "this one thing," says Peter, "that one day is with the Lord as a thousand years, and a thousand years as one day" (3:8). Only because God is longsuffering, "not willing that any should perish," do the scoffers even remain to carry on their false ways (3:9).

This final message leaves a challenge with the readers of the letter. "Wherefore, beloved, seeing that ye look for such things, be diligent that ye may be found of him in peace, without spot, and blameless . . . But grow in grace, and in the knowledge of our Lord and Savior Jesus Christ. To him be the glory both now and for ever" (3:14, 18).

JUDE

The letter that was to have been written concerning "our common faith" turned out, by constraint upon the writer, to be an exhortation to "earnestly contend for the faith" (v. 3). One of the chief differences between Jude and 2 Peter seems to be that while Peter warned that "there shall be false teachers" (2:1), Jude states that "there are certain men crept in unawares" (v. 4). One anticipates the problem, while the other realizes it as a present reality. Apparently, then, this epistle is somewhat later than 2 Peter. If Peter is dated about A.D. 65-67, Jude might be placed at A.D. 75-85.

Authorship

Jude was a "brother of James" and seems to fit into the pattern sketched earlier (chapter ten of James). Christ and James were recorded as having a brother named Jude (Matt. 13:55). James and Jude along with Jesus' other brothers appear as believers in Acts 1:14, and the author writes now as "a servant of Jesus Christ" (Jude 1).

Theme

As he begins to write, the author uses the interesting expression, "the faith which was once delivered unto the saints" (v. 3).[1] Here "the faith" has reference to "the body of doctrine" held in common by the church at that time. There is a note of finality about it—"which was once delivered." God has committed the Gospel to the church to be kept inviolate, as a trust (cf. Gal. 1:6-9; 1 Tim. 1:19; 6:3, 20, 21; 2 Tim. 1:13, 14). Doctrine, however, is not to be held in detachment from life. Correct teaching must result in holy living, else the practical purpose is lost. This is the error Jude combats—a kind of antinomianism or lawless libertinism that results in a denial of the rightful place of Christ in the life of the individual (v. 4).

Outline

Salutation	1, 2
Exhortation—Defense of the faith	3, 4
Illustration—Departures from the faith	5-16
Admonition—Progress in the faith	17-23
Conclusion—A doxology	24, 25

Purpose and Content

Jude, along with 2 Peter 2, turns to the Old Testament for illustrations of godlessness and makes clear God's judgment upon all such persons. A comparison of the two is as follows.

Ref.	Jude	Ref.	2 Peter 2
v. 5	Israel in the wilderness	____	_____
v. 6	The angels who fell	v. 4	The angels who fell
____	_____	v. 5	Sodom and Gomorrah
v. 11	The way of Cain	____	_____
v. 11	The error of Balaam	v. 15	The way of Balaam
v. 11	The disputing of Korah	____	_____

Jude employed these illustrations for a number of specific reasons.

First, he used them as a means of informing his readers of the serious consequences of unbelief. Israel illustrates unbelief (v. 5); the fallen angels illustrate disobedience (v. 6); Sodom and Gomorrah illustrate moral defilement (v. 7).

Second, Jude thus depicted the character of the false teachers of whom he warns his readers. Cain is a picture of willfulness, Balaam of greed, and Korah of presumption (v. 11).[2]

Third, by way of anticipation, Jude tells what will be the end of the false teachers. Using a quotation from the Jewish work, *The Book of Enoch*, he illustrates what God will do to these "ungodly sinners" (v. 14, 15).

In the face of all such dangers, the personal responsibility of the believer is (1) to remember the apostles' teaching (v. 17) and (2) to keep himself in the love of God (v. 21). This latter injunction is linked with a number of participial clauses: (a) building himself up in most holy faith (v. 20), (b) praying in the Holy Spirit (v. 20), and (c) looking for the mercy of our Lord Jesus Christ unto eternal life (v. 21). Along with these, the believer's responsibility to others is (1) to have mercy on some (v. 22, 23) and (2) to save some out of the fire (v. 23).

I JOHN

Background

John writes against the Gnostics who denied the reality of our Lord's humanity as well as His deity. John's epistles, especially the first, are powerful weapons against such heresies, whether in old or modern dress.

This letter is closely related to his Gospel (see chapter 4). Both concern the Lord Jesus and the eternal life that comes to those who trust in Him (John 20:30, 31; 1 John 5:13). The Gospel gives the declaration of salvation; the letter, the assurance of it. Both speak of "the Word," the term used for Christ as the revealer of God.[3] The vocabulary of the books is similar, both employing such important words as *beginning* (cf. 1:1 in each); *witness* (thirty-three times in John, six times in 1 John); *believe* (ninety-eight times and nine times); *eternal life* (John 3:15; 1 John 1:2); *love* (John 3:16; 1 John 4:9); *abide* (John 15:4; 1 John 2:28); and many others.

All of John's writings are usually dated near the end of the first century, somewhere between A.D. 85-95. Thus, as an old man, he looks back to his experiences with his Lord, upon which he had long meditated, and also at the current problems of the church.

Purpose and Content

John writes to define the nature of the person of Christ in the face of heretical teachings afflicting the church near the end of the first century. The general name given to this teaching was Gnosticism, a religio-philosophic school basically characterized by the idea that only spirit was good and matter was evil. As in other Greek and Oriental religious systems, the Gnostics believed that one must free himself from the material world and be occupied alone with spirit. The way of escape, for the Gnostics, was the way of superior knowledge. By learning the mysterious secrets of the universe, the initiate of the cult could supposedly attain freedom.

With regard to the teachings of Christianity, the opposition of this heresy centered in the person of Christ. Obviously, if matter (which involved the human body) was evil, God could not be manifest in the flesh, else He would be defiled. Therefore, Christ's humanity was not real; the disciples only saw a phantom; Christ only seemed to be real. If, as others taught, Jesus was truly man, the Christ-spirit did not actually unite with Him, except for the brief time between the baptism and the crucifixion.[4] This was, therefore, a denial of His deity.

When one becomes aware of these prevalent false claims, many of John's statements in the first epistle take on new meaning. John combats Docetism (see note 4) by his insistence on the reality of the humanity of Christ (1:1-3; 4:1-3). He utters severe words against Cerinthianism (see note 4) by emphasizing the fact that Jesus is the Christ, the Son of God (1:3, 7; 2:22, 23; 3:23; 4:15; 5:1, 20). This epistle should serve as a final answer to a heresy that persists until the present day.

The primary purpose of the epistle, as stated by John himself, is given in 5:13: "These things have I written unto you . . . that ye may know that ye have eternal life, and that ye may believe on the name of the Son of God." His remarks are addressed to "the children of God," those who have been "begotten of God." Thus it is a family letter and the word *fellowship* is used by John to describe the ideal relationship between God and His children (cf. 1:3, 6, 7).

Outline

Introduction—The reality of fellowship	1:1-4
The requirements for fellowship	1:5-10
The victorious character of fellowship	2:1-17
The enemies of fellowship	2:18-29
The reasons for fellowship	3:1-12
The tests of fellowship	3:13-24
The discernment of fellowship	4:1-6
The practice of fellowship	4:7-21
The foundation of fellowship	5:1-12
The privileges of fellowship	5:13-21

Characteristic Features

In this letter, John describes God as "light" (1:5) and "love" (4:8). "Light" has reference to God's holiness (cf. James 1:17) and is meant to stress to the believer the need for properly dealing with any sin in his life, that is, anything that would prevent fellowship with his Father. In 1:5–2:2 the remedy is given. The blood of Christ is the basis for cleansing (1:7); confession on the part of the believer is the condition for cleansing (1:9); and forgiveness by God is the accompaniment of cleansing (1:9). Those who deny the presence of a sin nature (1:8) only deceive themselves; those who deny they have committed acts of sin (1:10) make God a liar.

The other descriptive word, "love," refers to God's attitude toward us, and describes His nature (cf. 4:9). We learn the meaning of love by seeing what God has done for us (4:10). As a result of observing God's love, we are not only to love Him, but one another also (4:11).

Notice that John, as he writes, makes use of many contrasting terms and ideas. Things are "either black or white." He speaks in terms of "one or the other." Such passages as 1:6, 7; 2:4, 5, 9, 10, 17, 22, 23; 3:10, 18;

4:2, 3, 20; and 5:12 are outstanding examples of his technique. John's epistle is written to enable us to put our profession to the test.

Among all the New Testament writers, only John uses the now familiar expression "Antichrist." It is introduced in 1 John 2:18, then appears in 2:22; 4:3; and 2 John 7. The meaning of *anti* is "one who takes the place of" or "one who stands against (or opposes)." The essence of the nature of the Antichrist is the denial of the rightful place of the Father and the Son; the Antichrist himself would be supreme in the world. Furthermore, the spirit of antichrist is a denial of the reality of Christ's incarnation, thus attempting to do away with Christ's redemptive work, by which He laid the sentence of death upon Satan himself (cf. Heb. 2:14). "And we know that the Son of God is come, and hath given us an understanding, that we may know him that is true, and we are in him that is true, *even* in his Son" (1 John 5:20).

2 JOHN

Purpose and Content

Second John, together with 3 John, seems to be a sampling of John's personal correspondence. Both letters are addressed to individuals and have to do with a number of personal matters.

The key word of the letter is "truth." John stresses the need for "walking in the truth" (v. 4) because "many deceivers are entered into the world" (v. 7). He who denies the doctrine of Christ is not to be given Christian greetings, lest we find ourselves partaking in "his evil deeds" (v. 10, 11).

Outline

Salutation	1-3
Walking in the truth	4-11
The commandment of the Father	4-6
The message of the deceivers	7-11
Conclusion	12, 13

3 JOHN

Purpose and Content

The recipient of this final epistle of John is called only "well-beloved Gaius" (v. 1). He is identified no further, so must have been well known to the members of the Asian churches where John served during the last years of his life. The name itself was a familiar one, often appearing in the writings of Paul, where we see Gaius (of Corinth) in Romans 16:23, Paul's host in that city; Gaius of Macedonia in Acts 19:29; and Gaius of Derbe in Acts 20:4.

Third John's main theme is hospitality. The letter recognizes the kindnesses of Gaius in showing an open door to Christian workers and strangers alike (v. 5) and encourages him to continue this ministry (v. 6).

John promises to discipline the troublesome Diotrephes, who brazenly excommunicated those in the church who did not recognize his "preeminence" (v. 9, 10). By way of contrast, the man Demetrius is commended by all in the church (v. 12). John's commendation, "good report of all *men*, and of the truth itself," challenges the Christian to walk in truth.

Outline

Salutation	1
Prayer for Gaius's health	2-4
Praise for Gaius's hospitality	5-8
Condemnation of Diotrephes's policy	9-11
Commendation of Demetrius's character	12
Conclusion	13

DISCUSSION QUESTIONS

1. What emphasis is common among the last five New Testament Epistles?
2. How is the theme of 2 Peter emphasized by the writer?
3. What is the teaching of 2 Peter concerning the Scriptures?
4. Compare 2 Peter and Jude in reference to their statements concerning false teachers.
5. What illustrations of Old Testament godlessness are used by both Peter and Jude?
6. Compare the similarities of emphases by John in 1 John and his Gospel.
7. Justify calling 1 John a family letter.
8. What attitudes and teachings characterize the spirit of antichrist?
9. What was John's purpose in writing 2 and 3 John?

APPLICATION ACTIVITIES

1. Show from 1 John the tests by which a person today can know whether or not he is truly a Christian.
2. Compare present-day error with Gnosticism and indicate how 1 John provides answers for those denying Christ's deity or bodily existence.
3. From 2 Peter and 1 John, expand your findings on the true Christian in chapter 10, activity #6.
4. Without the use of aids, prepare an outline for one of the epistles studied in this chapter.

Chapter Twelve

BOOK OF THE
REVELATION

THE BOOK OF THE REVELATION, like the book of Daniel in the Old Testament, is apocalyptic. The term *apocalyptic* means "to unveil" or "to uncover;" thus, "to reveal" something that has been beforehand veiled, covered, or hidden. Several characteristics of apocalyptic writing are worthy of mention. Apocalyptic writing . . .

IS USUALLY WRITTEN IN TIMES OF TROUBLE AND DISTRESS

This is seen in both Daniel and Revelation. In Daniel, the days of the Babylonian captivity are vividly portrayed. In Revelation, the central issue is the beginnings of the conflict between the Roman Empire and the Church.

CONVEYS ITS MESSAGE BY MEANS OF SIGNS, SYMBOLS, DREAMS, AND VISIONS

John writes in Revelation 1:1 that his message was "sent and signified" (i.e., portrayed by the use of "signs," or physical figures having spiritual meanings attached to them). Within the framework of four great visions, John presents the main outlines of his message.

GIVES PROMISE OF THE EVENTUAL TRIUMPH OF GOOD OVER EVIL

By the appearance of the kingdom of God, together with the heavenly Lord (cf. "KING OF KINGS AND LORD OF LORDS," Rev. 19:16) as the sovereign ruler of the creation, all things shall be subjected to God's will (cf. Dan. 2:44; Rev. 11:15).

Despite the fact that the Revelation seems to many to be strange and foreboding, and thus is often neglected, the Revelation is the only book in the New Testament containing the promise of blessing to "he that readeth, and they that hear the words of this prophecy, and keep those things which are written therein" (1:3; cf. Josh. 1:7, 8). In addition, the book closes with a serious warning to any who would add to or take away from the contents of the prophecy (22:18, 19). Above all, it must be emphasized that this book is, according to its own statement, "the Revelation of Jesus Christ, which God gave unto him, to shew unto his servants" (1:1). With such character attached to it by so plain a statement, the contents are worthy of the diligent study of every believer.

Background

By reading the book itself, one sees readily that persecution and trouble were already threatening the Church. Serious problems were in evidence both from without and within. The church of Ephesus was commended for her endurance and discernment of evil men (2:2); the church of Smyrna would have tribulation ten days (2:10); in Pergamum, Antipas was martyred (2:13); "great tribulation" hung over Thyatira (2:22); and the church in Philadelphia was promised the Lord's protection amid the hour of trial (3:10).

The date of the writing of Revelation was about A.D. 90-95. During the first century, the Roman emperors held sway over the world, from Augustus to Domitian. All the Roman persecutions before the days of the Emperor Decius (A.D. 250) were local in nature. The Christians in certain places began to feel the sting of official opposition in A.D. 64, then again, it seems, during Domitian's time. The exile of John to Patmos was just one example of the present and impending tribulations spoken of within the Revelation (1:9).

Would this be the lot of the Church forever? Was it possible that Satan and his evil agents would win the victory? The book gives a decisive answer. The dragon would be cast down from heaven (12:9), and the saints would overcome him (12:11). Eventually, the dragon and his kind would be cast into "the lake of fire" (19:20; 20:10). Thus, God would be supreme and the Church established forever, "as a bride adorned for her husband" (21:2). Even as the Lord Jesus had said, so it would be: "the gates of hell shall not prevail against it" (Matt. 16:18).

Methods of Interpretation

Before attempting to investigate the details of the book, it is necessary to establish some methods of approaching it. Bible scholars recognize four basic methods.

THE PRETERIST METHOD

This approach asserts that the events in Revelation belong to the first century, and have, therefore, long ago been fulfilled. It maintains a past perspective. There is no prophetic or future aspect to the book. According to the preterist method, the setting for the visions was the existing conflict between the Church and Rome in the age of the apostles (i.e., up to A.D. 100).

This view emphasizes the relevance of the book to the churches to which it was written (1:11), but it hardly seems in keeping with the professed forward look of John's message, which specifically presents predictions of things to come (cf. 1:3, 19; 22:18, 19).

THE HISTORICIST METHOD

This approach sees the Revelation as a picture book of the conflict between the Church and the world (energized by Satan) from the time of the apostles until the end of the age. The approach gives full recognition to the relationship between the drama of the book and earthly events. The crises that have arisen in world history—the conquerors of past and present—are portrayed herein, and all are doomed to failure.

The major weakness of this method is the difficulty in equating events of the book with events in history. Serious and apparently irreconcilable disagreements between those who hold the view cast doubt upon the validity of the approach as a single solution to the book. Yet it does stress the tangency of the message to the realm of human history.

THE FUTURIST METHOD

With the exception of chapters 1–3, Revelation is viewed as wholly futuristic, depicting the drama that awaits the end of the age, the day of God's wrath, and the appearance of Christ from heaven. The opening section of the book, the letters to the seven churches (chaps. 1–3), is either regarded as limited to the first century or as a kind of sevenfold, symbolic sketch of the spiritual history of the Church from the apostolic age to the Second Advent.

In view of the prophetic language of the book (4:1) and the magnitude of the events predicted in chapters 4–22, this method seems to do greater justice to the interpretation than the previous methods. Yet the possible danger is that the book is thus rendered irrelevant to the first-century recipients of its message and, in a sense, to anyone prior to the end of the age itself. If this tendency is guarded against, the futurist method is of great value.

THE IDEALIST METHOD

This method should be distinguished from the three that have been discussed in that it is not tied to history, that is, the occurrence of literal events. It deals with spiritual, rather than historical, realities. Emphasizing the conflict between God and Satan, good and evil, righteousness and sin, it assures the reader, apart from concern with specific historical situations, that the victory will be won by the forces of right.

Certainly the spirit of the book has been caught by the idealist approach, but the virtual elimination of the historical setting is hardly in keeping with the biblical teaching of God's activity within the realm of human history. The symbolic element should not be the single emphasis; the predictive aspect must be maintained.

None of these approaches to the interpretation of this prophecy is singularly satisfactory. An attempt has been made to state concisely the strengths and weaknesses of all the methods, thus enabling students to cull from each the useful features and use them wisely in their own study. In this task, as in all Bible study, the guidance of the Holy Spirit is essential (1 Cor. 2:6-16; James 1:5).

Structure of the Book

In analyzing the Revelation with regard to its structure, notice that John uses a key phrase four times, thus dividing the book into major divisions based upon four visions that he saw. The phrase "in the Spirit" occurs in 1:10; 4:2; 17:3; and 21:10. It is used in the Old Testament regarding the prophets as they experienced the revelatory ministry of the Holy Spirit, conveying to them the Word of God (cf. Ezek. 3:12; 37:1). The chart that follows will aid in identifying the visions as they appear throughout the book.

Ref.	Location	Vision	Content
1:9–3:22	Patmos	One like unto a Son of Man	Christ as Lord amidst His churches
4:1–16:21	Heaven	The Throne and the Lamb	Christ as the Lamb; wrath of God
17:1–21:8	Wilderness	A Woman and the Beast	Christ as King of Kings and Victor over His enemies
21:9–22:6	Mountain	The New Jerusalem	Christ as Bridegroom with His bride in glory

Outline

The outline for the book is built around the four visions, together with the introduction (1:1-8) and the conclusion (22:6-21). It emphasizes the centrality of Christ throughout the entire portrayal.

Introduction	1:1-8
The first vision—Christ and the seven churches	1:9–3:22

The first vision, in one sense, is easier to understand than those that follow. As the Lord speaks to John (1:9-20) and then to the seven churches (chaps. 2, 3), we find language that, within the context of first-century conditions, is relatively clear. Emphasized here is the sovereignty of the Head as He walks among the lampstands (the churches) and holds the seven stars (the messengers, or leaders, of the churches) within His right hand, the place of authority and honor.

The seven churches of Asia, selected from a greater number then existing, are each analyzed by the Lord, and their spiritual condition is laid bare.[1] Christ follows a general pattern in speaking to each. Two exceptions are notable, however. Each church (as a whole) is commended except two, Sardis and Laodicea. Each church (as a whole) is condemned except two, Smyrna and Philadelphia.[2] The careful study of each letter, giving attention to the background and location of each church, the kinds of things said to each, and the spiritual counsel for the present day, will prove most rewarding.

The framework for the second vision (4:1–16:21) is the description of the three series of judgments upon the earth, each consisting of seven parts.[3] The magnitude of these events is breathtaking, and, whether interpreted literally or symbolically, they impress the reader with the fury of divine vengeance against unrepentant sinners (cf. Rom. 12:19; Heb. 10:30, 31).

In considering the three series of judgments, attention should be called to the problem of the relation of the judgments. Briefly it is this:

do they follow one another (consecutive)? Do they occur within the same period of time and end together (concurrent)? Or, do they all happen at the same time (simultaneous)? Each of the three positions has been adopted by equally sound commentators; no final solution has yet appeared.

Within this general framework a number of parenthetical events occur. They are found in 7:1-8; 7:9-17; 10:1-11; 11:1-13; 12:1-17; 13:1-18; 14:1-5; 14:6-12; 14:13; 14:14-20. These events, for the most part, appear to occur within the same time sequence as the judgments, but concentrate mainly upon persons, both human and angelic, showing their relation to the day of God's wrath.

The third vision (17:1–21:8) gives special attention to the victory of Christ over His enemies. In order of occurrence they are the harlot and the Beast of Babylon; the Beast and the false prophets with their followers; Satan and the rebels of earth; and unregenerate mankind. Thus the way is prepared for "the new heavens and the new earth." A crucial passage within this vision is 20:4-6, picturing the millennial reign of Christ, when He shall be vindicated upon the earth, the place of His rejection (cf. 1 Cor. 15:25-27). The saints shall reign with Him (cf. 1 Cor. 6:2) and shall exercise their function as "priests of God and of Christ."

Finally, in the fourth vision (21:9–22:5) dawns "the new heavens and the new earth." The spotless bride of Christ stands in vivid contrast to the scarlet woman, the harlot of Babylon (chap. 17). The perfections of the New Jerusalem are portrayed by John, centered in the unbroken fellowship between God and His people. With the banishment of death and the appearance of the tree of life, the pristine beauty of Eden reappears (cf. Gen. 2). That which sin has defiled is here restored and purified. Thus God shall be "all in all." The story of redemption is completed.

DISCUSSION QUESTIONS

1. List and illustrate from the Revelation three outstanding characteristics of apocalyptic writings.
2. Why is this book worthy of the diligent study of every believer?
3. Within what framework does John present the main outlines of his message?
4. Give a brief background for John's writing the book of Revelation.
5. Define and comment briefly on four methods of interpreting the Revelation.
6. What three possible views concerning the judgments divide Bible scholars?

7. What enemies of Christ are defeated in Revelation 17–20 in order to prepare the way for the new heavens and the new earth?
8. Briefly summarize the blessings of Revelation 21 and 22.

APPLICATION ACTIVITIES

1. Compare the presentation of the character of Christ in the letters to the seven churches with the depiction of Him in the Epistles.
2. Justify dividing the book into four sections on the basis of the phrase "in the Spirit." Compare our use of the term today.
3. From your Scripture reading give a brief account of the final events and the doom of Satan and his followers.
4. Write a paper of several paragraphs summarizing the message of the New Testament as it applies to your own life.

The Missionary Journeys of Paul

References	Places Visited	Personnel	Main Events	Main Results
First Journey Acts 13:4–14:28	Departure from Antioch (Syria) Seleucia Cyprus: Salamis Paphos Pamphylia: Perga Galatia: Antioch (Pisidia) Iconium Lystra Derbe Return to Antioch (Syria)	Paul Barnabas John Mark	Contest with Elymas at Paphos Sermon in synagogue at Antioch (Pisidia) Paul and Barnabas worshiped at Lystra Paul preaches, then is stoned at Lystra	Conversion of Sergius Paulus at Paphos Conversions and riot at Antioch (Pisidia) Churches founded and established in all Galatian cities; elders appointed Report of journey to the church in Antioch (Syria)
Second Journey Acts 15:36–18:22	Departure from Antioch (Syria) Syria and Cilicia Galatia: Derbe and Lystra Troas Macedonia: Philippi Thessalonica Berea Achaia: Athens Corinth Caesarea Return to Antioch (Syria)	Paul Silas Timothy (Luke)	Timothy added to party at Lystra Vision at Troas; Luke added to party Preaching and imprisonment at Philippi Preaching and persecution at Thessalonica Preaching at Berea Sermon on Mars' Hill in Athens Eighteen-month stay at Corinth, teaching, trial before Gallio Short stay at Ephesus, preaching	Conversion of Lydia and the jailer at Philippi; church founded Church founded at Thessalonica Conversion of Dionysius and Damaris at Athens Church founded at Corinth
Third Journey Acts 18:23–21:14	Departure from Antioch (Syria) Galatia and Phrygia Asia: Ephesus Macedonia Greece Macedonian cities Troas Asia: Melitus Syria: Tyre Ptolemais Caesarea Jerusalem	Paul Silas Timothy (Luke) Gaius Aristarchus Sopater Secundus Tychicus Trophimus	Teaching ministry in Ephesus (2–3 years) Riot of the Ephesian silversmiths Preaching at Troas Eutychus restored to life Farewell to the Ephesian elders at Miletus Warning to Paul at Tyre regarding Jerusalem Warning to Paul at Caesarea by Agabus regarding Jerusalem	Church established at Ephesus; center of evangelization of Asia Instruction to the Ephesian elders regarding official duties

The Letters to the Seven Churches of Asia

Church	Ephesus 2:1-7	Smyrna 2:8-11	Pergamum 2:12-17	Thyatira 2:18-29	Sardis 3:1-6	Philadelphia 3:7-13	Laodicea 3:14-22
Character of Christ	Sovereign Lord 2:1	Risen Lord 2:8	Warring Lord 2:12, 16	Judging Lord 2:18	Omniscient Lord 3:1	Authoritative Lord 3:7	Divine Lord 3:14
Commendation	Orthodoxy 2:2	Endurance 2:9	Faithfulness 2:13	Industry 2:19	(none?)	Endurance 3:10	(none)
Condemnation	Coldness 2:4	(none)	False Teaching 2:14, 15	Unfaithfulness 2:20	Unreality 3:1	(none)	Lukewarmness 3:15, 16
Counsel	Remember, repent, repeat first works 2:5	Be watchful unto death 2:10	Repent 2:16	Repent hold fast 2:22, 25	Be watchful; remember, repent 3:2, 3	Hold fast 3:11	Buy gold, garments, eyesalve 3:18, 19
Caution	Removal 2:5	(none)	War 2:16	Death 2:23	Invasion 3:3	(none)	Separation 3:16
Covenant with Overcomer	Eat of the tree of life 2:7	Not hurt by the second death 2:11	Hidden manna, white stone, new name 2:17	Rulership; morning star 2:26-28	White garments; name kept and confessed 3:5	New position; new name 3:12	Share Christ's throne 3:21

The Three Series of Judgments

	Seal Judgments	Trumpet Judgments	Vial Judgments
1	6:1, 2 Rider on a white horse Carried a bow Wore a crown *Object:* To conquer	8:7 Hail, fire, and blood on the earth *Result:* 1/3 part earth, 1/3 part trees, all green grass burned up	16:2 Poured into earth *Result:* Noisome and grievous sore upon worshipers of the Beast
2	6:3, 4 Rider on a red horse Carried a great sword *Object:* To take peace from the earth	8:8, 9 Fiery mountain cast into the sea *Result:* 1/3 of sea blood, 1/3 of sea creatures die, 1/3 of ships destroyed	16:3 Poured into the sea *Result:* All sea-life died
3	6:5, 6 Rider on a black horse Carried a balance *Object:* Produce famine conditions	8:10, 11 Burning star falls upon earth—named Wormwood *Result:* 1/3 of waters made bitter; many men die	16:4-7 Poured in rivers and sources of waters *Result:* Water became blood; revenge on murderers
4	6:7, 8 Rider on a pale horse Death followed by Hades *Object:* To kill by sword, famine, death, and wild beasts	8:12 Celestial disturbances *Result:* 1/3 of heavenly bodies darkened; day and night affected	16:8, 9 Poured upon the sun *Result:* Men scorched with fire; blasphemed God
5	6:9-11 Souls of martyrs under the altar *Object:* To cry for revenge against their murderers	9:1-11 Star (ruler) falls to earth; opens the pit; locusts emerge, led by Apollyon *Result:* Men tormented 5 months; unable to die	16:10, 11 Poured upon the throne of the beast *Result:* Kingdom darkened; men in pain; did not repent
6	6:12-17 Seismic and celestial disturbances *Object:* Day of God's wrath upon the earth	9:13-22 Four angels at Euphrates released; armies of horsemen proceed *Result:* 1/3 of men killed by horses that breathe fire, smoke, and brimstone	16:12-16 Poured upon Euphrates River *Result:* River dried up; eastern kings advance to Har-Magedon (Armageddon)
7	8:1, 2 Silence in heaven for a half-hour *Object:* Preparation for sounding of seven trumpets	11:15-19 Great voices in heaven and 24 elders sing praise to God *Result:* God's kingdom supreme over the earth	16:17-21 Poured upon the air *Result:* Voice announces "It is done;" disturbances and plague of hail; men blaspheme God

NOTES

1 BACKGROUND AND COMPOSITION OF THE NEW TESTAMENT

1. Others place the epistle later, about A.D. 62. If the early date is correct, it would give a date of only about fifteen years after the death of Christ.

3 GOSPEL OF JOHN

1. The most common words in the other Gospels are "powers" and "wonders." The former denotes the display of supernatural power in doing the miracle; the latter emphasizes the effect of the miracle upon the people—it left them awestruck.

4 BOOK OF ACTS

1. Chapter twelve is a glimpse into the persecution of some of the church leaders. James, the brother of John, was killed, and Peter was imprisoned. When released, Peter left the city, and James, the brother of Christ, became the leader of the Jerusalem church.

2. Between the record of the first and second journeys is the narrative of the Jerusalem Council. This council was occasioned by the teaching of certain men that the Gentiles must observe the Jewish law (cf. 15:19-21, 28, 29).

5 PAULINE EPISTLES: 1 AND 2 THESSALONIANS

1. The two prominent Rabbinical schools dated back to Hillel and Shammai. Hillel allowed his students greater freedom in their education, even to the reading of Greek writers.

2. Possibly Galatians 1:23 hints at a preaching ministry during these silent years, but the evidence is scant.

3. 1 Corinthians 5:9 indicates at least one such instance.

4. Although Galatians belongs in this group on the basis of its subject matter, it may well have been written earlier. Some place it as early as A.D. 48/49, others about A.D. 52/53. The date, however, does not affect its teaching.

5. The word translated "coming" in these passages literally meant "presence" in first-century usage (cf. 2 Cor. 10:10). But it also came to mean "arrival" and was used of the coming of a dignitary to some part of his domain.

6 PAULINE EPISTLES: 1 AND 2 CORINTHIANS

1. These are matters that relate to personal habits and scruples and for which Scripture allows liberty, i.e., habits of eating, dress, the use of time and such. See also Romans 14:1–15:13.

7 PAULINE EPISTLES: GALATIANS AND ROMANS

1. The Gospel came to him from Christ (1:12); he also has a new relationship to Christ (2:20).

2. The word *present* denotes an act of sacrifice; the words *be transformed* represent a process—a continual change from within. The latter is the basis for our English word *metamorphosis*.

8 THE PAULINE EPISTLES: COLOSSIANS, PHILEMON, EPHESIANS, PHILIPPIANS

1. "Put that to mine account" was a standard expression in bookkeeping in the first century. It referred to making an entry in the ledger. Sometimes the word is translated "reckon" (cf. Rom. 4:3-5).

2. Notice in this paragraph the repetition of the phrase "the praise of his glory" (1:6, 12, 14), distinguishing the work of the Father (v. 3-6), the Son (v. 7-12), and the Holy Spirit (v. 13, 14) in the creation of the Church.

3. In Colossians Paul gives most attention to the servant-master relationship (cf. Paul's letter to Philemon).

4. The term "wiles" (v. 11) is literally "strategy" or "methods" or "plans of attack." The companion expression, "fiery darts" (v. 16), refers to attacks of Satan upon the Christian.

9 PAULINE EPISTLES: 1 TIMOTHY, TITUS, 2 TIMOTHY

1. For a readable discussion, see D. Guthrie, *The Pastoral Epistles,* 11-52. A slightly more technical approach is taken by W. Hendricksen in *Exposition of the Pastoral Epistles,* 4-33.

10 THE CHURCH AND SUFFERING

1. The priestly and sacrificial system of the Old Testament (especially in the books of Exodus and Leviticus) forms the background for a proper understanding of Hebrews. This is particularly true in 4:14–10:18. Christ is presented as the High Priest who has no successor (chap. 7), the mediator of the New Covenant which has no terminal point (chap. 8), and the spotless sacrifice who, by His once-for-all offering, has dealt with sin completely and finally (chaps. 9 and 10).

2. See the outline for the character of each of the seven warnings.

3. The interpretation of these warning sections will be affected by the view one takes of the spiritual state of the recipients of the letter. Three major views are current: (1) they were only professing Christians, but never truly regenerated, and were in danger of "stopping short of salvation"; (2) they were believers, but could lose salvation by failing to maintain faith in Christ; (3) they were believers who were in danger of lapsing into a life of barrenness and uselessness, thus losing any reward.

4. It is also used with regard to Christ in 1:11; 2:21, 23; 3:18; 4:1, 13; 5:10—a total of seven times.

5. Notice also the occurrences of the word "grace" in the epistle—1:2, 10, 13; 2:19, 20; "acceptable"—3:7; 4:10; gift—5:5, 10, 12.

6. There are over thirty such statements in this short epistle. See M. C. Tenney, *New Testament Survey*, rev. ed., 351, 352.

11 THE CHURCH AND FALSE TEACHING: 2 PETER, JUDE, 1, 2, AND 3 JOHN

1. The same word is used to characterize the redemptive work of Christ in Hebrews 9:12; 10:10.

2. Jude also includes the devil as an example of blasphemy (v. 9, 10), although the incident is not included in any Old Testament book. It is taken from a Jewish intertestamental work and is used here as a graphic illustration of his characterization of the false teachers.

3. Even as the spoken word reveals the thought of the person, so the Lord Jesus revealed the Father (cf. John 1:18; 1 John 1:1, 2).

4. The former of these beliefs was called Docetism from the Greek word *dokeo*, "to seem (to be)"; the latter was called Cerinthianism, after the name of its champion, Cerinthus. Tradition informs us that John knew Cerinthus and regarded him as an enemy of the Gospel.

12 THE BOOK OF REVELATION

1. "The Letters to the Seven Churches of Asia" chart (page 105) will serve to present the characteristic words spoken by the Lord and the spiritual condition of each church.

2. Only these two among the seven cities are thriving communities today (although the names have been changed) and have maintained a Christian witness (Eastern Orthodox) in their locations. The Lord promised to each of them His protection and blessing because of their faithfulness (cf. John 17:15).

3. "The Three Series of Judgments" chart (page 106) gives a concise, consecutive analysis of the contents of each judgment. Reading it vertically will reveal the total impact of each series; reading it horizontally will show the contrasts and comparisons between each. This latter approach is especially important in relation to the trumpet and vial series.

BIBLIOGRAPHY

CHAPTER 1

Alexander, David and Pat, eds. *Eerdmans Handbook to the Bible*. Rev. ed. Grand Rapids: Eerdmans Publishing Co., 1983.

Bruce, F. F. *New Testament History*. Garden City, NY: Doubleday, 1972.

Gaebelein, Frank E., ed. *The Expositor's Bible Commentary: Vol. 1*. Grand Rapids: Zondervan Publishing House, 1979.

Geisler, N., and Nix, W. *From God to Us*. Chicago: Moody Press, 1974.

Halley, Henry H. *Halley's Bible Handbook*. Rev. ed. Grand Rapids: Zondervan Publishing House, 1976.

Metzger, B. M. *New Testament: Its Background, Growth and Content*. Nashville: Abingdon, 1979.

Morris, Leon., ed. *The Tyndale New Testament Commentary Series*. 20 vols. Grand Rapids: Eerdmans Publishing Co.

Scroggie, W. Graham. *A Guide to the Gospels*. Old Tappan, NJ: Fleming H. Revell Co. (Pickering & Inglis), 1975.

Tenney, Merrill C. *New Testament Survey*. Rev. ed. Grand Rapids: Eerdmans Publishing Co., 1985.

————. *New Testament Times*. Grand Rapids: Eerdmans Publishing Co., 1965.

Thomas, Robert L., and Gundry, Stanley N., eds. *A Harmony of the Gospels*. Chicago: Moody Press, 1978.

CHAPTER 2

Guthrie, Donald. *New Testament Introduction: Vol. 1*. Downers Grove, IL: InterVarsity Press, 1971.

Hunter, A. M. *The Parables Then & Now*. Philadelphia: Westminster Press, 1972.

Lane, William L. *Commentary on the Gospel of Mark*. Grand Rapids: Eerdmans Publishing Co., 1973.

Morris, Leon. *The Gospel According to St. Luke*. Grand Rapids: Eerdmans Publishing Co., 1974.

Stewart, J. S. *The Life & Teachings of Jesus Christ*. Nashville: Abingdon, 1982.

Thomas, Robert L., and Gundry, Stanley N. *A Harmony of the Gospels*. Chicago: Moody Press, 1978.

CHAPTER 3

Brown, R. E. *The Gospel According to John*. 2 vols. Garden City, NY: Doubleday, 1966, 1970.

Hendricksen, William. *John*. New Testament Commentary. Grand Rapids: Baker Book House, 1961.

Hunter, A. M. *Gospel According to John*. New York: Cambridge University Press, 1965.

Morris, Leon. *Gospel of John*. New International Commentary on the New Testament. Grand Rapids: Eerdmans Publishing Co., 1970.

Tenney, Merrill C. *John: The Gospel of Belief*. Grand Rapids: Eerdmans Publishing Co., 1948.

CHAPTER 4

Bruce, F. F. *The Book of the Acts*. New International Commentary on the New Testament. Grand Rapids: Eerdmans Publishing Co., 1954.

Longenecker, Richard. *Ministry & Message of Paul*. Grand Rapids: Zondervan Publishing House, 1971.

Vaughan, C. *Acts: A Study Guide Commentary*. Grand Rapids: Zondervan Publishing House, 1974.

CHAPTER 5

Bruce, F. F. *Paul: Apostle of the Heart Set Free*. Grand Rapids: Eerdmans Publishing Co., 1978.

Goodwin, Frank J. *A Harmony of the Life of St. Paul*. Grand Rapids: Baker Book House, 1964.

Hiebert, D. Edmond. *Thessalonian Epistles*. Chicago: Moody Press, 1971.

Morris, Leon. *First and Second Epistles to the Thessalonians*. New International Commentary on the New Testament. Grand Rapids: Eerdmans Publishing Co., 1959.

CHAPTER 6

Bruce, F. F. *Commentary on First & Second Corinthians*. The New Century Bible Commentary. Grand Rapids: Eerdmans Publishing Co., 1980.

Gaebelein, Frank E., ed. *The Expositor's Bible Commentary: Vol. 10*. Grand Rapids: Zondervan Publishing House, 1976.

Godet, Frederic L. *Commentary on First Corinthians*. Grand Rapids: Kregel Publications, 1977.

Hughes, Philip. *Commentary on the Second Epistle to the Corinthians*. Grand Rapids: Eerdmans Publishing Co., 1962.

CHAPTER 7

Moule, H. C. G. *Studies in Romans*. Grand Rapids: Kregel Publications, 1977.

Murray, John. *Epistle of Paul to the Romans*. 2 vols. New International Commentary on the New Testament. Grand Rapids: Eerdmans Publishing Co., 1960.

Tenney, Merrill C. *Galatians: The Charter of Christian Liberty*. Rev. ed. Grand Rapids: Eerdmans Publishing Co., 1960.

CHAPTER 8

Gaebelein, Frank E., ed. *The Expositor's Bible Commentary: Vol. 11*. Grand Rapids: Zondervan Publishing House, 1978.

Kent, Jr., Homer A. *Ephesians, the Glory of the Church*. Winona Lake, IN: BMH Books, 1971.

Moule, H. C. G. *Colossians and Philemon Studies*. Minneapolis: Klock & Klock, 1981.

_____. *Studies in Ephesians*. Grand Rapids: Kregel Publications, 1977.

_____. *Studies in Philippians*. Grand Rapids: Kregel Publications, 1977.

Muller, Jacobus J. *Epistles of Paul to the Philippians & Philemon*. New International Commentary on the New Testament. Grand Rapids: Eerdmans Publishing Co., 1961.

Simpson, E. K., and Bruce, F. F. *Epistles to the Ephesians and Colossians*. New International Commentary on the New Testament. Grand Rapids: Eerdmans Publishing Co., 1958.

CHAPTER 9

Kent, Jr., Homer A. *Pastoral Epistles*. Winona Lake, IN: BMH Books, 1982.

CHAPTER 10

Adamson, James B. *Commentary of the Epistle of James.* New International Commentary on the New Testament. Grand Rapids: Eerdmans Publishing Co., 1976.

Bruce, F. F. *The Epistle to the Hebrews.* New International Commentary on the New Testament. Grand Rapids: Eerdmans Publishing Co., 1964.

Kent, Jr., Homer A. *Epistle to the Hebrews.* Grand Rapids: Baker Book House, 1972.

Wiersbe, Warren W. *Be Mature.* Wheaton, IL: Victor Books, 1978.

CHAPTER 11

Boa, Kenneth. *Cults, World Religions, & You.* Wheaton, IL: Victor Books, 1977.

Breese, Dave. *Know the Marks of the Cults.* Wheaton, IL: Victor Books, 1975.

MacArthur, John, Jr. *Beware the Pretenders.* Wheaton, IL: Victor Books, 1980.

Marshall, I. H. *The New International Commentary on the New Testament: The Epistles of John.* Grand Rapids: Eerdmans Publishing Co., 1978.

Martin, Walter R. *The Kingdom of the Cults.* Rev. ed. Minneapolis, MN: Bethany Fellowship, 1985.

Wiersbe, Warren W. *Be Real.* Wheaton, IL: Victor Books, 1972.

CHAPTER 12

James, Edgar C. *The Day of the Lamb.* Wheaton, IL: Victor Books, 1980.

Ladd, G. E. *Commentary on the Book of Revelation of John.* Grand Rapids: Eerdmans Publishing Co., 1971.

Mounce, Robert H. *The Book of Revelation.* New International Commentary on the New Testament. Grand Rapids: Eerdmans Publishing Co., 1977.

Mounce, Robert H. *What Are We Waiting For?: A Commentary on Revelation.* Grand Rapids: Eerdmans Publishing Co., 1982.

Ryrie, C. C. *Revelation.* Chicago: Moody Press, 1968.

Tenney, Merrill C. *Interpreting Revelation.* Grand Rapids: Eerdmans Publishing Co., 1957.

Walvoord, John. *Revelation of Jesus Christ.* Chicago: Moody Press, 1966.

Since 1930

Evangelical Training Association

THE MINISTRIES OF EVANGELICAL TRAINING ASSOCIATION (ETA)

Experienced – Founded in 1930.
Doctrinally Dependable – Conservative and evangelical theology.
Education~~ally Sound~~ — ~~Engaging all adult learning styles.~~
Thorough **220.61 Exp**
Recomme~~nded~~   ~~sc~~hools.
Ministry **Exploring the Bible**   ~~fo~~r equip-
                                                                    ~~e~~ffectively

Affordabl~~e~~

For many lo~~cal churches looking for an effe~~ctive lay
leadership tr~~aining program, ETA offers an i~~nspiring,
motivational system of instruction. ETA curriculum is available as
traditional classroom courses, audio and video seminars, audio and video
CD-ROM packages, and other resources for your classroom teaching or
personal study.

Contact ETA today for free information and a 20-minute video presentation. Request Information Packet: Crossway Partner.

EVANGELICAL TRAINING ASSOCIATION
110 Bridge Street • PO Box 327 • Wheaton, IL 60189
800-369-8291 • FAX 630-668-8437 • www.etaworld.org